Mystical Bodies, Mystical Meals

Mystical Bodies, Mystical Meals

Eating and Embodiment in Medieval Kabbalah

JOEL HECKER

WAYNE STATE UNIVERSITY PRESS   DETROIT

© 2005 by Wayne State University Press,
Detroit, Michigan 48201. All rights reserved.
No part of this book may be reproduced without formal permission.
Manufactured in the United States of America.
09 08 07 06 05   5 4 3 2 1

Library of Congress Cataloging-in-Publication Data

Hecker, Joel.
  Mystical bodies, mystical meals : eating and embodiment in medieval
Kabbalah / Joel Hecker.
      p.   cm.—(Raphael Patai series in Jewish folklore and anthropology)
  Includes bibliographical references and index.
  ISBN 0-8143-3181-5 (hardcover : alk. paper)
  1. Cabala—History.   2. Dinners and dining—Religious aspects—Judaism.
3. Zohar.   4. Mysticism—Judaism.   5. Sacred meals.   I. Title.   II. Series.
  BM526.H43 2005
  296.8'2—dc22

                                                                    2004017355

∞ The paper used in this publication meets the minimum requirements
of the American National Standard for Information Sciences—
Permanence of Paper for Printed Library Materials, ANSI Z39.48–1984.

Grateful acknowledgment is made to the Koret Foundation
and to the Faculty Development Fund of the Reconstructionist
Rabbinical College for their generous support
of the publication of this volume.

To Mom and Dad

CONTENTS

ACKNOWLEDGMENTS

I AM GRATEFUL FOR the opportunity to express my gratitude to those who have helped me through the years it has taken to bring this project to fruition. First and foremost, I owe a considerable debt to my mentor in graduate school, Elliot R. Wolfson. In the years of my training and the time subsequent, his scholarship has helped me forge my own understanding of hermeneutics and gender in the kabbalah. I am thankful for his guidance into the *Pardes*.

During my graduate years, much cherished for their endless hours of study, I received support from the Social Sciences and Humanities Research Council of Canada, the National Foundation for Jewish Culture, and the Memorial Foundation for Jewish Culture. I am grateful for the freedoms that their financial support gave me.

My teachers, colleagues, and friends, Arthur Green, Shaul Magid, and Pinchas Giller offered detailed critiques and advice, enriching my work significantly. Special thanks to Moshe Idel who carefully read the entire manuscript, offering generous suggestions to improve points large and small. Friends and other colleagues who have read parts or all of this manuscript or discussed some of its finer points deserve my thanks as well: Daniel Abrams, Eddy Breuer, Joseph Davis, Lawrence Fine, Yechiel Goldberg, Tamar Kamionkowski, David Kraemer, Eric Lawee, Jacob Meskin, and Mark Smith. The professionals at Wayne State University Press have kindly shepherded me through the publication process. Mary Tederstrom, the freelance copyeditor, enhanced the manuscript's style considerably through her studious examination of the work. Kristin Harpster Lawrence, Adela Garcia, and Maya Rhodes helped steer the project through to completion. Jane Hoehner, director of the Press, was compassionate and patient throughout the process.

Over the last eight years, I have been teaching at the Reconstructionist Rabbinical College, an institution that is courageous in its honesty and integrity. It is peopled by individuals who are idealistic about Judaism and committed to its contemporary interpretations. The school has provided me with physical comforts, to be sure, but it is the institution's warmth and personal support that can hardly be equaled. I owe particular recognition to our librarians, Debbie Stern and Manel Frau, for their considerable labors on my behalf. The generous support of Bill Fern, chair of the school's College Committee was helpful in aiding me with research expenses.

My wife, Frani Pollack, and my two boys, Raz and Shai, create a haven of stability, reminding me of life's securities and so many of its deepest pleasures.

Last, I thank my parents to whom this book is dedicated. Harvey and Sheila Hecker have been psychic anchors for me throughout this project and most preceding ones as well. Their love, support, righteousness, and wisdom will nourish me always.

Thank you to the University of Chicago Press for granting permission to reprint as chapter 4 an article that initially appeared in *History of Religions*, copyright 2000 by the University of Chicago, all rights reserved; and to the Creighton University Press for granting permission to reprint as chapter 2 "The Blessing in the Belly: Mystical Meals in Medieval Kabbalah," which originally appeared in *Studies in Jewish Civilization*, vol. 14, copyright Creighton University Press, 2005.

Introduction

EATING, LIKE ALL HUMAN activities, is invested with symbolic significance. It is not so much that life is reflected upon with representations superimposed on dining, or that philosophical notions are translated into culinary practice; rather, this daily activity, practiced according to the norms of one's culture with the folkloric background that informs each bite, can be a sumptuous event, even when the portions and cuisine are quite modest. Like all physical acts that human beings share with the animal world, eating has been "cultured"; that is, although all animals feed, only human beings dine.[1] Akin to sexual intercourse in that it partakes of both the "order of need" and the "order of desire," to use Roland Barthes's distinction, eating is similarly bounded by the cultural constraints, goals, and ideal images that have variously tried to elevate, order, sanctify, or aestheticize this simple biological need.[2] In the Jewish tradition, eating (and restrictions on eating) is given considerable attention. From the biblical laws of kashrut serving to define the body politic, to the vast regulatory system established in rabbinic literature, to the tired stereotype of culinary excess in the modern Jewish experience, food and eating have been a rich template for the elaboration of cultural norms and self-representation in Jewish history.[3] In this study, I examine the symbolic nature of the eating experience for the kabbalists depicted in zoharic kabbalah, that is, the kabbalah of late-thirteenth- and early-fourteenth-century Spain, with special concentration on the kabbalah of the *Zohar*, the central and canonical text of Jewish mysticism.[4] I seek to uncover mystical experiences of the fictional rabbinic illuminates who populate the narratives and homilies of medieval kabbalah with an aim, ultimately, of finding the place of eating as an aspect of embodiment within the kabbalistic ethos. My focus on eating, then, will serve as a staging point for consideration of the larger issues of constructed embodiment.

Narratives entailing eating, and eating that conjures narratives, are primary structuring devices of the Torah and the subsequent development of Judaism. Many of the travails of the Israelites wandering through the wilderness concern their murmuring about the dearth of sufficient, or sufficiently delectable, fare to eat. Moralizing about God's graciousness—as if dissatisfied with the miraculous nature of the strange manna falling from the sky—the rabbis aggrandize the fantastic qualities of manna: the precious stones and jewelry that fell along with it; its multiple tastes varying like those of mother's milk; its multiple colors like a demon; its age-appropriate taste and texture; its ability to be absorbed throughout the body's limbs without need for elimination; the boxlike structure of dew that encased it; its enormous proportions; and so on.[5] The rabbis have, in effect, painted the tableau suggested by the verse in Psalm 78 that declares, "Each man ate an angel's meal" (Psalm 25). In postbiblical Judaism, the Passover seder is the exemplar of a meal that aims to instruct, requiring each individual to imagine herself actually present at the exodus.[6] These fusions of food and text, experience and memory, and imagination and eating are the focus of this study.

My contention is that, alongside the spiritual experiences located primarily in the mind or soul, other areas of the body, specifically the stomach and inward parts, also serve as locations for these experiences.[7] Thus, one of my aims is to account for the internal topography of the body as imaginatively conceived by the kabbalists. For them, the body is ideally a body of fullness, one whose boundaries are sufficiently permeable to allow for the intake of divine light and power and for the outward overflow of fruitfulness and generosity, but sufficiently closed to give the sense of completeness, as the perfect symbol for the Divine itself. As we will see exemplified in the practices and experiences surrounding the consumption of food but applicable to other aspects of embodiment as well, there is a spatiotemporal continuity of the body, allowing for unions between the kabbalistic devotee and his food, table, chair, and wine, as well as with his fellow. This fluidity, however, is not promiscuous but rather is explicitly or implicitly guided by halakhic norms and mystical aims; for example, leakages such as seminal emissions and menstruation, as well as forbidden mergers such as prohibited sexual unions, elicit horror in tandem with the delight in permitted unions. For the kabbalists, the act of eating entails a combination of daily, nonritualistic, physiologically required behavior; biblically and rabbinically enjoined requirements to recite blessings before and after eating; and specific dietary restrictions. Eating is thus uniquely suited for consideration of the way in which mundane aspects of living are transmuted in the kabbalistic lifestyle. Moreover, in a misprision of Lévi-Strauss's comment that "food is good for thinking," zoharic kabbalah would say that "food is good for interpreting." I submit that for the kabbalists, food does not serve merely a cognitive function; rather, there is a bodily intentionality in which, trained by the norms of Jewish practice, the kabbalistic body instinctively surges toward prescribed foods or away from that which is prohibited. Indeed, while the kabbalistic system certainly privileges spirit over matter in a conscious way, I aim to show some of the ways in which a more fluid relationship between the two exists. Sometimes the conceptual and ideational may influence and shape the physical; at other times, the bodily experience precedes the conception.[8] Elizabeth Grosz has written about body-morphologies in a similar manner:

> Body-morphologies are the results of the *social meaning* of the body. The morphological surface is a retracing of the anatomical and physiological foundation of the body by systems of social signifiers and signs traversing and even penetrating bodies. . . . The morphological dimension is a function of socialization and apprenticeship, and produces as its consequences a subject, soul, personality or inner depth. . . . What is mapped onto the body is not unaffected by the body onto which it is projected.[9]

In its treatment of the consumption of food, the classical kabbalah suggests that the physical body can be transformed through eating idealized foods or through eating with the appropriate spiritual or mystical intentions. The kabbalah views food as something other than physiologically sustaining, and it idealizes foods as providing a key to sundering the boundaries between the spiritual and the material, bringing that which is on high to the realm of the mundane and that which is brought forth from the ground to the realm of the ethereal. Nourishment imagery is used throughout the kabbalah as a metaphor signifying the flow of divine blessing from the upper worlds to the lower, from masculine to feminine, and from Israel to the Godhead. The primacy of the eating motif is not surprising, given the kabbalah's overwhelming use of the sexual metaphor. Both are physiological appetites and as such can be used to reflect the kabbalah's puritanical standpoint in which the physical appetites must be tended to for the sake of the maintenance of the body, whether human or divine. Simultaneously, they must be cautiously monitored, as they are prone to excess or profane indulgence. Moreover, as we will see at length in chapter 2, there are interesting parallels between the treatment of sexual union and that of eating (see text near notes 80–95). In eating, the human consumption of food signifies entry into various grades of the divine realm; in sexual intercourse, the human activity mirrors and engineers unions above, and concurrently, the partners participate in that supernal union. In each of these physical acts, paradoxically, penetration means containment, and consumption means entry. That is, as one ingests mystical edibles, one pierces the previously impenetrable and transcendent divine territory. In sexual intimacy, from the perspective of the male kabbalists, penetration marks the domination of masculine over feminine, but it also indicates an internalization and transformation of the masculine in the reciprocity that exists between the couple.

Frequently the term used to describe this nurturance is that of suckling (*yenikah*), indicating the intimacy of the mother-child relationship.[10] More often than not, however, it is used to suggest the relationship of the masculine to the feminine; in the action of union or intercourse with the *Shekhinah*, the feminine gradation within the Godhead or, on the human level, between husband and wife, the male figure is said to nourish his female companion. The benefit of nourishment is thus construed as a sexual act, and the sexual is construed as nourishing, each metaphor fructifying the other. Indeed, in one teaching from sixteenth-century Lurianic kabbalah, acts of sexual intercourse that occur in the supernal realm are termed "eating."[11] The satisfying of bodily needs through eating is thus homologized with the relationship between the masculine and feminine genders; in this manner, the act of nourishment is aligned with the broader matrices of power, knowledge, gender, and desire that are central elements of the medieval kabbalah's symbolic infrastructure. A significant part of this work explores the terms used to designate eating. Ingestion, eating, digesting, chewing, feeding, filling—these metaphors construct a semantic field that interplays with other semantic fields. In the interaction of the sexuality and eating metaphors, the two semantic fields used to signify these two human activities color each other reciprocally. When metaphors such as suckling signify sexual intercourse, or when eating signifies destruction, an imaginative world is created that invites analysis.[12] In this mystical literature, metaphors not only are linguistic instruments to communicate meaning but are ontological entities on their own; that is, a particular food or metaphor symbolizing eating is a linguistic device that opens onto aspects of the self and Divinity. The interaction of these terminological domains, then, has dramatic impact not only on the reader's experience but also on his soul, the cosmos, and Divinity itself.

Eating, however, plays another role in the lives of the zoharic mystics, both in setting the stage for the communal mystical experiences that they sought and in constituting a mystical event in its own right. Even setting the table acts as a portal to the holy or demonic realms; this stems from the fact that all appetitive bodily acts have a dual edge, resting on a foundation of positive or negative intentions. In Numbers 22:5, Balak, king of Moab, sends messengers to Petor to hire the sorcerer Balaam to curse the feared onslaught of the approaching Israelites. The biblical Hebrew for "to Petor" is *petorah,* which approximates the Aramaic word *petora,* meaning "table." Because Balaam of Petor is called upon to curse the Israelites from his table, he becomes the quintessential demonic chef, whereas the mystical fraternity of the *Zohar's* narrative exemplifies the holy uses of the meal.[13]

The lack of detail accorded to the preparation and contents of the meals themselves is noteworthy, given the amount of attention to eating itself; neither the identity of the food nor details of its appearance receive extended attention in the kabbalah's use of food as a trope for the mystical experience.[14] There are two reasons for this dearth. First, the eating that the kabbalists are engaged in is symbolic and sometimes imagined; because symbols acquire power through repetition and reinforcement, particular details of any given meal are unimportant. The ability to "see" the food as one of the idealized foods is more potent imaginatively and mystically. Second, in medieval kabbalistic literature, driven by powerful imaginations and suffused with the erotic, sensual detail is a sign of the demonic realm.[15] This spare treatment, however, does not restrict eating to a merely metaphorical role; rather, if one can extrapolate from exegetical passages and the zoharic narratives of the mystical fraternity to infer details about the lives of the mystics of the zoharic circle themselves, it would appear that food plays a significant role in preparing oneself for mystical encounters and for the mystical exegesis that is one of the primary modes of mystical praxis for the kabbalists.[16]

PNEUMATIC HERMENEUTICS AND EATING

A central component of my method will be reliance upon the pneumatic hermeneutics practiced by the kabbalists described in the zoharic kabbalah. Pneumatic, or spiritual, hermeneutics entails the reading of sacred texts as a vehicle to enter into the experiences described or imagined in the texts themselves. In the *Zohar's* narrative frames, the fictive kabbalists ruminate upon a verse or a ritual practice and, in experiential reverie, transcend their mundane existence to enjoy communion with the Divinity lying behind the text or practice. This is the technique by which the known authors of contemporaneous kabbalistic works read scripture and the rabbinic tradition. In the context of eating, this means that contemplating texts treating eating or foods, or contemplating food in response to considering texts, leads the mystics to profound encounters. For these kabbalists, the imaginative and subsequent psychosomatic experience follows a performative hermeneutics, an

idea propounded by Hans-Georg Gadamer.[17] For Gadamer, the very being
of the text, dramatic or musical, finds its embodiment—an expression of its
being—in its performance on the stage or in the concert hall. Similarly, for
the zoharic mystics (and, it has been argued, for mystics at different stages
in the Jewish esoteric tradition), the Torah serves as a full disclosure of
Divinity when it attains embodiment in the practices of its readership. It is
those experiences that this study documents, categorizes, and explains.[18]
Because eating is a physical event that one undertakes daily, it presents a different kind of imaginative activity than do other ritual practices or uses of
body symbolism. While all activities that one undertakes are by definition
mediated by the imagination, the work of the imagination will vary with the
object being imaginatively considered. Though eating can be viewed from
the perspective of gender and sexuality, as will be seen, it is somewhat innocent of these highly charged themes as well. Moreover, there is a daily engagement with material food that distinguishes eating from the more abstract,
ethereal, or cognitive events of vision, hermeneutics, and imagining gender.

This analysis of eating in zoharic kabbalah serves ultimately as a means to
trace the phenomenology of religious feasting of these mystics whose activities lie veiled beneath the literary cover of the text. In speaking of biblical
and rabbinic figures who are engaged in profound endeavors through acts
of eating, the kabbalists are in fact speaking of themselves; in their sacral dining, they are Temple priests eating the showbread, enlightened Israelites eating manna in the desert, and the righteous seated at the heavenly banquet in
the world-to-come. The evidence that the kabbalah of this period provides
is not history in a sociohistorical sense; rather, it proffers traces of the imaginative experience of the kabbalists. These are not merely literary fantasies
but are the end product of mystical experience and its concomitant literary
formulation. The ubiquitous assertions of the spiritual heights attributed to
the fictional characters of the zoharic narrative or related kabbalah strongly
suggest an identification with those practices and experiences by the kabbalists of late-thirteenth-century Spain. Moreover, the flowering of kabbalah
in late-thirteenth-century Castile through a profusion of books and treatises
illustrates that kabbalistic forms of thinking and behaving were exercising
the imaginations of a significant group of elite and secondary-elite figures.
The hermeneutical practices that these authors engage in, and the ideals that
they paint in nonpseudepigraphical works, indicate a personal sense of con-
nectedness on their part. Indeed, it has now become commonplace in kabbalah scholarship that one can infer the nature of the experiences enjoyed
and techniques employed by the circle(s) of mystics who write these texts

and for whom the kabbalistic companions of the *Zohar* serve as a veil.[19] This is precisely the model of what the classical kabbalah advocates in reading the narratives of the Bible; that is, I examine these texts for evidence of some concrete lived experience.

I am not unaware of the difficulties attending such efforts. One example shall suffice to illustrate the tangles one can encounter in assuming that the practices of the kabbalists represented in the *Zohar* mirror those of the *Zohar*'s authorship. In a section from the *Ra'aya Mehemna* that provides a series of eating practices, we read the injunction to recline at the table on Shabbat (*Zohar* 3:272b *Ra'aya Mehemna*).[20] In the following discussion, I draw attention to the centrality of sitting as part of kabbalistic praxis; this, however, is the only instance in which the *Zohar* calls for reclining (*haseibah*). Repeated emphasis in this passage on individual seating and having many cushions available reinforces the impression that the paradigmatic scenario is that of the Passover seder. The norm at the time of the *Zohar*'s authorship in Spain was to sit around a single table as in modern practice.[21] Were the kabbalists following this ancient practice as a pietistic or mystical pattern of eating? Or is the author of the *Ra'aya Mehemna* simply using this detail from classical texts to describe the ideal eating scenario? It is precisely in such instances in which the difficulty of musing about their lives, teased out from kabbalistic texts, becomes most acute. Regardless of the historical behavior of these men, the *Ra'aya Mehemna* relates the imaginative experience that the author and perhaps kabbalists of his acquaintance enjoyed.[22]

THE KABBALISTS AND THE BODY

The theosophic kabbalists—the kabbalists producing esoteric literature that sketches out the architectonics of the Godhead—employed the human body as one of their primary symbols to represent Divinity, Torah, and commandments. First appearing explicitly in *Sefer ha-Bahir* is a correspondence between the human body and the *sefirot*, the hypostatic entities that comprise the nature of the Divine.[23] With the development of theosophic kabbalah in Provence, Gerona, and Castile, the correlation of body/*sefirot* soon became a ubiquitous feature of theosophic kabbalah.[24] The limbs of the (male) body were also tied to the commandments.[25] Sometimes Moses de Leon, the primary author of the *Zohar*, attempts to vitiate the link between the image of the human body and the *sefirot*: "The body is not an image of the Creator, for a spiritual substance divorced from all physical accidents cannot be imaged in a body. What then is His image and His counterpart? The soul, without a doubt."[26] This defensive formulation succeeds better in reflecting the tension that de Leon felt at the audacity of the human-divine parallel, a parallel that he helped foster and reinforce, than as a definitive rejection of that correlation; it is, rather, the exception that proves the rule.

This aspect of the kabbalah's anthropology—the link of human body/divine body—points to the broader question of the ways in which embodied symbols shape the formation of identity. It has become a commonplace in scholarship to speak of various kinds of "bodies": the gendered body, the racial body, the consuming body, the performing body, and so on. These categories emerge from attention to the cultural constructedness of the human body, the idea that cultural and governmental institutions, cultural practice, and custom all function to consolidate particular forms of identity. Approaching the question of the nature of the body, as understood, experienced, and utilized by the kabbalists, this study assumes a constructivist understanding of the body, meaning that there is a history of the body that is variously constructed by different cultures in different places and times.[27] This stance is not intended to deny a transcultural reality to human physiology; undoubtedly, there are foundational, physiological aspects to the body that will assert themselves regardless of cultural construction. For example, with regard to the stomach and digestion specifically, it has been shown that the gastrointestinal tract has an independent nervous system, a holdover from a more primitive stage in evolutionary development, which can affect the brain just as the brain can affect the gut.[28] Thus the body is not wholly constructed inasmuch, in this example, as there is an independent aspect of mind, primitive as it may be, that is involved in shaping experience. Therefore, as we shall see, the physical processes of consumption, digestion, and satiation, as well as the various social, aesthetic, and ritual practices that animate the act of eating for the kabbalists, can be examined to see what they reveal about their particular experiences of eating.

To begin, we can posit three kinds of bodies in the medieval (kabbalistic) mind-set: divine body, ideal human body, and mundane human body. Each of these plays off the other dialectically, influencing both the conceptual parameters of what a body is and, as an immediate result, the experience of one's body. On the one hand, the more abstract, intellectual, or transcendent the conception of the Deity, the more distance one might seek from the body in order to attain the spiritual apex. On the other hand, theologies that place significant value on the individual person in her historical context can lead to a greater valuation of the world as an expression of divine being. Further, an examination of eating with its metaphors of incorporation and digestion facilitates an understanding of the way in which the mystic relates to his body and the world with regard to the openness or impermeability of the body's boundaries. Although not glorifying the material world as, say, Rabelais's grotesque does, the diner in the *Zohar* does engage and consume food of the material world as a primary avenue to uncovering mystical heights that lie behind it.[29] In eating with sacramental intent, the body is assimilated to the Divine even as it partakes of the world in the most material manner. The abyss between spirit and matter is thus vitiated as, in the kabbalah's spiritualized carnality, space is created for the spirit in the midst of the stomach. The script of the body as found in the classical kabbalah entails a contiguity of the theosophical system and the inner surfaces of the human body as the holy becomes incarnate in the act of eating.

The first topic that a medieval thinker considered when contemplating the meaning of the body was the relationship of the body to the soul. Neoplatonic dualism was rife with philosophically influenced religious thinking. The following questions emerged: What is the nature of the body as compared to the soul? How does one characterize the adversity between body and soul? Must one subdue the other? Could they cooperate? How were their respective talents to be yoked together for the greatest possible good? How was the body valued with respect to the soul? How is the body viewed as an instrument for gaining mystical experience? Where does the self reside, and how does it imagine that residence? Do scholarly constructions of the kabbalists' notions of the body correspond to broader dynamics within kabbalistic lore? What notions of symbolism are deployed to represent embodiment? On the most basic level, the *Zohar* can be said to have three primary conceptions of the body: first, the body in principle is evil beyond redemption; second, the body is predisposed to neither good nor evil but is capable of improvement and redemption; third, the body is modeled after the *sefirot* and assists man in his attempts to reach the Divine.[30] These different conceptions of the body lead in turn to different notions of the virtuous life and their impact on the body. The first view leads necessarily to an ascetic vision, one in which the body must be broken and humiliated to give supremacy to the soul.[31] According to the second position, the bodies of the righteous can be transformed rather than merely subjugated. Thus, through the soul's nocturnal, heavenly ascent, descending afterward saturated with divine light, the body can become imbued with the overflow of this light.[32] Harmony reigns between the otherwise hostile body and soul as a consequence of the study of Torah; the body becomes "a holy body." Isaiah Tishby explains, "A holy body such as this—like those of the mystics—is not dependent on gross material food, but can be nourished and sustained by food for souls that emanates from the divine wisdom."[33]

According to the third view, in which the human body is patterned after the image of the *sefirot,* one can learn about the divine realm through contemplation of the human body. In this way, there is no requirement for either denigration or transformation of the body: "By carrying out its ordinary functions the body performs as it were a holy service. This sacramental view of the physical life is mentioned by the *Zohar* in connection with various physical needs, and particularly with regard to the conjugal life, which is depicted as a corporeal representation of sacred intercourse in the world of the *sefirot*."[34] Is the body representational of supernal phenomena, thus furnishing epistemological significance, that is, knowledge of the divine realm? Or does the body operate in a sacramental modality, yielding meaning about being itself, that is, ontological significance?[35] The intersection of knowing and being is a crucial element of the kabbalistic experience of the world and will be a basic assumption of this work.

Although the first question for the medieval thinker about the body might have been one of valuation, for the contemporary scholar, the initial questions are the following: How is the body represented? How do its metaphors signify? How does a given culture construct bodies and shape the experience of embodiment? It is well known that the kabbalah uses the human body—specifically, the male body—as one of its primary symbols to signify the Divinity. Different aspects of the mind, the two arms, two legs, and the male sexual organ, all have correlates in the supernal realm and refer to divine qualities symbolized by these limbs. For some kabbalists, the relationship between signifier and signified, the human body and the Godhead, is expressly attenuated. Joseph Gikatilla, a contemporary and colleague of Moses de Leon, writes,

> What is the meaning of terms such as "hand," "leg," "ear," "eye," etc. that we read in the Torah [when they appear to ascribe physical characteristics to God]? Know and believe that with regard to all of these concepts, even though they instruct and testify to His greatness and truth, nobody can understand or contemplate those entities [in their essence] that are called "hand," "foot," "ear," etc. And even though we are fashioned in the image and likeness of God, do not imagine that an eye is in the form of a [divine] eye in actuality or a hand is in the form of a [divine] hand in actuality. Rather these are the most esoteric matters regarding the truth of the existence of YHVH, may He be blessed. It is from these [aspects of Divinity]

that the source and [divine] overflow proceeds to all existents through the decree of the Lord, may He be blessed. But the essence of "hand" [in reference to God in the Torah] is not the same as a [human] hand, nor is their structure at all similar, as it is written, "To whom, then, can you liken Me, / To whom can I be compared?" (Isa. 40:25) Know and understand that there is no essential or structural similarity between Him and ourselves. Rather the intention of the forms of our limbs is that they are made as signs, supernal, esoteric entities that the mind cannot know.[36]

Though the *Zohar* also offers such disclaimers at times, for the most part it abounds in anthropomorphic imagery with scarcely a concern for the philosophical dilemmas such a discourse creates.[37]

My own approach will be, first, to follow the assumption of the kabbalists and other medieval thinkers who made an essential link between knowing and being, between ontology and epistemology. For the kabbalists, symbols do not signify wholly recondite matters, but rather are transparent signs with correlates in both mundane realities and divine realms. Working with a phenomenological understanding of the human experience of embodiment, I contend that embodiment acts as a primary element comprising the kabbalist's horizon as he envisions the world. According to this model, the embodied symbol impacts on, and is generated by, the mystic, who is irreducibly embodied.[38] The following statement by Elliot Wolfson, treating symbolism in the context of visionary experience, offers an elegant formulation of this approach:

> Recourse to sensible images and symbols is part of the mystical experience itself and is not restricted to the description of an ineffable experience in oral or written communication. Mystical vision is such that the suprasensible world is experienced in sensory imagery and not simply described in terms of the sensible. . . . [Thus] religious symbolism is grounded in sensory perception. The power of the symbol, therefore, lies in its ability to affect the whole being, including sensory experiences, and not simply theological doctrines. . . . This overcoming of the boundary between spiritual and physical does not imply, in the moment of visualization, a negation or transcendence of the concrete image. In traversing the barrier between visible and spiritual worlds, the mystic experiences the latter in terms of the modalities of the former.[39]

How do the medieval kabbalists approach the problem of the body? Medieval Jewish thinkers wrestled mightily with the problem of carnality.[40] While Neoplatonism and neo-Aristotelianism and their concomitant spiritualizing influences most certainly had an impact on medieval thinkers, the body still retained its place as a significant focus for spiritual development.[41] In medieval Jewish literature, Maimonides excoriates the body's sensuality, following Aristotle, who refers to the sense of touch as the vilest sense, setting a touchstone for later discussants of the body.[42] In such a context, eating is treated functionally, as the activity that provides nourishment, instrumentally enabling more noble activity. The kabbalists, as we will see, designed a more complex conception of the body's significance. Among the kabbalists of Gerona, in the decades preceding the emergence of the *Zohar,* we find a range of approaches to the body. In Azriel of Gerona's soteriological discussions of Primordial Adam and the messiah, we find a desire, similar to that of Maimonides, to flee the body. Azriel teaches that, as at the beginning of time, so at its end will humanity reach its potential when it finally leaves the body for a purer existence.[43] This position has been contrasted with that of Moses ben Nahman.[44] In the eschatological treatise *Sha'ar ha-Gemul,* Moses ben Nahman describes Adam not as a spiritual entity but rather as a spiritualized body. In this text, one finds a utopian vision of the body, one that is no longer in need of physical food and that is sustained from the supernal splendor.[45] According to Moses ben Nahman's conception of the idealized body, Adam's "spiritualized body" can be regained through union (*devekut*) with the *Shekhinah.*[46]

The *Zohar* oscillates between these poles of the body perceived as material shackling and as the model for a future "spiritualized" form. Although the *Zohar* does indeed pose the body-soul relationship dichotomously, as has been shown by its modern interpreters, to some extent this polarity has been overstated.[47] The modern Cartesian mind-set that separates mind from body echoes the ancient and medieval divisions of form/matter and soul/body; it posits a binary of knowing subject versus inert body. This dualizing approach to the world inevitably colors the ways in which the kabbalistic texts have been interpreted. One of the ways in which the humanities and social sciences have been recalibrated in recent years has been a reconsideration of the role of embodiment, the way in which the body as subject impacts on culture rather than the other way around. People long thought in terms of the mind's ability to train the body and of metaphor's ability to point to something "out there." As anthropologist Michael Jackson has argued, "To treat body praxis as necessarily being an effect of semantic causes is to treat the body as a diminished version of itself."[48] The kabbalists would subscribe to this position, considering the world and its contents, including human bodies, to be linguistically constructed, not by a single Logos but rather by the complex permutations of the letters of the Hebrew alphabet. That attitude, however, is complemented by moments of ecstasy. In those moments, the symbolic relationship between a human arm and divine potency are recast; no longer is one "here" and the other "there." Ecstasy, indeed the very operation of mystical metaphor, ruptures the stasis of "below" and "above," revealing them to be coincident in both time and space. In Jackson's words, this

> implies a critique of the "intellectualist" approach to symbolism. . . . The meaning of a symbol . . . implied a presence and an absence; something always had to be brought from elsewhere to make the symbol complete, to round out its significance. For Freud, the absent element was a past event or unresolved trauma. A symbol was essentially and by definition an effect of some hidden or repressed psychic cause. . . . My objection to this way of thinking about symbols is that it departs radically from the original sense of symbol, which implied contemporaneity and equivalence between an object or event and the idea associated with it. It ranks the idea over the event or object. . . . In particular, my argument is against speaking of bodily behavior as symbolizing ideas conceived independently of it. In my view, utterances and body movements betoken the continuity of body-mind, and it is misleading to see the body as simply a representation of a prior idea or implicit cultural pattern.[49]

I have quoted at length from Jackson because he challenges received understandings of the workings of symbolism, bodies, and metaphors. In rethinking the kabbalah's treatment of the body and the metaphor of the body, I overturn some of these same assumptions.[50] Moses Cordovero, a prolific and influential kabbalist of sixteenth-century Safed, states the point plainly in a comment arguing that the earthly observance of the Sabbath causes, and is identical with, the ascent of the *Shekhinah* to higher gradations within the Godhead. He concludes his demonstration, saying bluntly that this occurs "because the manifest *is* the esoteric (*she-ha-peshat hu ha-nistar*)."[51] What I aim to show are some of the ways in which the authorship of the *Zohar* treats the body's actions to uncover the inner actions that occur simultaneously. To quote Jackson again, "Metaphor reveals unities; it is not a figurative way of denying dualities. Metaphor reveals, not the 'thisness of a that' but rather that 'this *is* that.'"[52]

Another question underlying this study concerns the kabbalists' bodily practices that serve wittingly as techniques and unwittingly by providing a physical context and environment for rituals performed with mystical intent to procure mystical experiences. Throughout my analysis I draw on insights regarding the body proposed by Marcel Mauss. In his landmark article "Body Techniques," Mauss suggests that many of the daily physical actions we perform, actions that are "second nature" for us, are, in fact, learned "techniques."[53] Thus, he argues, in different cultures there are different ways in which swimming, digging, marching, and walking have been taught. In order to study the "social nature of the *habitus*," a view of the "total man" is needed, accounting for psychological, biological, and social elements.[54] The last is gained through education as, he says, "there is perhaps no 'natural way' [of walking] for the adult. . . . It is commonly known that there is a link between certain acts (i.e., hunting) and the rituals accompanying them"; he points to "the confidence, the psychological *momentum*[55] that can be linked to an action which is primarily a fact of biological resistance, obtained thanks to some words and a magical object. Technical action, physical action, magico-religious action are confused for the actor."[56] He explains that "we are faced everywhere with physio-psycho-sociological assemblages of actions."[57]

Mauss refers to the body as "man's first and most natural instrument."[58] Thinking of the body instrumentally and of physical acts as techniques, he explains,

> I call technique an action which is *effective* and *traditional* (and you will see that in this it is no different from a magical, religious or symbolic action). . . . There is no technique and no transmission in the absence of tradition. . . . The constant adaptation to a physical, mechanical or chemical aim (e.g., when we drink) is pursued in a series of assembled actions, and assembled for the individual not by himself alone but by all his education, by the whole society to which he belongs.[59]

In other words, someone who is a proficient skier, tennis player, or cyclist has a certain "built-in" knowledge in her body. Consequently, she need not concentrate on all of the steps required for a turn on a mogul covered with powder-snow, a stroke that sends the ball toward the baseline, or the well-balanced leaning into a turn. Each of these actions is performed as if by instinct, though they are decidedly noninstinctual. Even actions as casual as walking or eating are learned habits, and the particular modes of practice of these actions in any given culture are freighted with meaning.[60]

In the analysis that follows, I explore the ways in which the body is represented in the *Zohar* as a site in which the soul acts and in which experience that one might have thought would be native to the soul in fact occurs in the body or, rather, in the constructed experience of the body. Thus, although the *Zohar* does not approach the somaphilic attitude that has been ascribed to the rabbis, there is an appreciation of the body as a site of religious experience that needs to be explored in greater depth.[61] This study provides an analysis of the several different kinds of "bodies" that are represented in the kabbalah of the late thirteenth century: a body of mystical knowledge, a body as theurgic instrument, an ethereal body, and a donor body, among others. What will issue as well is an understanding of mystical experience as one of psychosomatic unity in which spiritual experiences are located in the body, not only metaphorically but also in actuality. Because food is something that becomes oneself, the person eating the food and engaging it symbolically inevitably has some imaginative conception of the specific items of food that in turn bears upon the image that one has of oneself.[62] This discussion of food and ingestion thus bears directly on the larger issues of identity with ramifications for our own thinking about eating, food, and the body.

There are important historical questions regarding the kabbalists' consumption of food and the environments in which they ate for which we do not yet have answers. The *Zohar* and other kabbalistic texts of the period make no mention of food preparation: Were the men involved? Was it the task of wives or servant girls? Speaking in broad terms about the medieval kitchen, it has been noted that "the kitchen is essentially a feminine area where men play a secondary and passive role, confined to butchering animals or buying supplies in the market; they have no part in kneading bread and degreasing or bleeding meat, which is women's work."[63] Were the meals primarily acquired in or from inns that they came across in their peregrinations? Several passages in the *Zohar* locate meals in inns, and the innkeepers, though often represented as unlettered folk, frequently captivate the visiting rabbis with esoteric homilies from the finest cut. In fact, the late Middle Ages saw a new social phenomenon in the form of taverns and guest houses. Hans Peyer describes how in the late Middle Ages the inn created

a completely new, socially acceptable form of public hospitality, which forever shaped the world of hospitality.... This type of hospitality included unconditional, basic hospitality, primarily among the aristocracy, and simple hospitality without board, usually for merchants, pilgrims, and other travelers.... Rulers, monasteries, and the nobility built ... taverns in cities, places of pilgrimage, and at rest sites to function as retail locations for wine, beer, and the most necessary provisions—and, in some instances, as overnight shelter.... Because taverns provided owners with considerable income, they became a popular sovereign right, even though they continued to be regarded as places of ill repute. Yet they were visited by peasants, dealers, and carters, among others, though strictly condemned by both the clergy and nobility. . . . From the eleventh century until the late Middle Ages, taverns began appearing everywhere—in cities, villages, and along major routes. They provided provisions and lodging, and in some cases entire villages, even cities, developed around these taverns . . . long-distance merchants and occasionally other travelers began to stop regularly at commercial houses in cities, where hosts not only provided provisions but also assisted with business transactions. . . . Regional rulers, states, and communities assumed the protection of travelers, and many private homes in the city became a kind of commercial inn for better-class guests, while inns and taverns began more and more to resemble each other.[64]

In addition, it was often female innkeepers who were responsible for the provisions, part of what led to the concern about the reputation of some of these houses of hospitality.[65] What level of familiarity might the kabbalists have had with these institutions? We do not know what the travel practices of the kabbalists might have been, what sorts of business enterprises they might have been engaged in, or, significantly, whether they would have eaten provisions offered from, to use an anachronism, a nonkosher kitchen.[66] One of these scenes in the *Zohar* includes one of the womenfolk of the house, sitting demurely at the back of the room while the kabbalists are engaged in mystical talk. She stands in strong contrast to the types of women who were reputed to be running such establishments and suggests some small quotient of social commentary.

What were the eating habits of those around them and, particularly, of the monastic orders, whom the kabbalists might have viewed as alternate models of spiritual practice (albeit with ambivalence if not outright disdain)? Canonical institutions called for fasting during Advent, Lent, and established holy days, such that dietary restrictions covered roughly one-third of the year.[67] Did the kabbalists have grudging admiration for the members of the monastic orders? The latter had the freedom to devote themselves exclusively to service of God, unhampered by the burdens of mundane familial and religious obligations. The mendicants adopted vows of poverty that did not attract the kabbalists, but their sexual renunciation touched on issues that carried strains of ambivalence for the Castilian kabbalists. Arthur Green and Peter Schäfer have both argued that the monastic atmosphere, with its cult of the Virgin Mary, was influential on the kabbalists' development of symbolism for the *Shekhinah*. Furthermore, Yehuda Liebes has pointed to

Christian influences with regard to the love expressed between the kabbalists and that advocated in the New Testament (e.g., Romans 12:5) in addition to the celebration of Pentecost by Dominican friars in Spain, corresponding to the *Zohar*'s celebration of Shavuot as a central focus of devotion.[68] The Cistercian custom, following the Rule of Saint Benedict, had one main meal consisting of a generous portion of bread, two cooked vegetables, and fruit in season. Meat and meat products were completely excluded. Supper, when there was one, comprised green vegetables and fruits accompanied by the remaining bread. Bernard of Clairvaux, in one of his sermons on the Song of Songs (no. 66), explains the practice as follows: "I abstain from meat, because by overfeeding the body I also feed carnal desires; I strive to take even bread with moderation, lest my heavy stomach hinder me in standing up for prayer."[69] Centuries later, Thomas Aquinas opines that

> the Church rations the foods which afford most pleasure and stimulate our sexual appetites. Such is the flesh of animals who browse on earth and breathe the air, and their products, such as milk from mammals and eggs from birds. These foods we find more congenial; they afford us more pleasure and greater nourishment. A greater surplus for seminal matter is produced from their consumption, and its abundance sets up a pressure for lust. Here lies a reason for the Church's ordinance that we abstain from them when fasting.[70]

During festivals, a bit of white bread, fish, or similar monastic delicacies, called a pittance, would be added to dinner. Might the kabbalists have been exposed to and influenced by the practices of their Christian contemporaries? Whereas the sexual renunciation might well have impressed the kabbalists, there is little evidence that their dietary austerity registered in any convincing way. Although the kabbalistic passages that we will consider do not list the items on the menu at festive meals, jocularity rather than severity dominates the mood, and the metaphors used to describe food celebrate rather than disparage it. Lastly, we do not know exactly what the kabbalists of Castile were eating.[71] While we might make some assumptions about their economic class, judging them to be of the courtly class with at least some means, we cannot derive their culinary habits from those of their economic equals because of the restrictions of Jewish laws of kashrut. In the end we are left analyzing a work of the imagination, focused on ritual foods, largely freed of moorings in culinary history.[72]

The texts that I examine in this study are the zoharic library, from *Midrash ha-Ne'elam* through *Tikkunei ha-Zohar*, and contemporaneous works of theosophic kabbalah by Moses de Leon, Joseph Gikatilla, Joseph of Hamadan, Bahya ben Asher, and others. The texts that are from the *Midrash ha-Ne'elam* collection are assumed to have been written earlier than the main body of the *Zohar,* and they often have a philosophical flavor; but the main text of that collection I consider, that of *Midrash Ruth,* has been treated as a later stratum, and it bears many of the theosophic hallmarks of the main body of the *Zohar.*[73] The *Zohar* has been privileged because of the sheer volume of relevant material in the exegetical passages there, but also because of the narrative passages that bear some elements of cultural realia, be they historical or not.

Before I embark on close readings of the kabbalistic texts, I will survey in chapter 1 the religious significance of eating in Judaism, leading up to the time of the kabbalists. This chapter has a number of aims. First, because the kabbalists are interpreting tradition, it will be most helpful to the reader to have a broad sense of the eating traditions, texts, and understandings from which they had to draw. The difficulty of the kabbalistic texts on their own is made less so when the traditions from which the kabbalists mine their own material is made familiar. Second, in the earlier, canonical texts of the tradition, symbolism, allegory, miracle stories, and myth are all avenues through which food and eating are approached and from which the kabbalists choose their materials and strategies. The distinction of the kabbalistic material is the mystical and theosophic framework that is employed to provide coherence to this broad spectrum of eating lore. All of these earlier materials offer paths of interpretation from which they could choose.

I

"Give Heed to Me, and You Shall Eat Choice Food": The Religious Significance of Eating in Judaism from the Bible to the Kabbalah

> Ho, all who are thirsty,
> Come for water,
> Even if you have no money;
> Come, buy food and eat:
> Buy food without money,
> Wine and milk without cost.
> Why do you spend money for what is not bread,
> Your earnings for what does not satisfy?
> Give heed to Me,
> And you shall eat choice food
> And enjoy the richest viands.
> Incline your ear and come to Me;
> Hearken, and you shall be revived.
> And I will make with you
> an everlasting covenant.
> ISAIAH 55:1–3

SUSTENANCE THROUGH religious commitment is the promise that God offers in these words of Isaiah, and they are suggestive of the themes that I examine in this study. The food metaphors sensualize the covenantal relationship and salvation that God promises to those who turn to God. These are not promises for an eschatological age or fanciful imaginings but rather are

19

an inducement to a life fully committed to God's path. In this chapter, I offer a survey of the religious meaning of food, eating, and eating metaphors in Israelite and Jewish history preceding the development of the kabbalah. The parameters of this historical overview are circumscribed by the literatures that streamed into the kabbalists' imagination, bounded by the limits of canon. Noteworthy in their absence are the dynamics surrounding eating and the significance attached to food in the literatures of Qumran and the New Testament; indeed, in both these collections, because of their emphases on communal meals and the dogmatic assumptions that shape those communities, there are noteworthy parallels to kabbalistic patterns of thought. My interests here, however, are the narrative, mythic, and metaphorical ways in which eating was represented prior to the thirteenth century in the literary sources that present a backdrop for the mystical developments of zoharic kabbalah.

BIBLE

The biblical text could be repunctuated through highlighting the ways in which God defines and provides for people's diets. In his first communication with Adam, God says, "Of every tree of the garden you are free to eat; but as for the tree of knowledge of good and bad, you must not eat of it; for as soon as you eat of it, you shall die" (Genesis 2:16–17). After the sin, the punishment too is expressed partly through matters regarding food:

> Because you did as your wife said and ate of the tree about which I commanded you, "You shall not eat of it,"
> Cursed be the ground because of you;
> By toil shall you eat of it
> All the days of your life:
> Thorns and thistles shall it sprout for you.
> But your food shall be the grasses of the field;
> By the sweat of your brow
> Shall you get bread to eat.
>
> (Genesis 3:17–19)

It has been suggested that "the mutual ability of both woman and the land to bear fruit is a key dramatic element of biblical narrative which serves both to drive the plot, but also to assert God's ultimate control over these natural forces and God's unique ability to act in the world through them."[1] After the next destruction and re-creation of the world, God tells Noah, "Every creature that lives shall be yours to eat; as with the green grasses, I give you all these. You must not, however, eat flesh with its life-blood in it" (Genesis 9:3–4). Yet again, at the time of God's redemption of the Israelites from Egyptian bondage, he instructs the people about their present and future remembrance of this historical event through the consumption of foods, the unleavened bread, and the paschal offering. It is the miraculous foods that the Israelites eat in the desert, though, that truly differentiates one kind of food from another.

Miraculous Foods

In the Israelites' wanderings, God provides for their nourishment with a variety of foods, all appearing miraculously. The people had complained about the lack of leeks and garlic and of their longing for meat; God, in an irritable fit, responds by sending quail. The quail is not merely food but a meal bearing a moral message, and it is a meal that ends disastrously:

> A wind from the Lord started up, swept quail from the sea and strewed them over the camp, about a day's journey on this side and about a day's journey on that side, all around the camp, and some two cubits deep on the ground. The people set to gathering quail all that day and night and all the next day—even he who gathered least had ten *homers*—and they spread them out all around the camp. The meat was still between their teeth, nor yet chewed, when the anger of the Lord blazed forth against the people and the Lord struck the people with a very severe plague. That place was named *Kibroth-hattaavah,* because the people who had the craving were buried there. (Numbers 11:31–34)

Scripture emphasizes that God sends his wind, bearing the avian sustenance in direct response to Moses' prayer.[2] God dispenses both food to the relentlessly complaining Israelites and destruction to the gluttonous among them.

The initial momentous food miracle involves the rocks that give forth water. In this first instance, the Israelites complain about the lack of water. God instructs Moses, "'Pass before the people; take with you some of the elders of Israel, and take along the rod with which you struck the Nile, . . . I will be standing there before you on the rock at Horeb. Strike the rock and water will issue from it, and the people will drink.' And Moses did so in the sight of the elders of Israel" (Exodus 17:5–6). In response to yet another complaint from the people regarding the lack of adequate rations, Moses and Aaron appeal to God.

The Presence of the Lord appeared to them, and the Lord spoke to Moses, saying, "You and your brother Aaron take the rod and assemble the community, and before their very eyes order the rock to yield its water. Thus you shall produce water for them from the rock and provide drink for the congregation and their beasts." Moses took the rod from before the Lord, as he had commanded him. Moses and Aaron assembled the congregation in front of the rock and he said to them, "Listen, you rebels, shall we get water for you out of this rock?" And Moses raised his hand and struck the rock twice with his rod. Out came copious water, and the community and their beasts drank.

No food in biblical literature is as miraculous as the manna in fulfillment of God's promise to feed the Israelites:

And the Lord said to Moses, "I will rain down bread for you from the sky, and the people shall go out and gather each that day's portion—that I may thus test them, to see whether they will follow My instructions or not." . . . So Moses and Aaron said to all the Israelites, "By evening you shall know it was the Lord who brought you out from the land of Egypt; and in the morning you shall behold the Presence of the Lord because he has heard your grumblings against the Lord." . . . In the evening, quail appeared; in the morning, there was a fall of dew about the camp. When the fall of dew lifted, there, over the surface of the wilderness, lay a fine and flaky substance, as fine as frost on the ground. When the Israelites saw it, they said to one another, "What is it?" for they did not know what it was. And Moses said to them, "That is the bread which the Lord has given you to eat. This is what the Lord has commanded: 'Gather as much of it as each of you requires to eat, an *omer* to a person for as many of you as there are; each of you shall fetch for those in his tent.' The Israelites did so, some gathering much, some little. But when they measured it by the *omer*, he who had gathered much had no excess, and he who had gathered little had no deficiency; they had gathered as much as they needed to eat. (Exodus 16:4, 6–7, 13–18)

After his dramatic redemption of the Israelites from servitude in Egypt, God continues his providential treatment of the ancient Hebrews, providing the miraculous manna that would sustain them through their forty-year sojourn in the wilderness. Adding to the miracle is the manna's mysterious nature and the precise apportioning for each person according to need.[3] This breach of nature's normal boundaries serves as a marker of God's commitment to Abraham's descendants and as a test of the Israelites to determine if they will uphold their side of the covenantal arrangement.

The scriptural passage in Numbers offers a botanical and culinary description of this portentous food's qualities: "Now the manna was like coriander seed, and the appearance thereof as the appearance of bdellium. The people went about, and gathered it, and ground it in mills, or beat it in mortars, and seethed it in pots, and made cakes of it; and the taste of it was as the taste of a cake baked with oil" (Numbers 11:6–8). A midrashic reading of this passage views it as a scriptural argument, saying that it was "deliberately inserted here to refute each point in the people's complaint. The manna was (1) a seed, hence easy to pick; (2) white, hence easy to spot; (3) clean, since it fell on a layer of dew; (4) eaten raw or cooked, hence not monotonous fare; (5) like cream in taste and hence it would not shrivel the gullet."[4] Moreover, as the Psalmist notes, "[He] gave them in plenty the bread of heaven" (Psalm 105:40). These natural capacities are enhanced by metaphysical qualities as well. Numbers 11:6 records the Israelites' complaint: "Now our gullets are shriveled (ve-ata nafsheinu yeveishah). There is nothing at all! Nothing but this manna to look to!" This translation, from the 1985 JPS text, is a useful counterpoint to the 1917 version, which translates the complaint as "Now our soul is dried away." The term nefesh can refer both to the entire throat and to the metaphysical notion of soul, so that the verse testifies to the Hebrew sense of the unity of body and soul, physical and spiritual.[5]

At times the metaphysical merges with the metaphorical in instances that depict the hunger for, or consumption of, God's word. Thus, in the well-known words from Amos, "A time is coming—declares my Lord God—when I will send a famine upon the land: not a hunger for bread or a thirst for water, but hearing the words of the Lord" (Amos 8:11). Speaking personally, Jeremiah says,

When Your words were offered, I devoured them;
Your word brought me the delight and joy
Of knowing that Your name is attached to me,
O Lord, God of hosts.

(Jeremiah 15:16)

In more dramatic terms, in the book of Ezekiel, God enjoins the prophet,

"And you, mortal, heed what I say to you: Do not be rebellious like that rebellious breed. Open your mouth and eat what I am giving you." As I looked, there was a hand stretched out to me, holding a written scroll. He unrolled it before me, and it was inscribed on both the front and the back; on it were written lamentations, dirges, and woes. He said to me, "Mortal,

eat what is offered you; eat this scroll, and go speak to the House of Israel."
So, I opened my mouth, and He gave me this scroll to eat, as He said to
me, "Mortal, feed your stomach and fill your belly with this scroll that I
give you." I ate it, and it tasted as sweet as honey to me. (Ezekiel 2:8–3:3)

What precisely is the meaning of this image of eating the scroll, a centerpiece
in Ezekiel's call to ministry? In this example, the interplay among literary
metaphor, embodiment, and supernatural miracle is stretched to encompass
politics as well. Eating a scroll signifies control of language and internalization, even management, of God's word. For Ezekiel,

> verbal consumption is not a casual, voluntary gesture; it is the precondi-
> tion for public service. These words are not merely encountered; their
> authenticity and authority are unmistakable, for they come directly from
> the hand of God. But most strikingly, there is no longer any ambiguity
> about the form in which the prophet receives the edible revelation. It
> comes to Ezekiel already *as a text*. . . . Eating the scroll is part of a broader
> discourse dealing with the question of the very nature of prophecy, par-
> ticularly in light of the emergence of a fixed entity of scripture. The pas-
> sages that frame the "scroll" part of the "call narrative" (Ezek 2:4, 3:4) bear
> injunctions for extreme precision in delivering the divine word.[6]

This is linked to the precarious political situation at the time, making prophecy a more hazardous endeavor. In general, Ezekiel is greatly concerned with
establishing his own validity and the authentication of his mission and message. Could any performance do more to underscore that validity than his
act of ingesting God's textualized word and then falling silent to "let the
scroll which he has swallowed speak through him"?[7] When Moses produces
water from a rock, his success indicates his legitimacy as God's appointed
leader. In contrast, when Ezekiel eats the scroll, food, authority, and divine
message coalesce within the physical person of the prophet.

Covenantal Meals

A recurrent feature in the biblical narratives is the covenantal meal, a meal
that brings parties together to establish political agreements, confer blessings, or produce oracular pronouncements.[8] The paradigm for the covenantal meal is the sacrificial offering given to God. For the Mesopotamians, a
sacrifice was understood as a meal offered to God.[9] Central to covenant maintenance was the phenomenon of the cult meal in both the actual sense (food

shared among human participants) and the symbolic sense (food apportioned to God and burned on the altar).[10] The covenantal meal par excellence might be the one depicted in Exodus 24:

> Early in the morning, he [Moses] set up an altar at the foot of the moun-
> tain, with twelve pillars for the twelve tribes of Israel. He designated some
> young men among the Israelites, and they offered burnt offerings and sac-
> rificed bulls as offerings of well-being to the Lord. . . . Then he took the
> record of the covenant and read it aloud to the people. And they said, "All
> that the Lord has spoken we will faithfully do!" Moses took the blood and
> dashed it on the people and said, "This is the blood of the covenant that
> the Lord now makes with you concerning all these commands." Then
> Moses and Aaron, Nadav and Avihu, and seventy elders of Israel ascended;
> and they saw the God of Israel: under His feet there was the likeness of a
> pavement of sapphire, like the very sky for purity. Yet He did not raise His
> hand against the leaders of the Israelites; they beheld God, and they ate
> and drank. (Exodus 24:4–5, 7–11)

The Israelite leaders partake in a communal repast, sealing the covenant.[11]

The scenario here—covenant ratification accompanied by a meal—is
echoed in a variety of biblical passages.[12] In 1 Kings 18:41, Elijah has completed his successful showdown with the priests of Baal, they have been exe-
cuted, and he commands Ahab to ascend the mountain and to eat and drink
there in order to renew the covenant. When Josiah purges the kingdom of
the idolatrous cults, he reinstitutes the Passover, a festival in which the meal
is central (2 Kings 23). Similarly, when Hezekiah institutes his various reforms
and condemns the backsliding of the people, he too convenes the Passover (2
Chronicles 30–32). "Ritual eating and drinking not only seals the covenant
but also legitimates the enthronement of the human king and confers divine
approval."[13] To affirm Saul's sovereignty over Israel, Samuel offers a sacrifice
and sacred meal, followed by the anointing of the new king (1 Samuel 9). And
again, when David brings the ark onto the holy mountain in Jerusalem, he
offers sacrifices and distributes portions to the people (2 Samuel 6–7). In all
these episodes, eating and drinking, or simply eating a meal, designates confirmation of leadership and the establishment or renewal of covenant.[14] The
meal at the foot of the mountain in Exodus 24 would appear to signify both:
confirming the elite status of Moses and his entourage and signifying the val-
idation of the covenant established several chapters earlier.

In some instances meals establish the proper environment for the confer-
ral of blessings or the relating of oracles, whereas in others they conclude a
political compact. The pact of Isaac and Avimelekh, sealed with a covenantal

meal, serves as an example of the former (Genesis 26:24–30). Isaac enjoins Jacob, disguised as Esau, saying, "Serve me and let me eat of my son's game that I may give you my innermost blessing" (Genesis 27:25). Abraham prepares a luncheon for the angels, following which they proffer the announcement of Sarah's impending pregnancy (Genesis 18:1–9). Lot too offers hospitality, but the heavenly messengers bear a message of warning, not blessing (Genesis 19:3). Sometimes the political and cultic functions coincide. Thus we read in Genesis 14 that following Abraham's military victory, Melkizedek, the king of Shalem, "brought forth bread and wine; and he was priest of God the Most High. And he blessed him, and said, 'Blessed be Abram of God Most High, Maker of heaven and earth; and blessed be God the Most High, who has delivered your enemies into your hand'" (Exodus 14:18–20). Jacob convenes a meal with Laban in yet another instance of the meal as a vehicle that creates a feeling of friendship and mutual acceptability.

There are, of course, feasts of celebration and commemoration. After Isaac is weaned, Abraham throws a big feast (Genesis 21:8); the ceremony of the ordination of the priests in Leviticus 8 has both sacrifices to God and a meal eaten by priests; the arrival of the Ark of the Covenant in the City of David is marked by distribution of "a loaf of bread, a cake made in a pan and a raisin cake." The Levites are then invoked to praise the Lord, God of Israel (1 Chronicles 16); after the first public reading of the Torah after returning from the Babylonian conquest, the Levites declare a holiday and instruct the people to "eat choice foods and drink sweet drinks and send portions to whoever has nothing prepared, for the day is holy to our Lord. . . . Then all the people went to eat and drink and send portions and make great merriment, for they understood the things they were told" (Nehemiah 8:9–12). These are just samples among many, more of which we will have opportunity to discuss later.

Finally, the celebration of a banquet frequently marks the resolution of history in the eschatological age:

> The Lord of Hosts will make on this mount
> For all the peoples
> A banquet of rich viands,
> A banquet of choice wines —
> Of rich viands seasoned with marrow,
> Of choice wines well refined. . . .
> He will destroy death forever.
> My Lord God will wipe the tears away
> From all faces

And will put an end to the reproach of His people
Over all the earth—
For it is the Lord who has spoken.

(Isaiah 25:6, 8)

The flesh of the Leviathan is frequently said to be the main course at this
final banquet, with the righteous eating the creature's head.[15]

Metaphorical Meals

Much of the Pentateuch is organized according to the dramatic playing out
of God's covenant with the Israelites: they obey and receive reward, disobey
and are punished. Food is an apt instrument for reflecting this tension, both
in the wilderness, where food is scarce, and in promises for the Land of Israel
to which the former slaves are traveling. It also establishes food as a fulcrum
for evaluating the moral fiber of the people, to illustrate gratitude or ego-
centric rapacity. From the divine perspective, food can be either blessing or
curse: for example, the manna fell within the camp, whereas the quail fell outside the camp, the division serving as a topographic marker of the blessing-
curse distinction.[16] Much of the time the food and meals referred to in the
biblical text are synecdochical, standing for overall blessing, or metaphorical, using "devouring" in the sense of ravaging.

The blessing-curse alternatives are given clearly in the following proph-
esy from Isaiah:

"Come now, let us reason together," says the Lord.
Be your sins like crimson,
They can turn snow-white;
Be they red as dyed wool,
They can become like fleece." If, then, you agree and give heed,
You will eat the good things of the earth;
But if you refuse and disobey,
You will be fed the sword.

(Isaiah 1:18–20)

In this example, the prophet's poetics derive their power from the impact of
the imagery, the horror of the inversion of "eat the good things" and "fed
the sword," and the linguistic violence of shifting from a literal sensibility
("eat the good things") to one that is metaphorical ("fed the sword"). The

literal possibility of such a grisly end intensifies the metaphor. In other instances, such as the story of the quail noted earlier, God feeds the faithless with bad or poisonous food or lets them die of greed. In the punishments inflicted upon the greedy, wealthy man adduced by Zophar the Naamathite, all employ the imagery of consumption, corresponding to the greedy man's own "devouring" of the property of others (Job 20:10–23).[17]

Human Consumption of Sacrificial Offerings

Although sacrificial offerings are ostensibly proffered to God, they are in fact part of reciprocal exchange, and more often than not, the offerings are consumed by human participants in the rite. Among the sacrificial offerings, only the *shelamim* offering is generally available to the wider society, beyond the priestly elite. There are three different subtypes of the *shelamim* offering: *todah* (thanksgiving sacrifice), *neder* (vowed sacrifice), and *nedavah* (free-will offering).[18] The *pesah* (Passover offering) and *miluim* (supplemental offerings) had to be eaten on the day they were offered, distinguishing them from the other *shelamim* offerings. The reason for this distinction lies in the fact that the former offerings are obligatory, whereas most *shelamim* are not ordained; moreover, the requirement to eat within one day points to a higher level of sanctity. Mostly it appears that the *shelamim* serves as the accepted way for slaughtering meat for private consumption.[19] In addition, the *shelamim* offering comes to play an important role in the national festivals of Israel, not unconnected to covenant renewal.[20] The obligation to consume the *shelamim* offering serves an additional function as well; it has been argued that the most prominent feature of the *shelamim* is to fulfill the command to celebrate.

> In Deuteronomy the commandment to rejoice is found in very specific liturgical contexts, but the link between eating sacrificial food and rejoicing before the Lord is unmistakable. The specific occasions for joyous feasting include consumption of the tithe (14:26), the feast of weeks (16:11), the feast of Sukkot (16:14–15), consumption of the first fruits (26:11), and inauguration of the first cultic site in the promised land (27:7). . . . This performative aspect of the term "joy" is most evident in the biblical expression *yom simhah*, which means "feast day." The association of joy with the activity of eating at seasonal festivals is so strong that the preferable translation in these settings may be "to celebrate."[21]

It is not, as moderns or the ancient rabbis would expect, that eating and drinking *leads* to joy but rather that the performance itself is the mode of expression.

In addition to the sacrificial offerings that the priests consumed, they also ate the weekly showbread (*lehem ha-panim*), the twelve loaves displayed in the Temple.

> The Hebrew *lehem panim* has been variously translated, depending on the understanding of *panim,* which usually means "face, presence, interior." Ibn Ezra's explanation that they are perpetually set out before the Lord— hence "the bread of the presence"—is supported by the end of this verse and by 1 Samuel 21:7. Rashi takes the phrase figuratively: "bread fit for dignitaries." According to *b. Menahot* 94b, the loaves were flat and oblong-shaped, "like a broken box that has neither front nor back but only a base with two upright sides."[22]

In later biblical sources, the nomenclature is changed to *lehem ha-ma'arekhet, lehem,* or simply *ma'arekhet,* perhaps as a result of an aversion to anthropomorphic implications of the earlier formula (Nehemiah 10:34; 1 Chronicles 9:32; 2 Chronicles 2:3).[23] The scriptural treatment of the consecrated bread given to David in 1 Samuel 21:7, taken from the Presence of the Lord, would seem to privilege the latter translation. In this story, the priest cautions David that the consecrated bread could only be given from the sanctuary of Nob if David's men had not had sexual contact with women. David assures him that the vessels for eating have also retained a fit status for bearing consecrated bread. It has been submitted that "[t]wo different modes of sacrifice are reflected in the prescribed manner of offering the bread of display. The loaves themselves were a presentation to God for which no altar of burnt offerings was used. The bread was viewed by God and, by this means, accepted by Him. Subsequently, the loaves were apportioned to the priests. In an effort to adapt this widespread mode of sacrifice to the more distinctive method of burning offerings on the altar, frankincense was to be burned near the loaves of bread; just as with other offerings of grain, a small amount of flour was burned on the altar."[24] As with the cultic sacrifices, in which some parts are burnt and others are consumed by the human participants, here too there is a reciprocity insofar as both God and the priests are nourished.[25] The showbread was changed on the Sabbath and is called an eternal covenant (*brit olam*), as is the Sabbath; the showbread may then be connected to the Sabbath's status of serving as a "sign" (ot) and a remembrance (*zikkaron*), as well.

Food for God

What of God's food? Do the biblical writers and people of the period imagine that YHVH consumes the foods that are placed before him? Biblical literature treats God's food with some ambivalence. One part of the prophetic message is an angry reaction to the notion that God might require the cultic meals, denouncing such a conception as folly. Isaiah relates God's famous protestation:

> What need have I of all your sacrifices?
> I am sated with burnt offerings of rams
> And suet of fatlings,
> and blood of bulls;
> And I have no delight in lambs and he-goats.
>
> (Isaiah 1:11)

In clearer and more emphatic terms we read in the fiftieth chapter of Psalms,

> Mine is every animal of the forest,
> the beasts on a thousand mountains.
> I know every bird of the mountains,
> the creatures of the field are subject to me.
> Were I hungry, I would not tell you for Mine is the world and all it holds.
> Do I eat the flesh of bulls,
> or drink the blood of he-goats?
> Sacrifice a thank offering to God,
> and pay your vows to the Most High.
>
> (Psalm 50:10–14)

Or, in the subsequent chapter, the psalmist reflects the sentiment "You do not want me to bring sacrifices; you do not desire burnt offerings; True sacrifice to God is a contrite spirit" (Psalm 51:18–19a). The theological conundrum posed by the cultic offerings, that God might draw his sustenance from these meals, evokes a moralizing response. The attraction, however, of feeding God or somehow nourishing His being proves to be too powerful a religious image to be banished forever, and we will see how it undergoes several incarnations in the course of its historical interpretation. Nonetheless, the profusion of formulae that suggest cultic sacrifices are indeed food for YHVH make it difficult to accept the apologetic approaches of earlier biblical scholarship.[26] Thus we read about the altar described as "the table of YHVH"; the sacrifices are sometimes called "YHVH's food"; the aroma of the burnt offerings is said to be "a sweet savor to YHVH." Bread, oil, and wine are the staples of meals in the biblical period, and they are commonly offered as sacrifice (Numbers 15:1–12; Exodus 29:40). Lastly, we read in Judges (9:9, 13) and in Hosea (9:14) that bread and wine gladden the hearts of gods and men.

Dietary Laws

Of all the biblical issues surrounding eating, it is the dietary laws and their taxonomies that have drawn the most scholarly interest and, in the long run, have had the greatest impact on Jewish practice. To schematize, there have been three main approaches to categorizing the criteria for dividing pure from impure animals: to create a taxonomy of ordered categories, to reflect a humane ethic, and to aspire to holiness. Leviticus 11 states explicitly that the reason for observing these laws is in order to attain holiness: "You shall be holy, for I [the Lord] am holy" (Leviticus 11:45). The laws reflect the priestly value system, dedicated above all to the attainment of holiness, and "avoidance of the impure is a prerequisite for the attainment of holiness."[27] The book of Genesis indicates a distinction between pure and impure animals as Noah brings seven pairs of pure animals into the ark while bringing only two pairs of impure animals (Genesis 7:2–3).[28] The contrast of the scavenging raven and the seed-eating dove is yet another instance of the dissymmetry between pure and impure animals, beyond the specific discussion of food laws. Many modern commentators have built upon Mary Douglas's treatment in her classic work *Purity and Danger: An Analysis of Concepts of Pollution and Taboo.*[29] Douglas argues that the priestly taxonomy of foods as represented in the Holiness Code divided animals into tidy categories according to their methods of locomotion and digestion. The permitted animals are herbivorous ruminants, most of whom have a cloven hoof. Forbidden were the anomalies, those that did not fit "normal" categorization. Douglas writes that "in general the underlying principle of cleanness in animals is that they shall conform fully to their class. Those species are unclean which are imperfect members of their class, or whose class itself confounds the general scheme of the world."[30] Thus swarming insects, which both flew and crept, were anomalous and thus prohibited. Similarly, amphibians and reptiles who move about comfortably in water and on land transgress the pristine boundaries of the definitions of species. Fish with undulatory locomotion with fins may have been correlated with apparent feeding behavior; crustaceans were viewed as scavengers and hence undesirable.[31] Ultimately the Israelites prohibited "everything in the zoological realm that seemed in any way dissonant with the principle of ordered, shaped creation, everything that roused dim, uneasy recollections of the primordial chaos and void out of which God called the world into being."[32]

A second approach maintains that the preference for the herbivorous, the abhorrence of blood, the reduction of choice of flesh to a few animals, and the limiting to the "most humane way" of slaughter all indicate a moralistic rationale for the dietary system. In terms of the theology undergirding this approach, Milgrom contends that the eating practices evince an underlying, transcendent theology. He writes, "Holiness . . . is not innate. The source of holiness is assigned to God alone. Holiness is the extension of his nature; it is the agency of his will. If certain things are termed holy . . . they are so by virtue of divine dispensation. Moreover, this designation is always subject to recall. Thus the Bible exorcises the demoniac from nature; it makes all supernatural force coextensive with God."[33] In taking this approach, Milgrom sees the role of human will as a religious value of primary significance in the Bible's religious anthropology.

The third tack dissents, asserting instead that the dietary code is a means for achieving and maintaining holiness and that Israel affirms its status as a people consecrated to God by avoiding what he declares to be impure.[34] Israel would thus become impure and abominable if it eats that which God declares to be impure and abominable. Leviticus 20:24–26 states that in separating pure from impure, Israel emulates God's act in separating Israel from the nations.

> You shall faithfully observe all My laws and all My regulations, lest the land to which I bring you to settle in spew you out. You shall not follow the practices of the nation that I am driving out before you. For it is because they did all these things that I abhorred them and said to you: You shall possess their land, for I will give it to you to possess, a land flowing with milk and honey. I the Lord am your God who has set you apart from other peoples. So you shall set apart the clean beast from the unclean, the unclean bird from the clean. You shall not draw abomination upon yourselves through beast or bird or anything with which the ground is alive, which I have set apart for you to treat as unclean. You shall be holy to Me, for I the Lord am holy, and I have set you apart from other peoples to be Mine. (Leviticus 20:22–26)

Similarly, in Deuteronomy, we read, "You are children of the Lord your God. . . . The Lord your God chose you from among all other peoples on earth to be His treasured people. You shall not eat anything abhorrent. These are the animals you may eat" (Deuteronomy 14:1–3). The act of differentiating is the characteristic activity by which God created and organized the world. Thus the prohibition of particular animals should be understood as a requirement of God's will and not based on hygiene or other medical benefits.[35] While the prohibition against boiling a kid in its mother's milk would have arisen out of a humanitarian concern, probably as a response to a practice observed at pagan harvest festivals, the absence of an explicit comment linking dietary laws and ethical concern is, ultimately, a fatal blow to that middle position.[36] Moreover, the use of the word *abomination* to refer to the unclean animals (rather than using the word *unclean*) suggests that it is not reverence for animal life that is the point; the ideological thrust is for people to be holy.[37] Finally, as there is no limit on the amount of meat that can be eaten, only on the kinds of food, the argument for reverence for animal life is further weakened. Even at the earliest stages of the Jewish practices of food regulations, it appears that there was a desire to prevent pagan worship and to maintain distance between Israelites and their neighbors.[38]

Ritual Slaughter and the Blood Prohibition

Among ancient Israel's neighboring cults, the biblical prohibition against consuming blood is virtually unique.[39] This prohibition is mentioned five times in Leviticus 17 alone, indicating that this prohibition has primacy of place among the biblical dietary regulations.[40] This concern is first expressed in scripture's polemicizing laws commanded to Noah. He receives new permission to eat the flesh of animals and the prohibition "You must not, however, eat flesh with its life-blood in it" (Genesis 9:4). Because Noah is initially a vegetarian, God's permission for carnivorousness is hard-won; it has been argued that even this permission is restricted, reflecting an abiding uneasiness regarding man's uncontrolled power over animal life. Deeply embedded anxieties about the killing of animals led the priestly legislators to transform their guilt into an ethical imperative.[41]

There are two distinct trends in the Pentateuch regarding the consumption of meat. Leviticus 17 prohibits the slaughter of domestic quadrupeds outside of the central sanctuary, whereas Deuteronomy 12 makes an allowance for profane slaughter.[42] Perplexed by this incongruity, some scholars have attempted to reconcile the two positions. A talmudic debate posits Rabbi Ishmael's claim that the verses in Leviticus fully intend to prohibit profane slaughter and Rabbi Akiva's argument that only sacrificial offerings are restricted to the Temple precincts. Rabbi Akiva's position, that this law is one of cult centralization, solves a hermeneutical problem and has been taken up by modern scholars who find it hard to imagine a cultic law that would prohibit the slaughter of livestock away from the sanctuary.[43] This approach, however, does not stand up to philological scrutiny, as the cultic limits do not indicate a return to the antediluvian position in which animals were not permitted; permissible wildlife and fowl continued to be lawful foods provided that the blood prohibition not be transgressed.[44] From this perspective, all livestock fit for sacrifice could be eaten only as part of the peace-offering (*shelamim*) worship: "From the moment the Presence of YHVH entered the tabernacle, *all sacrificeable livestock had to be sacrificed* [italics in original]. From now on, the food of the deity had to be presented to Him in order for the Israelite to partake of it, to share in His repast by eating it in His presence. Before this time, [the construction of the tabernacle and establishment of cultic practice,] no such law was necessary."[45] This position is at odds with a more humanistic interpretation:

> No humane concern for animal rights, nor any ecological awareness, nor any moral opposition to the consumption of animal flesh can be detected in the priestly prohibition of extra-tabernacle slaughter of oxen, sheep and goats. Their flesh may be eaten without reservation, as long as the directives of the *shelamim*-ritual are carried out; and all other permitted animals may be eaten without compunction as long as the blood prohibition is observed. Priestly thought does indeed idealize the primeval era when neither man nor beast consumed any flesh. . . . The priestly prohibition does not stem from any ethical desire to keep man's consumption of meat to a minimum, [however,] but rather from P's theocentric insistence on the distinction between sacrificeable and non-sacrificeable animals. The former may not be eaten anywhere but at YHVH's table, since they are His food.[46]

The discrepancy has been explained by reference to texts ascribed to the "P" tradition and those ascribed to the "D" tradition, each bearing its own perspective on history: in the perspective of the former texts, the wilderness period was ideal, and profane slaughter belonged in the past and would forever remain prohibited. For "D," profane slaughter was permissible. The wilderness model was untenable in a state with expanded borders, and the prohibition against profane slaughter was short-lived.[47] The "P" tradition promotes a utopian vision of an everlasting cult, whereas the "D" tradition presupposes a life in the land that does not overly privilege the priestly cult.

Part of the concern about blood stems from the enormous symbolic power it carries. Thus, for the cult, "[blood] nullifies, overpowers, and absorbs the Israelites' impurities that adhere to the sanctuary, thereby allowing the divine presence to remain and Israel to survive."[48] In the sin offering, the animal's blood serves as a ritual "detergent," purging the sanctuary of its accumulated impurities. The substitution of sacrificial blood for the individual sinner's blood serves to expiate the sin; it has been argued that the blood is efficacious because it represents life, due to some intrinsic quality.[49] Here, too, a far more mundane reason for the association of blood with the life of the animal can be offered. The verse says, "For the life of the flesh is in the blood," (Leviticus 17:11) which, it can be asserted, provides neither theological nor metaphysical information, saying that the scriptural legislator used the loss of blood simply as a sign of an animal's death. Put simply, depriving a creature of its blood causes its death, but the blood is not actually the life, nor is there a life force contained in the blood that is independent of the body.[50] In the same chapter, we read a prescription for part of the method for killing an animal: "And if any Israelite or any stranger who resides among them hunts down an animal or a bird that may be eaten, he shall pour out its blood and cover it with earth" (Leviticus 17:13). Continuing in the same methodological vein, covering up the blood following the killing of an animal may be a provision for simply ensuring that one gets rid of the blood. That is, it is not for the sake of returning blood to God, nor is it a ritual substituting the earth for the earthen altar in Jerusalem; rather, it is merely an efficacious way of ensuring that one does not eat blood.[51]

The last item to be considered in this context is the prohibition of eating carrion. While the biblical legislator has limited this restriction to the priests (Leviticus 22:8), in Leviticus 17 common Israelites are encouraged to avoid eating carrion as well. In verses 15–16, Israelites are put on notice that if they eat carrion, they will become defiled and will be required to cleanse themselves and that there are consequences for failing to cleanse away the defilement. The legislator is powerless to outlaw the eating of carrion, with its subsequent inevitable consumption of blood, so he tries to dissuade the Israelites by including the law in the context of the prohibition against eating blood, referring to the subsequent defilement and noting that failure to do so invites excision.[52] Links between the eating of impure foods, sexual prohibitions, and pagan worship are barely under the surface in Leviticus 11, becoming explicit in Ezekiel: "Thus said the Lord God: You eat with the blood, you raise your eyes to your fetishes and you shed blood—yet you expect to possess the land! You have relied on your sword, you have committed abominations, you have all defiled other men's wives—yet you expect to possess the land!" (33:25–26).

"Thou Shalt Not Seethe a Kid in Its Mother's Milk"

In the history of interpretation of this thrice-repeated prohibition (Exodus 23:19; 34:26; Deuteronomy 14:21) there have been two primary thrusts to explicate its meaning.[53] The first explanation, initially promulgated by Maimonides, is that the practice of seething a calf in its mother's milk was a cultic practice of the pagan nations surrounding the ancient Israelites.[54] The prohibition, according to this reasoning, served as yet another means of distinguishing Israel from their religio-cultural environs.[55]

The second explanation is rooted in ethics: the mixing of meat and milk is problematic because it is tantamount to confusing life and death.[56] However, this symbolic argumentation seems forced upon the biblical text. A more transparent interpretation views this prohibition as stemming from a humanitarian concern as well, suggesting simply that it was viewed as barbaric. In Genesis 18:7–8, Abraham serves the angels a meat-based meal, accompanied by milk; the meal, including this particular combination, is portrayed as high cuisine. Incidentally, it has been a long-standing practice among Arabs to cook meat in *leben* (sour milk).[57] The Bible is well aware of this food practice and does not deride its status as a delicacy; it aims merely to preclude cooking a kid in its mother's milk because it is revolting.[58] This argument is bolstered with support from other humanitarian laws: an animal may not be taken for sacrifice before its eighth day (Exodus 22:29; Leviticus 22:27); no cow or ewe may be slaughtered on the same day as its young (Leviticus 22:28); if one is removing the baby birds from a nest, one is called upon to shoo away the mother bird first (Deuteronomy 22:6–7).[59] These rules are all intended to prevent acts of insensitivity against animals, and this rule would appear to be one more of this genre.[60]

Two literary issues remain. First, why does scripture specify a goat when one would assume that a humanitarian rule such as this was intended to be applied universally? One reason for this may be that goats were cheaper and more plentiful; further, goat meat in particular is in need of tenderizing. Second, how can one account for the contexts in which these appear? The third instance, in Deuteronomy 14:21, is the easiest to explain. The entire chapter is concerned with food prohibitions and regulations. The other two contexts, referring to the three pilgrimage festivals, are more mysterious. "Three times a year all your males shall appear before the Sovereign, the Lord. You shall not offer the blood of my sacrifice with anything leavened; and the fat of my festal offering shall not be left lying until morning. The choice first fruits of your soil you shall bring to the house of the Lord your God. You shall not boil a kid in its mother's milk" (Exodus 23:17–19). Although the text first specifies the three pilgrimage festivals, there appear to be rules for the first two only. Perhaps the rule of seething a kid in its mother's milk is connected to Sukkot, the Feast of Booths. It is the feast closest to the time of lambing and is coupled with the summer harvest. It is thus a joyous time, and scripture enjoins the Israelites to be humane even in times of jollity.[61]

Celebrating Passover

Biblical scholarship notes the presence of two separate festivals woven together in Exodus 12. The first is the Feast of Unleavened Bread, which symbolizes the experience of haste (Exodus 12:17–20, 29). The second festival is the festival of the Passover offering, commemorating the historic deliverance of the Israelites from Egypt (Exodus 12:13, 23–27). All biblical references to the evening rite assume the centrality of the sacrifice. In fact, the second Passover, designated to be observed one month after the main Passover festival, requires that the festival offering be brought and eaten with unleavened bread and bitter herbs; thus, the holiday cannot be celebrated without the paschal lamb.[62] In the book of Joshua, the Israelites maintain the practice of the Passover, circumcising themselves, eating the sacrificial offering, and eating produce of the land with unleavened bread (Joshua 5:2–12). Scripture indicates that on the anniversary of the exodus, the time of the Israelites' first consuming natural produce in their new land, the manna ceased to fall. Joshua's observance of the holiday marks the shift from supernatural existence and daily providential care to a more mundane form of living marked by the consumption of natural food and the ritualization of the Passover memorial. After the construction of the Temple, the Passover holiday becomes associated with pilgrimage, joyous festivity, and national holiday. This pattern of observance is then maintained throughout the Bible.[63]

The Passover offering and meal, as described in the Pentateuch, is distinctive in a host of respects:[64]

offering on the fourteenth of the first month, slaughtered at twilight
offering should be held from the tenth of the month
offering should be eaten by members of the household together
offering should be taken from the flock only, that is, goat or sheep
offering should be one-year-old male without blemish
blood from the offering should be smeared on the two doorposts and lintel
    of the house
eating takes place at night after sacrifice has been roasted over the fire (not
    raw and not boiled)
nothing can be left over until morning

eating is done hurriedly accompanied by dramatic-theatrical gestures: loins
  girded, sandals on feet, staff in hand, and only the circumcised may partake
none of the offering's flesh may be taken outside the house, no bone of it
  may be broken

There is no evidence before the end of the Second Temple period of a ceremony or ritual for eating the paschal lamb. Based on knowledge of similar
cultures, it is likely that the Passover feast served as an opportunity for the
community elders to recount the story of the exodus.[65] It has been suggested
that Psalms 77, 78, 105, and 106 point to the nature of the Passover evening
with their various retellings of the redemption from Egypt and/or tales of
the miracles of the sojourn through the desert. In Psalm 77, the distressed
psalmist reflects on God's great actions of the past:

> I recall the deeds of the Lord;
> yes, I recall Your wonders of old;
> I recount all Your works;
> I speak of Your acts. . . .
> You are the God who works wonders;
> You have manifested Your strength among the peoples.
> By Your arm You redeemed Your people,
> the children of Jacob and Joseph.
>
> (v.12–13, 15–16)

An early record of practice of the dietary laws is attested to in the book of
Daniel. We read that "Daniel resolved not to defile himself with the king's
food or the wine he drank, so he sought permission of the chief officer not
to defile himself" (Daniel 1:8). Under a self-imposed dietary regime of
legumes and water, he and his friends "looked better and healthier than all
the youths who were eating of the king's food" (Daniel 1:16).[66] The passage
is significant on a number of counts. First, simply as an early record of the
observance itself; second, we note the social function that the laws serve to
distinguish Israelites from others; third, and for my purposes the most significant, it foreshadows the ways in which biblical practices are internalized
but also recast. In this instance, obeying the food regulations leads to superior health and appearance, reflecting God's compensatory blessing.

In the discussion thus far of the role of food and eating in the Bible, we
have seen most of the themes that will be developed, interpreted, and
expanded upon in the subsequent layers of the Jewish tradition, including

that of the kabbalists. Food is a sign of God's power, used to establish covenants with men and with God, employed as a metaphor to signal God's grace or disapproval and to symbolize the eschaton, and understood as a means for regulating holiness, morality, and social interaction. In most cultures, food can carry this wide-ranging multivocity, but the mystics, as we shall see, are the heirs of a tradition that gives added weight to these practices, images, and customs with claims of their divine authority and their roles as conduits to Divinity itself.

FOOD REGULATIONS AMONG THE PHARISEES

In an analysis of the sect at Qumran, Morton Smith offers the following defining remarks about the Second Temple period:

> Differences as to the interpretation of the purity laws and especially regarding the consequent question of table fellowship were among the principal causes of the separation of Christianity from the rest of Judaism and the early fragmentation of Christianity itself. The same thing holds for the Qumran community and, within Pharisaic traditions, the *haburah*. They are essentially groups whose members observe the same interpretation of the purity rules and therefore can have table fellowship with each other. It is no accident that the essential act of communion in all these groups is participation in common meals.[67]

Recently Dennis Smith has broadened the discussion by considering ideology such as purity as only a part of the broader rubric of meal customs in the ancient Greco-Roman Near East. He contends that the Greco-Roman style of banquet, with all of its formal rules and conventions, cut across all ethnic and class lines and served as a social institution in the ancient world.[68] Everyday meals, mystery meals, symposia, everyday Jewish meals, Jewish festival meals, funerary banquets, sacrificial meals, Christian Eucharist, and Christian agape all draw from a common banquet tradition. Each of the varying traditions develops its own set of banquet customs, banquet ideology, and banquet social codes, the last referring to the subtle implicit ways in which values are communicated in a banquet setting. The Greco-Roman banquet template leads to "meals . . . [having] an integrative function in ancient society in which they combine the sacred and the secular into one ritual event."[69] In such a context, the term "sacred meal" loses its usefulness. Smith charts the following categories for his own analysis, but they play a role in subsequent literature as well: the idealized model of a banquet, social boundaries, social bonding, social obligation, social stratification, social equality, festive joy (*euphrosyne*), and banquet entertainment ranging from party games to philosophical conversation.[70]

The Pharisees developed their "*ḥavurah* (fellowship) program" as part of an articulation of a vision for a renewed Judaism.[71] This program is distinguished by its emphasis on the observance of ritual purity by nonpriests, a call for strict tithing, and distinctive practices on Shabbat and holidays. However, these differentiating practices do not necessarily indicate a social separation from the larger society. Indeed, the focus on tithing and other food rules is an expression of first-century Pharisees, who were in constant contact with the larger society and who were vigilant about the dangers of that contact. The Pharisees defined their fellowship over and against the *amei ha'arez*, literally, people of the land. There is no consensus as to whether "*amei ha-'arez*" is a technical term or how broadly it is applied; however, a series of rules set out in the mishnaic and toseftan tractates of *Demai* deal primarily with tithing, with accepting what one eats and with accepting the hospitality of an *am ha-arez*:[72]

> One who undertakes to become reliable must tithe what he eats, and what he sells, and what he buys, and he may not stay as a guest with an *am ha'arez*. Rabbi Judah says, "Even if he does stay as a guest with an *am ha'arez* he is still reliable." They said to him, "He is not reliable regarding himself, how can he be relied upon concerning what belongs to others!" One who undertakes to be a *ḥaver* may not sell to an *am ha'arez* either wet or dry produce, and may not stay as a guest with an *am ha'arez*, and may not have him as a guest in his garments. (*m. Demai* 2:2–3)[73]

The fellowship allows the members of the *ḥavurah* to eat together confidently, trusting in the tithing and purity practices of the other members of the association. Through restricting possibilities of commensality, however, it may also have induced significant hostility among Jews as a result.[74]

Jacob Neusner has estimated that "approximately 67 percent of all legal [Pharisaic] pericopae deal with dietary laws: ritual purity for meals and agricultural rules governing the fitness of food for Pharisaic consumption."[75] Contending that the pharisaic paradigm was to extend priestly behavior beyond the Temple precincts, he says, "The Pharisees held that even outside of the Temple, in one's own home, the laws of ritual purity were to be followed in the only circumstance in which they might apply, namely, at the table. Therefore, one must eat secular food (ordinary, everyday meals) in a state of ritual purity as if one were a Temple priest."[76] A passage from the Gospel of Mark, in which Jesus defends his disciples' eating with defiled hands, supports this view: "For the Pharisees, and all the Jews, do not eat unless they wash their hands, observing the tradition of the elders; and when they come from the marketplace, they do not eat unless they purify themselves."[77] This immersion is not mentioned in any biblical, rabbinic, apocryphal, or pseudepigraphic source, suggesting that this practice probably arose out of concern for incurring impurity through accidental contact, such as bumping into a non-Pharisee in the marketplace.[78]

Others have argued that Pharisees were not trying to live like priests and extend purity laws to themselves; rather, they were concerned for the purity of holy food—the second tithe, sacrifices, heave offerings—not of ordinary food.[79] Even if the Pharisees do not regard themselves quite as priests, they do "strive for a holiness above and beyond what the Torah prescribed for the lay Israelite."[80] Nonetheless, the Pharisees can be regarded as a reformist sect, the type of group that preserves hope of steering the mainstream back to correct practices.

Rabbinic Development of Eating Practices

The rabbinic corpus is vast, encompassing the literary output of Palestine and Babylon more than a half-millennium in duration, and my treatment of eating practices in this literature will be necessarily cursory. I have selected several topics to highlight some of the most significant developments with regard to eating, drawn from both the halakhic and aggadic genres. In the aggada, I discuss the themes of feeding based on merit and mystical nourishment. In the halakhic realm, I examine the celebration of Passover and the major aspects of the dietary laws.[81]

Food as God's Blessing in Response to Merit

In the biblical narrative, God provides food for the Israelites in response to their need and their complaints. Having rescued them from Egypt, he has taken responsibility not only for their salvation from slavery but for their continued well-being too. Although the biblical story intends to impart moral lessons, the values God expected are neither righteousness nor holiness but rather simple gratitude. As is well known, the Israelites are in store for harsh training because of their deficiencies in this department. Among the lessons the rabbis are interested in inculcating in their teachings are the legendary qualities of the Israelite heroes, Moses, Aaron, and Miriam. Their exalted status rides on merit. Rabbinic legends in first- and second-century midrashic materials describe Moses, Aaron, and Miriam as the benefactors to Israel of the manna, the pillar of cloud, and the well; upon their deaths, the blessings cease.[82] Thus we read in the midrashic collection *Mekhilta,* "When Miriam died, the well ceased; when Aaron died, the clouds of glory ceased; when Moses died, the manna ceased. Rabbi Joshua says: When Miriam died, the well was taken away, but it then came back because of the merits of Moses and Aaron. When Aaron died, the cloud of glory was taken away, but it then came back because of the merit of Moses. When Moses died, all three, the well, the cloud of glory, and the manna, were taken away and returned no more."[83] In this midrash, the manna derives not *from* Moses but rather in response to his merit, reflecting a broad-reaching emphasis on spiritual meritocracy in the rabbis' religious worldview.

"Nourished by the Splendor of the Shekhinah"[84]

In the biblical narrative, manna is a food that descends from a heavenly source, defying nature and demonstrating God's supernatural power and supreme beneficence. In the Second Temple period, religious figures transmute manna into a substance that, if not actually divine, is intimately connected to Divinity. Philo writes the following in reference to the biblical statement "I will rain down bread for you from the sky" (Exodus 16:4): "Of what food can He rightly say that it is rained from heaven, save of heavenly wisdom which is sent from above on souls which yearn for virtue" (*De Mut. Nom.,* 259–60). In a different but not unrelated approach in the Gospel of John, the apostles begin clamoring for a miracle, and Jesus answers them, "Truly, truly, I say to you, he who believes has eternal life. I am the bread of life. Your fathers ate the manna in the wilderness, and they died. This is the bread which comes down from heaven, that a man may eat of it and not die. I am the living bread which came down from heaven; if any one eats of this bread, he will live forever and the bread which I shall give for the life of the world is my flesh" (John 6:47–51). In each of these instances, the manna metaphor comes to stand for nourishment that is not merely from the heavens (i.e., above the terrestrial world) but truly of the heavenly realm, partially sharing in the divine source from which it originated.

The rabbis too adopt this line of interpretation, representing the manna not solely as a remarkable foodstuff but indeed as a transformative nutriment. A passage in the midrash *Mekhilta* comments on Exodus 13:17:

The Holy One, blessed be He, did not bring them by the direct way to the Land of Israel, but by way of the wilderness. He said, "If I bring Israel now to the Land, straightaway one will attach himself to his field, the other to his vineyard, and they will neglect the Torah. But I will cause them to go about in the wilderness for forty years so that they may eat the manna and drink the water of the well, and the Torah will be assimilated into their bodies."[85]

In this instance, the Jews as a whole undergo an "inlibration," a corporeal internalization of God's Torah achieved through eating the miraculous manna and well water.[86] Scholarship in the past had been inclined to view this kind of rabbinic exegesis as allegorical, but scholarship in midrash has been gradually retrieving the mythical qualities of rabbinic literature.[87] One might read such a passage as indicating a psychological internalization of the norms of the Torah, but a more literal approach gives the statement greater forcefulness and seems more plausible.

The line between the material and spiritual worlds fascinates and attracts the rabbis in their reading and assessment of the nourishment provided by manna and even more mundane foods. If God is responsible for the Jews' sustenance, and the Torah is his vehicle, statements about food can be reread metaphorically to refer to spiritual sustenance. Thus we find that it is virtually a commonplace to identify bread with wisdom. For example, Rabbi Joshua (b. Hananiah) teaches, "The bread is the Torah, as it is written: Eat of my bread" (Proverbs 9:5).[88] The following passage from *Shemot Rabah* explains Moses' remarkable abstinence from all food and drink for forty days through comparing the Torah to bread: "'He did neither eat bread,' eating only the bread of the Torah; 'nor drink water,' drinking only of the water of the Torah. He learnt Torah by day and dilated upon it by himself at night. Why did he do thus? In order to teach Israel to toil in the Torah both by day and night."[89] In yet another passage in the same collection, we read, "Another explanation: Whence did he derive his nourishment? From the Torah, as it says, '"Mortal, eat what is offered you; eat this scroll." . . . I ate it, and it tasted as sweet as honey to me' (Ezekiel 3:1, 3). Why so? Because the Torah is as sweet as honey, for it says, '[The judgments of the Lord are] sweeter than honey, than drippings of the comb' (Psalm 19:11). Another explanation is that he ate of the bread of the Torah, for it is written, 'Come eat my bread.'"[90] Not only nourishment but sensual delight are attained through the consumption of the Torah.[91]

An earlier passage from *Shemot Rabah* amplifies the divinity of the nourishment: "Another explanation of 'And he was there with the Lord. He did neither eat bread, nor drink water,' that is in this world; but in the world-to-come he will eat of the bread of the Torah and drink of its waters. For this reason 'He did neither eat bread, etc.' Whence did he derive his nourishment? From the luster of God's presence. Lest this seem surprising, . . . remember that the celestial creatures who bear the Divine Throne are also nourished from the splendor of the *Shekhinah*" (47:5, 540–41). Moses' physical needs are put into abeyance through the grandeur of the spiritual repletion. In the midrash's formulation, his experience is compared to that of those who are promoted to the world-to-come, with the Torah providing nourishment purely on a spiritual level.

The notion that one can be sustained by the radiance of the *Shekhinah* becomes a fully developed motif in rabbinic literature. We read that Rav, the third-century Babylonian rabbi, teaches, "The coming aeon is not like this aeon. In the coming aeon, there is neither eating nor drinking nor procreation nor trade and commerce, nor is there jealousy or hatred or competition; rather, the righteous sit with their crowns on their heads and feed upon the splendor of the *Shekhinah* [*nehenim mi-ziv ha-shekhinah*], as it is said, 'And they saw God and ate and drank'" (Exodus 24:11).[92] To behold God is a veritable feast, Rav suggests, and although it is generally reserved for souls in the world-to-come, the elite figures of the Bible were fortunate to partake as well. This midrash, and others like it, will lay the groundwork for much of the mystical eating that the later kabbalah will describe. In describing the theophany, a visible manifestation of God shared by the elders of Israel, scripture says, "They saw God, and ate and drank." Here the rabbis turn their backs on the mundane nature of the dining experience, mutating the actions of eating and drinking into sensual qualifiers of the theophanic experience.[93] We should note, however, that at this point the rabbi emphasizes the visual rather than the gustatory aspect of the experience. In *Heikhalot Rabbati,* a mystical collection that may have originated in this period, we are told, "Happy is the eye which is nourished and which gazes upon this wondrous light of God's throne, this wondrous and marvelous vision."[94] Other early rabbinic texts adopt the same adulatory approach. Thus in *Avot de-Rabbi Natan* we find "On the seventh day, what is recited? 'A psalm, a song for the Sabbath day': a day which is entirely rest, for on that day there is neither eating nor drinking nor trade and commerce; rather, the righteous sit with their crowns on their heads and are nourished by the splendor of the *Shekhinah,* as it is said, 'And they beheld God and ate and drank' like the ministering angels."[95]

The rabbis develop this phenomenon of feasting upon Divinity in an alternative mode, through the articulation of different realms between our world and the supernal world. That is, through delineating the categories of the righteous in this world, the righteous in the world-to-come, and angels, a topographical menu emerges: "Rabbi Abbahu (third-generation Palestinian amora) says . . . '[t]he creatures of the upper world and those of the lower world were created at the same instant. But the creatures of the upper world draw sustenance from the splendor of the presence of God, while, as to the lower realm of creation, if the created ones do not work, they will not eat.'"[96] This time the line between the upper and lower realms is reinscribed. Earlier we read Rav's assertion that the righteous in the world-to-come feast upon the shimmer of God's presence. That position is now more circumscribed. These strains between the different texts indicate the ambivalence regarding the possibility of such visions as well as the possibility that the sustenance of one realm can translate into nourishment in another. God's transcendence is preserved; the ethical and religious demands of the Torah, as prescribed in the growing rabbinic corpus, are the primary religious focus in this world. Similarly, in *Pesikta Rabbati,* we find that

> Rabbi Isaac says: "It is written, 'my sacrificial offering, my food' (Numbers 28:2). 'But is there any eating or drinking for Me? If you say that there is any eating or drinking for Me, learn from My angels, learn from My ministers, as it is written, "His ministers are burning fire"' (Psalm 104:4)." From whence are they nourished? Rabbi Yehudah says in the name of Rabbi Isaac: "From the splendor of the *Shekhinah,* as it is written, 'In the light of a king's face there is life' (Proverbs 16:15)."[97]

This text represents a conservative approach to the question of the viability of feasting upon God's glory: the angels are nourished from God's Presence; human beings are not. Nevertheless, the more that this boundary is reinforced, the more the stance appears defensive and can be seen to respond to some of the texts that wax enthusiastic about the possibility of transgressing that very boundary. A text from the *heikhalot* literature subscribes to a more tentative stance toward the goal of feasting on God's presence. A passage in *Heikhalot Zutarti,* cautioning about the dangers of "descending to the chariot," warns, "Be very careful about the glory of your Master, and do not descend to Him[.] But if you have descended to Him, do not feed upon Him. For if you have fed upon Him [*im neheneita mimenu*], you will end up being eliminated from the world."[98] Should such a statement be interpreted literally? Some have argued for an allegorical interpretation of this type of rabbinic exegesis, that no literal nourishment could be intended.[99] Conversely, the term *"nehenin"* might be translated as "enjoyed" or "feasted upon," with the latter intending a more sensual experience. Rav's proof text of Exodus 24:11 conveys a more literal, albeit spiritualized, interpretation—God's splendor is an eschatological food; the term "*nehenin*" is a substitute for "eating and drinking," not standing in opposition to it.[100]

Frequently the midrashic authors interpret a textual hook in Exodus 24:11 that describes the Israelite nobility eating, drinking, and gazing upon God. The verse concludes, "Yet He did not raise His hand against the leaders of the Israelites," suggesting to Rabbi Pinḥas, among others, that "it may be inferred that they deserved that a hand should be laid upon them," that eating in the presence of God would be horrendously inappropriate. Rabbi Hoshaiah responds rhetorically, "Were cakes taken up with them on Sinai, since it says, 'And they beheld God and ate and drank'? Rather it means that they glutted (*zanu*) their eyes upon the *Shekhinah,* like a man who gazes at his friend while eating and drinking." The genie has been put back in its bottle: sheer rudeness is the crime here, not mythical transgression. Rabbi Yohanan counters, however, saying, "It actually was eating, as it is said, 'In the light of a king's face there is life' (Proverbs 16:15)."[101] The last word is given to an apparently mystical interpretation of the problem: the nobles of Israel fed off and were physically sustained by the gleam of God's presence. Rabbi Yohanan is explicitly concerned that the metaphorical link between light and food not be taken merely metaphorically. Overall, "these midrashim reveal a continuing ambivalence: the vision of God in the context of revelation was seen to be positive and expressed in images of 'feeding,' but the danger of overstepping one's bounds was always present."[102]

Celebrating Passover

The Passover ceremony is first codified in the tenth chapter of the Mishnah and *Tosefta, Tractate Pesaḥim,* undergoing further development in the *Palestinian* and *Babylonian Talmudim.*[103] The explications sanctioned by Gamaliel and rabbinic successors in the Mishnah are not "an exposition of biblical text but of the food brought to the table, akin both to Jesus' explanation of the bread and wine which were served at the table and to sympotic custom . . . whereby it became common to explain the history and significance of foods brought to the table."[104] As noted earlier, the question of the similarities between the classical Greek symposia and the rabbinic crafting of the seder (Passover ceremony) has drawn considerable interest.[105] First, the nature of the symposium must be defined:

Symposium is an organization of all-male groups, aristocratic and egalitarian at the same time, which affirm their identity through ceremonial-
ized drinking. Prolonged drinking is separate from the meal proper; . . .
the participants, adorned with wreaths, lie on couches. The symposium
has private, political, and cultural dimensions: it is the place of *euphrosyne*
[joyfulness], of music, poetry, and other forms of entertainment; it is
bound up with sexuality, especially homosexuality; it guarantees the social
control of the *polis* by the aristocrats.[106]

Some of the main components of the symposium meal that prompt echoes
in the seder and demonstrate this influence include hand washing before and
after eating; hors d'oeuvres commonly consisting of salad stuffs, such as cel-
ery, herbs, olives, and eggs; and reclining at the meal as a sign of elite dining.[107] Even the enigmatic *afikoman* refers originally to prohibited revelry
but after a while comes to refer to dessert, the paschal offering, and ultimately, the concluding mazah.[108] Thus, even in opposing alcoholic excess,
the Passover ritual is operating within the larger rubric of the symposium.
A central component of the idealized symposium meal, and of the Passover
seder, is the educational role of the gatherings: they are as much about conversation, teaching, and group initiation as about wine, merriment, and
entertainment.[109]

The Mishnah prescribes a three-course meal consisting of hors d'oeuvres,
a main course, and dessert (*afikoman*), the same three parts as in the contemporary Greco-Roman festive meal.[110] Four cups of wine provide the basic
structure to which subsidiary parts were then added.[111] Specific quantities
are enjoined: one-fourth *log* for each cup, so that the four cups will contain
a total quantity equal to the volume of one and a half eggs. Before the hors
d'oeuvres, one is to wash one hand and then wash both before the meal
proper. While still eating the hors d'oeuvres, the diners have not yet formed
a table fellowship, so they recite their own blessings, only relying on the
leader once they come to sit together. When it is time for the blessing over
the second cup, uttered before commencing the discussion of the Exodus,
one of the diners says the blessing for the entire group, with the others
responding "*Amen*"; they now constitute a unified group rather than a collection of individuals, and this is marked by the leader's prominence.[112] Once
seated at the table, one's assigned position designated one's importance or
status in the group.[113] For the most part, the Haggadah, the literary text of
the evening's ritual, has no fixed form; the Mishnah gives two different ways

of recounting the events, both of which use foods as the point of departure.[114]

Perhaps the most notable aspect of the transformation of the practice of eating at the seder, though, is the treatment of foods as symbols to be eaten in symbolic quantities; as symbols, they evoke further exegesis, resulting in additional regulations about consumption, even preventing them being eaten at all.[115] The Passover, like the Eucharist, "require[s] a simultaneous translation to spell out the associations as the meal is eaten."[116] The first and most critical step that the rabbis devise is to transform the Passover meal from domestic, sacrificial meal into a nonsacrificial seder. Once the ceremony does develop, there are three parts to the evening ceremony: telling the story, a festive meal with special foods, and songs of praise intended to create a feeling of festivity.[117] The Mishnah calls for an ideological exposition of the foods per Rabban Gamaliel II, who required that the Passover offering, unleavened bread, and bitter herbs must all be specifically explicated in order to fulfill one's ritual obligation. This is achieved through the equation of eating unleavened bread and bitter herbs with the sacrifice, teaching that the unleavened bread and bitter herbs comprise the festival's three essentials.[118] The rabbis then retroject this behavior onto pre-70 CE practice, anachronistically reading back into history rituals that had not yet been adopted. The rabbis take several steps to transform the festival through ritualizing the seder. First, the verbalizing advocated by Gamaliel in *m. Pesaḥim* 10:5 has a double effect: it reverses the biblical perspective that *mazah* and bitter herbs are secondary to the paschal lamb, and it flattens any hierarchy that might have existed. All three verbal statements are now essentially equal.[119] Asserting that *mention* is what counts, the Mishnah takes an initial step away from the physical importance of the three elements.[120] As the Mishnah continues elaborating meanings, it develops this tendency further: by supplying rationales, it gives significance to what the three represent rather than to the literal act of eating, thus further limiting their physical presence. "The three elements have thus become ritual objects and not just foods to be consumed, and the ritual itself becomes speaking instead of eating."[121] According to the mishnah, it is now *mazah* that is about redemption, not the offering; the latter has now been relegated to a remembrance of Israel being spared the final plague.[122] The rabbinic transformation of the Passover ceremony is a testament to the rabbis' creativity at a time, following the Temple's destruction, in which Judaism needs to be recast and reimagined. Their efforts in the Mishnah and Talmudim are similar in their development of all biblical themes, and many more besides; in addition, the movement from being territory based and cult based to development of a "library" and its study as the core of their new Judaism has dramatic effects on the "simple" acts of eating and drinking at the table.

Dietary Laws

One of the most powerful and lasting contributions of the rabbis to Jewish religious practice has been the development of the Jewish dietary practices called kashrut, literally "fitness for consumption."[123] An enormous body of legislation developed around eating practices, but I will limit my discussion to a few of the central aspects of their edifice: the separation of meat and milk, the laws of forbidden mixtures, the *kashering* (making fit) of cooking vessels, and foods prohibited by rabbinic injunction. Perhaps the most outwardly noticeable aspect of the kashrut system is the separation of meat and milk cooking utensils and meals. At the outset, however, the limitations were rather rudimentary. The first indication of this restriction in rabbinic literature can be found in a mishnah in tractate *Hullin:* "It is forbidden to cook any flesh with milk, with the exception of the flesh of fish and grasshoppers, and it is forbidden to bring it upon the table with cheese, with the exception of the flesh of fish and grasshoppers" (8:1). In the Talmud, however, the justifications for the law and its expansion are dealt with at length. As noted earlier, there are three locations for the verse "Thou shall not seethe a kid in its mother's milk" (Exodus 23:19, 34:26; Deuteronomy 14:21). A central pillar of the rabbinic hermeneutic was the determination that biblical redundancies yield legislation and meaning. In this instance, the rabbis deduced three separate prohibitions from the threefold citation: to cook meat and milk together, to eat such a mixture, and to derive any benefit from such a mixture.[124] While the rabbis understood the biblical prohibitions to be limited to livestock, they extended the law's reach to apply to venison and fowl as well. The rabbis noted the anomalous nature of the meat-and-milk prohibition because each has an originally permissible status.[125]

One of the trajectories the rabbis pursued that further ramifies the complexity of the system is through their variety of definitions of what constitutes cooking. The prohibition ensues at the point at which there is a transfer of taste. At what point do meat and milk in a pot over the fire become cooked such that taste is transferred? Generally, the minimum temperature for the transfer of taste is deemed to be the amount of heat from which the hand recoils for fear of being burnt (*yad soledet bo*).[126]

There is considerable detail in rabbinic legal literature discussing forbidden mixtures and the consequences of unkosher food falling into a mixture of kosher food. The fundament of the rabbinic understanding is a principle called "the taste is like the essence" (*ta'am ke-ikar*). The primary statement of this principle is in the tractate *Avodah Zarah* 67a: "Rabbi Abahu said in the name of Rabbi Yohanan that any food which has taste and content [that are forbidden] is forbidden and one receives lashes. Any food which has [forbidden] taste but not [forbidden] content is prohibited but one does not receive lashes."[127] Talmudic reasoning proceeds to delineate the categories of foods and types of mixtures that run afoul of these restrictions. If discrete pieces of similar-tasting dry food become mixed together, and if the majority of the pieces are kosher, the entire group is determined to be fit. Thus if one piece of unkosher meat falls into a group of two other equally indistinguishable pieces of kosher meat, all three would be technically permissible, according to the rabbinic understanding of biblical law.[128] If, however, the portions that are mixed together are fluid or have been cooked together, the permissible food must exceed the unkosher food in quantity by a multiple of sixty. Thus if a drop of milk falls into a pot of meat stew, there must be sixty times as much of the latter than of the former in order to render the entirety permissible to eat.[129] Throughout all these laws, there are specifications of the volume eaten and the speed with which it must be consumed in order to constitute a violation of the *halakhah*. One may neither eat a *ke-zayit* (the volume of an olive) nor drink a *revi'it* (adjudicated by modern authorities to be roughly three ounces) of a forbidden mixture. Further, to incur an infraction one must have eaten or drunk the forbidden amount of food in the normal time that it would take to eat food of that size.

In addition to the expected boiling, roasting, baking, and the like, the rabbis considered soaking in water to be cooking as well.[130] This assessment arises because, if one were to soak meat that had not been salted and rinsed to remove its blood, after twenty-four hours the blood would be deemed to have fully pervaded the meat, rendering it inedible—as if it were cooked. As an incidental exception to this, meat and milk that are soaked together for a twenty-four-hour period are not considered to have been cooked together, though such a mixture remains forbidden by rabbinic injunction.

Another development is the duration of time that must elapse between the eating of dairy and meat meals. The following statement illustrates the issue colorfully: "Rav Ḥisda stated, 'One who ate meat is forbidden to eat cheese. One who ate cheese may eat meat.' Mar Ukba said, 'In this matter [of waiting between meals of meat and milk], I am as vinegar is to wine compared with my father. For if my father were to eat flesh now, he would not eat cheese until this very hour tomorrow, whereas I do not eat in the same meal but I do eat it in my next meal.'"[131] Thus the delay holds only after eating meat; after eating dairy foods, perhaps because they are understood to be digested more quickly, there is no waiting period.[132]

In addition to concern for the kashrut of the food itself, all vessels used for cooking and eating had to be maintained in a proper state of fitness. Pots had to be separated according to meat or dairy designations and had to be protected from invalidation through forbidden contact with prohibited food substances.[133] According to rabbinic "science," the taste of food is absorbed into pots and can then exude that same taste into the next food cooked in the same pot. Once a pot of food reaches the temperature of "*yad soledet bo*," taste-transfer occurs. If forbidden food were cooked in a pot, its forbidden taste, potentially contaminating to food that was cooked there subsequently, would be absorbed into the pot. In order to rehabilitate that pot, the principle of "as it was absorbed, so it is exuded"[134] was applied to remove the offending "taste." The rabbis developed this principle through the interpretation of verses in the books of Numbers and Leviticus: "Gold and silver, copper, iron, tin, and lead—any article that can withstand fire—these you shall pass through fire and they shall be clean, except that they must be cleaned with water of lustration; and anything that cannot withstand fire you must pass through water" (Numbers 31:22–23). "An earthen vessel in which it was boiled shall be broken; if it was boiled in a copper vessel, [the vessel] shall be scoured and rinsed with water" (Leviticus 6:21). A pot could be refurbished through heating a full pot of water beyond the point of *yad soledet bo;* this would cause the offending taste to be exuded into the water where it is nullified according to the principle of "nullification in sixty."

Beyond the foods forbidden by the Torah, either explicitly or derived through rabbinic interpretation of the Torah's intent, the rabbis saw fit to augment this list with other foods. These include the following:

Milk drawn from an animal by a non-Jew without the presence of a Jew is forbidden out of concern that the non-Jew mixed in milk from a non-kosher animal.[135]

Cheese produced by non-Jews is forbidden out of a similar concern that rennet from a non-kosher animal would be used.[136]

Wine touched or moved by a non-Jew is forbidden out of a concern that it was used for idolatrous worship.[137]

Each of these food restrictions constitutes a broadening of existing biblical interdictions. There are, in addition, other foods that the rabbis banned as a measure to prevent excessive social contact with non-Jews. These include

bread baked by a non-Jew;[138]
food cooked by non-Jew;[139]
wine prepared, moved, or touched by a non-Jew.[140]

This final category indicates the means by which the rabbinic sensibility moved beyond some of the inscrutable prohibitions regarding food to ruling with an eye toward social policy. The voluminous legislation on food law that the rabbis crafted, even when inexplicit, inevitably promoted separation between Jews and non-Jews; this likely was precisely what the authors had in mind. The level of restrictions designed by the rabbis virtually ensures that commensality will not reach beyond the Jewish community and, even then, only among those with the requisite know-how.

THE MEDIEVAL PERIOD

Moses Maimonides (1135–1204) had a profound influence on all subsequent Jewish literature, and our discussion of the medieval attitudes toward food will consequently focus strongly on some of the main lines of his approach. Although many came to disagree, his most prolific opponents came from within the kabbalistic camp, even if they were highly influenced by his thinking as well. Maimonides treats eating practices in both his legal code, *Mishneh Torah,* and his philosophical work, *The Guide of the Perplexed.* Perhaps the statement that could be read as an overall measure of his approach is in the Laws of Opinions:

> One should direct one's mind and all his actions exclusively to knowing God. Whether sitting, rising, or talking—all must be inclined in this direction. For example, when engaged in a business or in some wage-earning, one's aim should not be only to hoard money; instead, one is to do these things in order to obtain his physical needs: food, drink, shelter and marriage. Also, when he eats, drinks, or engages in sexual intercourse—he should not have in mind to do this only to gratify his physical needs, so that he is likely to eat and drink only what is sweet to the palate, and have sexual intercourse for the purpose of pleasure—but should have in his mind that he eats and drinks for the sole purpose of maintaining his body and its organs in good health. Hence, he will not eat everything that the

palate desires, like a dog or a donkey, but will use foods which do good to the body, whether bitter or sweet, avoiding those that are harmful to the body even though they are sweet to the palate. (Laws of Opinions 3:2)[141]

Maimonides' attitude toward food is utilitarian and rationalistic: one eats to sustain one's body in good health, with the ultimate aim of acquiring knowledge of God. In subsequent teachings, he cultivates an approach that is modest and private in style and moderate in quantity (Laws of Opinions 5:1–3). He quotes approvingly the talmudic statement "One should spend less than his means on food" (b. Ḥullin 84b).

In addition to his utilitarianism, which ties into his rationalistic theology, Maimonides' experience as a physician plays a considerable role in his legislation regarding diet. He devotes a full chapter of his Laws of Opinions (chapter 4) to details about conduct during a meal and specific types of foods that he recommends or rejects as unsuitable. More details of conduct during a meal can be found in Laws of Blessings, along with the arrangement of guests at the table and the hierarchy of host and guests with regard to different practices in the course of a meal.

In *The Guide of the Perplexed* 3:48, Maimonides offers his fullest discussion regarding forbidden foods. He writes,

I say, then, that to eat any of the various kinds of food that the Law has forbidden us is blameworthy. Among all those forbidden to us, only pork and fat may be imagined not to be harmful. But this is not so, for pork is more humid than is proper and contains much superfluous matter. The major reason why the Law abhors it is its being very dirty and feeding on dirty things. You know to what extent the Law insists upon the need to remove filth out of sight, even in the field and in a military camp, and all the more within cities. Now if swine were used for food, market-places and even houses would have been dirtier than latrines, as may be seen at present in the country of the Franks [i.e., of Western Europeans]. You know the dictum [of the Sages], may their memory be blessed: "The mouth of a swine is like walking excrement." The fat of the intestines, too, makes us full, spoils the digestion, and produces cold and thick blood. It is more suitable to burn it. Blood, on the one hand and carcasses of beasts that have died, on the other, are also difficult to digest and constitute a harmful nourishment. It is well known that a beast that is *terefah* [i.e., an animal that is diseased or wounded] is close to being a carcass. . . . As for the prohibition against eating meat [boiled] in milk, it is in my opinion not improbable that—in addition to this being undoubtedly very gross food and very filling—idolatry had something to do with it. Perhaps such food was eaten at one of the ceremonies of their cult or at one of their festivals. . . . In my opinion this is the most probable view regarding the reason for this prohibition, but I have not seen this set down in any of the books of the Sabians that I have read.[142]

Much of the argumentation that Maimonides provides here is of a medical sort: in general, the animals prohibited by the Torah in Leviticus 11:1–28 and Deuteronomy 14:12–18 are deemed harmful nourishment;[143] pork is said to be unhealthy by virtue of its excess humidity, thus being hard to digest; blood and carcasses, similarly, are hard to digest; with regard to meat cooked in milk he offers a medical reason—that this is "very gross food and very filling," but the primary justification that he offers for the prohibition is that cooking meat in milk was most likely an ancient pagan practice. Substantiating his scientific approach, he contends that the signs of an animal's permitted or forbidden status are not in and of themselves of any significance beyond helping to identify those animals that are beneficial and those that are not. Part of this argument seems designed to counter the possibility of symbolic interpretation, precisely the kind of reading that the kabbalists were soon to give.

Maimonides, a physician, followed Galen's approach in medicine; is it possible that Galen proposed a diet that so closely accorded with the commandments of Judaism? In fact, there are a range of foodstuffs that Maimonides recommends in his medical treatises whose consumption would contravene normative practice; these include the hare, wild ass,[144] and even pigs.[145] Moreover, he would have been familiar with the Arab custom of cooking meat in milk, which raises the question of the viability of his assertion that this is an unhealthy practice. It appears that the recommendations of prohibited food are only as remedies, not as food—this holds true for the hare, the ass, and the pig.[146] There is no mention of the prohibition of carcasses in his medical works, but he does refer to the danger of eating meat that is not fresh.[147] As to meat cooked in milk, in *The Regimen of Health* he says that "all that is cooked from milk or cooked in it are bad foods"; this coupled with the pagan practice is more than sufficient to explain the prohibition. In sum, "all Maimonides' works, and especially his medical works, lead us to the clear conclusion that in *The Guide of the Perplexed* he indeed expressed his expert opinion as a physician regarding the unhealthy quality of prohibited food, at least as concerns consumption by healthy persons."[148]

Maimonides' approach can be distilled to three essential sets of concerns: medical, rational, and theological, the latter reflected in his representation of Judaism as a battle for monotheism. This nexus of issues is representative of the Jewish elite of his time in Northern Africa and the Iberian peninsula. While Maimonides brought his philosophical, theological, and medical interests into intimate dialogue with his halakhic works, his younger contemporaries in Spain expended great energies explicating the talmudic laws regarding food and eating without explicit recourse to these seemingly external disciplines. Normative Jewish law reached its ripest development during the twelfth through fourteenth centuries in the hands of figures such as Rashi (Rabbi Solomon Yiẓḥaki, twelfth-century France), the Tosafists (twelfth-through fourteenth-century France), Rabbi Moses ben Naḥman (Moses ben Nahman, thirteenth-century Spain), Rabbi Solomon ben Adret (Rashba, thirteenth-century Spain), and Rabbi Yom Tov ben Ishvili (Ritva, fourteenth-century Spain), to mention a few. Moreover, the halakhic features in the *Zohar*, surprisingly, reflect more of the influence of the practice in Ashkenaz than in Spain.[149] Although much of the literary output of these figures had been written before or contemporaneously with the zoharic kabbalists, the latter seem to have taken little interest in or to have had limited access to such writings. The *Zohar* takes stands on quite a number of halakhic issues concerning matters of liturgy or ritual practice with regard to prayer, the Sabbath, and holidays, but few in the spheres of dietary practice or rituals related to eating.

Summary

This chapter has tracked the enormous range of significances attributed to eating practices and the elaboration of legislation regarding food consumption within the Judaic tradition as it developed through the thirteenth century. Among the broad strokes that we have examined are the propitiation of the Deity, symbolization, tensions around incarnation, spiritual qualms about the value of food, utilitarian approaches, legalistic development, and myth. Social separation is an important aspect of the dietary laws in the biblical through medieval periods. Whereas in biblical literature the laws aim to separate Israelites from other nations—an approach continued in the rabbinic tradition—the Pharisees use food laws to reinforce internal boundaries, defining which groups of Jews can eat with each other. The kabbalists, as we shall see, are invested in social hierarchies and yet are also committed to erasing strong boundaries among Jews, finding holiness in all social quarters. The biblical dietary laws—understood by scholars as aiming to establish order, ethics, or holiness—are interpreted in similar fashion by the kabbalists. Indeed, for the kabbalists, it is the immanent possibility of tying normative practice to themes of morality, holiness, or purity that animates much of their discussions about food. The rabbinic motif of nourishment from the luster of the *Shekhinah* becomes readily adapted in the Neoplatonic style of thinking about the relationship between God, people, and the foodstuffs that traverse the distance between them. The spiritualized luster approaches something far closer to incarnationalism in the hands of the medieval mystics. Lastly, the rabbinic habit of symbolization with food, most notably and explicitly at the Passover seder, becomes a normative approach in the hands of the kabbalists.

Although it is beyond the purview of this study, each of the eras that we have considered generates multiple conceptions of the body that the texts on eating could be forced to disgorge. For the kabbalistic writers, most of the literature I have considered was easily available to them as they contemplated the textualized food embodied in the Torah's narratives and commandments, and even as they contemplated their own food. Out of the profusion of materials, they carved out a coherent, if not homogeneous, set of approaches for thinking about food and ingesting and incorporating the divine blessing they sought.

2

"A Blessing in the Belly": Mystical Satiation

IN HIS *Major Trends in Jewish Mysticism,* Gershom Scholem cites Psalm 34:9 ("Taste and see that the Lord is good") as signifying the quintessence of the mystical experience. He explains that mysticism is the longing of the finite, mortal individual to cross the chasm that divides him from the divine Infinite.[1] While Scholem construes the Psalmist's locution in a purely metaphorical way, I will argue for a more transparent interpretation of the verse. I contend that to be able *to taste* that the Lord is good is to experience bodily the nature of Divinity. In another instance of a bodily metaphor, Psalm 40:9 says, "To do what pleases You, my God, is my desire; your law is in my heart (*mei'ai*)" or, alternatively, "Your Torah is in my inmost parts," or even "in my belly." Other biblical evidence and surrounding Near Eastern literature associate the term *mei'ai* with the liver, heart, and womb; it is also related to the emotions. For the zoharic kabbalists, however, this formulation signifies yet another mystical experience, an internalization of the Torah that goes beyond affiliation, loyalty, and behavior. It touches on the bodily transformation of the individual, representing him as a living expression of the Torah, having literally ingested Torah, and feeling fully satiated as a result.

The biblical trope of the Torah in the belly is surely not meant by the *author* to be taken literally, but rather intends that the poet's being is permeated with a fullness of devotion to God and His teaching.[2] An examination of passages from the *Zohar* and contemporaneous kabbalistic literature will demonstrate that, although some instances of these bodily metaphors may be understood as figures of speech, frequently the kabbalists are decoding the biblical text in a "hyper-literal" manner[3] and discovering their own bodies as the site of the mystical encounter.[4] These medieval kabbalists indicate a visceral quality of the mystical experience such that the Torah, even Divinity itself, is known through an encounter that entails eating, digestion, and repletion. Analogously, discussing mystical visionary ascents, Wolfson writes, "The soul undergoes kinesthetic and tactile experiences in the course of its ascent and ultimately enjoys a tangible sense of delight in the moment of the visual encounter with the divine."[5] Tishby comments similarly: "It is possible that in his presentation of *kavvanah* as a religious phenomenon that involves the human body *in toto,* the author of the *Zohar* has in mind a type of religious ecstasy that is accompanied by movements of the different parts of the body to help the soul to reach the peak of its mystical ascent."[6] In other words, the kabbalists ascribe physical attributes to spiritual experiences because that is the way they experienced them.

The technique used to engineer this process is called theurgy, a term that denotes working upon God, which is a central facet of the theosophic kabbalah. Generally, the kabbalah teaches that through Torah study, prayer, and the performance of the commandments one effects unions between the different *sefirot,* inducing cosmic harmony. In order to engage in theurgic praxis, the mystic must direct his attention in the performance of these ritual norms to one *sefirah* or another, or a combination of *sefirot.* A secondary benefit of successful theurgy is that one can draw down blessing from the *sefirot* with which one is interacting. When eating ritual foods, one of the aims of the mystical adept in his theurgic practice is to attain this "blessing in the belly." When the kabbalists sat down to dine they would theurgically invoke divine overflow from above and prompt its downward flow upon the individual's table, the bread upon it, and ultimately into his belly.

Before embarking on the analysis of the kabbalistic selections, it will be helpful to acquaint ourselves with the biblical models that the zoharic kabbalists have in mind in fashioning their own forms of mystical satiety. In chapter 1 I discussed the manna, which was provided according to the individual needs of each consumer: "He who had gathered much had no excess, and he who had gathered little had no deficiency: they had gathered as much as they needed to eat" (Exodus 16:18). While the story of the manna glorifies God's ability to manage scarce resources, the story of Elijah in the first book of Kings provides a true miracle of repletion and transformation of the foodstuff itself. The widow of Zarephath laments that she has

"nothing but a handful of flour in a jar and a little oil in a jug. I am just gathering a couple of sticks, so that I can go home and prepare it for me and my son; we shall eat it and then we shall die." "Don't be afraid," said Elijah to her. "Go and do as you have said; but first make me a small cake from what you have there, and bring it out to me; then make some for yourself and your son. For thus said the Lord, the God of Israel: 'The jar of flour shall not give out and the jug of oil shall not fail until the day that the Lord sends rain upon the ground.'" She went and did as Elijah had spoken, and she and he and her household had food for a long time. The jar of flour did not give out, nor did the jug of oil fail, just as the Lord had spoken through Elijah. (1 Kings 17:12–16)

Elijah's disciple Elisha performs similar feats. Scripture relates that "a man came from Baal-shalishah and he brought the man of God some bread of the first reaping—twenty loaves of barley bread, and some fresh grain in his sack. And [Elisha] said, 'Give it to the people and let them eat.' His attendant replied, 'How can I set this before a hundred men?' But he said, 'Give it to the people and let them eat'" (2 Kings 4:42–44). The *Zohar* takes these legendary histories and finds in their promise of God's grace a route to mystical satiation unmoored by historical confines. In the kabbalists' imaginative re-creation of these miraculous repasts, the satisfaction of bodily needs does not suffice as evidence of the mystical adhesion; the mystical initiates described further marvels that accompanied the mystical satiation.

In this chapter I examine the range of experiences associated with mystical satiation. A variety of foodstuffs and halakhic categories are marshaled in the kabbalistic texts to demonstrate feelings of physical and/or spiritual plenitude. The manna, the showbread, the halakhic category of the "olive's volume,"[7] and, sometimes, merely spiritual intention are all said to be capable of providing nourishment, even a feeling of fullness. This fusion of the parameters set by the imagination and the concomitant bodily experience is a form of psychosomatic unity. By use of the term "psychosomatic unity" I intend an experience in which a feeling that one would normally associate with the spiritual component of a person is vividly associated with her physical nature.[8] I do not mean that there is a full ontological identity between these two aspects of the individual; instead, it is the hyperliteral hermeneutic of the *Zohar* vivifying the meaning of the verse "Taste and see that the Lord is good."[9] This type of experience, then, is far from a "flight from physicality" or "escape into mysticism," but rather is more like a lived appreciation of "the possibilities provided by fleshliness."[10] It must be said that not all eating narratives result in a psychosomatic unity: there are certainly passages that, in emphasizing a body-soul dualism, militate against that kind of experience. Psychosomatic unity marks one place along a spectrum of experiences of body-soul interaction.

The existence of a phenomenon of psychosomatic unity raises important questions about the relationships of body and imagination, body and soul, and body and text. The different selections that I analyze in the following sections provide a range of responses to the following questions: To what extent is embodiment determined by one's spiritual intentions? What are the ways in which imagination about food shapes the visceral experiences of food? How do the biblical and rabbinic traditions shape the kabbalistic mindset and embodiment with regard to a feeling of surfeit in one's belly? Finally, what type of body emerges from the hyperliteral understanding of the Torah?

THE BLESSING IN THE BELLY

One dramatic homily from the *Zohar* recounts the miraculous experiences enjoyed by the Israelites when they consumed the heavenly manna:

> all of the faithful (literally: "scions of faith": *bnei mehemnuta*) went out and gathered [the manna] and blessed the holy name over it.[11] The manna emitted fragrances of all of the aromas of the Garden for it [the manna] was drawn from there and descended below.[12] Any taste that a person wanted he would find in it and would bless the supernal King.[13] He would then receive blessing in his belly (*mitbarekh be-mei'oi*) and would look and know above, seeing supernal wisdom. Hence they were called "a knowing generation." These are the faithful and the Torah was given to them to gaze into and to know its ways.[14] What is written about those who are not amongst the faithful? "The people would wander about and gather it" (Numbers 11:8). What is the meaning of "go about" (*shatu*)? They were taken to folly (*shetuta*) because they were not among the faithful. What is written about them? "[They would] grind it between millstones or pound it in a mortar." Who went to all this trouble? Those who were not among the faithful. Similarly, those who do not believe in the Holy One, blessed be He, are unable to look in His paths and they have to trouble themselves every day for food, day and night—perhaps they will not have bread. What causes this to befall them? It is because they are not of the faithful. (*Zohar* 2:62b–63a)

The sequence of experiences and techniques employed to attain them, as described in this section, can be distilled as follows. After gathering the manna, "the faithful" recite a blessing over it before eating. Its fragrance wafts over them, they taste it, and, after eating it, recite another blessing. The individual receives a blessing in his stomach, following which he looks above, seeing supernal wisdom. The recitation of the blessing, particularly after eating the manna, is instrumental in inducing the reception of divine blessing.[15] Most striking in this particular passage is that the descending blessing resides *in* the person's body. While in many passages it appears that the authorship of the *Zohar* thinks of the body as being inhabited by the soul, in this instance, the body itself partakes of the spirituality, yielding an experience of psychosomatic unity. The very experience of mystical repletion appears to originate from the fullness that one enjoys following a hearty meal. If that is so, the kabbalists' metaphor of choice—satiation—refers precisely to the literal experience itself. In other words, mystical plenitude is an extension of physical plenitude, the former being a translation of the physical experience into a mystical encounter.[16]

The act of eating that the kabbalists imagine, supplying a feeling of surfeit, provides a secondary benefit as well—the acquisition of enhanced hermeneutical abilities. In their reading of the biblical stories of miraculous eating, the kabbalists ascribe these augmented capabilities to biblical characters. The text of the *Zohar* analyzed earlier adduces a convergence of hermeneutical, ontological, and psychosomatic events: as the Israelites looked *into* the Torah, discerned the flavors *in* the manna, they would receive blessing *in* the belly. In the course of penetrating the Torah, itself an expression of Divinity, Divinity in turn penetrates the kabbalist. Thus wisdom is attained somatically, through eating.[17] Those who are unfamiliar with or, more likely, unappreciative of the esoteric approach, are doomed to "go about," unable to *enter into* the mystical knowledge promised to the faithful. They fail to realize that there is a mode of assimilating knowledge of the Torah that is immediate and effortless, an act of entry into an open door, as opposed to the travails of wandering and the drudgery of grinding. The wandering and grinding reflect spiritual itinerancy and intellectualistic study.[18]

In the Jewish mystical literature of the thirteenth century, this is a familiar polemic. A battle for the hearts and minds of the learned classes was a bête noire between the kabbalists and those who were following in the tradition of Maimonides. Kabbalists excoriated the rationalism of unnamed figures, blaming their rationalistic turn of mind for their refusal to recognize the mystical depths of the Torah. In *Sefer ha-Rimmon*, Moshe de Leon launches a two-pronged attack against those who have internalized the rationalistic approach:

I have seen men who used to occupy themselves with Torah and the teachings of the rabbis, may their memory be for a blessing, day and night; and they used to serve the Omnipresent with a full heart, as is appropriate. And then, one day, scholars of Greek wisdom came to confront the Lord, and Satan, too, came into their midst, causing them to leave the Source of Living Waters. They occupied themselves with those books [of Greek wisdom] and their minds were drawn after them until they left the teachings of the Torah and the commandments and cast them behind their backs.[19] According to the estimation of their alien thinking, they considered the teachings of the rabbis to be falsehood. "There was no sound and none who responded" (I Kings 18:29) for they were distant as a result of the Greeks and their supporters. There was no spirit of God within them such that they were transformed into other men, casting aspersion on their former selves and fine behaviors, according to which they conducted themselves in the past. They mocked and cast aspersions upon the teachings of [the rabbis], may their memory be for a blessing. . . . I have also seen them during the holiday of Sukkot standing in their place in the synagogue watching the servants of God circling the Torah scrolls in the ark with their lulavim, and the former were laughing and casting aspersions upon them. They said that they were fools, lacking in understanding, while they themselves had neither lulav nor etrog. They contended, "Did not the Torah say that this taking [of lulav and etrog] was on account of the verse 'And you shall rejoice before the Lord your God seven days'? (Exodus 23:40). You think that these [four] species will cause us to rejoice? Vessels of silver and gold and [valuable] garments will cause us to rejoice and delight!" And they said, "You who think that we must bless the Lord—He needs this? It is all folly!" Later, tefillin would no longer be seen on their heads and, when people asked them for the reason, they would say, "Is not the idea of tefillin precisely that which is written in Scripture, 'and as a reminder on your forehead?' (Exodus 13:9). Since there is no better memorial than verbally remembering our Creator several times a day, that is a better and more fitting memorial."[20]

The rationalists were accused of mercenary motives and antinomian behavior in their more philosophical approach to the Torah and God's will. When the author of the *Zohar* criticizes those who forage needlessly for the manna, he refers to those indicated in the previous passage, those who must look beyond the scope of the Torah for sustenance.

Mystical intention must be brought to the eating event, because eating manna is neither a mechanical nor an innocent act. This requirement ensures that only the faithful can enjoy the true rewards of the blessing and the food.

The *Zohar* is emphatic in its repetition that it was only the faithful that were able to gain the divine insight and blessing that came with the manna; others had to struggle to find it and then grind it in preparation for eating.[21] Interestingly, the activity of grinding has different valences in the *Zohar* depending on the agent. If the grinding is being done within the sefirotic realm, it is considered a necessary part of the process of causing the procession of divine flow; other times it is considered a necessary part of eating.[22] If, however, the grinding is being done by one who is not a "member of the faithful," it is disparaged and compared to the denigrated pilpulistic activity of those who deny a deeper meaning to the law. In its recasting of the biblical story of the manna, the *Zohar* offers an idealized economic system, in which privilege goes to the mystical elite, and the labor to forage and grind the food is the lot of the spiritual sluggards.[23]

Adam's curse, that he will gain sustenance only through toil and the sweat of his brow, has perennial currency, and the concern with economics that we saw earlier has other parallels. The *Zohar* avers that when the verse in 2 Samuel 9:7 says that Mephibosheth would always eat at King David's table, it means that he did not have to pursue other economic avenues to take care of his material needs; that is, he would be able to rely on providential care exclusively (*Zohar* 2:153a). In this instance the *Zohar* turns to a classically rabbinic approach, contending that the problem of economics is resolved through faith. The nature of satiation adopts different garbs: sometimes it occurs within the belly of the consumer; other times it is represented in terms of the daily search for food, rendered facile for the faithful and arduous for those of improper faith. The kabbalists' discussion of economic issues ultimately evinces a reflection on the biblical verse in Genesis regarding Adam's curse of working by the sweat of his brow more than a personal reflection on the exigencies of earning a living for oneself and one's family.[24] Indeed, the economic theme aims to overcome the mystical and soteriological challenge imposed by God's curse on Adam. The curse follows from a hermeneutical error, leading to economic misfortune. The foolish fail to comprehend that, unlike normal foodstuffs that require the manual labor of grinding in order to render it edible, the manna is ingested effortlessly.[25] Moreover, once ingested, as Joseph of Hamadan teaches, "When a person chews he opens his mouth; thus whoever eats the manna opens his heart and his mouth in the account of the chariot."[26] Here too the manna symbolizes mystical vision, and when one adopts the appropriate spiritual stance in approaching the Torah, one can speak the mystical truths. In a more miraculous and fantastic vein, Baḥya ben Asher says that in the future one will no longer have to work for bread; rather, bread will emerge whole from the ground. In his vision, the world had been transformed as a result of original sin and will ultimately be restored to its idyllic stage.[27]

The *Tikkunei ha-Zohar* continues with the motifs of chewing and grinding to identify the benighted ones who do not apprehend the Torah clearly, while offering yet another way of interpreting the difference between those who acquired the manna with ease and those who struggled to find it.

> "The stomach grinds (*korkevan tohen*)" (*b. Berakhot* 61b): If a person is meritorious, it [the supernal stomach] grinds manna for the righteous because their limbs have been sanctified through the positive commandments. And if they do not conduct themselves in the way of the good commandments, they are sustained by *lehem kelokel* ("miserable food," from Number 21:5), meager (*KaLa*) food, in disgrace (*be-KaLOn*)—throat (*Veshet*)—["The people] would wander about (ShaTU) and gather it" (Numbers 11:8). They would wander and gather in foolishness. "Grind it between millstones"—with great effort. They would grind it in their mouths. "Or pound it in a mortar,"—this is the palate. . . . This is a supernal secret: If Israel is meritorious, the Torah will descend from the heavens for them with no strain and a person will not need to teach his fellow. This is as it is written, "I will rain down bread for you from the heavens" (Exodus 16:4), for there is no bread other than Torah. If they do not merit, it is because of the mixed multitude who are fools. "The people would wander about and gather it" refers to them—they strained to teach each other, each one with difficulty; whereas for the wise, a hint is sufficient. But in the time to come, the mixed multitude will be extinguished from the world and it is said about them, "No longer will they teach one another" (Jeremiah 31:34). (*Tikkunei ha-Zohar* §30, 140b)[28]

Although the verse in Jeremiah looks forward to a day in which God's glory is evident to all, the author of this text construes it to refer to the wicked who share the secrets of their evil ways. Moreover, because the author of *Tikkunei ha-Zohar* is contemplating his contemporary scene and not a final utopia, his comments shed light on his vision of an epistemological ideal. It is unmediated access to divine wisdom that he claims for the elite, whereas others are trapped in conventional learning techniques: education from a teacher or a peer. In essence, then, this appears to be a part of the author's continuing polemic against the rabbinic establishment and a claim for prophecy for the privileged few.

The ambivalence toward work indicated by the curse of wandering and grinding tacitly implies that food procurement is not understood as an independent protocol but rather as one that is driven wholly by exegesis. Thus, when grinding is referred to in a rabbinic text as an activity performed in the heavens, it adopts a holy visage; when it is performed by nonbelievers, the activity itself is deplored. One of medieval kabbalah's primary structural axes is a binary, pitting the holy against the demonic. A prominent example is the kabbalistic transformation of the scapegoat in Leviticus 16. The biblical scapegoat is sent off to the desert, to Azazel, a being or place that is left obscure. The author of *Pirke R. Eliezer* (chapter 46) indicates that this goat is being sent off as a bribe to Samael on Yom Kippur not to prosecute Israel when they stand before God awaiting judgment. Moses ben Nahman carefully explains that this goat is presented to the archon of destruction, not as service but rather because God has commanded this act. The first goat is offered as a sin offering to God, whereas the second is intended to appease the Other Side, distracting it from the sancta of the Temple and dissuading it from acting as accuser to Israel.[29] The *Zohar* expands upon this description, explaining that this goat was offered to the *Sitra Aḥra,* the Other Side, so that it too has something to eat from the King's banquet and so that it would lose interest in the primary offering in the Temple precincts. In each of these examples—grinding and the scapegoat—it is the approbation or condemnation insinuated in canonical texts, as inferred by the kabbalistic interpretation, that determines the ontology, sacred or evil, of a given subject or activity.

A somewhat similar approach is taken by Isaac of Acre in comparing two different kinds of food, this time with a turn of the hermeneutic wheel toward faith rather than openness to esoteric interpretation. He poses two different kinds of food—manna and quail—as two different kinds of requests from God:

When they asked for the quail with a complaint, and not in an appropriate manner (*ve-lo ke-halakhah*), the blessed Holy One satisfied their desire to demonstrate His Greatness. Was the hand of the Lord not restrained? Indeed, He gave it to them with the attribute of night, as it is written, "[By evening] you shall know it was the Lord who brought you out from the land of Egypt." Use of the term "evening" attests to the attribute of nighttime (*Shekhinah*). With regard to the manna, which they asked for in an appropriate manner (*ke-halakhah*), for a man cannot be sustained without eating, they trusted in the blessed Holy One, gathering enough each day, except for the Sabbath [when there is a double portion].[30] This is the full trust (*bitaḥon*) that one should have in God, that He will provide one's daily sustenance. He gave them [the manna] with an illuminated visage, that is, the attribute of daytime (*Tif'eret*). This is as it is written, "and in the morning you shall behold the Glory of the Lord" (Exodus 16:7) and I say that the term "morning" attests to the attribute of daytime.[31]

Two naturally occurring events, the appearance at dawn of the manna and the nighttime resting of the migrating quail, are first explained by scripture as miraculous provisions by God for the Israelites. Exegetical hooks such as day and night, and the Glory of God in relation to the former, allow Isaac of Acre to interpret the two events along dualistic lines, here emphasizing faith and its lack.

The binaries of good food/bad food, manna/quail, and good intentions/bad intentions are treated by the author of the *Tikkunei ha-Zohar* as well.[32] He notes that it is the mixed multitude that, according to the midrashic tradition, asks for the meat. This meat cannot be demonized in a facile way because of a teaching in the Talmud that states that this meat fell from heaven, and nothing impure falls from heaven.[33] The esoteric meaning of this meat, the homily continues, can be discerned in the verse "[My breath shall not abide in man forever,] since he too is flesh (*be-she-gam hu basar*)" (Genesis 6:3). Because the *gematriyah* (numerical value) of *be-she-gam* equals the *gematriyah* of Moses, the kabbalistic reading of the verse yields an identification of Moses with *be-she-gam*. *Be-she-gam*, in turn, is flesh according to the verse, yielding a theosophic link of the quail with the *sefirah* with which Moses is identified *Tif'eret*.[34] Thus, just as the manna comes from *Tif'eret*, so does the quail. The problem then is not the source but rather the way in which the individual Jew relates to flesh per se. One approach is through the kabbalistic interpretation of "from my flesh I shall see God"; through proper observance of biblical legislation regarding sexuality, one preserves the covenant of the flesh and merits a vision of God. If, however, one violates these norms, the flesh (*bsr*) is turned into famine (*Shbr*). The linchpin, determining whether one receives flesh or famine, is one's guarding of the fleshly covenant.[35] One kind of *basar* is edible and damaging, the other opens onto visionary experience.[36] Sexual behavior—and here the text intends to include purity of thought as well—calibrates the quality of divine overflow. In each of these instances, the dualism hinges on the essential correctness of one's hermeneutics, but the question is intimately connected to pure action and, one assumes, proper social affiliations. Similarly, the *Zohar* asserts that the children of Israel were privileged to eat the manna but the mixed multitude were not (*Zohar* 191b). It is no surprise that the medieval kabbalah uses binaries to inscribe its spiritual, social, and political ideology. It is noteworthy, though, to see how this manifests itself in practice through belief and social demarcation.

INDUCED SATIETY AND THE VOLUME OF AN OLIVE

In contrast to the somewhat materialist nature of the *Zohar*'s approach discussed earlier, elsewhere the *Zohar* treats the concept of satiety by spiritualizing it:

> Rabbi Ḥiyya began, saying, "'When you have eaten and been sated you shall bless the Lord your God' (Deuteronomy 8:10). Is it the case that unless one has eaten to satiety and filled his stomach that he should not bless the Holy One, blessed be He? [If that is so,] to what [amount of food] do we apply the verse 'When you have eaten and been sated you shall bless [the Lord your God]?' Rather, even if a person only eats an olive's-worth (*ke-zayit*) [of bread] and his 'intention' (*re'uteih*) is upon it and he has considered it (that morsel) to be the essence of his meal, he is deemed 'sated.'[37] This is as it is written, 'You open your hand and feed every creature as it wills (*razon*)' (Psalm 145:16). It is not written 'every creature,' rather [it is written, 'every creature] as it wills.' That intention (*razon*) which he directs to that food is called 'satiety' and even if there is only a small olive's-worth and nothing more before this person. Thus it is the intention of 'satiety' that he has accorded to it. Therefore, [it is written,] 'and feed every creature as it wills.' It is written 'as it wills' and not ['feed every creature] its food.' For this reason it is written 'and you will bless,' in actuality (*vadai*), and a person is obligated to bless the Holy One, blessed be He, in order to give pleasure above." (*Zohar* 2:153a–b)

The author is responding to the fact that, according to normative Jewish law, one recites Grace after a *ke-zayit* of bread rather than after actual satiety.[38] Responding to the contradiction between holy writ and norm, the writer contends that the blessing should follow upon either satiety or a contemplation-induced satiety. Because scripture specifies satiety, satiety there must be. "Satiety" emerges as a technical term not necessarily referring to an experience of physical fullness. Physical repletion is not entirely irrelevant: the physical state prescribed by the normative halakhah is textually associated with the minimal amount required to be eaten to invoke the requirement of Grace. The physical, then, is important, but mostly as a cue: one must eat in order to invoke the commandment of Grace; in the verse, then, the term "satiety" refers to a particular kind of contemplation rather than a physical experience. The *Zohar* is referring to an "induced satiation," a somatized feeling of mystical fullness in which the contemplative application of *kavvanah* to one's meal results in both a unitive mystical experience and a physical sensation of saturation that is consequent upon that experience.

We see how, in Steven Katz's words, "beliefs shape experience, just as experience shapes belief."[39] The operative mechanism that enables this satiation by a *ke-zayit* is the textualization of the kabbalistic body; that is, the mystic has a visceral cognition of the olive's volume before him by virtue of his internalization of the textual practices, laws, and beliefs that inform his diet. The hermeneutical key that facilitates the bodily transformation is the kabbalistic use of the term *vadai* ("in actuality"). In context, the term explains, actually *responds to,* the implicit question of how a mortal could confer blessing onto God. The *Zohar*'s assumed readership has an inculcated assumption that, while people may utter blessings, the metaphysical content of blessing can proceed only downward, from the supernal realm to the human. The author of the *Zohar* here attests to the possibility of translation of a human blessing to the supernal realm. This translation occurs bilaterally: the *ke-zayit* of food that he ingests is energized by *razon,* and in this bridging of holy and mundane worlds, the liturgy can then travel upward as blessing "in actuality."[40]

A gap exists between the law requiring grace after eating a *ke-zayit* and the plain meaning of the biblical verse, which calls for a blessing after satiety, which is not likely to ensue after eating an olive's volume of bread. The author of the *Zohar* capitalizes on this gap, making contemplation the central aim of the practice through his exegesis of the verse "and feed every creature as it wills." What one "wills," in terms of satiety, is a state of contemplation. The *Zohar* concludes, saying that one has an obligation to bless in order to give pleasure above; although this is not overtly talking about physical pleasure, especially because it is referring to the divine realm, it does return the reader's attention to the factor of physical experience and pleasure. Throughout the kabbalah, there is a ubiquitous pairing of the human realm and the sefirotic in which the human anthropos is said to be modeled after the divine anthropos. Consequently, the joy given to the Divine, as described at the end of the passage, follows upon a sensual experience on the part of the mystic or, at the very least, the ritualized behaviors associated with satiety. "Satiety" thus acts as both a technical term and a reference to a felt experience. I suggest that the *Zohar* is referring to an "induced satiation," a somatized feeling of mystical fullness in which the contemplative application of *kavvanah* to one's meal results in both a unitive mystical experience and a physical sensation of saturation that is consequent upon that experience.[41]

Joseph of Hamadan offers a similar rendition of satiation from a *ke-zayit* of bread:

> [It is a commandment to] set forth bread and frankincense before the Lord on each Sabbath, as it is said, "And on the table you shall set the face-bread (*lehem ha-panim:* usually, showbread) before me always." The essence of this commandment has already been stated by our masters, may their memory be for a blessing, with regard to the face-bread. Why is it called face-bread? Because each and every side has a face and since it is all faces, it is called face-bread.[42] The Holy One, blessed be He, caused blessing to descend there. When the priests would eat of the face-bread, seventy faces, they would eat a *ke-zayit,* since, "There the Lord ordained blessing, everlasting life" (Psalm 133:3), and the priests were nourished [from the bread] because the blessing and everlasting life descend there.[43]

In this example, the *ke-zayit* also serves as a marker not only of physical satiation or psychosomatic plenitude but also of ultimate redemption: upon eating this meager portion of bread one gains "blessing and everlasting life." It can be inferred that the kabbalist-cum-priest gains the physical experience of satiety through a meager portion of bread.[44] We see a return to the economic theme that if one can eat food that has been blessed by God, one can survive on considerably less than a normal person. Moreover, Hamadan portrays the idealized food as a substance that has been energized so that its functionality has been enhanced. The priests gain physical nourishment and both physical and spiritual satiety through eating yet a different idealized food—idealized because of its sacred function but also because of the legendary attributes ascribed to it. For example, the "face-bread" bears seventy faces, a number that signifies completion in the rabbinic and kabbalistic mindsets. Thus, even though Hamadan does not associate the bread with any particular *sefirah* or suggest that Divinity itself has somehow descended into the bread, the plenitude is a cipher for a rendezvous with perfection itself.

SATIETY FROM *RAZON* VERSUS REAL FOOD

The previous discussion maintained that satiety can be achieved with a morsel and a bit of *kavvanah.* Spirituality meets economics in another passage of the

Zohar that distinguishes between different grades of satiety: that of the rich man, of the poor man, and finally, of all people:

> In all, three kinds of food are described here. ["The eyes of all look to You expectantly] and you give them their food when it is due" (Psalm 145:15). This is the food of the wealthy to whom an abundance of food is given at the appropriate time (*be'ito*)—that is one [type of food].[45] The second [kind of food corresponds to that which] is written, "and sate all creatures with favor (*razon*)" (Psalm 145:16). This is the food of the poor who are sated with favor (*razon*) and not with an abundance of food.[46] The third is, as it is written, "You open Your hand [and sate all creatures with favor (*razon*)]" (Psalm 145:16). This is the power of that place through which favor and satiation emerge for all when He opens His hand." (*Zohar* 3:226a).

This passage invokes the question of the sympathy or identification that the kabbalists had for the poor. Anger toward the moneyed class is sprinkled liberally in the *Ra'aya Mehemna* and the *Tikkunei ha-Zohar*, the latter strata of the *Zohar*. In fact, Yizhak Baer argued that the authorship of the *Ra'aya Mehemna* and the *Tikkunei ha-Zohar* were much influenced by the model of their Franciscan counterparts who esteemed poverty as a religious value. Although this position was critiqued in later scholarship, the ethical stance of these latter strata of the *Zohar* and even of the *Zohar* itself stand out.[47] The poor represent the lowly and humble and are associated with the *Shekhinah* and, as such, are worthy models for the kabbalists.

There are two possible interpretations that one can adopt with regard to the similarity of the poor to the kabbalists, both of whom are able to subsist on *razon*, through reading each in light of the other. The kabbalists may be poor themselves and through kabbalistic concentration are able to defeat their hunger. The previous passage would then have to be understood as one of the polemical pieces in the *Zohar* that critique the upper classes—the wealthy attend to their material needs while the impoverished kabbalists remain focused on spiritual ends. The other interpretation would be to suggest that the poor, by virtue of their misfortune, inexorably attain a spiritual grade that is superior to that of their more affluent counterparts. The *Zohar* claims that King David is able to transform himself into a poor person through contemplation, attested to by the opening line of Psalm 102: "A prayer of the lowly man when he is faint and pours forth his plea before the Lord."[48] This transformative capacity is valued because God is said to be more attentive to the petitions of the lowly. Is this attentiveness experienced through the dispatch of food or the ability to be satisfied with *razon* alone? The closing sentence of the previously cited passage suggests the latter: ultimately, all creatures will be sated with God's favor as strength is given to *Malkhut,* "that place," which then disseminates favor and satisfaction to all. Further, the poor are nourished from the *sefirah* of *Keter,* the highest of the *sefirot,* whereas the wealthy are receiving their abundant food from the relatively lowly *Yesod* and *Shekhinah.* In this nexus of the material, spiritual, and economic spheres, the entire populace is not promised the boon of wealth and comfort; rather, the advantages normally conferred upon the poor will ideally be given to all creatures. Unless "satiety" is given a privileged meaning that refers to an experience resulting from a large quantity of food, it seems safe to assume that the ideal is a somatized spirituality, that is, satiety without food.[49]

The consequence is that, inasmuch as the "experience" of satiety can be attained through a somatized spiritual event, and this event corresponds to the experience of the impoverished, there is a dialectic of opposites that constitutes the existing, consuming body. The idealized body, in dialogue with the actual body, a body that knows hunger full well, is determined in the exchange. In other words, in imagining a body above and a body below, religious writers inevitably create a dialectic of the actual human body and the idealized human body—the body that is and the body that could be.[50] In other words, the kabbalists, adequately fed, identify with the poor and meld their own experience with that which they project onto the poor. Their own superlative experiences interact imaginatively with the presumably quite different experiences of the pious poor. Further, this "body-technique" of experiencing satiation with minimal provisions underscores and harmonizes well with the ascetic inclinations of the kabbalists.[51] In this manner, their mystical experience is wed to their ethical program: not only should one not eat too much but, in constraint, the practicing kabbalist will experience a "real" physical satiation, a far cry from the clearly metaphorical satiety that one acquires through spiritual activities such as Torah study.[52] In a slightly different way the author of the *Ra'aya Mehemna* gives an apologetic accounting for the less privileged condition of the Jews in his day, making a virtue of necessity in discussing a lack of sufficient food. He writes that Israel does not have food in this world as compared to that of the other nations of the world; Israel will find theirs is in the world-to-come (*Zohar* 3:232a *Ra'aya Mehemna*). Although this is not advocacy for or against fasting, it intimates that historical contingencies occasionally affected kabbalistic attitudes toward food.

Fasting, Sacrifices of the Flesh, and Embodied Spirituality

Mystics are commonly conceived of as ascetic, solitary individuals, but the zoharic kabbalists are not asocial, and their asceticism is moderate. Nonetheless, the biblical and rabbinic traditions they have inherited has a host of legislated fast days, including Yom Kippur, the Ninth of Av—commemorating the destruction of the Temple in Jerusalem—and a series of minor fasts, as well. Indeed, fasting is a venerated practice in both biblical and rabbinic traditions, intended to command God's attention and elicit his mercies during times of affliction and distress. Moreover, the spirit-matter dualism that is a central structuring feature of kabbalistic theology inclines toward fasting or other forms of self-sacrifice as the means of mending this rift. Before commencing with my analysis of kabbalistic fasting, some brief observations on fasting in biblical and rabbinic literature are in order. Fasting is a paradigmatic form of ascetic behavior intended to induce repentance and to display that intention to God. Preeminent examples include the psalmist's lament of the social disgrace he suffers as a result of his fasting (Psalm 69: 10–12); in the book of Esther, when news of Haman's plotting spreads, the Jews of Shushan begin to display penitent behavior upon Esther's instruction (Esther 4:3); in the book of Daniel, the hero fasts on several occasions as part of a regimen to induce God to have mercy upon Israel (chapters 9–10); in preparation for the return to Jerusalem, Ezra says, "I proclaimed a fast there by the river Ahava to afflict ourselves before our God to beseech Him for a smooth journey for us and for our children, and for all our possessions" (Ezra 8:21) While the stories of Daniel, with their sackcloth and prayer, serve as templates for later normative practice, it is the model of Moses that deeply impressed the medieval kabbalists. Moses neither eats nor drinks for forty days while up on the mountain, during which time he has the most exalted prophecy in the Jewish tradition. This extended period of abstinence and the resulting reward signal a transformation of the self and is echoed in various forms throughout the succeeding development of the spiritual tradition in Judaism.

In rabbinic literature, various figures adopt fasting practices for disparate purposes, ranging from the penitential to the petitionary to preparation for visionary experience.[53] In the Babylonian Talmud, tractate *Bava Mezia* 85a, there are a series of stories about fasting: Rav Joseph is said to have fasted for forty days on three successive occasions so that the Torah would not lapse from him, his children, or his grandchildren. As an example of the one-upmanship that is sometimes found in rabbinic literature, Rabbi Zeira fasted for 100 days on three separate occasions: after he arrived in the Land of Israel in order to forget the Babylonian Talmud, to protect Rabbi Eleazar from the pressures of public office, and to be spared from the punishing fires of Gehennom. At the beginning of the ninth-century midrashic work *Pirke Rabbi Eliezer,* the spiritually ambitious youth, Eliezer, fasts for eight consecutive days and gains a vision of the prophet Elijah. Here, fasting is not designed to attract God's favorable disposition, but rather, in line with magical or mystical tradition, Eliezer undertakes this abstinence as a spiritual technique. Elsewhere, Rabbi Akiva refers to fasting as a technique to gain both holy and demonic illumination.[54] In the *heikhalot* literature, mystical adepts fast in order to gain visions of the supernal realm or to attain encyclopedic knowledge of the Torah.[55]

Following the rabbinic tradition that there is no eating in the world-to-come, members of the medieval philosophical tradition, such as Judah Halevi, Abraham ibn Ezra, and Maimonides, found support for their spiritualizing approach.[56] For example, Abraham ibn Ezra, citing Judah Halevi, contrasts Moses' ability to fast for forty days during his experience of the Divine, while the elders of Israel had to persist in their eating.[57] Rabbi Ezra of Gerona, the mid-thirteenth-century kabbalist who was strongly influenced by Neoplatonic thought, comments on Exodus 24:11, saying that "when the power of the soul, which adheres to its creator [in *devekut*] increases, the senses, thirsting after the pleasures of the lower world, become redundant."[58] Here, the ascetic moment is identified with the ecstatic, and the eating described in the verse is replaced by mystical union.

Visionary illumination is one aim of fasting in the *Zohar* as well. In one narrative, Rabbi Ḥiyya cries over the insurmountability of mortality. When Rabbi Yose joins him, they fast in order to secure a vision of Rabbi Shimon. Though denied once, they persist in another fast and then are granted their request: they see Rabbi Shimon and his son Eliezer studying the Torah, with an audience of thousands. Subsequently a flock of angels whisks Rabbi Shimon and his son up to the supernal academy.[59] The form of vision preferred in the zoharic kabbalah is hermeneutical, and this too can be gained through fasting. The Talmud claims that Rabbi Zadoq fasted for forty years to prevent the destruction of the Temple (*b. Gittin* 56a). The *Zohar* expands upon this tradition, with Rabbi Shimon talking about the physical weakness of Rabbi Zadok. He explains that "he is called weak because he fasted for forty days on behalf of Jerusalem so that it should not be destroyed during his lifetime. He explained the supernal secrets that are [contained] in each and every word of the Torah and, thereby, gave the people a path by which to conduct themselves" (*Zohar* 1:149a). Fasting endows a person with the ability to prevent historical cataclysm and transform society, grand ambitions that are not unusual in the zoharic corpus. Fasting, moreover, has the same powers for enhancing Torah study that certain kinds of eating does, as we saw earlier. This indicates that, ultimately, the human body is a pliable tool resilient enough to produce desired spiritual effects, provided that there is an established rubric for the practice. In other words, either fasting or eating heightens the hermeneut's skill.

Among the reasons that the fasting regimen is effective is the dualistic ontology to which the author adheres. In diminishing the dominance of the physical, the spiritual can be in ascendancy. While no explicit explanation is given in the *Zohar,* Moses de Leon treats the subject in his Hebrew work *She'eilot u-Teshuvot le-Rabbi Moshe de Leon be-Inyanei ha-Kabbalah.* The text is structured as an imaginary dialogue, and de Leon puts the issue in the mouth of his questioner. The student marvels about the nature of Moses' body, given that the latter was able to abstain from all material sustenance for forty days. He argues that the biblical praise for Moses' fasting for forty days is misplaced, given that body and soul are separate; that is, if only his soul ascended, Moses' abstinence is unremarkable. Moreover, the verse says, "Moses was not aware that the skin of his face was radiant when he was speaking with Him" (Exodus 34:28); Moses' body must have indeed ascended as well if his face was shining from his interaction with God.[60] It is the dualistic presumption that irks the questioner regarding the biblical contradictions. The rejoinder is that Moses enjoyed unparalleled status as a unique human being in terms of the nature of his physical being. None other could reach the purity and pristine quality of Moses' body.

This is the meaning, de Leon says here and as it is presented throughout the *Zohar,* of the biblical statement that Moses was called "husband of God" (*ish ha-Elohim*).[61] In his erotic union with the *Shekhinah,* Moses did not have to abandon his physical being. At the same time, de Leon retains a certain sensitivity to the philosophical dualism of body and soul, arguing that, though Moses made his ascent bodily, he resided in the cloud that mediated between him and God. The cloud is undoubtedly symbolic of the *Shekhinah,* indicating that there is some reserve in allowing Moses an apotheosis beyond this level. Moses' uniqueness, however, appears to be that of an ideal human specimen, distinct from Elijah who is not born of a woman and thus not truly human.[62] Therefore, de Leon concludes, Moses' body as well as his soul must have made the supernal ascent. The mentor in the dialogue affirms this speculation, saying that Moses' body was unlike any other in its refinement and hence was able to transcend the body's normal limitations.[63] This bodily configuration of Israel's most remarkable son is deemed miraculous and becomes a supreme aspiration for the kabbalists. It also proves the rule of matter's incompatibility with things of the spirit, reinscribing the dualism even as it details an instance of its transgression.

Not unrelated to the issue of fasting is sacrifice. Indeed, first the rabbis of the Talmud and then the *Zohar* translate ritual fasting into self-sacrifice. After a penitential fast, Rav Sheshet prays "that my fat and blood which have diminished [through fasting] be as if (*ke'ilu*) I sacrificed them on the altar before You, and You favored me (with forgiveness)."[64] The *Zohar* injects its understanding of the intersection of human physiology and theosophy, explaining that fasting is an act of sacrificing food and drink from the human liver to the supernal liver. Guided by his will, the individual gives up his own fat and blood:

> [Rabbi Yeisa the Younger] began, saying, "'Who gives food to all flesh, His steadfast love is eternal' (Psalm 136:25). What did David see that led him to conclude the Great Hallel with this verse? There are three rulers above through which the Holy One, blessed be He, is known and they are His glorious mystery. They are the brain, heart, and liver.[65] These are set in the inverse order of this world. The brain above takes its [provisions] first and then gives provision to the heart and the heart takes and gives [provision] to the liver. The liver then divides everything among the various springs of the lower world, each and every one as is appropriate to it. In the lower world, the liver takes first and then sacrifices everything to the heart; the heart takes the best portion of the provision. Once it has taken it and been strengthened by this strength and will, it gives to the brain, arousing it. Then the liver distributes nourishment to all of the limbs of the body. On a fast day, a person sacrifices his food and drink to the supernal liver. What is it that he sacrifices? His fat, his blood, and his will. The supernal liver takes everything with desire. When everything is in it, it brings it all to the heart, which is greater and rules over it. Once the heart has taken and is strengthened by the will, it brings all of this [nourishment] to the brain, which is the supernal ruler over all the body. Then the liver divides up the portions to all of the springs and limbs below."[66] (*Zohar* 2:153a)

The paradox of this teaching is that it is the fasting body that nourishes the divine body through its own very lacking. It is not merely the deprivation that is effective in this matter, however; rather it is the spiritually directed use of the body that confers benefit to the supernal realm.[67] This approach betokens an antagonistic relationship between body and spirit, registering the idea that the two are irreconcilable and that the way to advance the agenda of the supernal realm is through repression of the human body. Another teaching takes a similar approach in explaining the verse "It is for your sake that we are slain all day long, that we are regarded as sheep to be slaughtered" (Psalm 44:23). The *Zohar* says that it is through fasting that the observant are killed.[68] In other words, the "killing" is the subjugation of the body, marking a harsher ascetical stance. The attempt is to experience abstinence as the ultimate existential sacrifice to God.[69] Another teaching continues with the same basic paradigm but shifts the focus to the positive. The homily signals its preference for ethereal intake over and above more eating, saying that the human windpipe is like the world-to-come, whereas the esophagus, transferring food, is like this world.[70]

A more moderate approach to the body-soul relationship is brought out in a zoharic justification for the offering of animal sacrifices. Human beings, in their precarnivorous state were sin free, but once sin was absorbed into the body through eating, adopting the form of the evil inclination, God felt that it was necessary to concede permission to be carnivorous. Animal sacrifices are offered because flesh and blood are increased by eating meat, and it is from the flesh that sin originates. By sacrificing meat, one kills a substitute for the flesh that is the source of sin.[71] Eating is understood as an assimilatory activity, and through the offering of a meat sacrifice, one cedes the fuel of sin. This teaching is different from the previous examples insofar as one's body remains implicated in the sin, but it is not the body itself that is held accountable (*Zohar* 1:89b).

Elsewhere, the dynamic of fasting fulfills a different function, poised to achieve affliction, physically and psychologically. With regard to Yom Kippur, the *Zohar* refers to the rabbinic dictum that if one eats on the ninth of Tishrei and fasts on the tenth, it is deemed that he has fasted on both days[72] (*Zohar* 3:68b). Here, intense physical experience is used for spiritual instrumentality: "'Afflict your souls' (Leviticus 16:29). It says 'your souls' (*et nafshoteikhem*) [specifically]. This [is instructed] so that Israel will be deemed meritorious before the Holy King; their will should be directed toward the Holy One, blessed be He, and they should cleave to Him so that He will grant atonement to them for their sins. Therefore, one should eat and drink on the ninth and delight his soul (*nefesh*) with food and drink so that his soul will be afflicted on the tenth in two aspects. It will be as if he had fasted on the ninth and the tenth."[73] The superfluous definitive marker *et* in the biblical verse commands the author's attention, and he resolves the problem by alleging that one must afflict two components of the soul. There is suffering on the tenth of Tishrei, both from the abstinence of food and through the simulated experience of feast and famine: the sudden shift engenders a spiritual trauma, thus fulfilling the presumed scriptural requirement for two days of affliction. Hunger is experienced on a number of levels, and each of those experiences is marshaled in fulfillment of scripture's injunction.[74] It is noteworthy that both body and soul are manipulated to gain the desired effect; the soul is not merely a more ethereal version of the body. This activity does not, therefore, rise out of abhorrence for the body but rather out of an appreciation of its instrumentality for spiritual athleticism. Furthermore, if we read this teaching in conjunction with one in *Sod Eser Sefirot Belimah*, we observe a phenomenon of union rather than division. Moses de Leon compares the ninth and tenth of Tishrei to the *sefirot Yesod* and *Shekhinah,* the masculine and feminine potencies of the Godhead. While *Yesod* "eats constantly," it satiates the latter, which is nourished from above.[75] Fasting thus becomes a part of the general economy of theurgic activities, not simply a focus of ethico-spiritual behaviors.[76] In fact, there is relatively little mention of fasting or of other forms of asceticism.

The relationship to food and eating, as suggested by the homilies of the *Zohar,* indicate a disciplined approach that moderates intake and fashions it with the rabbinic regimen of blessings and kashrut requirements as well as the kabbalistic emphasis on distinctive *kavvanot*. The zoharic kabbalists were not a circle who castigated the body, perhaps because they viewed their primary tasks as fostering the study of the Torah and enhancing religious observance. Indeed, study and prayer remain the preferred methods for achieving the same spiritual objectives. In one episode, Rabbi Shimon and his son find themselves in ecstatic study, faces illuminated, with their Torah novellae ascending heavenward before they realize that two days have elapsed without their eating any food or water. Rabbi Shimon marvels at how profound the experience of Moses must have been, given that he had abstained from eating for forty days. The fasting of Rabbi Shimon and Rabbi Eleazar, the *Zohar* says, leads them to a state in which they no longer know the difference between day and night. Because day and night signify *Tif'eret* and *Shekhinah* respectively—the masculine and feminine aspects of Divinity—the difference between these is not obscured, but rather the differences evaporate as the kabbalists join in the divine union[77] (*Zohar* 2:15a).

Fasting is not an unequivocally praised behavior. For example, if one fasts on the Sabbath one fails to perfect his *ru'ah* (spirit) in this world and as a result does not perfect the *ru'aḥ* above.[78] Both the supernal spirit and the angel who supervises that individual issue complaints before God and are only overruled when such a person fasts again during the week. In contrast to earlier examples, here the fasting deprives the supernal world rather than contributes to it. In its unceasing efforts to craft the lower and upper worlds as a seamless unity, the *Zohar* requires that one's bodily delight correspond to the supernal realm, and it is on the Sabbath that the angel of delight is active. Failing to do so indicates one's indifference to God.[79] There is a rabbinic tradition, however, that praises the one who fasts on the Sabbath, assuring him that evil decrees passed upon him will be annulled, and a number of zoharic passages follow in its wake.[80]

EATING, THEURGY, AND PHALLIC POTENCY

In Moses de Leon's *Sefer ha-Rimmon* we find a passage similar to the ones previously mentioned in that it displays the same heightened assumptions about the *ke-zayit*. What distinguishes it from the previous examples is its adoption of two different attitudes toward the body at the same time:

> A person who recites the Grace after eating gives power to the attribute of Goodness (*tov*), which is the attribute that receives from *Ḥesed*. The appearance of this known attribute that receives food is satiated, totally filled with goodness. The lighting and sparking of the brilliant light is good and satiating, without causing harm. In any event, when he recites the Grace after he has been sated, his blessing is a good blessing (*berakhah tovah*), as it is said, "For then we had plenty to eat, we were good ones (*tovim*)" (Jeremiah 44:17).[81] Therefore, it is incumbent upon each person to bless His Creator as we have said, as it is written, "When you have eaten and been sated you shall bless the Lord" (Deuteronomy 8:10). For this reason, they [the rabbis] have said, may their memory be a blessing, in the tractate *Berakhot* regarding the mystery of that which it says, "The Lord lift up His countenance (*yissa panav*) to you and grant you peace!" (Numbers 6:26): the ministering angels said before the Holy One, blessed be He, "Master of the universe, is it not written in your Torah, '[For the Lord your God is God supreme and Lord supreme] who shows no favor (*lo yissa fanim*) and takes no bribe?' (Deuteronomy 10:17). How can you show favor to Israel?!" He said to them, "How can I not show favor to Israel? I have written in my Torah, 'When you have eaten and been sated, you shall bless . . .' and they eat only an olive's-worth and bless before Me."[82] In any event, when a person is sated or appears sated with regard to his food, he should bless His

master. This causes the ascent of favor above and increases the attribute of goodness according to the matter as we have said.[83]

The conclusion of this section seems to follow the same line of thought as that of the *Zohar*: whether one is actually sated or has only eaten a *ke-zayit*, he should recite the grace. Satiety bears significance, therefore, as a sign of the normative requirement for the blessing; blessing is incumbent upon the individual as a mark of piety, at a stage that precedes satiation. It marks the religious intention that one should have in turning to God. This foodless satiation is an example of the embodied experience of transcending the body, that is, a representation of the "body that is not a body."[84] That is, there are various ways in which the mystical experience entails transcendence of the body's normal limits.

At the beginning of the passage cited, however, it appears that the embodied experience of satiety results in a blessing of superior quality. Although it might be suggested that de Leon intends that the resultant feeling of comfort and joy will give one greater ability to bless with the desired *kavvanah*, there is no such suggestion being made here.[85] Further, the use of terms in both the human and divine realms strongly anchors the experience in the physical. When a person recites the grace, he draws blessing from the *sefirah* of *Ḥesed*, causing it to flow onto the *sefirah* of *Yesod*, referred to by the cognomen *tov* in this instance.[86] The *sefirah Yesod*, referring to the phallus of the divine anthropos, is said to be sated with food. Consequent upon its satiation, the *sefirah Yesod* provides nourishment to the feminine *Malkhut*.[87] Similarly, those reciting the grace following their own satiation are said to be *tovim* (good ones). The kabbalist thus bodily expresses his satiety in terms of sexual potency; in the anagogic relationship between human and Divine, there is a commonality of sexual potency as a result of the food consumed. God and the kabbalist are both full and potent. Satiety is linked to sexual potency, and this potency expresses itself theurgically in the quality of the blessing directed toward the Divine.

One can conceive of the individual as a sharply dichotomized combination of body and soul, irreparably divided against itself until the time of spiritual redemption, which is only achieved through the soul's transcendence of its material habit. In this instance, we can see the *Zohar* conceptualizing the individual instead as a being whose mystically energized body contributes to the blessing that he gives to the divine realm. The body eclipses its normal alienation from the spiritual, becoming assimilated to the divine flow. What emerges is not so much a spiritualization of the body, but rather the spirit-matter binarism is overcome, and the body is transformed into something that is neither wholly material nor wholly spiritual. The body that has emerged is one of psychosomatic unity.[88] This ideal yields a construction of the individual as an ensouled body in which the exclusive primacy of the soul has faded.

In this fashion, we observe an instance of the zoharic kabbalah's ambivalence. In the same passage, de Leon considers two different constructions of the body: one that focuses on the spiritual and the other presenting an alternative of a union that depends quite palpably on both partners, spirit and body. The transformation of the physical body evidenced here is one of the various spiritual goals of the *Zohar*. This, in fact, is the force of the biblical proof text: "For then we had plenty to eat, we were good ones (*tovim*)." In the act of eating, one becomes an actual manifestation of that *sefirah* from which one benefits, provided that one recognizes the relationship. The experience is one of psychosomatic fullness, in which both body and soul receive external overflow and respond with an overflow of their own.[89]

The ambivalence toward the body noted previously can be seen in the *Zohar*'s equivocal attitude toward physical pleasure derived from eating and drinking. When the verse from the book of Ruth says, "Boaz ate and drank and his heart was joyful (*va-yitav libo*)" (Ruth 3:7), the *Zohar*, drawing on a rabbinic teaching, interprets Boaz's good mood to mean that he recited the grace after the meal.[90] While, in the biblical context, Boaz's pleasure both results from his meal and foreshadows the impending intercourse with Ruth, a consummation of soteriological import, the *Zohar* says that this blessing was directed to the place called *lev*, that is, the *Shekhinah* (*Zohar Hadash Ruth* 86c).[91] The *Zohar* could have drawn on midrashic teachings that stressed the sensual nature of the food or the aphrodisiacal effects of the eating but instead chose the midrash that could be best used for theurgic purposes.[92] At this textual moment, the author felt more drawn to the theurgic potential than the potential for ecstasy during the act of eating. It is significant that each of these traditional avenues of interpretation was available with obvious zoharic application, and yet it was the least sensual of the options that was chosen. This may be explained by the fact that it is the term *va-yitav* (was joyful) that led to the allusion to the grace.[93] As we saw earlier, the term *tovim* (good ones) had a technical meaning referring to those who had recited the grace after the meal. Thus the *Zohar*'s interpretative approach is steered here by its own idiosyncratic understanding of certain terms. As noted earlier, the term *tovim* has a phallic valence. Boaz too is associated with the *sefirah Yesod*, which corresponds to the phallus of the divine anthropos.[94] Moreover, the phrase *va-yitav libo* ("and his heart was joyful"), referring to his recital of the grace, takes on phallic significance as well through the extension of the kabbalistic code. Indeed, the blessing of God is understood to be the automatic response of eating, a verbal ejaculation that reinforces Boaz's status as human correlate to the *sefirah Yesod*.[95] Boaz's joy, the *va-yitav libo*, builds on the same root *tov*, which played a sexual role in the previous discussion. The *Zohar*'s chain of associations conflates the joy from the food, the recital of *birkat ha-mazon*, and the act of sexual union with the *Shekhinah*, which Boaz achieves through intercourse with Ruth, the repast that follows his meal. From this vantage point, even the eating and drinking itself can be seen to be metaphorical for the sexual moment.

Throughout the preceding discussion, we have seen a variety of strategies for dealing with the mind-body problem, to use an anachronism. Many of them have displayed a psychosomatic unity as a means of resolving the predicament. Whether it is the manna, the showbread, or the foodstuff no bigger than an olive, biblically or rabbinically ordained foodstuffs have the capacity to provide feelings of surfeit in the body as a result of the imagination's mediation. This feeling of bodily surplus is an overflow of the kabbalist's predilections as determined by the tradition. The overflow is multidirectional as well, creating a feeling of abundance on a visceral level as well as a mystical level. In this dynamic, one cannot isolate an initial experience; rather, the psychosomatic unity that the kabbalists experience is one that knits together body and soul in a way that further reifies the spirit/matter divide even as it defies it, paradoxically being the exception that proves the rule.

The experiences that they have emerge from their pneumatic, even performative, exegesis of the biblical text. When the biblical text says, "You shall eat and be satiated and shall bless the Lord your God," the kabbalists assume that it is incumbent upon them to be satiated regardless of the quantity of food that they have eaten. They are told that they will be satiated, and satiated they are. This triad of eating, satiation, and blessing is understood in a causal way so that satiation is understood as a prerequisite for theurgic activity. Feelings of satiation and the eating of idealized foods lead to enhanced hermeneutical ability—indeed, one could say that eating and satiation are themselves hermeneutical activities.[96]

3

"The Bread of Angels": The Role
of Idealized Foods

MANY BIBLICAL VERSES and rabbinic teachings attest to God's beneficence to his creatures through his sustenance of them with abundant food. As chapter 1 noted, food is often the instrument God uses to indicate his approval or disapproval of humanity's or Israel's behavior, disbursing or withholding it respectively. On the most basic level, the kabbalists are interested in the morality and piety required to influence God's decision. The following passage illustrates this point:

> What does the Holy Blessed One do with this gift? [This can be compared to] a King who eats at his table on which every type is served: fine flour, middling flour, and waste. He distributes from his table to all those at the banquet, through those he has appointed, to each one as befits him. From the bread made with the fine flour, that which the king eats, he designates that it should be given to those he loves. . . . This is from the side of the Tree of Life. But [the food that comes] from the Tree of Knowledge of Good and Evil he designates that it is middling food that should be given to the angels. And the waste should be given to the demons and the angels of destruction who serve the horses and the riders of the king. (*Zohar* 3:253a, *Ra'aya Mehemna*)

This general apportioning delineates the general gradations of divine overflow and the intended recipients of their respective bounty. What exactly is the nature of the "bread made with the fine flour," that is, God's ideal nourishment for humanity below? Bahya ben Asher addresses this question in his treatment of the episode of the meal eaten by the nobles at the foot of Mount Sinai, described in Exodus 24:11. Bahya contends that "human eating is illusory (*dimyon*), not a true event (*davar amiti*) nor an actual action (*pe'ulah vada'it*), for it is a disgraceful matter, transitory, passing through the mediating limbs. . . . But pure ideas [that reside] in wisdom and in the cleaving of thought to the light of the Intellect in the Supernal Wisdom—this is truly sustaining eating."[1] Alternatively, he offers that the prophetic vision that they gained was of the same attribute from which they ate and drank.[2] As Baḥya continues, with his exploration of that idealized food, he opines that another possible interpretation of the food eaten by the nobles is that it is the same as the manna insofar as manna too is a product of the supernal light.[3] Pursuing an ascetic line of thinking, he counsels that the one who fears God should have his thoughts tied to the supernal entities, eating for sustenance and not pleasure, as pleasure is a pursuit of the transitory body. Eating leads one to forget God and induces haughtiness; his proof text is the episode in which Joseph's brothers sold him after a meal. Further, because eating causes one to stray from Torah and divine worship, so one should offer blessings to God after eating. Just when eating leads one to divest oneself of the yoke of the kingdom of heaven, he adjures, bless God and accept the yoke instead.[4] Echoing Maimonides, he intones that one should eat only for the sake of sustenance and pursue pleasure only for the sake of opening one's mind's eye. Those that do so are angels of God; those that do not, like beasts.

As I will suggest in this chapter, the approach that Baḥya takes here is atypical of the zoharic descriptions; this approach is represented with an intellectualist, spiritualizing, and ascetic orientation, whereas the *Zohar*, and its contemporaries, assimilate the ideal food eaten by biblical figures to the mystical achievements that can be attained by kabbalists in the performance of eating-related rituals. When the zoharic kabbalists turned their gaze toward *maẓah*, wine, and Sabbath loaves, foodstuffs eaten by scripture's Israelites or prescribed in halakhah, they enwrapped these familiar foods in characteristic kabbalistic garb, identifying them with the various *sefirot*. Because of their role in contemporary ritual, temple ritual, or even that of the Israelites in the desert, these foods are ripe for the spiritual hermeneutic employed by the authorship of the *Zohar*. Indeed, food comes from, or is associated with, each of these *sefirot*: *Keter*,[5] *Ḥokhmah*,[6] *Binah*,[7] *Gevurah*,[8] *Tif'eret*,[9] *Neẓaḥ* and *Hod*,[10] *Yesod*,[11] and *Malkhut*.[12] With the full range of *sefirot* correlated to various foodstuffs, the potential exists for mystical interaction with Divinity at all of its gradations through the otherwise mundane act of eating.[13] For example, food is generally assumed to come from the upper world (*Zohar* 3:186b);[14] when the Jews emerge from Egypt they eat *maẓah* that comes from the *Shekhinah*; in the desert, they were ready to eat comestibles from a higher level, the manna from *Tif'eret*.[15] The pieces of bread distributed by the host at the Sabbath meal comprise points of the holy name and are called the crumbs of the *ke-zayit* (olive's worth), that is, the *Shekhinah* (*Zohar* 3:272a); bread is the written law (*Tif'eret*),[16] and wine is the oral law (*Shekhinah*; *Zohar* 1:240a; 3:271b *Pikkudin*); bread in general is associated with the Torah;[17] olives produce the oil for the bread, that is, as *Nezah* they convey the divine flow toward *Yesod* (*Zohar* 3:272a); and one passage says that all food comes from All (*kol*), that is, *Yesod* (*Zohar* 2:156b).

In each instance of eating, a certain food is idealized by virtue of either its being enjoined by the halakhah or its being one of the foods discussed in the biblical text; eating one of these foods leads to mystical union with a particular *sefirah*. The inverse is predicated of prohibited foods, so that one will have the same kind of engagement with the demonic counterpart of the Godhead as represented by the *sefirot*, that is, the *Sitra Ahra*.[18] The foods that are emphasized in the *Zohar* are significant because they are ritual foods: the source of their meaning derives from their authoritative status in the Torah and halakhah as revelations of God. These ritual items symbolize Divinity and, as such, serve as portals, entry points, for mystical adhesion. Although these material foods do not take on a fully incarnational quality, as symbols of the *sefirot*, they are the site of a concentration of divine power and presence. This chapter will survey and analyze the various foods, material and spiritual, that are idealized in the *Zohar*, as well as the different kinds of nourishment yielded. The kabbalists evoke images of physical nourishment from spiritual substance or mystical experience; the success of these forms of nourishment are predicated upon unconventional understandings of how the body functions and flourishes. They also describe how eating manna, and even unleavened bread, is not only healthful but actually promote a bodily resilience. They view contemporary, that is, thirteenth-century bodies, as being comparatively inferior. Ultimately, the kabbalists' aim in these and other tacks is to discover the appropriate hermeneutical stance to adopt in relation to their food, the texts, and their bodies in order to attain a transformation of their bodily persons.

BODILY NOURISHMENT FROM SPIRITUAL STUFF: WISDOM, WORDS OF TORAH, AND SEFIROTIC EFFLUX

The foods of revelation—those made normative in Jewish law—are liminal in that they originate in the divine realm and descend to the human. The zoharic kabbalists feel that it is incumbent upon them to seek that threshold of religious experience and consume those foods that transgress the line dividing the sacred and the profane. It is quite often the case that the anthropomorphic actions of the Divine in the kabbalah represent an idealized picture of the mystics' notions of their own human activities. In the case of eating, however, the human actions closely approximate those projected onto the Godhead. Thus, as we shall see, in the same way that God eats spiritual entities such as souls, words of Torah, prayers, and the like, the kabbalists consume a variety of sublime foods in their diet as well.[19] This phenomenon allows us to observe the dialectic of the actual human body and the idealized human body. While, of course, the anthropomorphic form of the Divine in the *Zohar* is modeled in the imagination of the kabbalists after their own bodies, they conceive of the human body as following the divine paradigm. As God eats spiritual entities, so, too, must his human devotees.

To understand the enterprise of consuming idealized foods, there are several questions that must be addressed. What exactly is the nature of the food being consumed? Moreover, what is the nature of the act of eating? Is it a passive event of being nourished by a superior entity, or is it an aggressive act of integrating, absorbing, and incorporating a foreign entity? The very first biblical food that is primed for idealization is the fruit of the Tree of Life, which Joseph of Hamadan discusses: "[Adam's sin] had the effect that there would be little emanation in bread; when there was the Tree [of Life] he enjoyed the supernal bread bearing the taste of manna. Its seed was larger than the form of man and tasted like a honey-cake. Every day it grew, causing no lack [in man's nourishment]. His form in the Garden of Eden was beautiful because he drew upon the supernal bread."[20] The reference to a honey cake is a reference to Ezekiel's repast, which he had said was "sweet as honey," as well as to the Ashkenazi rite for initiating a young boy to Torah study.[21] Among the rituals at the ceremony, he is summoned to eat a honey-cake with verses from Ezekiel inscribed upon it. Hamadan conflates the bread from the Tree of Life, the manna, the Torah—symbolized by the Tree of Life and alluded to by the honey cake—and Ezekiel's meal of the scroll. Although most of these symbols hearken back to the hoary past, the link to the Torah and to Torah study roots his own practices to those times and, more importantly, to the *sefirot* denoted by these foods. Study is imagined as an act of consumption and can be best expressed, even experienced, through the use of sensual metaphors.

Regarding the manna, the *Zohar* teaches the following homily:

Come and see. The manna which descended for Israel in the desert, that manna was from the supernal dew that descended from the Ancient

One, the most hidden of all hidden things. When it descended, its light illuminated all of the worlds. From it were nourished the Field of Apples [*Shekhinah*] and the supernal angels. When it descended below and the air of the world ruled over it, its splendor was congealed and altered, and its splendor was only as it is written, "Now the manna was like coriander seed . . ." (Numbers 11:7), and nothing more. All the more so is the case with angels when they descend and the air rules over them that they are altered from their previous status. (*Zohar* 3:208a)[22]

Following a Neoplatonic scheme in which entities that emanate from the Divine are marked by progressive concretization and degeneration, the overflow, called dew, from the Divine changes and congeals into an oily substance that looks like coriander extract.[23] The theological benefit of this approach is that it maintains the transcendence of the Divine even as it allows for some measure of immanence. Eating the manna signifies participation in a glorious feast by virtue of the manna's origin but, at the same time, avoids a pantheistic blurring of boundaries. The worlds above are illuminated, and presumably the same can be expected of the individual consumer. Perhaps in deliberate contrast to the Christian model,[24] however, the possibility that the mystic is actually eating the substance of the Divine in this example is mitigated through the emphasis on the steady degradation of the divine influence.[25] Whatever acquisitiveness or aggressiveness may reside in the act of eating is vitiated by the assertion of the hierarchy.[26] This representation of an act of feeding as a nourishing of subordinate entities thus remains an expression of the *Zohar*'s pervasive reliance on a dynamic of superior/inferior binaries. Still, the stress in kabbalistic texts is on the miraculous, not the cautionary. As remarked upon by Joseph of Hamadan, "When the manna fell everyone knew the wisdom of the words of God; they were all astonished that something so transcendent could be earthly."[27]

In other passages, we find that the kabbalists are nourished by spiritual commodities emanating not from God but from their comrades. For example, the *Zohar* states that, during his lifetime, Rabbi Shimon bar Yohai had been a source of manna and good fragrances that were no longer available after his death (*Zohar* 1:217a). The manna and good fragrances are used figuratively to signify the esoteric and kabbalistic lore that bar Yohai taught the mystical fraternity. Notwithstanding the figurative nature of this trope, the choice of metaphor is significant. It is an experience of nourishment and fragrance, physiological metaphors suggesting fullness and satisfaction.[28] Also significant about this passage is the relationship of bar Yohai to the *sefirot* of *Nezah*, *Hod*, and *Yesod*. He is compared to the millstones (*shehakim*) that produce the manna, which, in the divine model, correspond to these *sefirot;* on the structure of the divine anthropos, these are the testicles and the phallus. Thus Rabbi Shimon serves as the human counterpart of *Zaddiq*/*Yesod,* the divine phallus.[29]

Sometimes the *Zohar* has a strategy of maintaining distance between the Divine and the human by emphasizing the ontological gap between the two; an instance of this approach is the text's assertion that the ideal eating occurs in the world-to-come. Here, the *Zohar* maintains the same strategy, questioning whether souls in the world-to-come eat and answering that the angels do, as well. In addition, it adopts a historical strategy: though Israel is angelicized in their ability to eat angelic food, it is, in this instance, the Israel of old that has this capacity.[30] People in latter days, because of the decline of the generations, would have to wait until their final residence in the world-to-come before having that dining experience. In the very next breath, however, boundaries are transgressed as eating in this world leads to the ability to eat in the next world; that eating, in turn, resembles the eating practices of angels, which is the same that Israel had in the desert (*Zohar* 2:156b–157a).[31] The *Zohar*'s mystical fluidity and midrashic quality is exemplified in these abrupt shifts; what remains constant, however, is the use of embodied metaphors.

Moreover, there are passages in which it is considered undesirable to eat foods that are connected to certain *sefirot.* For instance, in *Sefer ha-Rimmon,* Moses de Leon says that the reason for the restriction against eating the sciatic nerve is that eating from this place in an animal's thigh would highlight Jacob's point of vulnerability, sustained in his battle with the angel.[32] The patriarch Jacob symbolizes the *sefirah* Tif'eret, which is the point of sustenance for the sefirotic structure.[33] What is perplexing is that, although foods associated with certain *sefirot* are normally considered desirable to eat, here, eating it would immodestly reveal the divine phallus. Usually, eating such foods implies *devekut* with the relevant *sefirah;* in this instance, it implies an inappropriate revelation. Consumption, ostensibly an act of concealment, is instead an act of disclosure, and some things may not be revealed. Like the forbidden fruit or the wine drunk by Nadav and Avihu, this food reflects an inappropriate view of the Divine.[34] From the previous discussion we observe the extent to which the *Zohar* is exegesis driven rather than systematic in its theology, at times idealizing food from a particular *sefirah,* at other times avoiding it; this variance may also suggest an ambivalence about being overly connected to any one *sefirah.*[35] Last, we see the jockeying of the various streams of influence on the *Zohar:* food as point of direct access to particular *sefirot;* food regulation from the halakhah, and issues of aesthetics and propriety.

Physical Nourishment through Mystical Experience

The *Zohar* assumes several different postures with regard to the relationship of nourishing the body and nourishing the soul. One phenomenon that emerges is the nourishment of the body via the nourishment of the soul, that is, through the adept's mystical experience of the Divinity. In one passage, the *Zohar* affirms that those involved with Torah are nourished from a higher place than regular members of Israel, by virtue of the verse that attests, "Wisdom (*Hokhmah*) preserves the life of him who possesses it" (Ecclesiastes 7:12), that is, from the *sefirah* of *Hokhmah* (*Zohar* 2:61b). The passage continues:

> Come and see. All food for the people of the world comes from above. That food which comes from the heaven and earth is the food for the entire world . . . and it is coarse, heavy food. That food which comes from a more supernal place, the finer food, comes from a place above the locale of Judgment and that is the food that Israel ate when they were in the desert.[36] It comes from a supernal place called "Heavens."[37] It is a finer food that goes into the soul more than any other food and is more distinct from the body. It is called the "bread of angels". . . . The finest food of all is the food of the companions, those who study the Torah, for they eat the food of the *ru'ah* and the *neshamah,* and do not eat the food of the body at all. It comes from a most exalted and honorable place, called *Hokhmah*. For this reason, the bodies of the companions are weaker than those of other people, because they do not eat the food of the body at all. They eat the food of the *ru'ah* and the *neshamah* that comes from a distant place, the most exalted and honorable of all. Their portion is meritorious. This is as it is written, "Wisdom (*Hokhmah*) preserves the life of him who possesses it." Happy is the portion of the body that can be nourished by the food of the soul. (*Zohar* 2:61b–62a)[38]

Tishby explains that the holy bodies of the righteous kabbalists have been purified and so can receive light and influence from the soul.[39] It is worth noting, however, that the bodies are not nourished by the soul but rather from the food of the soul itself. Thus, in this instance, it would appear that the soul does not mediate or transform the food so that it can be integrated by the body; rather, these bodies are purified to the extent that they do not require the mediation of the soul in any mechanical way and are able to assimilate the supernal nourishment directly. A model for this spiritual diet exists in the midrash: when Abraham offers food to the angels he says, "Let me fetch a morsel of bread that you may comfort/nourish your heart"[40] (Genesis 18:5). "Rabbi Isaac teaches that in the Torah, Prophets, and the Writings we find that bread is the food of the heart"[41]

Further, there is a taxonomy of bodies with diverse populations receiving their nourishment from disparate places within the sefirotic structure. Thus the bodies of non-Jews are sustained by the material food of this world, with no sefirotic derivation; that of Israel immediately upon their departure from Egypt was from *Malkhut;* during the desert sojourn Israel ate food, manna, deriving from *Tif'eret;* and last, those who are engaged with Torah receive nutritive support from the *sefirah Ḥokhmah.* Paradoxically, the *Zohar* notes, those who receive the most favor from God have the weakest bodies. Apologetically explaining this apparent strange turn of events, the *Zohar* argues that bodies are normally nourished by coarse food while the members of the fraternity are spiritually nourished by a supernal source.[42] The "nutrients" in turn are passed into the body, but it is the ethereal quality of this nourishment that engenders the physical weakness.

At the same time, however, the *Zohar* lauds the accomplishment of these kabbalistic sages who are able to be sustained by their mystical engagement with holy texts. In this dialectic between the ideal body and the actual body, the actual body is reread as an ideal body in spite of its apparent weaknesses: weakness is read as an expression of strength.[43] Human bodies are employed as confirmation of the esoteric hermeneutic: it is the hidden strength of the body rather than its outer trappings that is the true referent of the term "strength." There are two inversions here: first, strength refers to an inner faculty rather than an outward one; second, the apparent weakness of the body is just that—the kabbalist's body is stronger than that of the non-Jew by virtue of its superior nutriment. Strength is disclosed through weakness, and weakness through strength.

As the previous passage continues, it contends that the highest food is the food of the companions, which is the food of the Holy One, blessed be He, Himself, coming from the *sefirah Ḥokhmah* (*Zohar* 2:62a). In and of itself, this appears no different from the representations of the food above; however, the alternate version in the zoharic text, as attested to in some manuscripts, seeking to identify "God's food," identifies this spiritual food as blood and forbidden fat.[44] The antinomian implications of this passage are clear. In the same way that God "eats" the sacrifices of blood and fat, foods that are forbidden for human consumption, whether on or off the altar, so shall they be shared with the kabbalists. The symbolism of sitting at the table of the king is thus intensified—they not only sit at his table, but they eat his food, as well. While the meaning here is not that they will eat actual blood and forbidden fat but rather that they will consume the spiritual correlate of those foods, it remains suggestive that this desire—to transcend the limitations of the law—exists. Indeed, there are zoharic passages that distinguish between permitted and forbidden foods by associating them with the holy and demonic realms, respectively; here, those associations have fallen away. As the boundaries between human and Divine blur, so do those between permitted and forbidden. Further, as we shall see, limiting one's diet to kosher food serves apotropaically to protect from harm; this alternate version of the text, with its antinomian impulse, runs counter to that perspective.

In describing the eating of the soul itself, the semantic field of the text is bounded by the soul's being modeled after the body such that its experiences can only be expressed in terms of the body.[45] Thus, while no physical eating occurs, suggesting that the eating is "spiritual" leads to a withering of the text's intent. The metaphor is extended as Rabbi Isaac says that the righteous man eats after sating his soul with prayer and Torah (*Zohar* 2:62b).[46] Using the manna as a barometer, a distinction is drawn between the righteous kabbalists and the wicked: the righteous will eat and be crowned with *Hesed* while the wicked will remain hungry.[47] At times, these distinctions take on the aura of class warfare. The mixed multitude does not merit eating the manna, only the chaff, the same as Israel would give to their slaves (*Zohar* 2:191b).[48]

PURIFYING THE BODY

One property of these ideal foods is that they can effect purification of the body, permeating the body, and ridding it of harmful contents. The unleavened bread (*mazah*) eaten at the Passover rite is one of these perfect foods, and its treatment in the *Zohar* suggests one aspect of the kabbalistic experience of eating. This particular nutriment has an enduring impact on the body, effectively purifying it so that it is no longer vulnerable to the pernicious effects of the harmful leaven (*hamez*). The substance of this edible protecting agent is revealed in an interesting zoharic passage. Scripture prescribes that during the feast of Shavuot, the Israelites should bring two loaves of leavened bread as part of their offering of first fruits.[49] Subsequent to the festival of Passover, in which even the possession of leavened bread results in excision, the Torah prescribes leaven as part of the sacrificial offering, ostensibly confounding the author of the *Zohar*:

Now we must look carefully. On Passover, Israel went out from the bread which is called leaven, as it is written, "You shall not see any leaven" (Exodus 13:7). . . . What is the reason? On account of the honor of that bread which is called unleavened. Now that Israel merited the highest bread, it was not appropriate for the leaven to be wiped out and not seen at all. And why was this sacrifice from leaven? . . . For on that very day [Shavuot] the evil inclination was wiped out because the Torah, which is called freedom, was to be found. (*Zohar* 2:183a–b)[50]

The offering of leaven that is prescribed for the festival of Shavuot can be justified, because at that point, having eradicated the danger of the leaven, Israel has been purified and liberated from the evil inclination.[51] The bodily nature of that eradication is made plain by the medical parable that follows. The *Zohar* says,

This may be compared to a king who had an only son who was sick. One day, the son desired to eat. They said to him: The king's son should eat this medicine, and until he eats it, no other food will be found in the house. So it was done. When he ate the medicine, he [the king] said to him: From now on you may eat whatever you desire, and it will not harm you. Similarly, when Israel left Egypt, they did not know the essence or secret of faith. The Holy One, blessed be He, said: Israel shall eat medicine, and until they eat the medicine, no other food shall be shown to them. When they ate the unleavened bread, which was medicine, in order to enter and to know the secret of faith, the Holy One said: From now on, leaven shall be shown to them, and they can eat it, for it cannot harm them.[52] And all the more so on the day of Shavuot which is a complete medicine. Therefore, leaven is offered to be burnt upon the altar with two other loaves of bread that are brought as one.[53] The leaven is burnt in flames upon the altar and it cannot rule over nor harm Israel. On account of this the holy ones of Israel cleave to the Holy One, blessed be He, on this very day with the remedy of the Torah. And if Israel had not been properly protected, the two sides of the bread would never have rightly ascended. (*Zohar* 2:183b)[54]

This passage moves fluidly between the literal understanding of eating, both in the parable and in its analogue and the more attenuated meaning of the eating metaphor as the homily continues. While referring to the unleavened bread and the leaven offerings of the Shavuot, as well as in the case of the king's son, the *Zohar* is quite clearly referring to concrete nutriments. Their mystical meaning is revealed as the discussion explains how the Torah, symbolizing freedom, is encountered in that eating. In the continuation of the homily the *Zohar* refers to the New Year, saying that if someone had not fully eradicated his leaven, that is, his sin, the leaven would arise as his prosecutor, calling him to account for his misdeeds. At this point, the material leaven has been internalized and accusing. Nonetheless, it is quite clear that it is not only the Torah, the receipt of which is commemorated at Shavuot, that acts as the remedy for the offending inclination but rather that the prescribed and proscribed eatings themselves are integral to the remediating process.[55] Thus the *Zohar* is not allegorizing here, but rather talking about the psychosomatic results of eating the two kinds of bread.[56] Moses de Leon, in *Sefer ha-Rimmon,* tells a similar medical parable expressing the need for the right kind of medication that wholly eradicates the illness. De Leon explains that healing the body depends not only on medication but also on healing the soul. In this source, the medical model is used to recommend total eradication of the harmful foodstuff *without* recourse to it after a return to healthfulness.[57] Here again, we see the intricate intertwining of body and soul, notwithstanding ideological posturing in other passages that express a more strongly dualistic picture. The ideal of psychosomatic unity is apparent as de Leon comments about how pleasant it is to have both of them healthy together.

Perhaps because of the potential antinomian application of this principle—that the erstwhile demonic leaven is now rehabilitated as part of a divine commandment—the *Zohar* displays some discomfort with the meaning of its parable. Retreating, the text argues that on the festival of Shavuot, one receives the most elevated bread, a kind of supermedication, and the evidence for this is that the leaven offering is burnt. The *Zohar* says that the leaven should not be absent, then says that it is destroyed, then says that it should be brought so that it can be burnt. To a certain extent, the *Zohar*'s parable dissolves in its bifurcated attempt to both redeem and castigate the leaven.[58] It is possible that the contradiction here should be noted without attempting to resolve it for the sake of consistency. The *Zohar*'s suggestion that there is an injunction that the leaven be burnt, a departure from the biblical prescription that it be eaten, calls for consideration of this side of the contradiction.[59] The *Zohar*'s misconstrual of this requirement may be taken to be a subconscious aversion to the priests' actually internalizing the leaven by consuming it. The most that the author can allow is that the leaven should be brought to the Temple, but it is destroyed—full rehabilitation of the demonic effectively means its annihilation. Notwithstanding the *Zohar*'s typical fluidity, once it has vilified the leaven, rehabilitation is well nigh impossible. The trope of unleavened bread as medication takes on a slightly different guise in the hands of Joseph of Hamadan. He says that eating unleavened bread on the night of Passover acts as a temporal apotropaic from the harmful spirits and the evil inclination, accustoming the body to the good inclination. Unleavened bread is an unusual apotropaic, inasmuch as it functions not as an external guard, as is the case with *mezuzah* or circumcision, which are "superficial," but rather as an internal mechanism, like medication. Hamadan's sketch for a topography of the body illustrates the physically internal battle with the evil inclination.[60]

In another manna-related passage, we read the following:

> There [it is written] "she shall count off seven days" (Leviticus 15:28), here [it is written] "[you shall count off] seven weeks" (Leviticus 23:15). . . . Regarding this, [scripture means] seven weeks, in actuality, in order to give them merit. This is like a woman whose purification comes at night, enabling her to have sexual relations with her husband; thus it is written, "When the dew fell on the camp at night, [the manna would fall upon it]" (Numbers 11:9). . . . And when does that dew fall? When Israel approached Mount Sinai, that very dew fell in its perfected form, and it purified them, causing their filth to depart from them and they cleaved to the Holy King. And the Assembly of Israel accepted the Torah, and thus it is established. (*Zohar* 3:97b)

Here, too, the manna, the highest bread, causes the "filth" to pass away from them. This homily builds on the rabbinic legend that the spiritual event of Eve's sin is self-profanation, incurred through the disobedient eating from the Tree of Knowledge and represented as the serpent's insemination of her; in the words of the Talmud, he deposited his "filth" into her. That filth then passes out of the Israelites at the point of revelation at Mt. Sinai.[61] The string of associations fuses manna, revelation, Torah, and ritual immersion after menstruation, but it also exemplifies a psychosomatic spirituality that militates against a rarefying allegoresis. That women undergo ritual purification and that manna was eaten is beyond question for the kabbalist, but the event resonates on both historical and mythical or external and internal levels.

In *Shushan Edut*, one of Moses de Leon's Hebrew writings, we find a similar treatment of the original sin: "For when he ate from that tree [the Tree of Knowledge] his limbs drew from it and that food was absorbed throughout his limbs so that his offspring and later descendants would all have that nature [of the Tree of Knowledge] in actuality. That sickness cleaved to each and every one [of humanity] since it exists by virtue of that nature."[62] Sin is consumed through eating and then pervades not only that individual's body but his offspring in generations to come: sin bears a component of bodily corruption as well as a genetic component, causing that which one eats to be replicated in the succeeding generation.[63] De Leon emphasizes that this is food in actuality (*vadai*) that is being referred to—that it is symbolic food and that it corresponds directly to the supernal realm—not merely allegorical food.[64]

De Leon's model of spiritual digestion follows directly from his understanding of the physiology of digestion.[65] He discusses the prohibition against eating blood from a slaughtered animal.[66] When food is digested, it becomes blood, that blood being identified with the *nefesh,* the lowest part of the tripartite soul.[67] Because of the difficulty of digesting meat, only the finest aspect of it is absorbed. In contrast, the blood is easily digested, and so, in eating it, one assimilates the animal nature of its soul that is contained within the blood. The animal's soul then intermingles with that of the person.[68] The digestive system acts as a filtration system, extracting the spiritually elevated aspect of the animal's flesh. The term that de Leon uses to describe the choice part that is desired to be absorbed is "*tamzit,*" which, in the rabbinic context, means either the last blood to spurt out of a vein or that can be squeezed from an animal's flesh.[69] Though this liquid is most bloodlike in its fluidity, it lacks the stigma of actually bearing the soul of the animal. Problematically, it is not immediately clear what aspect of the animal could be more exalted than its soul, but de Leon operates in a system in which ontological stratification is the rule, and so the notion that there would be purer and coarser aspects to the animal, though not formally divided into different parts as in a human being, is not wholly surprising. Consequently, blood that is absorbed indiscriminately is inferior to the flesh that is processed for its "spiritual nutrients."

De Leon explains that man is the most elevated among God's creatures and that it is the perfection of his nature as evidenced in his blood and soul that give him the unique ability to understand his Creator; the outcome is that human understanding is integrally related to the blood. It is for this reason that God picked the foods that perfect or have adverse effects upon the *nefesh* (animal soul): blood is specified because it is "the basis of the whole structure." Each part of the soul supports the one below it, ultimately constituting a single unit—this is the mystery of the soul. The *ru'ah*—the middle aspect of the tripartite soul—is the form for the *nefesh* that is like darkness on its own; everything is then comprised within the *neshamah,* the supersoul. Although the *nefesh* is usually drawn after the desires of the body, it can get drawn into the *neshamah,* because, in actuality, it is the mystery (*sod*) of the *neshamah*.[70] The esoteric meaning of the supersoul is the animal soul; that is, the core of the supersoul's life is invested in the success of the supersoul; indeed, without it, it would not exist. The result is a unity through the length of the vertical axis of soul and body: the *nefesh* is intimately related to the body through the blood and is tied to the *neshamah*, comprising a unified soul; the entirety is a human being who, ideally, has perfected himself even while eating the flesh of an animal. Maintaining sharp ontological distinctions within the human being becomes increasingly difficult.

Gikatilla resolves the dilemma differently. He addresses the issue in the context of Isaac's choice to give a blessing to his wicked son Esau, and his request for a meal in advance of the blessing. Gikatilla wonders how Isaac could ingest food before uttering the blessing (a violation of rabbinic norms). He suggests that Isaac agreed to give Esau the blessing of *this* world, reserving the blessing of the next world for Jacob/Israel. Because material food of this world contributes sustenance to the *nefesh*, Isaac preferred to let Esau bring the food so that the blessing would issue from this lower soul rather than from the *neshamah*, whose blessing Isaac reserved for Jacob. In contrast to Hamadan, whose efforts effaced the distinctions between strata of the soul, Gikatilla reinforces them, with each compartment of the soul responsible, like a bureaucracy, for its own circumscribed functions.[71]

In discussing the ban against eating blood, de Leon alludes to the rabbinic restriction against eating before prayer but limits the injunction, perhaps inadvertently, to judges.[72] De Leon does not elaborate, saying that "the details of this commandment are known to every enlightened person." It is unclear whether this last comment refers to the commandment as a whole or only to the prohibition against judges' early eating. If it is the prohibition against the judges, though, perhaps he invokes the esotericizing formula—"this matter is known to every enlightened person" (*maskil*)—because the task is too difficult for common folk and so only has the elite "judges" in mind; the "judges," then, could be a reference to the kabbalists. Alternatively, he thinks of the judges because, according to many of de Leon's contemporaries, it is only those versed in kabbalah that could slaughter and eat meat with the appropriate intentions to rectify the fate of those souls who were reincarnated into animals.[73]

One unusually folksy passage from *Sha'arei Orah* explains the complexities of meat eating at length:

Let me give you a great key. Why did God, may He be blessed, see fit to issue a commandment in the Torah to slaughter animals for human consumption? Is it not written, "The Lord is good to all and His mercy is over

all His works?" (Ps. 145:19). If He is indeed merciful, how could He command to slaughter this animal for man's consumption? Where is His
mercy? But the mystery of this verse comes in its first clause, which says,
"The Lord is good to all"—good, indeed, and therefore, "His mercy is over
all His works." This is the explanation: During creation, it was predeter-
mined that this particular animal was to be slaughtered and the animal said
"good." What is the reason for this? The animal does not have an upper
soul (*neshamah elyonah*) that could comprehend God and His mighty
works. So God decreed during the creation of the world that all of the animals should be brought before Him, and He said, "Do you wish to be
slaughtered and eaten by people so that you will ascend from the level of
an animal, knowing nothing, to the level of a person who knows and recognizes the Lord, may He be blessed?" And the animals responded:
"Good, and this is merciful to us." For when a person eats a part of the animal, it becomes a part of the person. Thus, the animal becomes a person
and its slaughter is merciful, for it has left the status of animal and entered
the status of a person. In this way, a person's death is life for him, for he
ascends to the level of the angels. And this is the mystery of "man and beast
you deliver, O Lord" (Ps. 36:7). Since this is the case, consider carefully
the mystery of slaughtering animals, as it is all from His great mercy and
graciousness to all His creatures. For this reason, consider that which the
rabbis said in *Tractate Pesaḥim:* "It is forbidden for an ignoramus (*am
ha'arez*) to eat meat" (*b. Pesaḥim* 49b), since He commanded in the Torah
that only one who is educated in the teachings about domesticated beasts,
wild animals, and fowl may slaughter [animals]. Anyone who is engaged
with the Torah is permitted to eat meat and anyone who is not engaged in
the Torah is forbidden to eat meat. Therefore, an ignoramus may not eat
meat for he is like an animal, without a soul, and [God] did not command
that an animal should be slaughtered to be eaten by another animal.[74]

This passage illuminates several different aspects of kabbalistic notions of
eating. Consumption entails the assimilation of eaten matter, such that the
animal is metaphysically transformed, becoming part of the person eating.
The human soul, in turn, upon being consumed in death, attains angelic status. Gikatilla thus reverses the familiar maxim "You are what you eat," yielding instead "You are that which eats you." One unusual characteristic of this
teaching is that the animals appear to retain some aspect of their identity,
because the metaphysical ascent benefits them; this is, of course, in line with
the desire to maintain personal human identity even upon angelification or
apotheosis. In *unio mystica,* identity is erased as the mystical adept dissolves
into an all-encompassing deity. But this is not the only kind of mystical

adhesion available to the kabbalist, and while *unio mystica* has an appeal as an ultimate experience, other kinds of mystical communion have their own appeal as well. The kind of transformation indicated here arises from a position that is either skeptical of the possibility of *unio mystica* or that values the retention of the ego and self. The popular tone of this legend might indicate that the intended audience holds onto classical notions of reward in the world-to-come, compensation that is certainly personal. Thus it may not be the humanity or the animal nature that these respective subjects desire to hold onto; rather it is the core self that appreciates its transcendence because it has retained its own personal subjectivity. Eating, then, is an act that is both "form preserving and form destroying."[75]

In the preceding example, death equals salvation for both animals and man; it is the deleterious nature of the flesh that induces the pain of death and impedes an easier end. Gikatilla contends that it is because of this potential soteriological benefit that an ignoramus may not perform ritual slaughter or eat meat.[76] In other words, the animal should acquire a true ascent, something that would not occur should it be eaten by a person whose own status is little above that of an animal. In a very different interpretation of the same rabbinic teaching, Joseph of Hamadan explains that the proscription against the ignoramus eating meat exists in the context of concerns about reincarnation. Because the ignoramus can be reincarnated as a beast, the sage is allowed to eat meat, but the ignoramus, being but a beast himself, cannot eat this beast.[77] The food chain of the kabbalists, in which a superior soul (human) consumes the inferior soul (animal), is further ramified in this teaching where we see a spiritual anthropophagy (cannibalism), in which one person consumes another. In another instance of anthropophagy, Hamadan says that the permission to eat the flesh of animals that have split hooves and the prohibition against eating the flesh of the pig are related to the doctrine of the reincarnation of souls. Most people's souls are taken in beneath the chariot and thus, one assumes, are like the creatures supporting the chariot. Therefore, a permissible animal, presumably bearing the soul of a righteous person, may be eaten. The pig's split hooves symbolize the person who spreads his legs during prayer, in contravention of the halakhic requirement to keep them together. In the description of the creatures bearing the divine chariot, Ezekiel explains, "the legs of each were [fused into] a single rigid leg" (Ezekiel 1:7); thus the injunction to keep one's legs together is designed to give the praying individual a semblance of these same celestial figures. All livestock that is kosher has split hooves. Why are the pig's offensive? The midrash draws attention to the fact that the pig stretches

out its split hooves, sharing the characteristic of permissible animals, though
it is in truth one of the unclean animals.[78] Both the pig and the person who
prays with legs splayed epitomize the kabbalistic anathema of separation,
represented here by falsehood. The wicked person praying represents himself as pure intentioned when in fact he divides that which should be joined.
This is similar to the pig, which misrepresents itself. Self-representation and
internal truth do not coincide, an act of wickedness that can, in turn, lead to
a fissure within the Divine. The pig can therefore be assumed to be a reincarnation of the wicked who transgress the law in this way, and this is why
the pig may not be consumed.[79] Hamadan, in contrast to Gikatilla, is not as
interested in the ontology of the consumed creature—where its soul will
go—as he is in the anthropology of this religious norm.

The gap between the individual and his food has been bridged: one does
Eating marks the reconstitution of one creature by another. The outcome
is an organic model in which a worthier entity may absorb, and thus bestow
greater dignity upon, another. Further, it merits comparison to a related
notion that could be formulated as a commandment: you may eat that which
you have engendered.[80] This idea is presented in Moses de Leon's explanation for God's granting permission for people to eat meat after Noah brings
all the animals into the ark. The ark is a cognomen for the *Shekhinah,* and
Noah, the righteous, is a cognomen for *Yesod;* as such, his entry into the ark
symbolizes the supernal union of *Yesod* and *Malkhut*—when the animals
emerge, they represent the divine overflow, the offspring of that union. The
reason for the permission is that, through Noah's union with the *Shekhinah*
upon entry to the ark and the subsequent safe exit of the animals from the
ark, Noah has, in effect, created these animals, and one is allowed to eat that
which one has engendered.[81]

The gap between the individual and his food has been bridged: one does
not eat something that is wholly other but rather something that has been
brought into existence by the self. Both the violence of carnivorousness and
the rent between self and other are vitiated by this innovation. The resolution of the chasm between self and other is obtained through a denial of the
otherness of the other; the other now has its ontological origin in the self,
and its incorporation is merely a return of that which has been lost. The perfect analogy for this is Adam's rib, restored to him when Adam and Eve
become "as one flesh." Eating and parenting have been abstracted to divulge
their essence: ontological relationships in which one entity (Noah) vouch-
safes another (animals) and thus attains complete mastery of the latter.[82]
In a recasting of Levinas's words from *Totality and Infinity,* Grace Jantzen
writes the following: "If knowledge is the apprehension or appropriation of

being to myself, then knowledge is like digestion, making what is taken in, part of me. Everything becomes part of 'the same.'"[83] The story of Noah, for the theosophic kabbalists, never retreats into allegory but rather maintains a mythical valence so that eating, to this day, is an affirmation of that continuing covenant between humankind and the animal kingdom.

THE EPISTEMOLOGY OF EATING

In addition to the cathartic or medical effects of idealized foods, another property that the *Zohar* ascribes to idealized foods is the provision of wisdom, the supernal Torah, and knowledge of the *sefirot*. This noetic quality is a common component of mystical experience in a variety of mystical traditions, but it is in scripture that the grounds for this association are laid.[84] When Moses recounts the delivery of the manna, the idealized food par excellence, he says, "[God] subjected you to the hardship of hunger and then gave you manna to eat, which neither you nor your fathers had ever known, in order to teach you that man does not live on bread alone, but that man may live on anything that the Lord decrees" (Deuteronomy 8:3).[85] Although the biblical statement refers to God's ability to manipulate nature, for the rabbis, the manna, like the other articles that emerge from the Lord's mouth (*kol moza fi ha-shem*), must also be a bearer of wisdom.[86] For the *Zohar*, there is sometimes merely a correspondence cited, while in other instances it is made clear that, in the performance of a commandment, food plays an integral role in the mystic's attainment of supernal wisdom.[87] In the analogue to the previously cited parable, the manna corresponds to the Torah, while elsewhere wine is said to correspond to the Torah.[88] At the beginning of the previously cited passage the *Zohar* says, "Bread is the essential thing, as it is written, 'With the bread you shall present, as burnt offerings [to the Lord] seven yearling lambs . . .' (Leviticus 23:18), [and] 'You shall bring from your settlements two loaves of bread as an elevation offering'; (Leviticus 23:17), because, on account of this bread, Israel attained the supernal wisdom of the Torah and they walked in its ways" (*Zohar* 2:183a).[89] In this instance it is the bringing of the bread that elicits the gift of knowledge. The manna is identified with the bread offering of the festival of Shavuot, creating a confluence of the metaphors of sacrifice, mystical gnosis, and consumption.[90] As is to be expected, it is frequently indicated that through eating these idealized foods one gains knowledge of esoteric secrets, so it is through the consumption of manna that one gains this gnosis.[91] In *Sefer Tashak*, Joseph of

Hamadan comments that when the manna fell, everyone knew the wisdom of the words of God. They were all astonished that something so transcendent could be earthly.[92] This statement by Hamadan exemplifies the value of the concrete and the ways in which immanent instantiations of holiness mark the theosophic kabbalist's interaction with the world.

One passage that stresses the cognitive value of eating the manna explains the import of eating in general.

> Rabbi Hiyya said, "Regarding this verse that you have cited [Job 28:5], I remember a supernal teaching that I learned from the Old Man regarding Passover. The Holy One, blessed be He, gave Israel this bread [unleavened bread] from the Land of Life [*Shekhinah*] and after that [gave them] bread from the heavens [*Tif'eret*]—this refers to this bread [of the verse from Job], and this idea has already been established. He said further that when a person enters this world he does not know anything until he tastes bread; once he has tasted food he is aroused to know and to be informed. Similarly, when Israel left Egypt they did not know anything until the Holy One, blessed be He, gave them bread from this land to taste, as it is written, 'Earth, out of which food grows' (Job 28:5). Then Israel ascended to know and to become known by the Holy One, blessed be He. The infant does not know anything nor is he known until he has tasted bread of this world.[93] Israel did not know nor were they known by the supernal entities until they ate the supernal bread. Once they knew and were known by that place [*Shekhinah*], the Holy One, blessed be He, desired that Israel should know more about that place, which can be seen from that Land [i.e., *Tif'eret*] but they would not be able to until they tasted bread from that place. And what is it [that place]? Heaven [*Tif'eret*], as it is written, 'I will rain down bread for you from heaven' (Exodus 16:4). Then they knew and gazed upon that place but until they ate bread from that place, they did not know anything nor were they known." Rabbi Yose came and kissed him. He said, "It is certain that the Holy One, blessed be He, aroused us with this [teaching] and that the beginning of Israel's knowledge [about supernal matters] was with this bread." (*Zohar* 1:157a–b)[94]

The motif of the child's gaining certain cognitive abilities only after eating bread, while probably arising from a rough chronological coincidence with the development of a child's diet, points to a belief that bread somehow introduces a child to the verbal world. Although, for the rabbis, there is undoubtedly a crucial developmental stage that is traversed when a child first eats bread, for the kabbalists, different kinds of bread now serve as vehicles to mystical gnosis. When the text says that the infant "does not know anything . . . until he has tasted bread of this world," it is evident that it is through the consumption of something from a given realm that one acquires knowledge and entry into that realm. The child is not fully of this world, being unknowing and nonverbal, before he eats bread. Similarly, it is through the consumption of the bread, whether the unleavened bread from the *Shekhinah* or the manna from *Tif'eret,* that a person comes to know these worlds. Further, this is an inevitable event that may be contingent upon the individual's readiness, but is not dependent on any specific preparation. It is clear that one has to eat the bread that comes from a particular *sefirah* before one can experience and have knowledge of the *sefirah* itself. Thus it is not learning certain esoteric knowledge that will give them this experience, but rather it is as a result of God's grace that one consumes his emanant and thereby comes to know it.

The manna and the unleavened bread have emerged as the perfect test cases for the kabbalists' epistemology of food and eating. In a discussion of the unleavened bread, Gikatilla explains that the *mazah* is not called poor bread because it is inferior to leavened bread; in truth, he says, the leavened bread is the poor bread. It is, instead, an indication of the weakness of the recipient who cannot see the bright, supernal light until he mixes in a portion of darkness and dims the light—at that point, he can see it. Rich food connotes spiritual opacity, but it is a necessary concession to the human state. Blending Neoplatonic and symbolic thought, Gikatilla argues that intelligibles have to be rendered in corporeal form in order to be comprehended; for the same reason, Israel is not required to, nor can they, eat *mazah* all the time. As if working at cross-purposes, however, he says that yeast actually causes a loss of comprehension (*hasagah*). There was a need upon leaving Egypt for Israel to separate from the sensibles so that there should be no impediment to apprehension. It was essential that their bread not have the possibility of leavening because the leaven suggests an overinvolvement in the material world and would have meant that they would have deserved slavery.[95] The food that one eats is thus an index for the degree of mystical cognition that one enjoys.[96]

The Edenic sin is obviously fertile ground for elaborating epistemological models regarding the knowledge gained by the original couple and acquired subsequent to their sinful eating. Commenting on the biblical verse "When the woman saw that the tree was good for eating" (Genesis 3:6), the *Zohar* says that she saw the measure of the tree and gave that to Adam, thus separating the *sefirah* of *Malkhut* from *Tif'eret* (*Zohar* 1:36a). This particular eating gave visionary knowledge of the Divine but in such a way that its import was misunderstood. It also apparently bestowed demonic knowledge upon them. Adam and Eve are said to cover themselves with the leaves of the tree (*tarfei de-ilana*) from which they had just eaten, a code formula for knowledge of forbidden magic.[97] Previously, they had been covered with a supernal aura (*zohara*), but now their eyes were opened, and they saw that they had been stripped of that aura; now they saw the sins of the world, which they had not seen previously (*Zohar* 1:36a). Eating, then, is an avenue into both supernal insight and degraded insight.[98] The knowledge Adam and Eve gained, upon realizing that they were "naked," also reflects self-knowledge, as they have gained insight into their degraded ontological status; the knowledge itself is debased. Demonic or flawed perception of the Divine can be found in the case of the Sabbath meals as well, because skipping one of the three prescribed meals causes a blemish in the supernal world, which, in turn, induces punishment (*Zohar* 2:88b). The *Zohar* says, "If a man impairs just one meal, he causes a defect to appear in the world above, and shows that he does not belong among the scions of the supernal King, among the scions of the royal palace, or to the holy seed of Israel."[99] Eating can thus be seen to serve a crucial role both in one's understanding of the Divine and in the constitution of the Divine, as well. While always connected to the question of obedience to the law and the religious correlate of affiliation with one realm or another, the significance of proper eating is that it brings one to the threshold of either holy or demonic experience and understanding.

One of the paradigmatic foods serving kabbalistic purposes is the nut. Most commonly, the nut is used as a metaphor to describe the layers of the divine realm, with the fruit inside symbolizing the purest aspect, and the shell symbolizing the least pristine or even demonic aspect that is able to attach itself to the purity of the fruit.[100] In other instances, the layers of the nut are said to symbolize the different ways in which the Torah can be read: "The words of Torah may be compared to a nut. How? . . . Just as a nut has a shell outside and a kernel inside, so the words of Torah contain *ma'aseh, midrash, haggadah,* and *sod,* one within the other" (*Zohar Hadash* 83a *Midrash Ruth*).[101] Similar are the passages that describe the kabbalistic understanding of the Torah as eating the wheat or the kernel as opposed to those who adhere to the simple meaning alone as eating the chaff or straw.[102] We see another example of the same usage of food metaphors with regard to the waters of Marah, where the biblical text itself has provided the metaphor.[103] Thus, once one throws the "Tree of Life" into the bitter waters, they become sweet to drink.[104] The *Zohar* also relies extensively on the rabbinic trope of the Torah as a well of living waters, altering it so that it is the kabbalah specifically that fits that description.[105] Elsewhere the loaves of bread that are brought for Shavuot are considered to represent the two stone tablets that were originally intended to be given to the people.[106] In these instances, the usage is metaphorical: one does not eat a nut in order to gain knowledge of the Torah; rather, the way in which one learns is compared to different aspects of the nut.[107] What is significant for my purposes about this passage, however, is that Torah or wisdom is understood as something that one can consume and internalize. That which is tasty and nourishing is the truest Torah; that which is discarded is the more mundane Torah.

In one instance of the *Zohar*'s treatment of the story of Elisha and the poor woman, we find the link between bread and wisdom.[108] The homily concludes: "This is the mystery of 'I have granted wisdom to all who are wise' (Exodus 31:6); and it is written, 'He gives wisdom to the wise' (Dan. 2:21). The table of the showbread refers to this mystery, as it is written, '. . . on the table you shall set the bread of display, to be before Me always'" (Exodus 25:30) (*Zohar* 2:157b). Here the mystery stands exposed. Divine wisdom is experienced in the bread, both that which is in the temple of old and that which is in the home of the kabbalist.[109]

The parable from the introduction to the *Sifra di-Zeni'uta* underscores the conception of Torah as something that is consumed:

There was a man who lived in the mountains. He knew nothing about those who lived in the city. He sowed wheat and ate the kernels raw. One day, he entered the city. They brought him good bread. He said, "What is this for?" They said, "Bread, to eat!" He ate, and it tasted very good. He said, "What is it made of?" They said, "Wheat." Later, they brought him cakes kneaded in oil. He tasted them and said, "What are these made of?" They said, "Wheat." Finally, they brought him royal pastry made with honey and oil. He said, "And what are these made of?" They said, "Wheat." He said, "I am the master of all of these, for I eat the essence of all of these: wheat!" Because of that view, he knew nothing of the delight of the world; they were lost to him. So it is with one who grasps the principle and does not know all those delectable delights deriving and diverging from that principle. (*Zohar* 2:176a–b)[110]

This wonderful parable speaks more about hermeneutics than it does about food, but the *Zohar*'s dwelling upon the delights that food brings certainly is not the mark of an abstemious orientation. The parable suggests a veritably sensual delight taken in gaining knowledge of the realm of *sod*. Here, it is not only the satisfaction of satiety but the luxurious and complex tastes of the food that are summoned. In another body of literature, we might consider this to be an apt but unessential metaphor; in the *Zohar*, however, where the visionary and experiential elements are so pronounced, such metaphors suggest visceral engagement. The end of the passage suggests that the straw man is not a literalist but rather a stereotypical philosopher who, having grasped the essential nature of God, rejects religion. In this reading, the fancy foods represent the *sefirot*, the divine complexity that the philosopher rejects and does not comprehend.[111]

UNITIVE EXPERIENCE

In the kabbalah, knowledge of the Torah is always intimately linked with knowledge of the Godhead.[112] If consumption of food leads to esoteric Torah knowledge, then it should lead to knowledge of God as well.[113] This knowing is sometimes expressed in terms of gnosis and sometimes as mystical or unitive experience. Although the *Zohar* repeatedly refers to the sefirotic associations that various foods have, it is rare that the obvious result of eating these foods—that is, that the person has consumed the Divine—is expressed.[114] It is in respect to this phenomenon that we see the *Zohar*'s slippery symbology. While the unleavened bread, the Sabbath loaves, or the wine are understood quite literally to be affiliated with particular *sefirot*, that aspect of the Divine is *not* considered to pass literally through the mouth, the esophagus, the stomach, the intestines, and the organs of elimination.[115] Although there are instances of "blessing in the belly," the *Zohar* generally avoids formulations that suggest the concretizing of the Divine within the human body. Meanwhile, in some sense, according to the *Zohar*'s conception, this is in fact occurring. The reticence is understandable: the problem requires a thoroughgoing reconciliation of God's transcendence with the immanence and incorporation that these correspondences suggest.

The kabbalistic ethic in the *Zohar* portrays virtually all human action as stepping into either the holy or demonic realm. Often, it is the intention (*kavvanah*) with which one performs the deed that determines which path one follows. The result is *devekut* with some aspect of the Godhead. Thus, when one eats *maẓah*, unleavened bread, one steps into the camp of the Shekhinah; whereas when one eats leaven (*ḥameẓ*) during Passover or eats some other forbidden food, one becomes part of the demonic realm. This binary representation usually suggests that one is wholly within one realm or the other, but there is some nuance, and psychological insight, inasmuch as there can be gradual movement into or out of one realm or the other. Perhaps the most common example of the two domains as represented in the context of food and eating occurs in discussions of the leaven and unleavened bread. These are clearly presented as two different domains in which the *ḥamez* represents the domain of uncleanness, and the *mazah* represents the *Shekhinah*. In eliminating all *ḥamez* from one's home and then, on the festival of Passover, eating the unleavened bread, one has effectively moved from one realm to the other.[116]

> Rabbi Hiyya and Rabbi Yose were walking along the road. Rabbi Yose said to Rabbi Hiyya, "Whenever we are walking along the road and we are studying Torah, the Holy One, blessed be He, performs miracles for us. Now, this is a long path ahead of us; let us occupy ourselves with the Torah and the Holy One, blessed be He, will unite (*yizdaveg*) with us." Rabbi Hiyya began, saying, "'In the first month on the evening of the fourteenth of the month you shall eat unleavened bread' (Exodus 12:18). It is also written, 'For seven days you shall eat unleavened bread, a poor bread' (Deuteronomy 16:3). . . . Come and hear. When the Israelites were in Egypt, they were in another domain.[117] When the Holy One, blessed be He, desired to bring them closer to Him, He gave them the place of the poor bread.[118] What does 'poor' signify? This refers to King David, about whom it is written, 'For I am poor and indigent' (Ps. 86:1), and this bread is called 'poor.'[119] It is called *mazah*. The feminine without the masculine is impoverished. First, they came close to the *mazah*. Upon coming closer, the Holy One, blessed be He, raised them to other levels and the masculine united (*ithaber*) with the feminine. When the *mazah* is united with the masculine, it is called *mizvah* with the addition of *vav*.[120] This is as it is written, 'For this *mizvah*'" (Deuteronomy 30:11). (*Zohar* 1:157a)[121]

In this passage, there are a series of movements from domain to domain: first, from Egypt and the *Sitra Ahra* to that of the *Shekhinah/mazah;* second, from *Shekhinah/mazah* to *Tif'eret*/manna/*mizvah*. The formulations that are used for these different unifications are numerous: they are "in the domain" or "under the sovereignty" of the *Sitra Ahra* ("*bi-reshuta ahra*"); God "gives them the place" of the *Shekhinah;* then they, having joined with or been assimilated to the *Shekhinah*, are "raised to other levels" and "joined" to the masculine. There are both theurgic and ecstatic events occurring here. In other instances, they "depart from the bread that is called leaven"[122] or "depart from their domain, from the other domain, from that domain which is called *ḥamez*, evil bread."[123] In each of these, they appear to be dominated by the divine or demonic entity with which they are joined, except for the feminine *Shekhinah,* whom they are given as a place. These different unifications are understood to be the direct result of the different dining activities that the Israelites engage in: eating first the *maẓah* and then the manna.[124]

Elsewhere, the eating and moving from one realm to another is given a stronger ethical cast, as the eating of the leaven is represented as a unification with the evil inclination (*yeẓer ha-ra*):

> It is written, "You shall make for yourself no molten gods" (Exodus 34:17), and the next verse states, "You shall keep the feast of unleavened bread." What has one to do with the other? They have explained it in this way: One who eats leaven on Passover is like an idol worshiper.[125] Come and see: When the Israelites departed from Egypt, they departed from their domain, from the other domain, the domain called leaven, evil bread. That is why idolatry is given the same name. This, too, is the mystery of the evil inclination, foreign worship, which is also called leaven. This is the evil inclination, for such is the evil inclination in man. It is like leaven in the dough.[126] It enters a person's belly (*mei'oi*) little by little,[127] and then grows until it permeates the whole body. And this is idolatry. That is why it is written, "There shall be no strange god in you" (Ps. 81:10) —"no strange god" indeed. (*Zohar* 2:182a)[128]

Here, the unification with the demonic occurs both inside and outside one's body upon the eating of the prohibited leaven. The leaven exercises a transformation of the individual by slowly occupying his body in the form of the evil inclination, but also, as is apparent from the beginning of the passage, places the person ontologically in a different realm. Thus, when one's body is internally changed, one is said to occupy a different domain ontologically.

In a disquisition on the meaning of Passover and, in particular, the eating of unleavened bread, Joseph of Hamadan writes similarly of the movement from one realm to another, with a similar focus on internal and embodied aspects:

> *Maẓah* is the side of purity and leaven symbolizes the camps of Samael and the evil inclination. The *maẓah* symbolizes the camp of Michael, the High Priest of the heavens, and it annuls the evil inclination, because the latter is not of its type.[129] Also, in order to subdue the evil inclination at the beginning of the year in the face of the good inclination; and to accustom [oneself] to the camps of Michael, the High Priest; and to distance oneself from the camps of Samael, the Lord, may He be blessed, forbade us

to eat leavened bread on Passover. . . . [He forbade leavened bread] since leavened bread is symbolic of (*dumya*) the evil inclination. As an egg's volume of leaven slowly transforms the dough, so did the Evil Inclination, bit by bit, draw Adam and Eve according to his own will, causing them to err. . . . In order to weaken his strength and to alleviate his burdensome yoke from us, our Creator, the Lord, may He be blessed, commanded us to eat *mazah* on Passover eve, at the beginning of the year in order to recognize and know and to destroy the evil inclination, to hate evil and choose the good. This is another reason according to the simple meaning. . . . According to the way of the kabbalah, . . . since that night is protected from agents of destruction, [we eat the *mazah*] in order to uproot the agents of destruction (*mazikin*) and the evil inclination from the world, and in order to inculcate the good inclination in the body. The *mazah* symbolizes the *Shekhinah* so that the Holy One, blessed be He, will cause His *Shekhinah* to dwell there.[130]

Deploying a variety of metaphors, Hamadan demonstrates how the consumption of *mazah* brings about a transformation of the individual and the world. The individual metamorphoses not only through a redirection of attention or an imbibing of ethical norms; rather, his very body is transformed as, bit by bit, the evil inclination is driven out, and the good inclination is absorbed.[131] Moreover, the agents of destruction, populating the world as world-conquering variants of the evil inclination, are eradicated as well. In addition, purifying the individual body serves to purify the world body.

Bahya ben Asher also describes a purification of the body through eating idealized foods. He writes,

The aim of mystical intention in the course of these corporeal [eschatological] meals is that they should be an avenue to purify the body and matter, to sharpen the intellect (*sekhel*) in order to apprehend knowledge of the Blessed Creator, and to contemplate the intelligibles. Then souls will transcend their bodies, now fit for the feast of the intellect from which the ministering angels themselves, who are closest to the *Shekhinah*, eat. Then the soul will apprehend the brilliant light, which it is unable to apprehend when it is sunken in matter.[132]

This stance complements Bahya's approach noted at the beginning of the chapter. His discomfort with food and its pleasures led to a utilitarian disposition, similar to that of Maimonides. Here, he imagines idealized foods, the flesh of the Leviathan, and indicates that its value is that it purifies the body, leading to the ultimate religious aim, apprehension of God in the purest sense. Certain kinds of foods have a unique subtlety such that they practically transcend the category of food itself. They are "brain foods" rather than culinary delights. This food that transcends food feeds the body so that it too can be transcended. As the manna is divine dew congealing into food, manna and other foods lead rarefied persons to make the reverse journey, slipping out of the snare of materiality to gaze upon, even "eat" from supernal realms. Baḥya's eschatological scheme is complicated by ambivalence toward resurrection, but at one point in his discourse he says that we can anticipate an intellectual meal at the resurrection enjoyed by the soul and the body. At that time, humans will be restored to their bodies and have ethereal meals that are consumed bodily.[133]

Moses de Leon, in his Hebrew work *Sefer ha-Rimmon*, relates the eating of the unleavened bread to the beginning of knowledge of and unification with the Divine:

> This is the beginning of the tying into the mystery of His Name, may He be blessed, this is the opening to enter. This is, as we have said, the first bread to know, to recognize, and to be tied with a supernal knot. This is the opening, as it says, "This is the gate to the Lord, the righteous will enter into it" (Ps.118:20). And with this we know and recognize that it is this bread that gives the one who is enlightened and knowledgeable the ability to know his Creator.[134]

As de Leon continues, he explains that the eating results further in the theurgic union of *Malkhut* with *Tif'eret* above, and with Israel below. As is frequently the case, unitive experiences are accompanied by theurgic abilities. Manipulating the sefirotic realms entails full engagement, communion, and even union with them.

The quality of one's intention in eating determines if the diner resides in a place of holiness or impurity, and the same holds true for one's table. The Mishnah teaches that if no words of Torah are uttered at a meal, the table is considered like a table of vomit and filth.[135] The *Zohar* adds that it is forbidden to recite the grace after the meal there (*Zohar* 2:154a).[136] This table is considered to be parallel to the holy table, that is, the *Shekhinah*, but does not partake of its holiness. In fact, it elicits disgust, a revulsion of good taste. There is the potential for God to make the table "His portion." In such an instance, the angel Suria takes all of these words of Torah recited at the meal, brings an image (*deyoqna*) of the table before God, the words ascend to the table, at which point it is crowned. The crowning is an act of completion, but it marks the assimilation and integration of the feminine table into the masculine God. As noted in similar passages, the words of Torah act as adornments for the bride, thus leading to the final coronation.[137]

Finally, the experience of unification is often described as receiving a seat at the king's table. It is a rabbinic trope that in the eschatological age the righteous will sit at the table of the king.[138] In the *Zohar*, this becomes a common description of the lived experience of righteous personalities in this world. Eating is represented as the ultimate experience in benefiting from divine beneficence. In one passage, Satan berates Job before God, saying that it is only because Job sits at the table of the king that the former maintains his righteousness; once that privilege is removed, he will abandon his good works (*Zohar* 2:33b). The table stands metaphorically for all of the benefits conferred upon Job, conveyed through the *Shekhinah*, that is, symbolized by the table. It is not only the kabbalist who sits at the king's table, however. In some instances, all of Israel is said to benefit, provided that they are fulfilling the will of God or that they are living in the idealized, sin-free existence of preexilic Israel.[139]

In its exegesis of Psalm 23:6—"You spread a table for me in full view of my enemies; you anoint my head with oil; my drink is abundant"—the *Zohar* comments,

> "You spread a table for me"— this is the feast of the king. "In full view of my enemies"—these are the dogs [foreign peoples] who sit before the king, hoping for a portion of the bones, and he [King David] sits with the king in the delight of the feast at the table [the *Shekhinah*].[140] "You anoint my head with oil"—this is the beginning of the feast, as all the oil, delicacies, and trimmings of the meal are given at the beginning to the king's beloved—[the *Shekhinah* and the mystic]. That which remains afterwards is given to the dogs and to the table-servers. "My drink is abundant"—the cup is always full before the king's beloved and he does not need to ask [for it to be filled]. (*Zohar* 2:152b)

To explain the notion that the Israelites receive the most select portion when they are living in the Land of Israel, giving the remains to the other nations, the *Zohar* offers a parable of a king who seats the members of his household at his table who then cast the bones to the dogs.[141] When the members of his household do not find his favor, the king throws the food and bones to the dogs directly. Returning from the parable to the main subject, the *Zohar* indicates that when Israel follows the will of God, they eat at the table of the king and the whole feast is prepared for them (*Zohar* 2:152b).[142]

This passage is descriptive of a communative experience as indicated by the proximity between Israel and God in the parable. One delights in God's gifts while sitting in his presence.[143] Last, the table too is a symbol for the *Shekhinah,* and in sitting at the table one has attained union with the *Shekhinah* and is prepared for union with the king, *Tif'eret.* It is consequent upon the host's distributing the food, emulating *Tif'eret,* that the latter union is attained. The degree of the union extends to apotheosis as, in some instances, the *sefirot* themselves are said to be the guests at the king's meal.[144] This places the mystics on the same ontological level as, and in considerable intimacy with, aspects of the Godhead itself.

KOSHER FOOD AND MAGICAL PROTECTION

In contrast to the demonic chef Balaam, the righteous Jew invokes divine effulgence onto his table. This theurgic and magical activity has benefits on both personal and divine levels. In an example of food's apotropaic effects, Daniel, Mishael, and Azaryah are reputed to be saved from the lions by virtue of the fact that they did not defile themselves with the king's nonkosher food (*Zohar* 2:125b).[145] The author asserts that the king was serving "*patbag*" (Daniel 1:15), which the *Zohar* claims is a combination of meat and cheese. The seventeenth-century commentator Azulai explains that this term is a *notarikon* (acronym) for *pat, basar,* and *gevinah*—bread, meat, and cheese.[146] Through the avoidance of this forbidden and contaminating combination, Daniel was able to retain his divinized visage, causing trepidation among the leonine denizens of the lair. The *Zohar* cites Daniel 1:3, which describes the youths sought out by the king ("youths without blemish, handsome") to corroborate this interpretation. Nebuchadnezzar's face, however, did change (Daniel 3:19), and the *Zohar* contends that this was due to his persistent eating of milk and meat.[147] In Moses de Leon's *Commentary on the Chariot,* the barren hill upon which an ensign will announce the restoration of the nobles is employed to refer to the consumption of the king's nonkosher food as in Daniel.[148]

The divine image, guarded by Daniel and forfeited by Nebuchadnezzar, is not merely a physiognomic metaphor for a spiritual capacity; the *Zohar* is concerned with practical issues of physiognomy.[149] This is evident from the fact that, in the *Zohar*'s account, the animals could discern a physiognomic difference. As noted earlier, the rationalist philosophers, and Maimonides in particular, believed that the food regulations of the Torah were designed to promote health and prevent disease.[150] It is an innovation of the mystics to say that there will be a change in physiognomy as a result of the violation of this practice. The labile image is both physical and spiritual, denoting the actual physical appearance of Daniel and Nebuchadnezzar and, implicitly, its spiritual correlate. The biomagical nature of the laws of kashrut is apparent in the fact that Nebuchadnezzar, a non-Jew who is not bound by the norms of the Torah, is, nonetheless, detrimentally affected by this diet. The effects of the Torah's norms about food are universalized and taken out of the narrower compass of intentionality that so often characterizes the *Zohar*'s stance with regard to the commandments.[151]

In one narrative, the *Zohar*'s mystical rabbis encounter an herbalist burning grape leaves. He informs the rabbis that they are suffering from a certain illness, but that if they eat garlic they will be healed (*Zohar* 2:80a). This kind of folk medicine is common enough, both in the Talmud and in the society contemporary with the *Zohar*, but the *Zohar* gives this herbalist the same kind of mysterious aura of esoteric knowledge that it attaches to the Old Man of *Mishpatim*, the *yanuka*, and the various anonymous donkey drivers. The herbalist explains that this kind of naturalist lore, demonstrating the wisdom that God planted within nature, has been rendered esoteric only to prevent people from relying on the lore and forgetting God's ways, that is, normative practice.[152] His other magical herbal practice, inducing a snake to emerge from a certain hole, further establishes his connection with the standard motifs of the *Zohar*'s religious imagination (*Zohar* 2:80a–b). The lines between magic, science, and religion blur, demonstrating how tenuously these different categories can be divided.[153] What is at stake here are the respective abilities of God's law and esoteric instruction to keep one's health: apparently, God's laws keep people healthy, but not as healthy as esoteric magic.

EATING, GENDER, AND SEXUALITY

Eating and sexuality are prominently linked in the *Zohar*.[154] Because the sexual act is portrayed as an event that has active and passive partners, the *Zohar* tends to regard it as analogous to the activity of nourishment, where one party is feeding, the other being fed. Indeed, the term "to nourish" (*zan*) is found ubiquitously in the *Zohar*, often as a term parallel to "to support" (*mefarnes*). In some places the analogous treatment, or homologization, of these two becomes explicit, and the male of the divine couple is said to nourish and support the female.[155] For example, in a description of God's autogenesis in the *Zohar,* we read the following:

> When the world above (*Binah*) was filled and impregnated [by *Ḥokhmah*], like a female impregnated by a male, it generated two children as one, male and female, who are Heaven (*Tif'eret*) and Earth (*Shekhinah*), . . . Earth is nourished by the waters of Heaven, released into Her, though the upper are male and the lower female, the lower nourished by the male. The lower waters call to the upper, like a female opening to the male, pouring out water toward the water of the male to form seed. The female is nourished by the male, ...[156] (*Zohar* 1:30a)

It is a rabbinic model of nature that provides incentive for this identification of Heaven/*Tif'eret*/masculine/water with Earth/*Shekhinah*/feminine/earth as we seen in the aggadic midrash *Bereshit Raba:*

> Rabbi Shimon son of Eleazar said, "Every single handbreadth [of water] descending from above is met by two handbreadths emitted by the earth. What is the reason? Deep calls to deep . . . (Psalm 42:8)." Rabbi Levi said, "The upper waters are male; the lower, female. The former cry to the latter, 'Receive us! You are creatures of the Holy One, blessed be He, and we are His messengers.' They immediately receive them, as is written: 'Let the earth open' (Isaiah 45:8)—like a female opening to a male."[157]

Mythically, the heavenly Father quenches Mother Earth with rain, nourishing and impregnating. The rabbis and then the *Zohar* slide effortlessly between these two models, substantiated by the ancient and medieval models of human anatomy that were available to them. On the human plane, the delicacies of the Sabbath table are said to effect the union of the masculine and feminine potencies of the Divine.[158] When kabbalistic texts speak of delightful delicacies, food serves both erotic and gastronomic functions. Barthes avers that natural appetite arises from the order of need and that the appetite for luxury arises from the order of desire. At the same time, he notes, however, that food gives more of a sense of repletion than of climax or crisis—there are no paroxystic effects in eating.[159]

The priestly meal of the showbread in the Temple serves as another opportunity to link sexuality and eating. According to the mishnah, the priests partook of this meal each Friday afternoon; in reflecting upon the meaning of this meal, the author of the *Zohar* uses the same locution that is employed in regard to scholars' conjugal responsibilities on the eve of the Sabbath (*"me-'erev Shabbat le-'erev Shabbat"*) (*Zohar* 2:154b).[160] Homologizing showbread to wives, the kabbalist feminizes the bread, inviting his contemporary male mystics to confront the feminine bread by consuming it, mastering it, and incorporating it.[161] The relationship of eating to the sexual dynamic, in which the male incorporates (might we say consumes?) the female, is evident. Further, because this bread is the product of the sacred union between masculine and feminine potencies above, this text has instituted a formal parallel between sexuality and gastronomy on both supernal and mundane levels: in the upper realm, sexual union produces bread while sexual union in the lower realm is identified with eating the showbread and procreation. Eating is an indication of the receiving of the divine flow, and in receiving sustenance, the one being fed is enclosed within the one providing the nourishment; feeding propagates the divine flow and, in disseminating that flow, contains those who receive it.[162] Both the receiving female and the nursing child are penetrated by the issue of the donor entity. Although food is eroticized in this manner, zoharic kabbalah displays its usual puritanism with regard to food when it bears on real human sexual activity.[163] For example, de Leon avers that the mixture of meat and milk serves as an aphrodisiac, hence its prohibition. God has given this commandment because he hates promiscuity.[164]

A striking example of the meaning of food and the experience of eating in the *Zohar* occurs in another passage involving the manna: "'Now the manna was like coriander seed (*ke-zera gad*)' (Numbers 11:7). R. Yose said, 'To establish seed (*zar'a*) and strength in the land, as it is said, "Gad will be raided by raiders" (Genesis 49:19). As the seed of Gad takes its portion in another land,[165] so the manna rests upon those of Israel who are outside of the Holy Land.' Another teaching: "'like coriander seed'—like coriander seed—white and congealing when it came down to earth and materialized in the body, and this has been established by the companions" (*Zohar* 3:155b).[166] Driven by an imagination exulting in male virility, the *Zohar* considers the manna, partly because of the comparison to the coriander seed, to be the divine seminal fluid.[167] Manna's relationship to seminal fluid is established in the first teaching, in which it is compared to strength or forces, common synonyms for the divine potency.[168] The next homily says that the "seed" congeals and materializes in this world in the bodies of those who consume it.[169] While not saying so explicitly, the physiological model for a seed entering a body and "congealing" is conception; thus analogizing

manna eating to impregnation. The implication is that men are eating
and being symbolically impregnated with the divine seed. Drawing the eat-
ing/impregnation comparison explicitly, one passage refers to the *Shekhinah*'s consumption of souls, saying, "All of those souls are contained within
that point and She takes them at once like one who has swallowed up words,
becoming pregnant like a pregnant woman" (*Zohar* 2:213b).

Gender transformations are not uncommon in theosophic kabbalah, and
this passage constitutes one more example of this phenomenon.[170] In this
instance the male body is feminized and is regarded as subject to penetration; pregnancy has been transvalued from a feminine to a masculine valence.
Further, although the seed's movement from the supernal realm to the earthly
is a spiritual descent insofar as it is an event of materialization, there is no
overt negative value judgment assigned to this occurrence, in contrast to the
previous passage about manna. Nourishment is described as a passive event,
corresponding to the medieval notion of impregnation in which the mas-
culinization of pregnancy and giving birth render the female as essentially
passive.[171] In the previous passage, the value accorded to eating the manna
is limited as a homiletical means to emphasize the scale of the fall of the two
angels; in this last passage, the eating is equated with the essential act of continued transmission of the divine seed.

This interpretation is first offered in a homily by the Saba, found in
Tikkunei ha-Zohar, written in the early years of the fourteenth century: "'And
the manna was like coriander seed.' What does it mean that it was *like* coriander seed? Rather it means *GaD* (coriander) which is the right and the left,
beneficence to the lowly (*Gemul Dalim*). 'Like coriander seed' refers to Jonah.
The letter *yod*, in actuality, a white drop through which *GaD* is fulfilled and
becomes *GYD* (*membrum virile*). Of this seed, which is the *yod*, which is the
holy seed, it is said, 'and it vomited Jonah upon the dry land' (Jonah 2:11),
which is the feminine. [The letter] *heh* is called land which produces seeds
and fruits. This is as it is written, 'And God called the dry land earth (Genesis
1:10),' . . . The source of the flow from that seed that was drawn from the
supernal mind and that drop which is the small *yod* originates when the *alef*
emerges from the mind" (*Tikkunei ha-Zohar* 21, 54a). The word for coriander is composed of the letters *gimmel* and *dalet,* which are related, by the
text's etymology, to the words *gemul dalim,* beneficence to the lowly. The
letter *yod* is the first letter of God's ineffable name, YHVH, and as such represents the most recondite aspect of the divinity. Zoharic kabbalah associates it with the masculine *sefirah Ḥokhmah,* who sows seed in his feminine
partner, *Binah.*[172] Although many zoharic passages link the initial flow from

Hokhmah to *Binah* with a seminal emission, this is one of a few passages in the *Tikkunei ha-Zohar* that explicitly identify divine seminal fluid with manna.[173] It is the ejaculation that enables the *membrum virile* to attain its true, potential nature, as we see with the example of Jonah. Jonah is vomited out and can now bring divine admonition and mercy to the people of Nineveh. Moreover, the discharge fertilizes the primordial "dry land," that is, the *Shekhinah*. Inferring back from this passage to the one in *Zohar* 3:155b, we find that those eating the manna attain their fulfillment through the consumption of the supernal semen.

We have seen that there is a wide range of mystical and magical experiences in which the *Zohar*'s kabbalists partake through ritual eatings, informal meals, and engaged contemplation of the foodstuffs discussed in both biblical and rabbinic literature. These experiences are noteworthy for the ways in which they help us to understand the nature of embodiment experienced by the kabbalists. The body is revealed as an entity that can ingest knowledge and distribute it throughout one's limbs. Eating metaphors are used to describe unitive experiences and magical protection. All of these suggest a remarkably embodied spirituality enjoyed by the kabbalists; I have argued that they delight in a psychosomatic spirituality in which the spiritual experience is enjoyed and engineered by the body as well as the soul. As noted at the outset, this helps us to see how these figures grounded their spiritual experience as an occurrence that does not transpire exclusively in the mind or in the soul, detached from one's corporeal existence, but rather is part of one's fleshly, lived experience. From the evidence provided here, it is evident that the kabbalists engrossed themselves in their food in a concentrated, albeit abstemious, way, using it and thinking about it as if it were God himself.

4

"I Am So Glad to See the Face of the Shekhinah!*":*
The Social Aspects of Meals

THE *ZOHAR*'S NARRATIVE frequently uses meals as the occasion for the delivery of mystical sermons and as the site of mystical experience. If walking in pairs or groups serves as the most frequent opportunity for members of the mystical fraternity to impart their homilies, sitting down for a meal certainly ranks second.[1] Michel Jeanneret, in his work *A Feast of Words: Banquets and Table Talk in the Renaissance,* notes that there is a tendency to use banquet material in literature as a way of rooting the text in material reality and thus serving as a bridge to the reader.[2] What is the nature of the social interaction providing the backdrop for conversation or sermons? How does the engagement with food function as part of a social, mystical praxis? To be sure, there is a supernal realm with which the kabbalists engage that is of primary concern; however, it should be stressed that access to that realm lies only through active engagement with the physical realm. Although mystical symbolism can be understood as a deflection from the material and social world, I argue that, on the contrary, this symbolism places special emphasis on these lower domains.

Regarding the significance of the three Sabbath meals, Isaiah Tishby offers the following remarks:

> The various links between the Sabbath meals and the *sefirot* are presented in the *Zohar* not only as formal pattern, but as media of living contact with the divine powers, which attend and take part in these sacred meals. . . .

But it was not only at spiritual-mystical meals, arranged instead of the normal physical meals, that the supernal King would be invited to attend and join those participating. At every Sabbath meal, "Rabbi Shimon would say . . . Sabbath meals are called in the Zohar 'meals of faith,' which means 'meals of the mysteries,' like the sacred meal of the ancient mystery cults, where the spirit of God would be present in the divine images of *Atika Kadisha, Ze'ir Anpin,* or 'the Field of Holy Apples.'"[3]

Tishby, referring to meals as "media of living contact with the divine powers," pinpoints the phenomenon to which I now turn. That living contact occurs not only in a cognitive sense but also as an embodied experience, occurring at the table, in the kabbalists' mouths, and in their stomachs. In the following discussion, I examine the social aspects of the meals of the kabbalists and the ways in which their interactions and styles of eating lead to mystical experience and practice.

APPROACHING THE TABLE

The table acts as one of the many zoharic symbols for the *Shekhinah,* and sitting at the table invariably implies an engagement with the *Shekhinah.*[4] The connection of the male kabbalists eating at the table, *cum Shekhinah,* is erotically charged. These two appetitive acts are thus assimilated to each other in a larger framework of the erotic.

At least a partial motive for using the meal and its setting at the table as an opportunity for the delivery of mystical sermons comes from the dictum in the Mishnah:

> Rabbi Shimon [bar Yoḥai] said: "If three have eaten at one table and have not spoken over it words of the Torah, it is as though they had eaten of the sacrifices of the dead, for it is written, 'Yea all tables are covered with vomit and filth without God' (Isaiah 28:8).[5] But if three have eaten at one table and have spoken over it words of the Torah, it is as if they had eaten from the table of God for it is written, 'And he said unto me, "This is the table that stands before the Lord."'" (Ezekiel 41:22) (*Avot* 3:3).[6]

In Tractate *Berakhot* we read, "Rabbi Yoḥanan and Rabbi Eleazar both explain that as long as the Temple stood, the altar atoned for Israel, but now a man's table atones for him."[7] Together, these two rabbinic teachings provide literary grounding and motive for the zoharic practice. The teaching from *Berakhot* is an expression of the pietistic approach to the meals adopted by the Pharisees, in which they tried to project some of the sanctity of temple norms into the domestic realm; the kabbalists move in the opposite direction, imaginatively projecting themselves into the Temple and translating themselves into priests.

The frequency and nature of the table discourse in the *Zohar* indicate that the meal serves as more than merely nutritive and social ends.[8] In one instance, the itinerant rabbis are treated to a meal in an inn: "The companions rejoiced on the road. . . . When they arrived there [at a certain town] they went to an inn and [the innkeepers] set a table before them with various kinds of foods to eat. Rabbi Ḥiyya said, 'Certainly this table is like the world-to-come and we should raise this table and crown it with words of Torah'" (*Zohar* 2:157a). The table and its delicacies serve as a symbol for the world-to-come, signifying the *Shekhinah* in this instance.[9] How did the table come to bear this significance? Ronald Grimes, in his work on ritual studies, considers the ways in which objects are consecrated or ritualized with power by asking the following questions:

> What, and how many, objects are associated with the rite? What are their physical dimensions, shape, weight, and color? . . . Are the making and disposition of the object ritualized? . . . What uses would profane it? Must it be in some special position? What does it symbolize? How did the object become special? What stories are told about it? . . . Is power said to be resident in it, or does its power come and go, depending on its use? . . . Is it valued more for what it means or for what it does?[10]

Here, no magical act is performed, meditative mantra repeated, or kabbalistic intention explicitly adduced. The table and its meal evoke the thought of the commandments to be performed there; they are automatically assimilated to the rabbinic-kabbalistic mindset, which reads the world in terms of its legalistic and theosophic import. Sitting down to a meal becomes a hermeneutical act: the kabbalists read the scene of table and food as exemplars of the textual paradigm. At the same time, sitting down to a meal, even if ritualized, is a daily and usually mundane experience. What they bring to the table is a coalescence of religious, mystical, and bodily expectations.

Two aims reside in the desire to "raise the table": one is the theurgic concern to join the *Shekhinah* to her lover, *Tif'eret;* the other is the desire to elevate the food, that is, to turn the gathering into a spiritual communing, resisting the downward tug of the potentially coarse, material food. The mystical activity in this instance is theurgic in the desire to adorn the *Shekhinah* and unite her to *Tif'eret* and unitive when the kabbalists join together. The table is the locus and inspiration for this mystical event. Is it the food's appearance or taste that elicits this semblance between table and world-to-come?[11] In the courtly dining rooms of medieval European Christians, a great deal of attention was paid to the appearance and presentation of a meal, and less to its actual taste.[12] Because the delicacies are often compared to adornments for the Divine Bride and given the preponderance of visionary mysticism in the *Zohar,* it is most likely the visual modality and the ritualizing context that is being accentuated here.

Elsewhere, the meal itself is the instrument for the mystical experience. One of the most charming figures in the *Zohar* is a figure called *yanuka,* child. Like many of the mysterious characters that Rabbi Shimon bar Yohai and his companions meet up with, the unnamed *yanuka* is a hidden kabbalist, the son of "the late" Rav Mehemnuna Saba, who is himself an acclaimed kabbalist in the *Zohar.* Much of the scholars' argy-bargy with the sagely *yanuka* consists of discussion of the esoteric meaning of different foods and rituals associated with dining.[13] Following one such delivery, the child remarks,

"Friends! Bread and wine are the essentials of the table, and all other foods follow in their path. The Torah deals with them broadly for us and they are Her concerns.[14] The Torah requires that you ask for mercy and says, 'Come, eat my food and drink the wine that I have mixed' (Proverbs 9:5). Since the Torah invites you and requires this matter [eating] of you, you should do Her bidding. I invite you [to join me in eating], since She invites you to do Her bidding." They sat and ate and rejoiced with him. Once (or: since) they had eaten, they remained at the table. He began his discourse and said, . . ."[15] (*Zohar* 3:189b)

The parallelism of "I [*yanuka*] invite you . . . since She [Torah/*Shekhinah*] invites you" signals the equation of sacred acts in the mundane world with correlative acts in the supernal world. A key structuring device is the child's teaching that all the other foods "follow in the path" of bread and wine, the central foods of the Jewish liturgical economy. According to the normative halakhah, the blessings recited before eating bread and before drinking wine exempt the requirement for further blessings of any subsequent eating or drinking. The same goes for the blessings following the consumption of these two staples. Employing bread and wine as paradigmatic foods, the *Zohar* is less interested in a variety of delicacies or in the sensual experience of eating them than in the functional and symbolic value of food.[16] Distinct, identifying characteristics among foods are lost, as they are all enfolded in the broader categories of bread and wine. That is, it is the sefirotic correlates of food that intrigue the author of the *Zohar* rather than, overtly, their sensual nature; their symbolic stature is attained through their ritual status. This convergence of material, symbolic entities around exemplars (bread and wine) eases the path to connection with the most abstract entity of all, God. This pattern of disparate articles coalescing around larger symbols is a central feature of the zoharic kabbalah. At the same time, however, these ritualized foods are transvalued so that they become the portals through which the Divine is accessible.

Also central to this episode's transaction is the sequence in which mystical words of Torah lead into the meal, which, in turn, leads to more mystical homilies. In this spiritualized physiology, the body is prepared for proper eating through preprandial mystical discussion, and the eating in turn gives the nourishment to continue with the task of further mystical exegesis.[17] Praxis leading to experience leading to further praxis is a common phenomenon within the zoharic circle, a type of performative hermeneutics.[18] Another passage makes the point quite explicitly. At the end of a long homily by Rabbi Isaac,

> Rabbi Ḥiyya came and kissed him on the head. He said to him, "You are just a young person and yet supernal wisdom rests in your heart." Then they saw that Rabbi Ḥizkiah had come. Rabbi Ḥiyya said, "Certainly, the Holy One, blessed be He, will join (*yitḥaber*) with us, because Torah novellae will be introduced here." They sat down to eat. They said, "Let each one say words of Torah at this meal."[19] Rabbi Yeissa said, "This is not a full meal, but nevertheless it is called a meal.[20] Moreover, this is called a meal from which the Holy One, blessed be He, benefits. About this it is written, 'This is the table that stands before the Lord' (Ezekiel 42:22), because words of Torah surround that place." (*Zohar* 2:153a)

In the kabbalists' joining together and offering words of Torah, the words serve to unite the kabbalists with each other as well as with the *Shekhinah*, the feminine potency within the Divine; this leads to the Holy One, *Tif'eret*, the masculine potency, joining them as well.[21]

In the world of the zoharic narrative, arriving at someone's home inevitably presages hospitality and food. When the senior rabbis first arrive at the home of the *yanuka*, he stuns them with his occult knowledge that they had not recited the daily *keri'at shema*,[22] a fact that he deduced by the "fragrance of their garments."[23] They proceed to sit, ritually lave their hands, and break bread; the child in turn proceeds with his mystical homilies.[24]

Eating and mystical discourse are strongly linked for the members of the fraternity: there is no formal break between the first homily, the ritual acts, and the next homily, which takes the ritual washing as its point of departure. The bread they were eating might as well have been the mystical Torah to which they were listening. The lines between these two acts—consuming food and consuming Torah—are thus effectively and explicitly analogized. Elsewhere it is the great spread of food served by the *yanuka* that elicits recollective comments.[25] The intent of the rabbis' appreciative remarks refer metaphorically to the abundance and wonder of the mystical homilies that the child delivered; however, the first source is not intended to be taken merely metaphorically.[26] In both instances, the use of the food metaphor points to an understanding of the discourse as a gustatory event upon which Jeanneret has remarked, "Eating and learning are the same: two ways of absorbing the world."[27] Undoubtedly the "eating" of mystical homilies refers to an intellectual process, but it is a process that can be best understood with the consumption metaphor. It is precisely this permeability of boundaries, of both the body and the mind, that expresses the nature of the *Zohar*'s ideal human being.

SITTING DOWN TO EAT

In the symposiac atmosphere of the meals in the *Zohar*'s narrative, the meals are always prefaced by the gesture of sitting. Keeping Mauss's assumptions regarding the significance of bodily gestures in mind, sitting at the table must be seen in the broader context of the gesture of sitting as depicted in the *Zohar*.[28] An analysis of the act of sitting reveals that it was frequently an essential, preparatory component of the contemplative process, leading to study, gnosis, visionary experience, union with the *Shekhinah*, and union of the individual kabbalist with his companions.[29] Significantly, sitting is most commonly represented as an action of the rabbinic kabbalists rather than attributed to biblical characters in the exegetical portions of the *Zohar*. Sitting is also a common feature in many talmudic narratives, as one rabbi prepares to address another. The most likely talmudic source for the zoharic practice is from the *merkavah* narratives in *b. Ḥagigah* 14b. Rabbi Yoḥanan ben Zakkai is described descending from his donkey, wrapping himself in a prayer shawl, and sitting on a stone underneath an olive tree. Sitting was also a central part of the mystical praxis of the heikhalot mystics. Indeed, "the visionary experience was facilitated by his [the mystic's] sitting down before the throne of glory."[30] The *Zohar* further ensconces sitting among a range of mystical techniques. Ubiquitous in the zoharic passages describing the traipsing about of Rabbi Shimon and his companions are the formulae "they sat in a field,"[31] "they sat in a garden,"[32] "they sat under a tree,"[33] "they sat under a rock,"[34] or "they sat in a cave."[35] Each of these sites refers to self-locating in relation to either the *Shekhinah* (field, garden, rock, cave) or the *sefirot Yesod* and *Tif'eret* (under a tree or by a spring). Further, the term "they sat," meaning "they remained in a place," rather than the actual gesture of sitting, recalls the previous discussion about locating oneself in a certain place and how such an act is expressive of a particular spiritual and ethical affiliation.[36] For example, sitting in a ruined building next to graves evokes in the mystic an identification with his surroundings and the more general state of exile and destruction of Israel as he experiences it.[37] In some instances, one is "sitting," or staying, to pray.[38] Sitting suggests constancy and settledness, and it is only in a condition of constancy, the *Zohar* avers, that wisdom can truly rest.[39] There is, then, a complex of meanings for the image of sitting that all converge on the general meaning of union, usually with the *Shekhinah*.

One might object that a gesture such as sitting is a part of regular everyday movement without the automatic mystical results that one would associate with mystical techniques. I suggest that we speak of two different kinds of techniques: innovative techniques and naturalized techniques. The former would be those, such as breathing exercises, specific *kavvanot*, or contemplative foci, that are expected to arouse the mystical state of mind required for *devekut* or mystical illumination. The latter would be those acts that help create a singular environment in preparation for the desired experience but do so through reliance upon the constructed embodiment of the practitioner, building upon inherited gestures. Sitting would certainly be counted as one of these components, necessary and yet not expressly part of the contemplative process.

Germane to my concerns is the fact that the gesture of sitting is apparently the first stage in preparing oneself for a particular kind of mystical or spiritual experience.[40] This reading is affirmed by Hayyim Yosef David Azulai, the seventeenth-century emissary, halakhist, and kabbalist, who notes in a gloss that the appropriate physical preparation for mystical interpretation of texts is that one be dressed; the appropriate spiritual preparation is that one have the appropriate *kavvanah* and that one sit down.[41] The most common form in the *Zohar* of representing these naturalized sitting acts is the act of sitting in order to study. Although, obviously, sitting is the most likely position in which people would engage in study or mystical exegesis, the fact that the *Zohar* tells us that the company, in fact, did this makes it worthy of analysis. Consider the following:

> Fortunate are the righteous who have the Holy One, blessed be He, as their crown, and they serve as a crown for Him. They are fortunate in this world and they are fortunate in the world-to-come. It is written about them, "And your people, all of them righteous, shall possess the land for all time" (Isaiah 60:21). And it is written, "The path of the righteous is like radiant sunlight, ever brightening until noon" (Proverbs 4:18). They continued [walking] until they arrived at a field and they sat. (*Zohar* 1:84a)

Interpreting a verse that speaks of a path, the kabbalists follow its injunction, continuing on their way, presumably until noon, at which point the sun's heat would lead them to seek out a place to rest, notably in a field. Both "the land" and "the field" serve as cognomens for the *Shekhinah* in the *Zohar*'s parlance, homologized here. Because the *Zohar* considers both the literal interpretation of the "path" part of the verse and its mystical significance, the sitting here should be understood as both having a literal, physical gesture and bearing mystical import. Consider the following case in point: "[Rabbi Shimon] approached a cave and Rabbi Eleazar and Rabbi Abba emerged. Rabbi Shimon said, 'I can see from the walls of this cave that the *Shekhinah* is here.' They sat. Rabbi Shimon said, 'On what topic shall we discourse?' Rabbi Abba said, '[Let us talk] about the love of the Assembly of Israel for the Holy One, blessed be He'" (*Zohar* 1:245a).[42] The deliberate phrasing of "They sat" underscores the intentional role of sitting.

In one narrative passage, we read the following: "Rabbi Bun and Rabbi Jose, son of Rabbi Ḥanina, were walking on the road to redeem hostages. They happened upon a town and descended into an inn. At midnight they arose to study Torah. The woman of the house arose and lit a candle for them. When they were all sitting, she sat down behind them to hear the words of Torah They noted her . . ." (*Zohar Ḥadash* 86d *Midrash Ruth*). Sitting here evidently refers to the establishment of place in conformity with some established pattern—they sit down, then she, representing the *Shekhinah,* sits down behind them; in this manner, sitting is an act both of establishing position and of theurgic and possibly unitive significance. This expressionistic narrative frame that animates the *Shekhinah* in the form of a female innkeeper renders the links of study, sitting, and *devekut* with the *Shekhinah* in an especially charming way.[43]

In one of the zoharic passages that outlines the etiquette of the meal, the *Zohar* explains that the superior member of the group should sit at the table's head, the person of second greatest honor in the secondary place, and the same for the third figure. From there on, the text does not fix a seating plan.

Although these prescriptions are talmudic in origin,[44] the *Zohar* describes the arrangement as if it were commonly practiced by the kabbalistic elite: "Come and see. The masters of the King's banquet had many good and beautiful practices to show that they are among the members of the King's table. . . . The senior person would be seated at the head, the second [most senior] beneath him, and the third beneath the second. These [figures] are designated as three beds (*mitot*) receiving the three patriarchs and receiving the priests, Levites, and Israelites" (*Zohar* 3:271b–272a). The rabbinic source of this practice describes the seating arrangement as an arrangement of "couches" (*mitot*), the furniture used for seating at that time.[45] When the *Zohar* uses the same term (*mitot*), it intends that the kabbalists are "beds" or "resting places" for the *sefirot;* that is, they are the points of "resting" in this world, and there is a gendered and sexual valence accompanying this union.[46] This association is flagged by an express statement by Joseph of Hamadan, who refers to a woman as a chariot.[47]

While the seating arrangement demonstrates a social structuring of the kabbalistic fraternity, it also reflects a theurgic concern. The seating plan at the *Idra Raba* (Great Assembly)—with three senior members presiding over a total of ten participants—reflects the duty of each of the members to assume the position and role of one of the ten *sefirot*.[48] After the first two speakers, Rabbi Shimon issues an injunction to each figure following, saying, "Stand at your place."[49] One might presume that it is the gravity of the *tikkunim*— the various kinds of religious acts, whether ritualistic, liturgical, or scholarly, that act on and influence the Godhead to restore its primordial unity—which are performed at the *Idra Raba,* that leads to the distinction of standing rather than sitting. The spatial arrangement of the figures in the *Idra* is clearly construed as a physical model of the supernal world above. Further, the meaning of one's gestures in one's place reflects the meaning of the event. Sitting, as we have seen, is often a posture of mystical praxis and, when performed in a group at a table, requires a particular arrangement; standing would appear to be one degree superior—while the positioning remains the same, one stands as did the angels in Ezekiel's vision and as one does in the statutory prayer.[50]

One is led to conclude that the act of sitting at a table or sitting to eat, like sitting in a field, in a cave, or under a tree, have similar valences. Each is an act that involves contemplation and that can induce a variety of mystical experiences.[51] Moreover, the fact that one must locate oneself in one of these various sites not only indicates the significance of these material or geographical entities as part of the general symbol system but also points to the nature of embodiment: one's physical backdrop helps to create the desired spiritual environment. Indeed, the body that is suggested by this trope of sitting is a "body of communication," in which one is not engaged in a self-contained or self-referential system; rather, one situates oneself in a social setting, interacting with both one's fellows and one's environment.[52] The body of the mystic is open to the influence of his surroundings, both personal and inanimate, as it is all suffused with the symbolic potential of union and gnosis. This is the way in which the *Zohar* endows these acts with meanings so that readers can begin to see, and to live, their own lives inside this frame of meaning, thereby engendering mystical experiences themselves.[53]

Last, it must be noted that this sitting is not explicitly characterized as enthronement. Visions of the divine enthronement and experiencing such enthronement oneself were important aspects of earlier forms of Jewish mysticism upon which the *Zohar* draws heavily, and the naturalized enthronement in these instances in the *Zohar* must be read in light of those traditions: the sitting here is the naturalized experience of enthronement, even when not explicitly described in this manner. Put plainly, when a kabbalist is sitting, he is enthroned. Catherine Bell refers to a long-standing distinction that asserts that rituals "do" one of two things: communicate and symbolize or effect and instrumentalize.[54] Though there is something of both of these aspects in the kabbalistic sitting, the kabbalists are ultimately doing more than either of these options; they have internalized the ritual so that its formality is attenuated and its communication muted. Still instrumental, sitting is not primarily effecting something beyond the mystical adept, but rather it is his very basis for interaction with the Divine. The kabbalist's body is thus an exemplar of the ritualized body, the body invested with a sense of ritual.[55]

ETIQUETTE

Virtually any group in which people eat meals together develops a system of conventional rules delineating acceptable behaviors while dining; in a number of passages, the *Zohar* enumerates the various rules of this system.[56] The *Zohar* does not prescribe an elaborate code of behavior, as was developing contemporaneously in non-Jewish society, but there is nonetheless a concern, largely growing out of rabbinic prescriptions and proscriptions, regarding the way in which one should conduct oneself at a meal.[57] These rules encompass a wide variety of concerns, from the ethical to the mystical, but rarely relate to the mundane issues that concerned contemporary gastronomes. They are treated primarily in terms of their theurgic functioning, so that the ten aspects of the table refer to the *Shekhinah* and, as such, are part of the augmentation theurgy to be discussed later.[58]

There are two main discussions of etiquette in the *Zohar*. They are found in *Zohar* 3:271b–274a (*Ra'aya Mehemna*) and in *Midrash Ruth, Zohar Ḥadash* 86d–87d. Note that, in *Sefer ha-Rimmon,* de Leon says that it is by virtue of the various *tikkunim* established by the rabbis that one is able to elicit the flow of divine efflux onto one's table and gain atonement for one's sins.[59] The section in the *Ra'aya Mehemna* begins by saying, "Come and see. There are many good and fine practices performed by the masters of the feast of the King *to demonstrate* that they were from the table of the king" (*Zohar* 3:271b). The performative or dramaturgical behavior emerges again, stressing that one will be desirous to show that one is, indeed, from the table of the King. Quickly retreating from this kind of literalistic reading, however, the author expounds that there is no bread other than the Torah, though the meaning of the statement on "fine practices" no longer makes literal or contextual sense in this figurative mode.[60]

Gluttony is one of the primary sins in the kabbalah's standards of etiquette. Using Esau as the negative paradigm, the *Zohar* says that blessing will not rest in the stomach of a person who eats ravenously, but rather only in the stomach of one who is not a glutton (*Zohar Ḥadash* 86d, 87b *Midrash Ruth*).[61] Gluttonous behavior is rude and unfitting for a person eating at the table of a king.[62] Such a person has the serpent, the *Sitra Aḥra,* resting in his stomach, and the serpent is never sated. Lustful insatiability, as suggested by scripture—"the belly of the wicked is empty" (Proverbs 13:25)—is thus contrasted with the mystical contentment that both follows and accompanies eating done by the righteous.[63] Personal conduct in eating is thus raised to the mythical level; not only ritual conduct, but even the private actions of a person affect one's spiritual state, relegating one to the particular realm—holy or demonic—with which a person is currently affiliated.[64] To avoid the demonic result, "one should eat at his table calmly, like one who is sitting before the king."

It should be noted that, in the previous example, there are two different reasons given for avoiding the sin of gluttony: one is the motivating thought that one is sitting at the table of the king; the second is that one's belly will be suffused either with divine blessing or with the *Sitra Aḥra.*[65] While the borders of the bodies of both holy and sinful gourmands are interrupted, the holy diner has blessing, a nonpersonal entity, suffusing his innards, whereas the sinner has a living, growing, personal being sitting in his stomach. The body of the holy man retains a certain amount of bodily integrity and control and is enhanced by the experience; the transgressor suffers invasion and internal discontinuity. This rupture within the personality and physical being of the glutton mirrors, on a human level, the cutting of the shoots, the paradigmatic sin that occurs on the sefirotic level. The ethic of continence is thus promoted as the capacity to be sated emerges as a sign of righteousness.

FOOD AND MASCULINITY

In a text as strongly concerned with issues of masculinity and virility as is the *Zohar*, it is unsurprising that eating should also be understood as a function of these issues. Elliot Wolfson has argued that in Jewish esoteric literature, the "perfected" male sexual organ is frequently identified as a site for the mystical experiences of union, prophecy, vision, and hermeneutical abilities.[66] Maleness is thus the determinant of a host of mystical capacities and has an impact in the realm of one's eating as well. For example, one's ability to consume the angelic foodstuffs is determined by the presence of the mark of circumcision. Another experience resulting from the circumcision rite is that one can enjoy *devekut* with God and eat "higher bread" (*Zohar* 2:61b).[67] The manna is understood to originate at a higher place within the sefirotic structure than does the *mazah*, inasmuch as it is from the heavens, a cognomen for *Tif'eret*. Thus, before the circumcision that took place in the desert, the Israelites were only able to eat *mazah* but afterward could eat the bread of angels.[68] What made that earlier period different was that it marked a union with the *Shekhinah* alone and was thus considered to be "flawed bread."

The movement from *Shekhinah* to *Tif'eret*, from *mazah* to manna, is also marked by the movement from the first to the second part of the rite of circumcision, from *milah* to *peri'ah*;[69] similarly, the Passover offering can only be eaten by a Jew, that is, one who bears the mark of circumcision (*Zohar* 3:73a).[70] The *Zohar* links these two, conflating the eating of the Passover offering with that of the manna (*Zohar* 2:41a *Ra'aya Mehemna*). The ability to eat "higher bread," in this instance, is certainly synonymous with the attainment of union with a particular grade of the Godhead; it is nevertheless significant that the *Zohar* has chosen the metaphor of eating to express this experience of union. This implies that an internalized and somatic experience follows from the unitive event. Further, there is a hierarchy of bodies in which the circumcised body is not only superior by virtue of the kind of mystical union that it can attain but also in terms of the actual food that it can consume.[71] The manna is, of course, not merely food but the vehicle for union with, and gnosis of, the Divine. When this metaphor of unification is concretized and read back into the Bible's historical narrative, however, there is a merging of the material and spiritual realms such that the material serves as an entryway to the spiritual.[72]

One particular aspect of masculinity merits attention in this context, namely, the ways in which masculinity is represented in the interactions among pairs or groups of men. One example of this feature of gender dynamics involves Moses in the role of a food producer who is reportedly pleased with the manna that issues consequent upon his merit.[73] When Israel rejects the manna, calling it "miserable bread," he reevaluates his status, assuming that it is his own spiritual level that must be impaired:

> Come and see. Moses united and ascended to [a place] with which no other prophet had united. At the time that the Holy One, blessed be He, said to Moses, "I will rain down bread for you from the sky" (Exodus 16:4). Moses was delighted and said, "It is certain now that wholeness is found in me, for it is because of me that Israel has its manna." When Moses saw that they had returned to descend to that other level and asked for meat, saying, "Our souls[74] have come to loathe this miserable food!" (Numbers 21:5) he said, "If this is so, my spiritual degree must be flawed,[75] for it is through me that Israel eats manna in the desert—now I am flawed, and Aharon is flawed, and Nahshon son of Aminadav is flawed."[76] He said, "If you would deal thus with me, kill me rather, I beg you" (Numbers 11:15), for I am considered a female with respect to their food. I will descend from the heavens, a high level descending to the level of the female. I am superior to the rest of the prophets of the world, and regarding this he said, "and let me see no more of my wretchedness"—certainly that is descending to the lower level. (Zohar 3:156a)

The quality of food is determined by the person who elicits it; this capacity is explicated explicitly in terms of male virility.[77] Moses understands the spiritual backsliding of the Israelites as a personal failure that is, essentially, his. The merit of manna that the rabbinic text ascribes to Moses is automatically turned into a function of masculinity, the inference being that if one is a good disseminator of Torah, one is fully masculine; to have failed in one's leadership suggests emasculation, understood as death. Indeed, the feminine, figured oppositionally to the masculine, is nothing short of death.[78]

In this treatment of the story of the manna, we see how the *Zohar*'s authorship transmutes gender following opportunities in the biblical text; it is the movement of the biblical text itself that guides the *Zohar* in its exegesis. Death and failure are construed as feminine; success, life, and piety are associated with the masculine. When scripture represents the manna as "seed," the *Zohar* has a wonderful opportunity upon which to capitalize. In theosophic kabbalah, the ability to produce food is understood as a masculine trait that can be traced back to ancient and medieval notions of physiology.[79] While Moses' sex has not been changed, in terms of gender he has become a woman. In the same way that the idealized functions of prophet, visionary, and exegete correspond to the phallus as roles in which there is a revealing of that which is hidden, so does the food producer—the one who causes manna/seed to rain down from the heavens—correspond to the phallus.[80] It is, of course, no small irony that Moses—a male—construes the inability to produce proper nourishment as a characteristic of femininity.

In an amusing vein, normal assumptions about gender and food production are short-circuited in the narratives of the *yanuka*.[81] One of the primary characteristics of the kabbalists' interpersonal relations is a masculine competitiveness in which one's power is determined by the strength of one's creativity. Although the sword of the non-Jewish model may have been turned into the pen, the word is translated back into a sword by the kabbalists in their jousting as they compare the name of God to a battle sword and esoteric homilies to a variety of weapons (*Zohar* 3:272a *Ra'aya Mehemna*).[82] Interestingly, the power to deliver homilies is related explicitly to virility in the *Zohar*'s uses of the rabbinic teaching: "All seed that does not shoot like a bow will fail to procreate."[83] The *yanuka*, who delivers these homilies declares, "'Now it has been made clear to you that I know how to bring down great men with swords, the spear, the bow, and the sling.'[84] We [the rabbis] were astonished and we could not speak before him. He said to them, 'Rabbis, now we see who is the one that will profit with bread, that is, the bread of the blessing recited over bread.'" Like Moses, who was superior to all of his competitors and was thus able to produce food for Israel, so does the *yanuka* win the right to produce food for the table.[85] The concepts of masculinity and virility are transvalued as the child overtakes the men with his superior weapons, that is, masculine potency, as expressed in his ability to deliver superior homilies. The irony here is enhanced by the fact that the word *yanuka* means, literally, "one who suckles," when, in fact, it is the child who nurtures the rabbis. The bread that the *yanuka* gains is at once the bread of the meal, the bread of Torah, and the bread that is the fruit of the *sefirah* *Yesod,* the *sefirah* that corresponds to the male member of the divine anthropos.[86] The meal is thus seasoned with elements of competition, humor, and the sharing of mystical gnosis.[87]

AFFECTIVE PERFORMANCE

In *The Presentation of Self in Everyday Life,* Erving Goffman argues that every group dynamic displays some theatricality, inasmuch as there is an awareness of how one's actions are being perceived by others or how one's self-representation is being assimilated.[88] In the *Zohar,* this dynamic rests prominently on the possibility of being recognized as "the faithful" or as "the scions of the king," as represented in the main discussion of the Sabbath feasts.[89] It is by virtue of observance of the Sabbath meals that Israel is recognized as "the faithful," "the members of the palace," and "the scions of the King" (*Zohar* 2:88b).[90] In context, it is not immediately clear how they merit this distinction other than the simple observance of the meals and the testimony they give to the arrangement of the *sefirot.* Further, the ontic nature of the status of "scions of the palace" or "scions of the King" is also left unclear.[91] What is apparent, though, is that one who neglects these meals causes a flaw to appear in the *sefirot* and demonstrates that he is not a "member of the palace."[92] At the same time that this miscreant causes an ontological flaw within the Divine, he demonstrates to his fellows that he is not a worthy member of the community. An ethic of watchfulness prevails in which one's performance, or lack thereof, serves as the criterion for evaluation by others. One's perception of one's fellow is, unsurprisingly, affected by the simple observance of his behavior.[93]

There is another aspect to this phenomenon of theatricality and self-representation. One of the most interesting of the praxes employed in the course of eating to gain the desired mystical experiences may be called "affective performance." By affective performance, I mean the adoption of not only a mood but also the demonstrative expression of that mood—in a word, a mask. The adoption of such a visible affect is intended to express the internal state of the subject, to create a feeling of unity and love among the group, to affirm shared values and practices, and to promote rectifications (*tikkunim*) in the supernal realm.[94] Thus, in a straightforward example, we read as follows:

> "I therefore praised enjoyment. For the only good a man can have under
> the sun is to eat and drink and enjoy himself. That much can accompany

him, in exchange for his wealth, through the days of life that God has granted him under the sun" (Ecclesiastes 8:15). "I therefore praised enjoyment": King Solomon praised this?! Rather, "I therefore praised enjoyment": this is the joy of the Holy King when He rules on the Sabbath and festivals. For out of all the good deeds that a person might do, there is nothing better for a person . . . than to eat and drink and to display joy to that side [of holiness] so that he will have a portion in the world-to-come. (*Zohar* 2:255a)

Not only festive eating is required during these sacred times, but joy too is normative. Another important normative emotion is love. Rabbi Shimon frequently exhorts his band to be loving in their fraternal congregation, asserting that it is that mood itself, as evidenced in their facial expressions, that creates the proper environment for the mystical communion.[95] The need for love is stated emphatically:

When the companions came before Rabbi Shimon, he saw a sign in their faces [that there was love among them], and he said: Come my holy children, come beloved of the King, come my cherished ones who love one another. For, as Rabbi Abba once said: All those companions who do not love one another pass from the world before their time. All the companions in the days of Rabbi Shimon loved one another in soul and spirit. That is why [the secrets of the Torah] were disclosed in Rabbi Shimon's generation. As Rabbi Shimon was wont to say: All the Companions who do not love one another divert from the straight path, and cause blemish to the Torah, for the Torah is love, brotherhood, and truth. The Companions must follow this example and not blemish [the Torah]. (*Zohar* 2:190b)[96]

The descriptions of physiognomy in the *Zohar* are primarily interested in examining the hair, forehead, eyes, lips, face, ears, and lines on the hands.[97] In examining these various characteristics, the *Zohar* concerns itself with character traits that they indicate: anger, integrity, honesty, aggressiveness, selfishness, garrulousness, libelousness, and so on. These indicators are physically based rather than being rooted in affective displays, and one wonders to what extent they were used for inclusionary or exclusionary practices within the fraternity. The ethical or spiritual nature of these evaluations in the *Zohar* can be seen in the following passage:

At a time when anger rules over a person, another judgment is given by which he is known . . . but to look at a face in the true way is at the time when the face is illuminated and a person is established in his place. Then these markings can be seen in a true way, because then, with *that* visual examination, his nature can be better evaluated. Of course, the wise are able to look [at and evaluate a person by his facial markings] in any situation. (*Zohar* 2:76a)

The *Zohar* spiritualizes this lore by proceeding to discount its value, saying that Moses did not need this science to be able to select the appropriate leaders, but rather was able to do so by virtue of inspiration by the holy spirit (*Zohar* 2:78a).

The relationship between outer affect and inner experience varies as one surveys different cultures. As Clifford Geertz writes, "[Religion is] a system of symbols which acts to establish powerful, pervasive, and long-lasting moods and motivations in men by formulating conceptions of a general order of existence and clothing these conceptions with such an aura of factuality that the moods and motivations seem uniquely realistic. . . . [Religious systems shape experience by] inducing within the worshiper a certain distinctive set of dispositions."[98] Building on this notion, Gary Anderson has noted that, for modern readers, "[e]motional experience is thought to occur prior to any behavioral expression, so to understand the behavioral mode as the primary dimension appears to do violence to the integrity of the emotional life. For the ancients [biblical era], however, such isolation of performative elements was quite natural. The emotional experiences of grief and joy were inseparable from their behavioral components."[99] Further, for ancient practitioners of Judaism, ritual activity creates sentiment rather than, in expressivist fashion, stemming from it.[100] For the ancients, at least, this is a reversal of contemporary notions of the relation between the inner and outer.[101] George Lindbeck employs this approach, calling it a "cultural-linguistic alternative" to the study of religion. He writes,

A religion can be viewed as a kind of cultural and/or linguistic framework or medium that shapes the entirety of life and thought. . . . It is not primarily an array of beliefs about the true and the good [though it may involve these), or a symbolism expressive of basic attitudes, feelings, or sentiments (though these will be generated.) Rather, it is similar to an idiom that makes possible the description of realities, the form of beliefs, and the experiencing of inner attitudes, feelings, and sentiments. Like a culture or language, it is a communal phenomenon that shapes the subjectivities of individuals rather than being primarily a manifestation of those subjectivities. . . . Instead of deriving external features of a religion from inner experience, it is the inner experiences which are viewed as derivative.[102]

How then does the inner/outer dynamic play itself out in the *Zohar,* a literature that bears the strong markings of medieval Jewish philosophy, where the question of the compatibility or incompatibility of soul and body is pronounced?

Earlier, I drew attention to a passage in Moses de Leon's *Sefer ha-Rimmon* in my discussion of satiety from an olive's-worth of food.[103] De Leon writes,

> A person who recites the Grace after eating gives power to the attribute of *tov* (Goodness), which is the attribute that receives from *Ḥesed.* The appearance of this known attribute that receives food is satiated, totally filled with goodness. The lighting and sparking of the brilliant light (*or ha-bahir*) is good and satiating, without causing harm. . . . In any event, when a person is sated or appears sated with regard to his food He should bless His master.[104]

It is not necessarily a physical experience or even the adoption of a spiritual stance that is required: in order to have the requisite status for reciting the blessing, the individual diner and his supernal correlate are either sated *or bear the appearance of satiety.* If a person has had an olive's-worth of food before him and has eaten it, that gives the *appearance* of satiety, because the halakhah defines an olive's volume as the point at which one recites the grace, ostensibly the minimal point at which one might be sated.[105]

Both in this passage from *Sefer ha-Rimmon* and in the zoharic parallel, the reference to the filling of the individual diner and the correlate *sefirah* are symbolic of the erectile filling of the divine sexual organ and its earthly representative, the kabbalist, as he is about to bless the Divine. The performative dimension on the part of the mystic serves as a mark of his own fullness and, as such, constitutes an act of *imitatio dei.* The kabbalist mirrors the appearance of the sated *sefirah Yesod,* the phallic member of the Godhead. The text says that if one *appears* to be sated, one has fulfilled a halakhic requirement and is considered by the kabbalah to be imbued with a privileged status according to which one must then act in accordance—that is, recite the blessing. Satiation is associated with fullness, which translates into spiritual satiation in the divine realm.[106] It is apparent that one is emulating the appearance of the Divine not only in terms of the performance of the various rituals but also in terms of the affect of the Divine; the kabbalist emulates God's joy and satiety as well.[107] Here the phallic fullness is expressed bodily by the kabbalist. Once the mystic resembles the supernal paradigm, fullness comes from above and enables him to direct his blessing upward; the kabbalist's act of *imitatio dei* endows him with theurgic capacity.

Satiety, and the subsequent overflow—one might call it generosity—is analogous to sexuality both conceptually and morphologically. In each instance, there is a filling of the subject and an inexorable response of love to the other, whether it be a poor person (as we shall see in chapter 5) or the beloved. In one of the *yanuka* passages, the companions celebrate the child's genius, dancing him around on their shoulders.

> They pronounced three words upon him: "Out of the eater came some-thing to eat, out of the strong came something sweet" (Judges 14:14). . . . He opened and said, . . . "We have support for this verse, 'Out of the eater'—this is the Righteous One (*zaddik*), as it is written, 'The Righteous One (*zaddik/Yesod*) eats to sate his soul' (Proverbs 1:13).[108] 'The Righteous One eats'—in actuality—and He takes everything [from above]. What is the meaning of 'to sate His soul?' He gives satiety to that place that is called 'His soul'—of David (*Shekhinah*). 'Out . . . came something sweet'— if not for that Righteous One, food would not proceed to the worlds, and the world would not be able to subsist." (*Zohar* 1:240a)

The gifted child imitates Samson offering the "true" explanation of the mys-terious riddle and, as Samson is analogous to the virile and powerful lion, so too is the child similar to the lion yielding sweetness and the *sefirah Yesod* that he describes. In his exegesis, the boy identifies the food eaten with the efflux from above. Once full, the eater/*Yesod*, endows fullness onto his soul/*Shekhinah,* which then confers the divine overflow, now materialized into food, onto the world below. Supernal food is translated into material food by means of the juncture of masculine and feminine potencies above, an event mirrored below in the child's actions—giving food to the compan-ions and sharing esoteric insight. Verily, the mystics' meal and its subsequent satiety comprise the mechanism that facilitates the surplus, spilling over below.

In each of these passages, we see that it is desirable to enact and model a certain appearance to gain an esteemed spiritual status. This modeling or stylized eating is another kind of body technique advocated by the *Zohar* as a means for turning oneself into a vessel and instrument for divine bless-ing.[109] Although there is no injunction in the passage from *Sefer ha-Rimmon* to assume a particular expression or affect, it is clearly desirable to be able to express a certain mood, even if it is not spontaneously felt. It is reasonable to assume that this appearance is not a spiritual appearance, noted only by God or charismatics, but rather the more commonplace manifestations of appearance that can be evaluated by ordinary individuals. Furthermore, the adopted similitude to the *sefirah Yesod* is characteristic of zoharic theurgy, as it is through emulating the Divine that one attains likeness and communion with it. *Imitatio dei* takes on a particularly morphological meaning.[111] The *Sefer ha-Rimmon* text proceeds to say that one should run with an erect posture when one is headed toward the synagogue because this shows people that he is blessed by God. Further, one must sit in the synagogue with humility and awe to demonstrate that the synagogue is a unique place. These ritual expressions perform a didactic role as the pious behavior expected to visually express to others the nature of the building in which they sit. The emphasis on gesture here fully accords with the demand for certain norms of affective expression.

In this passage and others, we see that it is the affective dimension of emulation that is required.[112] In one instance, the *Zohar* proffers that, because food and satiety emerge from the place to which the grace after meals is directed, the *sefirot* of *Tif'eret* and *Malkhut,* one should display satiety and joy before that place (*Zohar* 2:153b).[113] In prayer, in which the gesture of standing with one's mind trained upon the higher *sefirah* of *Binah,* there is no eating and drinking; in contrast, in the recital of the grace after meals, when one directs one's intention toward the *sefirot* of *Tif'eret* and *Malkhut,* who are responsible for disseminating food to the lower realms, one should not only eat and drink but also model the paradigmatic appearance suggestive of those *sefirot.* At this juncture, we see how the *Zohar* creates different models of the body as it lays out the different regions of the Divine and its modes of physicality. There is the consuming body, for which proper sensuality is permitted, and the prayerful body, which requires neither physical sustenance nor the sensual stimulation of eating and drinking.[114]

A passage in *Zohar Ḥadash,* however, makes this mood adoption a normative behavior: "On the Sabbath, one has to give the appearance of satiation to overturn the maidservant Lilith. And in the place of sadness of Shabbatai, [one must] give the appearance of delight; in a place of darkness, a candle; in a place of suffering, delight. [All of this is done] in order to effect a transformation in everything" (*Zohar Ḥadash* 33d).[115] Affected satiation is not the dominant motif in these instances, but, rather, they are part of a broader emotional idiom.[116] Referring to the hazards of the day on which there is a particular constellational configuration, another passage continues this theme: "We have to comport ourselves with joy and food and drink and white clothes or beautiful colors, cleaning the house and setting the table on this day" (*Zohar Ḥadash* 37a).[117] Here the performative nature is evident, as one is instructed to change one's facial appearance with the same perfunctory tone as one is told to set the table. Elsewhere one is exhorted to display oneself as sitting under the shade of faith (*Zohar* 3:103a); to adopt a deathlike appearance after the statutory prayer (*Zohar* 3:120b); or to exhibit oneself as a free person during the Passover holiday (*Zohar* 3:95b).[118] At other times, the performance is explicitly intended to have a theurgic effect; thus, tasting the Sabbath food with gusto increases the strength of desire above (*Zohar Ḥadash* 48d *Sitrei Torah*). Proper emotional comportment is so important that even artificial means may be used to induce the desired reaction: "[It is good to drink] wine below in order to display joy to that other supernal wine [*Gevurah*]" (*Zohar* 1:248a). The import of this injunction is that one's emotional mood augments the Divinity.[119]

The test case to evaluate the way in which this mood is effected and the extent to which this is a norm would be best seen in instances of failure, in which the initiates are unable to evoke internally or to sustain the required emotional modality: To what extent is failure allowed? How are the norms enforced? What transpires at the margins? The *Idra de-vei Mashkena*, in which a number of the kabbalists die, not having loved one another sufficiently, might be the best scene to shed light on these questions.[120] Death in this episode is catastrophic rather than ecstatic, as the moment of *tikkun* of self, cosmos, and Divine is elsewhere—because the normative emotion was absent. Although it is unstated whether Rabbi Shimon evaluates their lessthan-exemplary mood by observing their actions or their faces, it is their ideal features that reflect their good mood. It seems reasonable to conclude that it was their faces, as transparent templates of their feelings, that enable his assessment of their lack of love.

Dynamics of gender and sexuality also play a role in the affective dimension at zoharic meals. There are instances in which the joy that is being expressed or experienced is related to the *Shekhinah* in such a way that it marks the sexual-spiritual completion of the individual mystic. For example, the *Zohar* comments upon the verse "You shall rejoice before the Lord your God" (Deuteronomy 12:18), saying, "This [the rejoicing] is the cup of blessing. When a person says the blessing [after a meal] with a cup of blessing he must rejoice and display his joy with no sadness at all. When a person lifts up the cup of blessing the Holy One, blessed be He, is upon him[121] and he must enwrap his head with joy" (*Zohar* 2:168b). The coronation motif here, in which the kabbalist covers his head with joy, signals the erotic moment between the kabbalist and his *kiddush* cup, the cup of blessing.[122] Further, the *Zohar* adduces the scriptural verse "[It is a land] . . . on which the Lord your God always keeps His eye" (Deuteronomy 11:12) to indicate that as God keeps his eye upon the Land of Israel—the *Shekhinah*—so should you keep your eye on your cup of blessing, also identified with the *Shekhinah* (*Zohar Ḥadash* 87c *Midrash Ruth*).[123] As an emulation of the divine action, one is supposed to keep one's eyes upon the cup. As Wolfson has argued, the eye acts as a displacement of the phallus, so that the act of gazing upon the *kiddush* cup is in itself an erotic act—as the masculine aspect of the Divinity unites with the *Shekhinah* at this moment, so should the individual kabbalist.[124] In the act of *imitatio dei*—gazing at the cup—the adept both effects the divine union and attains union himself with the *Shekhinah*.

Moreover, the *Zohar* states explicitly that one must display this joy, reinforcing the sense that it is an outward demonstration and not merely an inward emotional response that is required. In one joyous outburst, Rabbi Yose's proclaims his delight upon greeting Rabbi Ḥiyya: "I am so glad to see the face of the *Shekhinah*!" (*Zohar* 2:94b).[125] In a different passage we read that the mystical companions "are called the face of the *Shekhinah* because the *Shekhinah* is hidden within them. She is concealed and they are revealed" (*Zohar* 2:163b).[126] The kabbalists were not the first to ascribe an aspect of divinity to one's encounter with a rabbi; the *Talmud Yerushalmi* remarks that greeting one's teacher (*rav*) is like receiving the face of the *Shekhinah*.[127] What is distinctive here, though, is that the passage collapses the implied simile that seeing a fellow kabbalist is like seeing the face of the *Shekhinah*.[128] If the talmudic passage that lies at the root of these teachings was intended as a simile, here the myth is intended as written: meeting up with one's fellow kabbalist has both theophanic and latently homoerotic valences. The eros of seeing the *Shekhinah* is certainly underlying such an expression.

Once again, the sensualities of eating and eros merge. The "joy" of the verse is identified by the author of the *Zohar* with the *kiddush* cup, but it is also the crown upon his head and is thus related to the *Shekhinah* itself. As Wolfson has shown, coronation is generally an erotic motif in which there is a restoration of the feminine gender within the masculine body.[129] This dynamic is repeated with the Sabbath guest. Discussing the crowning that takes place upon the holiday and Sabbath feasts, the *Zohar* says, "A person who invites someone [as a guest] has to show him joy and an illuminated face in order to crown the path of this guest" (*Zohar* 3:94a). We have already seen the link of Sabbath joy and crowning as an erotic nexus that the individual has with the *Shekhinah* on his own. In this instance, the host pre-

pares the coronation of his guest, strongly suggesting an implicit homosocial dynamic.[130]

While it is generally assumed that the behaviors prescribed in the *Zohar*
apply to the male kabbalistic initiates, it is possible that women were
involved in some small measure as well. Consider the following passage
from *Zohar Ḥadash:*

> [When the Sabbath is sanctified on Friday evening] two supernal spirits
> are aroused, one from the side of light and one from the side of darkness:
> Michael and Gabriel. They are engraved upon the 60 myriads of troops
> that rule over the evening. For their pleasure, with one on the right and
> one on the left, they set a table for each and every one [of the troops]. When
> the troops above see the tables below within the renowned palace, they all
> have their places set out on this evening. Each one is great and honored in
> his own place above all the other powers and the troops are appointed
> under his command. From these forces, two supernal ones emerge from
> among them and take one table from the right side and one from the left
> side. Every table that is not brought close between these two [tables] is
> not a Shabbat table and is not a table before the Holy King. When a woman
> and her husband rejoice [on the Sabbath], that table is crowned. When
> that table is brought closer with the six loaves from one angel on one side
> and six loaves from the other angel on the other side, that is a table that is
> crowned with its crowns. These two that take the tables must guard the
> table so that the six loaves from one side do not become mixed with the
> six from the other side. When this table is brought before the one who is
> master and superior to them, one [loaf] is taken from one side and one
> [loaf] is taken from the other side and one recites a blessing over them.
> Each one says to his troops: "This is the table before the Lord." (*Zohar
> Ḥadash* 48d)

The idealized Sabbath table abounds with harmonious balances: two
supernal angels, two supernal tables, six loaves on one side and six on the
other, one loaf taken from each side. Crowns and blessing denote the successful pairing and harmonious balance of the two; it is, indeed, somewhat
striking that neither side is privileged, but rather the integrity of each one
is maintained. In the midst of this vision, the text states, "When a woman
and her husband rejoice [on the Sabbath], that table is crowned." Here too
the balance is maintained, but in the human realm, the focus is on emotion.
If the affective performance is successfully enacted, the *Shekhinah* announces
that this table belongs to her; if not, the table and family are left to the
devices of the evil inclination and the food itself is rendered impure. In this

instance, notably, one's wife is called upon to perform as well. It could be argued that we cannot deduce historical practice from the *Zohar*, no more than mystical reveries can be assumed—these women, constructed in the imagination of the kabbalists, complete an idealized picture. Although the actual history remains speculative, if it is a correct assumption that charismatic hermeneutics lead to practice, then there seems little reason to exclude women from the practice.[131]

There are other instances in which the adopted affect is not prescribed, but its description as an effective theurgic catalyst would inevitably prompt the kabbalists to adopt this pose. In a homily extolling the holiness of the Land of Israel and its impenetrability with regard to the *Sitra Aḥra*, the text says,

> This is why, even though Israel is now outside of the Holy Land, nonetheless it is from the power and merit of the land that there is food and sustenance for the whole world. Therefore it is written, "[When you have eaten your fill,] you shall bless the Lord your God for the good land which He has given you" (Deuteronomy 8:10). "For the good land"—in actuality! For it is due to it [the land] that there is food and sustenance in the world. One who has delight at his table and enjoys his food should remember and worry about the holiness of the Holy Land and about the King's tabernacle that was destroyed. As a consequence of that sadness that he experiences at his table at which there had been joy and feasting, the Holy One, blessed be He, will consider it as if he had built His house and built all of the destroyed structures, for the Temple will increase his portion. (*Zohar* 2:157b)

This passage is noteworthy because of the demonstrated affect of sadness, commingled with the joy that one has experienced in the sadness. It resonates with the motif of bribes or gifts offered to the *Sitra Aḥra*, although that motive is not mentioned here. The table that has served as a site of joyous celebration and dining is now to be mourned: The ceremonious decoration of the table as bride is tempered with the gloom of her lost status. Moods are adopted and cast off, each acting as the appropriate response to a particular context.

Drama is truly the nature of the event transpiring here. The kabbalists are performers manipulating not only the material world and the sefirotic world but their mood as well. One attains the proper atmosphere through the embrace of a particular emotional expression that makes its impression not only upon God and men but upon demonic spirits and the self as well.

Clearly, the desired mystical mood could not be attained if there were any distance between the normative affect and the natural affect of the kabbalist.[132] I submit that once a particular reading of a text has been offered, or once a particular norm has been prescribed, the kabbalists *naturally* adopt the same pneumatic hermeneutic—the space between the normative affect and the natural affect is collapsed. Unlike the ancients, for whom the performance itself serves as a marker of mood, for the kabbalists, the need to resolve the inner-outer relationship is more deeply felt.[133] At the same time, however, the previously cited passage renders it clear that there is a performative aspect to this technique, as one is instructed to adopt a variety of moods depending on the context.

In a study of the performative aspects of ritual, Stanley Tambiah writes about the inevitable distancing between internal feeling and ritualized feeling that accompanies ritualized expression.[134] For the kabbalists, however, affective performance is intended as a masking that reveals truest feeling. Ronald Grimes, in writing of masks, says that there is a monistic moment of embodiment in which interior and exterior, affect and feeling are so harmonized as to be virtually indistinguishable.

> One's exterior mask, or persona, . . . begins to resound with presence . . . spirit can become fully resonant in exteriority—in the skin, demeanor, and style of action. . . . In this moment, masking—or, for that matter, any form of facial stylization—is denied and a claim is made for naturalness and spontaneity. A totally embodied mask would, of course, lose its dialectical relation to a hitherto trapped internality or transcendent other. . . . In the embodied moment of masking, the distinction between wearer and thing worn is no longer made.[135]

Reflecting Grimes's insights onto the kabbalistic material, I suggest that the pneumatic reading of a text both creates the mask and reveals it to be transparent, such that the space between normative affect and spontaneous affect is collapsed.

To conclude this discussion of affective modeling, note that the outcome of this emphasis on the performative or dramaturgical aspect in the fraternity's lived theater is that *imitatio hominis* becomes as important as *imitatio dei*. That is, assuming the theatrical quality of the affective performance, the kabbalists model for each other and learn from each other about the ways to express the appropriate emotions in any given context. It can only be presumed that, in the course of admonitions given by Rabbi Shimon with regard to the need for love among the group, it is the illumined face that both receives blessing and, more importantly, is a sign of blessing. The logical outcome is that the adepts adopted certain modes of facial expression and bodily gestures to communicate and effect a mood of repose, equanimity, and joy. This affective performance thus takes on a pedagogic quality that is close to the heart of this kabbalistic homiletical work.[136]

The question that the kabbalists' affective performance raises in the mind of a modern reader is the question of sincerity. The Western mind is so accustomed to outward affect being an expression of inner feeling that it is challenging to imagine a mask as the key to revealing inner truths. The central hub of kabbalistic activity, however, is an attempt to pierce the surface to see the truth within and then to discover the underlying integrity, even identity, of the two. Yet it is precisely this program that allows one kabbalist to greet his fellow with the exclamation "How glad I am to see the face of the *Shekhinah*!"

5

"Blessing Does Not Rest on an Empty Place": Talismanic Theurgy

IN THE KABBALAH, theurgy refers to the working, or exerting influence, upon the Divinity and is one of the primary functions of the commandments. Moshe Idel offers the following definition, saying that theurgy refers to "operations intended to influence the Divinity, mostly in its own inner state or dynamics, but sometimes also in its relationship to man. In contrast to the magician, the ancient and medieval Jewish theurgist focused his activity on accepted religious values."[1] In the following discussion about eating practices, I will consider how theurgy serves as a method through which an individual worshiper engages the Divinity to procure sustenance. Through the fulfillment of the various rites with the proper kabbalistic intent, the individual is able to restore the primordial unity of the sefirotic order; consummate the romantic union of *Tif'eret* and *Malkhut;* reconstitute the male androgyne; establish the ultimate oneness of the *sefirot,* cosmos, and lower realms; and draw blessing down upon himself and the lower world. There is a subgroup of theurgic practice that I refer to as "talismanic theurgy." By talismanic theurgy I refer to the use of a material object as a locus into which divine energies will be drawn down from the *sefirot.*[2] Divine overflow is invoked from above and, through ritual behaviors and/or spiritual intentions, is induced to flow down upon the individual's table, the bread sitting on it, or even into his belly. Further, ritual has often been treated as an act that can symbolize and communicate or effect and instrumentalize.[3] Characteristic of the kabbalistic phenomena that I will be examining is a merging of these two categories, stemming from the fusion of hermeneutics and experience.

TALISMANIC THEURGY AND FOOD

As we saw in the example of Moses' frustration with the Israelites' dissatisfaction with their food provisions, food production is one marker of the righteous individual who is able to invoke food for those in need through his mystical practice. The priestly figure, King Melkhiẓedeq, who presents an offering of food to Abraham, is a case in point. In the *Zohar*'s reworking of the scriptural story, Melkhiẓedeq is deemed analogous to both the *Shekhinah* and *Tif'eret* and, as such, is able to bring out bread and wine because these are "within" him (*Zohar* 1:87a). Moreover, Melkhiẓedeq "serves the world [*Shekhinah*] in order to receive the world." He is able to bless Abraham because, as a priest, he comes from the side of *Ḥesed* with which the priests are identified. In the subsequent homily, this ability to elicit bread and wine is compared, by virtue of a linguistic similarity, to the earth's ability to bring forth trees.[4] It is the verb denoting fruitfulness—"bringing out"—that links these quite different activities. The ability to be fruitful and to bring food for the world establishes Melkhiẓedeq as a paradigm for the righteous on whose behalf blessing is brought to the entire world. Acting on both cosmic and human realms, he is able to draw the nourishing flow for both the supernal and mundane worlds. In this latter homily, clearly uncomfortable with the theological implications of the first teaching, the *Zohar* represents God as the source of power, limiting the theurgic potential of the kabbalists and saying that the blessing is brought *for* the righteous rather than *by* them[5] (*Zohar* 1:87b).

The way in which theurgy is most commonly employed to trigger the flow of food is through prayer and the performance of commandments. For example, normative halakhah prescribes that one recite Psalm 145 ("*Ashrei*") thrice daily during the statutory prayers, as per the prescribed rite: twice to draw down food for the world and the third time "to give strength to that place that opens Its hands [the *Shekhinah*]"[6] (*Zohar* 3:226a). In the subsequent parable we are told that, normally, the king eats first and then the servants. Moving from the parable back to its analogue, the text says that it is inappropriate to ask for nurturance for oneself before giving nurturance first to one's master. In the movement between parable and "real" analogue, no distinction is drawn between giving "strength" (*toqfa*) and giving food, so it is apparent that that which one must give to God before eating oneself is in effect God's food.[7] The *Tikkunei ha-Zohar* expands upon this notion, equating prayers with the sacrificial offerings that are offered as food for God and, alternately, identifying the positive commandments as foods for God, whereas negative commandments (when violated) nurture the *Sitra Aḥra*.[8] Furthermore, it is through the recital of verses about food, specifically Psalm 145:16, that gives food to God and thus legitimates asking for food for oneself. Indeed, it is obligatory to ask for food daily.[9]

The requirement to ask for food is illustrated in a delightful biographical tidbit rendered of the Rabbi Yeisa Saba, one of the *Zohar*'s mysterious hierophants. Yeisa Saba would not proceed with his meal, even if he had food present in the house, unless he first prayed for food.[10] The explanation of this behavior can be deduced by virtue of his being portrayed as the paradigmatic expression of Proverbs 28:20: "A man of faith will abound with blessings." The blessings intended by the verse, as understood by the *Zohar*, flow bilaterally, both upward toward the Divinity and downward upon him and his table. Although it is customary not to eat until one has first prayed,[11] the text emphasizes that Yeisa Saba uttered an additional petition following his regular prayers in order to receive food: "We cannot prepare until we have been given from the house of the King."[12] Evidently, even once there is food upon the table, there is still a need for a procession of the divine flow into the food.[13]

The desire to have God's blessing *in* one's food is intimated by the mysterious sage and is confirmed in a broad theme.[14] For the *Zohar*, the fundamental condition for the drawing-down theurgy connected to the table is that the table never be left empty.[15] Biblical and rabbinic precepts prefigure the kabbalistic divinizing of the table and the ever-present food as they figure in the *Zohar*. The biblical commandment to ensure that there will always be showbread in the Temple, replaced weekly on the Sabbath, acts as one of the more common models for idealized food in the *Zohar*. The perception of it as an idealized food begins with the biblical injunction "on the table you shall set the bread of display, to be before Me always" (Exodus 25:30). This requirement of permanent presence is developed by the rabbis, who explain the procedure by which the showbread would be replaced in such a manner that the Temple's bread table, a special bread rack, would never lack for bread.[16] As will be seen, this permanent foodstuff accords neatly with the theological stance of the *Zohar* in which divine blessing continually rains down unless somehow interrupted.

A rabbinic teaching avers that "blessing does not rest in an empty place," and this statement comes to be widely cited by the *Zohar* and contemporaneous kabbalah.[17] The talmudic context for this statement is a distinction drawn between the ways of human beings and those of God: "A mortal can put something into an empty vessel but not into a full one. But for the Holy One, blessed be He, this is not so; He puts more into a full vessel but not into an empty one; for it says, 'If you listen you will hear,' implying that if you listen once you will go on hearing, and if not, you will not hear" (*b. Berakhot* 40a). God grants wisdom to the wise but not to the foolish, in which the wise are "full" and the foolish "empty." While a person can fill an empty vessel but not a full one, God only gives to full vessels; that is, he bestows wisdom upon the wise of heart. Returning to the zoharic context, we witness the linking of wisdom, a prerequisite to receive yet more, with food and blessing; this series of links will be central to our discussion. Joined to this comment is Rabbi Eleazar's teaching that "one who does not leave crumbs of bread upon his table will not see a sign of blessing," apparently suggesting that one must leave charitable remains for the poor at the end of one's meal.[18] This is an important theme in the discussion of food in the medieval kabbalah: in one's satiety one must always remember the poor. One fulfills the commandment of *imitatio dei* by maintaining the divine flow; as God's blessing descends upon one's table, one sustains that blessing by causing blessing to flow down to those less fortunate. The circuit of blessing from presence to absence is fulfilled beyond oneself—taking care of the poor once one's own needs are satisfied—and in one's house—providing food for the table before reciting the grace after the meal.

The *Zohar* interprets these various biblical and rabbinic statements to develop a theurgy that is talismanic inasmuch as the food item has acquired a ritual focus and acts as a magnet for God's blessing.[19] Acting like a lightning rod, it is through the maintenance of an avenue along which a continued flow of divine blessing can travel, that is, through leaving some crumbs on the table following one's meal, that such blessing will descend.[20] Moreover, the table being spoken of corresponds to three distinct "tables": the table in the Temple bearing the showbread, a person's individual table, and the table in the supernal realm, the *sefirah* of *Malkhut*. A series of passages in the *Zohar* commenting on the showbread and its table develops this complex set of associations. Consider the following:

"You shall make a table of acacia wood . . ." (Exodus 25:23). This table is intended to be established in the tabernacle. Blessing from above rests upon it and food proceeds from it to the entire world. This table must not be empty for even a moment but rather there should [always] be food upon it because blessing does not rest upon an empty place. Consequently, there must always be bread upon it so that there will always be supernal blessing found in it. It is from that table that blessings and food proceed to all other tables of the world that are blessed because of it. Each person's table must be [full] like this when he blesses the Holy One, blessed be He, so that blessing from above should rest upon it and so that it should not appear empty, for supernal blessings do not rest upon an empty place, as it is written, "Tell me, what have you in the house?" (II Kings 4:2), and the companions have established this. (*Zohar* 2:153b)[21]

The statement that the table should not be left empty intends, in the most literal sense, that there should be bread left on the table during the recitation of the final grace over the meal.[22] It should be observed that the blessing that proceeds from the divinity in response to the recitation of grace and words of Torah appears to rest within the bread itself and that the blessing proceeds from the table itself: divine blessing resides within these physical entities. It is the bread as lightning rod that calls for our attention in this citation. The recurrent emphasis on the need for the table to have bread resting on it so that divine blessing will rest on it makes it obvious that the table itself is the conveyor and the bread the final bearer of God's blessing.

We also note that the table must not "appear empty." The blessing will proceed to the table and its bread, provided that the right image of it is maintained, in the imagination and available to the physical sense of vision as well. The theurgic process, then, entails two requirements: the physical act of retaining bread upon the table and retaining a particular vision of the table in the imaginative faculty. Both, I surmise, are indispensable to effect the transfer of blessing from the upper realm to the lower.[23] Thus it is insufficient to have imaginal bread alone upon the table; its physical presence is required as well. Success demands transparency between the physical reality and the idealized impress in the mind of the kabbalist.

The passage continues, trying to determine the symbolic hierarchy of the bread and table. On the one hand, the table serves to present the bread, thus appearing to be subservient; further, the table rests below the bread, offering a visible paradigm of the spiritual hierarchy. The responding voice counters, however, that "it is not so. Rather the table is the essence in this ordering, receiving supernal blessings and food for the world. Food for the world emerges from the mystery of this table as it was given to it from above. That bread is the fruit and food that emerges from the table, demonstrating that it is from this table that fruit and food emerge for the world" (*Zohar* 2:154b). Responding to a debate that concerned the author either internally or with his cohorts, the author finds a solution to the contradiction that his visual perception of the table-bread relationship posed to his notion that the table was a symbol of the *Shekhinah* and the bread thereon was fully material, to be consumed by men. The author's creativity often lies in the ability to perceive the world visually as a template for the sefirotic structure; in this instance, the ensuing contradictions demand resolution. While this passage explicitly treats the table in the Temple with the showbread, it has the added resonance of one's table at home.[24]

Divine blessing is transmitted through the mechanics of talismanic theurgy. That blessing does not rest on an empty place is the trope used to refer to this particular talismanic theurgy:

Rabbi Yehudah began, "'I am my beloved's and his desire is for me' (Song 7:11). This has been established but the arousal from above is contained within the arousal below for there is no arousal from above until there is arousal below. Thus, blessings from above are only found in a place where there is something of substance, a place that is not empty. From where [do we know this]? From the wife of Obadiahu who was asked by Elisha, 'Tell me, what have you in the house?' (2 Kings 4:2), for supernal blessings do not rest upon an empty table nor in an empty place. What is written? She replied, 'Your maidservant has nothing at all in the house, except a jug of oil.' How much is a "jug"? She said to him, 'There is only enough oil here to anoint a little finger.' He said to her, 'You have comforted me, for I did not know how the blessings from above would rest upon an empty place but now that you have this oil, it will be the place where the blessings will be found.' From where do we know this? It is written, 'It is like fine oil . . .' and what is written at the end. 'There the Lord ordained blessing, everlasting life' (Psalm 133:2–3). In that place blessings will rest." (*Zohar* 1:88a)

The physical bread is not only required as a symbolic marker that one has demonstrated one's commitment to the divine commandment; ontologically, the bread serves as the receptor point for the divine flow. According to this homily, for movement to occur from the supernal realm to the material realm, there must be some material body there; the nonmaterial words of Torah or grace after the meal will not suffice. Here the text crosses over into the realm of the magical, as the requirement in the biblical story entails no normative practices, merely the presence of a jug of oil.[25] The question of *kavvanah* rises again because, although one might assume that the onus for such intention would rest upon the prophet, it is the woman's merit that draws the divine efflux downward.[26]

Bahya ben Asher attempts to explain the mechanics of talismanic theurgy, basing his explanation on a particular philosophical approach to miracles. He asserts that it is crucial to have bread on the table so that the blessing should apply to it for, if there were no bread, how could the blessing take hold?[27] He proceeds, saying that blessing spreads to all the food of the world from the *lehem ha-panim* because blessing is transmitted *yesh mi-yesh* (creation from something material) and not *yesh me-ayin* (*creatio ex nihilo*). Only during creation did God create *yesh me-ayin* and, subsequently, everything is merely generated from that which is already existent. Bahya concludes that one should therefore leave a bit of bread "so that the blessing should rest upon it and the energy of expansiveness should spread out within a trifle."[28] The bread serves as both the receiving point and transmitter for supernal blessing.

The verse from the second book of Kings, so often cited by the Castilian kabbalists ("Tell me, what have you in the house?" [2 Kings 4:2]) in the context of eating, is also found in the context of a discussion of the resurrection of the dead. Moses de Leon explains that when the body decays one bone remains, and God will rebuild the person from that bone. There is a need for material continuity for there to be a proper resurrection, and it is as if the secret of that person's identity is encoded within that bone. De Leon draws the connection to the requirement that one not utter a blessing at an empty table; the blessing of food that rests in the food remaining on the table is like resurrection. As a proof text, he cites Jeremiah 23:29: "Behold my word is like fire—declares the Lord—and like a hammer that shatters rock!"[29] In other words, there need only be a morsel of bread or a fleck of bone for God's blessing to sprout nourishment and new life.

Bahya ben Asher, one of the late-thirteenth-century kabbalists who was among the first to cite passages from the *Zohar* and may well have been one of its contributors, writes a passage in his essay *Shulhan Shel Arba* that offers an explanation for the mechanics of talismanic theurgy:

> One must be careful when one is about to bless [after a meal] that there is bread left on the table, as they said in [the tractate] *Sanhedrin:* "Whoever does not leave bread on his table [when he is about to bless following a meal] Scripture says the following about him, 'There was nothing left after he had eaten, His goodness will not take hold'" (Job 20:21) (*b. Sanhedrin* 92a).[30] The reason for the practice is so that the blessing will rest upon that which remains; if nothing remains, the blessing has nothing to rest upon.

For blessing does not apply to a vacuum but rather to an existing entity. The witness for this is the table in the Temple that was never without bread. That bread fed the Kohanim who served the Temple and the small amount sufficed for the great numbers. And the rabbis, of blessed memory, said similarly, "Any Kohen who would receive [his portion of showbread] doubled over (i.e., less than the requisite amount) would be sated" (*b. Yoma* 39a). From that bread that was on the table the blessing would proceed and be dispersed in all the food of the world from the showbread, through the means of something from something and not something from nothing. . . . For only the Holy One, blessed be He, the Creator, created His world as *creatio ex nihilo* and even He, in His glory only did so in the six days of creation, and from then on, everything has been creation from a pre-existent entity. . . . When a person is about to say the grace after meals he should leave some bread on the table—even if only a little bit—so that blessing should rest upon it and the power of increase will disperse within that small amount, in the manner of the hidden miracles that are done for us every day, and we do not know or recognize them.[31]

God too is said to be limited to creating, nowadays, from that which exists, not creating anything anew since the first creation of the world. This gives the theurgy of the practice something of a scientific patina—operating within the rules of the universe, not relying primarily on God's grace.

Another route for the divine blessing is also available as the *Zohar* reveals the nature of the blessing or food that is descending. The twelve loaves of the showbread that are on the table of the Temple are understood to represent the twelve channels through which the divine flow from the *Shekhinah* emanates.[32] These twelve loaves of showbread (*lehem ha-panim*) refer to the "internal mysteries" (*razin di-penim*), revealing the innermost nature of the Divinity.[33] Moreover, the bread itself is the mystery: "This bread is the innermost one of all in the supernal mystery, as is fitting. The showbread, the food that comes from these countenances, the food and the sustenance that comes forth from them to the world, comes and settles upon this table because this table receives food and sustenance from those upper countenances, and it then produces food and sustenance from those innermost countenances. And the food that it produces is bread, as we have said" (*Zohar* 2:155a).[34] To engage in talismanic theurgy, then, means to invoke like with like, an act of sympathetic imitation.[35] Through placing bread upon the table and infusing the table with (mystical) words of Torah, one induces "sustenance" and "food" to descend from the upper countenances which then turn into food for the entire world. The blessing moves from the showbread and its table to bread on tables everywhere. Once the theurgic process has been engineered, the result is that the table both receives and produces food. The circuit of constant flow is thus maintained.

Inevitably, in a discussion of the topic of the direction of blessing, one touches upon the *Zohar*'s conception of gender. The repeated refrain that "there is no arousal above until there is arousal from below" frequently refers to the initiation of the mating rite of the *sefirot* of *Shekhinah* and *Tif'eret*.[36] The feminine *Shekhinah* must direct her attention upward to her mate before he will direct his attention downward. On a theological level, this refers to the need for Israel to be observant of the commandments, thus "adorning" the bride and drawing the attention of the Divinity in its masculine aspect to look down upon and unite with the *Shekhinah*. This same dynamic is invoked in passages relating to the showbread and the food on an individual's table. The table, representing the *Shekhinah*, is thus the locus for the divine blessing that descends in the form of food. The showbread must rest on the table in the Temple as should bread on private tables so that the arousal from below occurs before blessing will descend from above. In the example of food on the table, the food functions as both the spiritual and erotic effort exerted from the lower realm, ensuring that the blessing from the upper reaches of the sefirotic structure will find an appropriate site of reception.

Joseph of Hamadan explains the dynamic in stark terms, putting the gendered aspects into high relief. Considering Pharaoh's dreams about the stalks of grain, he reports that the parched stalks represent degrees of impurity. The degrees of impurity and the years of famine are linked because satiety cannot rest in either one; this is because they are always in the position of recipient, never giving. They are consumed by hunger.[37] An important set of inferences can be drawn from these associations. First, redemption from impurity is achieved through transformation from a recipient to a donor, which in gendered terms, means the possibility of moving from feminine status to masculine status. The feminine, negatively charged as we saw earlier in a variety of instances, is in the position of recipient from her husband but performs the role of patron when she is a mother. In fact, the possibility of gender transformations allows for the frequent casting and recasting of males as feminine and females as masculine; these makeovers also occur in the instance of a male student hearing a lesson and then proceeding to teach others. Fulfillment transpires when one continues the flow of blessing. What is the human correlate for the entity that only receives? Joseph explains by offering another correlation for the seven parched stalks of wheat, recounting that "this is the secret of 'These are the kings who reigned in the land of Edom,'" referring to one of the more recondite mysteries in zoharic kabbalah. Genesis 36:31–39 enumerates a series of eight kings who ruled over Edom. The first seven of these die, apparently without marrying or fathering children. There is perhaps no figure more abhorrent to the kabbalists than the bachelor, the moral and spiritual equivalent of a nihilist, one who receives blessing and does nothing to promote its propagation. Such a person, it is assumed, spills his seed rather than "sowing" it and, as nature is said to abhor a vacuum, so do the kabbalists in their own fashion. This is not merely a sexual crime with moral overtones; rather, the sexual component is only one, if primary, part of the kabbalah's predilection for generativity writ large: in terms of biology, blessing, light, and morality. It is greed that is being critiqued, the greed that resists further spawning of blessing that has been passed down from supernal to terrestrial levels.[38] We will see the development of this rhetorical style when we discuss generosity and greed on a social scale in the following section.

TALISMANIC THEURGY AND THE BODY

It is not only one's table and its appurtenances that are determinative of success for the theurgic flow, but one's body must also contribute to an unimpeded downward stream:

> One's table must be accompanied by a clean body since one should not come to eat unless he himself is clean. Therefore one should eliminate his waste before eating because the Holy One, blessed be He, desires a pure table with the food prepared on it so that it should not be a table of filth and vomit which would be from the mystery of the *Sitra Aḥra*. In this way, the *Sitra Aḥra* will not receive any of the food that is on the table. After a person eats and delights he must give a small portion to that side. What is that [portion]? The final waters: the filth from one's hands must be given to that side, that is the portion that it needs. (*Zohar* 2:154b)

The maintenance of the divine flow is attained through proper body upkeep. The whole environment must be one that is free of waste, expressive of fullness, and enlightened by the illumination of words of Torah. Normally, elimination is required antecedent to the recital of any liturgical passages so that one would not utter God's name when in an inappropriate physical condition.[39] This extra-halakhic condition ensures a situation in which even one's body participates in the holiness of the table; eating itself has become a supra-halakhic scenario—a liturgical act—invoking holiness into the world and one's daily activities.

Ritual hand washing must be performed to remove the impurity that rests upon the hands; if not, the blessing that one recites over the bread will be ineffectual as "blessing only rests on a pure place" (*Zohar* 3:272b).[40] The *Zohar* not only attaches ontological significance to the various rituals regarding purity but also delineates the path that blessing follows through the human body to the food itself. Each part of the body, individually and as a group, must bear this purity. The water used in the hand washing must extend until the wrist so that all fourteen joints of the hand are included in the blessing. The added value of the number fourteen is that it is the numerical equivalent of the letters in the word "*yad*" (hand), according to the practice of *gematriyah*, the calculation of numerical values to establish correspondences with other words or phrases. The *Ra'aya Mehemna* understands that it is the hand of God or the hand of the side of *Ḥesed* that is directly involved in transmitting this blessing (*Zohar* 3:272b).[41] Once the hands are washed the *Shekhinah* can rest in the fingers' joints (*Zohar* 3:273a).[42] The four fingers of the hand are raised because they are cast in the image of the Divinity, representing the four letters of the tetragrammaton, with their twelve joints representing the faces on the divine chariot. The two joints of the thumb represent the two letters of the hidden name.[43]

The left hand washes the right so that the left is serving the right, preserving the correct order above and below; one then raises one's hands, joining them together, effecting the union of the right and left sides.[44] The raising of the hands is enjoined rabbinically, but the joining is the *Zohar*'s innovation.[45] This raising is the same as is found during prayer, and the *Zohar* warns against adopting this gesture at inappropriate times.[46] It is a gesture of the lower arousing the upper as the lower fingers arouse the upper ones. Even the blessing for the washing fulfills this supernal duty (*Zohar Ḥadash* 86d *Midrash Ruth*). The washing of the hands after the meal does not require a blessing, in contrast to the hand washing that precedes the meal, thereby distinguishing between the waters that serve God and those that serve the *Sitra Aḥra*.[47] Further, the filth that is removed from the hands after the meal, being the residue of food, appears to be of greater contaminating capacity than whatever impurity may have been removed before the meal. I have digressed regarding the hand washing because, ultimately, the aim in the washing is to attain the status of angels who eat in holiness:

Eating requires cleanliness like that of the ministering angels above. This is what Rav Hamnuna Saba said, "What is the meaning of the verse 'Each man ate an angel's meal?' (Psalm 78:25). It refers to the bread that the ministering angels eat. What is the practical consequence? As the ministering angels eat in holiness, purity, and cleanliness, so must Israel eat in holiness and purity. . . . And they have said that anyone who eats in holiness, purity, and cleanliness is compared to the ministering angels who are holy." (*Zohar Ḥadash* 86d *Midrash Ruth*)[48]

Thus one's entire environment, hands, bowels, table, and so on must be prepared for the now-holy rite of eating.

THE IMAGE OF THE SET TABLE

In one passage, the *Zohar* provides a more complex model to which one should conform in order to summon the divine efflux—bread on the table and cup of wine in the right hand:

Come and see. One who is reciting the grace over bread should not bless in front of an empty table and there must be bread upon the table and a cup of wine in his right hand. Why? In order to connect the left to the right. Also so that the bread, from which one is blessed, should be connected to them, so that all of it should be connected together as one to bless the Holy Name as is proper. For bread is connected to wine and wine to the right side and then blessing rests upon the world and the table is perfected as is proper. Rabbi Isaac said, "If we had the opportunity to have this guest to hear these words alone, it would have been sufficient for us." (*Zohar* 1:240a)[49]

In this configuration, the bread, corresponding to *Yesod*, is deemed to be contained within the wine, representing the *sefirah Gevurah*, which in turn is contained in the right hand, symbolizing the *sefirah* of *Ḥesed*. This series of containments results in the lower contained in the upper and the left contained in the right so that all of the *sefirot* are united as one entity, resulting in an overflow onto the table, blessing the bread. Through the adoption of this physical gesture and domestic layout, the mystic and his table become a veritable replica of the *sefirot*, affirming, demonstrating, and effecting the unity of the Divinity.[50] Culinary gesturing also plays a role in the *Zohar*'s injunction that one eat from all of the different dishes that were prepared for the Sabbath to show that the "tabernacle of peace" (*Shekhinah*) is comprised of everything (*Zohar* 1:48b).[51] In these various examples a presumed audience enables these performances to serve double duty: as theurgy above and as demonstrations below.[52]

Another mode of preparing the table for blessing is through the actual physical setting of the table and the preparation of the meal. For instance, setting the table with a variety of delicacies is an invitation for divine blessing (*Zohar Ḥadash* 48d *Sitrei Torah*).[53] Adapting the popular dictum that two angels follow a person home from the synagogue on the Sabbath eve to examine his Sabbath preparations, the *Zohar* says that when a person's table is elevated, these two angels offer the talmudic blessing if the person's table is in fact meritorious (*Zohar* 2:154a)[54] The table, translated by the Talmud into a domestic altar, is here transformed into an offering, for it is not only the food upon the table that the angels elevate but truly the whole visual image. Rabbi Abba urges that the table be covered so that it should be presented modestly to the king's messengers. The author thus views the table as a kind of feminine representative of the kabbalist, engaging in the same erotic hiding-and-revealing dynamic that is so central to the *Zohar*'s erotic thrust.[55]

The themes of food and the erotic are further blended by the zoharic prescription that one must set one's table on Friday night, mirroring the activity of the *Shekhinah* who sets the table for her mate, in preparation for the divine intercourse (*Zohar* 2:63b). As the intercourse is prepared above through a meal, the same is done below in preparation for the human intercourse. Food plays an aphrodisiacal role; presumably it is not only the intimacy of the social contact but also the sensual impact of the presentation of the food that precipitates the union following the meal. In this instance, eating plays an important preparatory role for the maintenance of the divine flow that is achieved through procreation.[56] Further, the initiate is instructed to set the table "so that supernal blessings will rest upon it and blessing does not rest upon an empty table." The two themes intertwine: the union of masculine and feminine produces the "fruit" that sustains the lower world and causes rejoicing, leading to the human conjugation that perpetuates the divine process. Gastronomically sustained by the divine coupling, the kabbalists have thus constructed an unusual model of nourishment.

Hunger is the corollary to this scheme and follows when there is a lack of proper heterosexual union. A passage from Joseph of Hamadan's *Sefer ha-Malkhut* demonstrates this point. Hamadan relates the biblical Joseph's interpretation of Pharaoh's dreams as follows:

[Joseph] said, "All dreams follow their interpretation.[57] Certainly the upper *sefirot* instruct about the 'sevens' in the world.[58] These seven good years and the satiety will be manifest in the world. This is the appropriate way to interpret this dream. The seven [parched] sheaves and the sickly cows signify the impure classes. They certainly manifest as hunger and they are called 'dogs.' As the dogs are never sated so these classes are never sated. This is the esoteric meaning of 'Like a dog who returns to his vomit,' they receive the divine efflux and they return and vomit it.[59] This is the aggadic teaching taught by our sages: "'If dogs are laughing Elijah will come to the city": this is when there is no female dog among them. When there are dogs crying the Angel of Death has come to the city.'[60] These [latter] dogs correspond to the dogs to which I referred that belong to the classes of impurity. Therefore they display hunger in the world, and therefore Joseph the Righteous interpreted the dream of hunger with regard to the ten degrees of impurity. They are insatiable because they are always receiving. How could they be sated? They emerged from Hunger and Hunger will consume them. This is the mystery of "These are the kings who reigned in the land of Edom before any king reigned over the Israelites" (Genesis 37:31; 1 Chronicles 1:43). (*Sefer ha-Malkhut* 77b)

The unsated dogs are representatives of the *Sitra Aḥra* and as such bear many of its traits. They are bound to impurity in their origin and in their future; they manifest hunger and suffering. They are identified with the notorious (for the kabbalists) seven kings of Edom, notorious for having died without having been married. For the kabbalists, this lack of marital and procreative fulfillment indicates that they have subverted the human responsibility of continuing to reproduce the image of God. What is unusual is the statement that "[t]hey are insatiable because they are always receiving." Being a recipient in a kabbalistic hierarchy indicates one's status as feminine: the masculine gives, the feminine receives. Females and feminine *sefirot* are redeemed from insatiability, presumably through their assimilation to the masculine status during marriage and intercourse; these emasculated dogs remain perpetually in that feminine state, never procreating, always standing in opposition to their nature. Satiability has thus been reconfigured as a distinctly masculine trait.

One benefit of setting one's table with the appropriate care is that one's table in this world enables him to eat at another table in the next world (*Zohar* 2:156b). The *Zohar* also says, "One who has attained the degree of faith should set his table and prepare the meal on the eve of the Sabbath so that his table should be blessed for all of the other six days [of the week.]"[61]

For it is at that time that blessing is invoked for the six days of the week and blessing is not found on an empty table. Therefore one should set his table on the eve of the Sabbath with bread and food. Rabbi Isaac said, 'Even on the day of the Sabbath [he should make these preparations.]'" (*Zohar* 2:88a).[62] Because this passage speaks of one's having had to attain a degree of spiritual perfection to be able to set the table properly so that blessing will descend upon it for the other six days of the week, there appears to be a requirement for *kavvanah;* only a person of such lofty stature would be sufficiently able to evoke the blessing from above and draw it onto the table.[63]

Sitting down to a meal, the kabbalists would make pronouncements about the sefirotic correspondences of the various meals:

> When Rav Hamnuna Saba was seated at a Sabbath meal he would rejoice in each one, and he would pronounce: "This is a holy meal of *Atika Kadisha*, the most recondite of all." And at another meal he would say: "This is a meal of the Holy One, blessed be He." And so on with every meal. And he would rejoice in each one of them. And when he had finished the meals he would say: "The meals of faith have been completed." Rabbi Shimon would say when he came to the table: "Prepare the meal of supernal faith, prepare the meal of the King."[64] And then he would sit and rejoice. And when he had finished the third meal a proclamation would be made about him: "You shall take delight in the Lord; and I will make you ride upon the high places of the earth; and I will feed you with the heritage of Jacob your father." (Isaiah 58:14) (*Zohar* 2:88a–b)[65]

In this way another kind of stylized behavior that is part of the general Sabbath performance indicates how a declaration was intended to arouse a certain intention.

BALAAM, THE DEMONIC CHEF

The dividing line between theurgy and magic can be drawn by counterposing the model of the non-Jewish prophet Balaam with that of the kabbalists; this demarcation also underscores the significance of mystical intention. Balaam is one of the *Zohar*'s favorite targets for vilification, rivaled in human ignominy only by Pharaoh and Esau. Unlike the other two, Balaam is strongly associated with magic and is said to use his table for demonic purposes.[66] The initial association of Balaam performing magical acts at his table arises from Balaam's place of origin, "Petor," which, in the form *Petorah,* means "to Petor" in Hebrew, and means "table" in Aramaic.[67] Because of the verse in Isaiah—"But as for you who forsake the Lord, who ignore My holy mountain, who set a table for Luck and fill a mixing bowl for Destiny" (Isaiah 65:11), with Luck and Destiny being names of actual Canaanite heathen gods—the *Zohar* assumes that a table can be used for demonic purposes:

> "[Balak] sent messengers to Balaam son of Beor in Petor. . ." (Numbers 22:4–5). There are twenty-eight words [in this verse] to receive the twenty-eight levels of magic performed by the sorcerers of Zippor. . . . Petorah was the name of a place, as it says," . . from Petor of Aramnaharaim, to curse you" (Deuteronomy 23:5). Why is it called by this name? Because it is written, "Who set a table for Luck [and filled a mixing bowl for Destiny]" (Isaiah 65:11). He [Balaam] would set a table there every day because this is the perfection (*tikkuna*) of the evil sides: one sets a table before them of food and drink, performs magic, and burns incense before the table. All impure spirits enter there and they [the spirits] respond to all their requests. All forms of the world's magic and sorcery are found in that table. That is why that place is called Petora: this is what they call a table in Aramnaharaim—"Petora." (*Zohar* 3:192a)

This passage offers a clear expression of the qualities latent in food and the table. They are instrumental in the magical exercises performed by Balaam for both oracular purposes and magical aims, the cursing of Israel. Balaam's magical activity is thus the demonic counterpart to the talismanic theurgy of the holy realm.[68] The primary aim of the mystical dining exercises of the *hevraya*, the mystical fellowship, is an experience of, or *devekut* with, those aspects of the Divinity that are found in the table; Balaam's aim is the acquisition of knowledge from the demonic side. In other instances, Balaam explicitly consults the table as if it were an oracle (*Zohar* 3:193a).[69]

In the homily adjacent to the previously cited one, the contrast with sanctified behavior is explicitly delineated:

> He [Rabbi Yose] began his discourse and said: "You shall make a table of acacia wood" (Exodus 25:23), and it is written, "And on the table you shall set the bread of display" (Exodus 25:30). The Holy One, blessed be He, desired that all of these holy vessels should be made before Him to draw the Holy Spirit from the upper realms to the lower realms. The wicked Balaam would arrange the same setting for the *Sitra Ahra*. He would arrange a table and bread, called "repulsive bread." This is as it is said that the *Sitra Ahra* is to holiness as a monkey is to a man. (*Zohar* 3:192a)

In this passage, the two opposing realms are starkly contrasted. It is unclear how the bread itself is distinguished between being holy or "repulsive." It could be a different kind of bread, it could result from different magical practices performed upon it in preparation, or it could be the mark of different mystical intention.[70] The phrase "repulsive bread" (*leḥem mego'al*) is used by the prophet Malachi, who denounces the execrable offerings of Israel, saying, "You offer repulsive bread on My altar" (Malachi 1:7). In the biblical usage, the term refers to offerings given with insincere motivations or in an atmosphere of concomitant social ills. An interest in intention is certainly a plausible explanation of the *Zohar*'s use of this verse. The identity of table and altar, in the mind of the zoharic authorship, is made clear in its adaptation of this verse. That Balaam performs magic, burns incense, and always sets his table on the same river reinforces the impression that a particular magical praxis is being performed.[71]

THE DIVINE NAME, WORDS OF TORAH, AND OTHER MEDIA OF TALISMANIC THEURGY

Talismanic theurgy finds its needs fulfilled in a host of media brought to the table. One instance of the axiom "blessing does not rest upon an empty place" helps contextualize the meaning of the comment. The axiom prescribes that a person should place a piece or more of bread on his table; if that is impossible he should leave over something from his meal so that the blessing can be recited over it (*Zohar* 2:87b–88a). When the Shunamite responds to Elisha that she has only a small container of oil, and this appears to satisfy the prophet, the *Zohar* interprets this in light of scripture: "A good name comes from fragrant oil" (Ecclesiastes 7:1).[72] "A good name," that is, God's name, can be uttered in the blessing over oil, the *Zohar* infers. Not only bread but other kinds of foodstuffs as well serve as the drawing card for the supernal blessing, and in the case of the Shunamite, the oil that she has in her house suffices. Oil functions in this way because it is one of the Bible's highly valued fluids and is often deployed by the *Zohar* to describe the flow of intrasefirotic blessing. According to this passage, at least, the reason that the mechanics outlined earlier perform as desired is not because of some magical quality of the bread and oil but rather because blessings will be recited over those foods. The foods serve merely as a technical or material prompt eliciting the human contribution to the spiritual dynamic that eventuates in God's response, divine blessing.

The meaning of the bread-on-the-table motif evolves into a concern that the divine name not be uttered in isolation, that is, without the appropriate blessing context. The *Zohar* contends emphatically that it would be better for one not to have been born than to recite the name of God in isolation. Even scripture observes this rule, says the *Zohar*, placing the holy name after two words, as in the opening words of Genesis, "In the beginning, God created" (*Bereshit bara Elohim*).[73] Another "opinion" says that God's name, the tetragrammaton, is only uttered upon an entire world; that is, after the end of creation as in Genesis 2:4, the first instance of the tetragrammaton.[74] The zoharic passage continues, citing the commandment that God's name should not be said in vain and thus should only be uttered in the context of prayers or a blessing. The homily closes, identifying the divine name with blessing.[75] Eventually it is emptiness itself that is abhorred by divinity (*Zohar* 2:67a). Similarly, because blessing does not rest in an empty place, one should only raise one's hands in making a blessing or in prayer. Because raising the hands is such a powerful implement for perfecting the Divinity and drawing blessing downward, that action should only be performed in the context of the performance of sacred rituals. Moreover, if the hands are raised without this intention, impurity would rest upon them. All of these instances—the bread, divine name, and praying hands—point to the need for "arousal from below" and to anxiety regarding the "cutting of the shoots," central dynamic structures of the *Zohar*'s theosophy.[76]

As we have seen, there is a strong concern with the appearance of things worldly as the zoharic kabbalist seeks to replicate in his home environment the supernal world he imagines above. In offering both spiritual and material modes of interpretation of the rabbinic axiom that "blessing does not rest in an empty place," the *Zohar* demonstrates its fluidity and flexibility. Although there is no lack of assertions in the zoharic kabbalah that privilege the spiritual world over the material, and the system that it lays out certainly does the same, nevertheless, at other moments, the author is able to plumb the depths of spiritual experience and fulfillment in the most material of settings. Furthermore, this literary expression would seem to arise from his personal engagement with foodstuffs every week: as he sits down at his Sabbath table, recites the *kiddush,* places his hands and fingers upon the bread, recites the blessings, leaves the crumbs on the table, and so forth. To bifurcate the literary product and the religious experience would be to forget the traditional and ritualistic element that pervades these people's lives.

Michel de Certeau proposes a model for thinking about the body in which the body is composed of a triad of forces—events, symbolic discourse, and social practices. If we adopt de Certeau's model, episodes in which words of Torah are recited at a meal would constitute a balance of these three.[77] This is the case because the recital of homilies, the primary activity of the zoharic fraternity, also serves as a vehicle for talismanic theurgy. An event of Torah study at a meal knits together the pleasure of the meal, the symbolic discourse (both literally and figuratively) of linking words of Torah to food and the recitation of blessings, and the social practice of a communal meal, fulfilling the rabbinic stricture of reciting words of Torah at the meal. The kabbalists have instituted, using the words of de Certeau, "a style that articulates itself into *practices* defining a *modus loquendi*."[78]

Reciting mystical homilies is a prerequisite to the ability to consume the angel's meal as referred to in Psalm 78:25. The *Zohar* reports that the Israelites in the desert fed on the very emanatory substance that drips from *Atika Kadisha* (the Holy Ancient One) onto *Ze'ir Anpin* (the Impatient One) and from there onto the *Hakal Tapuhin Kadishin* (the Field of Holy Apples). The passage says, "Rabbi Shimon said, 'How many people in this time are nourished from this [substance,] and who are they? These are the companions who exert themselves in Torah study day and night. If you think that it was from that very food in actuality, it is not so. Rather, it is like that food in actuality, receiving a double portion'" (*Zohar* 2:61b).[79] Manna is identified with wisdom and is the reward of assiduous Torah students of any day. In this particular passage, however, the *Zohar* is more cautious in terms of the mystical claims that it makes with regard to the miraculous nature of this reward. Hedging its bets, it says that it was not from this heavenly food in actuality that the kabbalists were nourished, but rather from something "like" that food. The distinction between the kabbalists and the saints of the desert rides not only upon the author's concession that manna was not falling from the heavens in second-century Palestine (nor in thirteenth-century Spain for that matter) but also from a desire to mythologize the experiences of the Israelites and acknowledge the relatively mundane nature of the author's experience in Spain. Nonetheless, there is a spiritual component that remains consistent. The sages of the text (*talmidei hakhamim*), referring to the mystagogues of the zoharic circle, are given a status similar to that of the Israelites.[80] Continual study emerges as another method for attaining the "eating" experience of the desert, with the assimilatory nature of that study being best expressed with the nourishment metaphor.

Quite often, though, the talismanic need for food to remain on the table is employed to affirm the importance of reciting words of Torah while sitting at the table. Like the bread, oil, and blessings, words of Torah recited over the table fill the table so that it should be worthy of receiving supernal blessing:

> It is written about a table over which words of Torah are not recited that "Yea, all tables are covered with vomit and filth, so that no space is left" (Isaiah 28:8), and it is prohibited to recite a blessing over such a table.[81] Why is this so? Because there is one kind of table and another kind of table. There is a table that is prepared before the Holy One, blessed be He, above and it is always prepared to have words of Torah recited upon it and to comprise the letters of the words of Torah within it. He gathers them toward Himself comprising them within Himself and they are perfected and rejoice in Him and He [also] rejoices. It is said about this table, "This is the table that stands before the Lord" (Ezekiel 41:22). There is another table that does not have a portion in the Torah and does not have a portion in the holiness of the Torah, and that table is called "vomit and filth" and this is the one that has no place inasmuch as it has no portion in the side of holiness. Consequently, a table over which words of Torah are not recited is a table of vomit and filth. (*Zohar* 2:153b–154a)[82]

The two tables referred to in this homily are the two potential tables that a person could set before himself, one holy and one demonic. The determinant of identity is the religious intention that one brings to the table and the religious activities performed there. This is already indicated in the rabbinic teaching that originally plays upon the verse from Isaiah. When scripture says, "no place is left" (*beli makom*), the rabbis understand this to be a lack of awareness of God, drawing upon the rabbinic cognomen for God of *makom,* meaning place. In the zoharic rendering, the table is infused with words of Torah and is thus inducted into the realm of holiness; the lack of words of Torah effects an induction into the inverse realm. Thus, returning to the rabbinic statement that introduced the homily—that blessing will not reside in an empty place—the *Zohar* explains how one maintains the "fullness" of a table: through investing the table with one's own "blessing" that is analogous to the divine blessing being invoked.

In this manner, the chain is complete: the person invests wisdom into the table, which in turn draws food wisdom from above so that the table remains continually full. Such a table is properly configured as the letters of the words of Torah have been contained within it. In this way it has been prevented from becoming, according to the rabbinic warning, a table full of filth and vomit. These two visions, that of the table composed of the letters of the Torah and that of the table full of filth and vomit, compete for the kabbalist's intention in his performance of the commandments. That these vivid tables act as visualized imaginative models is apparent from the *Zohar*'s emphasis in the first part of the homily: "[the table] should not be *seen* to be empty."[83] Last, the *Zohar* asserts that the table, now associated with *Gevurah* on the left, is completed by words of Torah coming from the right (*Zohar* 3:273a). Because "procuring food for people is as difficult [for God] as splitting the sea," and the task is related to the side of Judgment, affiliated with one's own table, it is important that these words of Torah bring Grace from the right side to ease that strain.[84] In his generosity, God gives food even to the wicked, and so, though food comes from the left, he passes over that side, being gracious to all. Simply setting the table, as best as one can do, achieves this aim (*Zohar Ḥadash* 86d *Midrash Ruth*).

6

"He Makes Peace and Increases Peace between the Supernal Realm and the Lower Realm": Augmentation Theurgy at Mystical Meals

THE KABBALISTS OF late-thirteenth-century Castile are highly pietistic and, in many ways, deeply conservative figures. In particular, the popularistic coloring of the *Zohar* reveals their concern that Jews be deeply committed to the punctilious observance of Jewish law. The theosophic overlay that they contribute provides added incentive and theological structure to the performance of the commandments, but it is to traditional practice, rather than nonnormative techniques, that they devote most of their attention. Analysis of the kabbalistic discussions of dining rituals reveals the kind of theurgy that kabbalah scholarship has long dealt with: augmentation theurgy. The term "augmentation theurgy" signifies theurgic acts that are intended to unite *sefirot,* link masculine and feminine potencies, or otherwise enhance the grandeur and glory of the supernal realm.[1] Moreover, in the discussion that follows, we will observe the range of roles that the kabbalist adopts to influence the supernal realm. He is alternately supplicant, caretaker, and lover, attending to the Divinity in many of the social roles that human experience furnishes. Last, this analysis will continue to delineate the construction of the body that is entailed by use of the mouth and the stomach through eating activities in the performance of theurgic operations.

AUGMENTATION THEURGY

The following list details some of the ways in which food items and table settings symbolize the various *sefirot* and thus enable repair and augmentation
of the Godhead:

Each of the three Sabbath meals is designed to give joy to one of the supernal countenances—specific groupings of the *sefirot* (*Zohar* 2:88a–b).[2] The
meal on Friday night helps the Field of Holy Apples—*Shekhinah*—to
rejoice, the Sabbath morning meal does the same for *Atika Kadisha*—*Keter,*
and the third meal similarly enhances *Ze'ir Anpin*—*Hokhmah* through
Yesod.[3]

Theurgic benefit extends to all *sefirot* from the three meals, as they are considered to supplement the seven blessings of the Sabbath statutory prayers,
thus comprising ten. If this practice is not fulfilled, the delight (*oneg*) that
one is supposed to have on the Sabbath is instead turned to affliction
(*nega*) (*Zohar* 3:273a *Ra'aya Mehemna*).

Wine is required for the sanctification (*kiddush*) of the Sabbath to cause the
King to rejoice and to adorn him with his crowns (*Zohar* 3:95a).

The loaves of bread used at the different meals are explained in a variety of
ways: as uniting *Tif'eret* and *Malkhut;*[4] as causing a flow from *Binah* to
Malkhut;[5] as symbolically unifying the four letters of the tetragrammaton;[6] as four loaves at each meal, representing the four faces of each creature of Ezekiel's chariot;[7] and as four loaves at each meal to represent the
four limbs of the *Shekhinah,* who is constructed as a body for *Tif'eret.*[8]

Four cups of wine are drunk at the Passover feast in order to unite the four
letters of the tetragrammaton (*Zohar* 3:95b).

Unleavened bread (*MaZaH*) with an additional letter *vav,* symbolizing the
male *Tif'eret,* turns the word into *MiZVaH,* meaning commandment, and
this linguistic move is understood to symbolize the ontological and experiential transformation that the Israelites underwent in their progress
from eating unleavened bread upon emerging from Egypt to their consumption of manna/Torah at Mount Sinai.

Upon breaking the bread at a meal, the kabbalist is instructed to take from
the place that is baked best, "because it is the point of the finished fruit
and that [symbolizes] the letter *vav*" (*Zohar* 3:272b *Ra'aya Mehemna*).[9] In
zoharic kabbalah, fruit is usually associated with the feminine and the letter *vav,* the third letter of the tetragrammaton, represents the masculine,
then completion of "the fruit" represents the letter *vav;* the feminine, ultimately, is not overtly represented in the final constitution of the bread.[10]

Because the letter *vav* corresponds to the masculine potency of the Godhead, the marked part of the bread corresponds to the point of the mark of circumcision of the divine phallus: this is the food that the kabbalists are supposed to ingest. The table must be illuminated by a candelabrum, referring symbolically to the illumination of *Gevurah* from *Ḥesed* (*Zohar* 3:272b–273a). Although the rabbinic sources refer to the table and the candle, they are not linked as the *Zohar* links them. The *Zohar* connects them because of the layout in the Temple in which the candelabrum is in the south and the table is in the south; for the *Zohar*, these associations adhere to its symbolic system in which *Ḥesed* is affiliated with the south, illuminating *Gevurah*, which is affiliated to the north.[11]

In each of these examples, food does not only stand for a supernal entity, prompting cognitive attention to one *sefirah* or another. Every sensual action—biting, cup holding, gazing—is a tactile or otherwise physical engagement with food that is simultaneously a unitive and theurgic action. In each of these practices, one's own body is the first medium for interacting with the upper realms.

The *Zohar* enjoins that when one recites the blessing "who brings forth (*ha-moẓi*) bread from the earth" before eating bread, one accentuates the "*ha*" prefix, which, signified by the letter *heh*, corresponds to the *Shekhinah* (*Zohar* 3:272a–b *Ra'aya Mehemna*).[12] One thus raises the *Shekhinah*, restoring sefirotic unity after Adam's sin; that sin was the improper consumption of fruit—wheat—from the Tree of Knowledge, rendering Adam's sin epistemological.[13] The speech act of accenting the "*ha*" sound affirms the immanence of the lower levels of the sefirotic structure as epitomized by the meaning of the formula "who brings forth."[14] This emphatic consonant expresses the notion that the divine act of self-revelation is intended for the benefit of humankind alone (*Zohar Ḥadash* 87b *Midrash Ruth*).[15] Although the atomizing hermeneutical tendencies in kabbalah are well noted, here that mode of reading extends itself into ritual practice, or rather the ritual practice has extended itself into the mode of reading, eliciting a stylized manner of articulating the words of the blessing. The mouth serves two different functions in this example: speaking and eating, each of which is enlisted in holy activity. The mouth is first paired with holy physical activity in the earliest Jewish mystical text, *Sefer Yeẓirah*.[16] In that work, the text identifies two separate yet related covenants, the covenant of the mouth (*brit lashon*) and the covenant of circumcision (*brit ma'or*).[17] The sign of circumcision corresponds to the *sefirah Malkhut*, which in our text is signified by the utterance of the letter *heh;* eating and circumcision are linked as well by not only being physiological phenomena, but also representing two primary bodily appetites. Hence the speech act of stressing the article "*ha*" corresponds to the ingestion of the bread, each of which is enacted with the sense of exclusivity and sacredness that the notion of covenant commands. Hermeneutics, speech, and eating thus all converge around the definite article "the."

Kabbalistic orthography interprets the twenty-two letters of the Hebrew alphabet through a variety of methods, among which is the discerning of masculine and feminine qualities within the letters themselves.[18] In the previous example, I noted how the letter *vav,* written essentially with a single vertical stroke, represents the masculine aspect of the Godhead; the author acquires this impression because of the phallic quality of the letter. The cup of blessing used for both the sanctification of the Sabbath and the grace after the meal has a variety of symbolic correspondences, among which is reliance on the masculine nature of the letter *vav.* The wine in the cup of blessing is considered to be the wine of Torah; the value in *gematriyah* of the word *kos* (cup)—eighty-six—is the same as that of the divine name Elohim; the number of words recited over the cup at the sanctification of the Sabbath is seventy-two, corresponding to the number of channels through which the divine blessing proceeds from the Holy Bride down to the world; last, the cup must be full and not ritually disqualified or one will have caused a similar flaw above.[19] That is, because the word for cup, *kos,* if written without the middle letter *vav,* is the same word as the incomplete "throne"—*kes* from Exodus 17:16, understood in kabbalistic literature to refer to the flaw in God's throne—then a flaw in the cup implies a flaw in the Divinity.[20] Ideally, the cup draws food down from the triad of *Hesed, Gevurah,* and *Tif'eret,* and the food is then dispatched to the lower world. Each of these rituals of the cup of blessing connotes completion: the numbers seventy and seventy-two are both identified with God's name; the letter *aleph,* missing from God's throne, signifies the number one, and therefore God. Further, the phrase of the *zimun* blessing, recited while holding the cup—"Let us bless the one of whose bounty we have eaten and whose goodness sustains us"—is said to refer specifically to the cup of blessing. That reading of the liturgical text conveys the symbolic truth that the cup of wine is the food of the *Shekhinah,* and it is her food that we have eaten (*Zohar Hadash* 87c *Midrash Ruth*). With this combination of utterances and hermeneutical devices, the cup of blessing operates as a multifaceted sacrament to be consumed by every male householder.

As is usually the case in the medieval kabbalah, epistemological achievement is linked to ontological rank; in the previous example, the bread on the kabbalist's table serves as a medium for both epistemological and ontological change. Raising the *Shekhinah* through the careful utterance of the letter *heh* of the blessing redeems the *Shekhinah* from the *Sitra Aḥra* and, in doing so, redeems the bread from the demonic realm in preparation for eating it. This redemption is repeated in the emphasis on the rabbinic requirement that one ritually wash one's hands before eating bread.[21] The ritual, it is said, rescues one from suffering (*Zohar Ḥadash* 86d–87a *Midrash Ruth*). In this instance, with regard to the blessing, the bread itself begins with a status of contamination and is called "evil eye."[22] It is only secondarily that the *Zohar* says that, in addition to this form of corruption, the food also becomes impure.

Although the rabbis had instituted hand washing as a norm, modeled after the priestly hand washing that was required before eating the heave offering, the *Zohar* truncates the purported rabbinic reason for a particular act in favor of its mystical explanation.[23] The *Zohar* similarly reifies another ritual, splitting it off from its overt reason in the case of *havdalah*—the ritual that distinguishes the Sabbath from the other days of the week. In the ritual, one ceremoniously lights a candle, recites the blessing "who creates the lights of fire," and then gazes upon one's fingernails. The reason that the rabbis supply for looking at the fingernails is to see if the candle is throwing off enough light to determine the border between flesh and nail. Looking at one's fingers and fingernails, then, is not so much the essence of the candle part of the ceremony; rather, this gazing is merely an instrumental measure of the quantity of light, to ensure that it is sufficiently luminous. The *Zohar* lets this mundane reasoning slip away and offers instead a mystical explanation for gazing at one's fingernails without any reference to the border of the flesh. The homily explains that with the departure of the Sabbath one can no longer look at the "internal light" as reflected by the palm and the "insides" of the finger; instead, one must settle for the "backs" of the fingers, representing the outer aspect of Divinity rather than its internal core, as experienced on the Sabbath.[24]

KAVVANAH AND THE ROLE OF FOOD AS MYSTICAL AND LITURGICAL OPPORTUNITY

The divide between the side of holiness and the side of impurity is a tension-laden boundary that religious thinkers regularly exploit. In medieval Jewish philosophical writing, the twelfth-century ethicist Bahya ibn Pakuda is the first to teach that every action brings one either closer to God or further away.

It can also be argued that, for the thirteenth-century German-Jewish pietists, it is precisely this tension that drives the religio-ethical model of *Sefer Hasidim*.[25] Building on this religious heritage, the most basic religious task, as construed in the medieval kabbalah, is to direct one's thoughts and actions toward the side of holiness and away from the side of impurity; the issue of *kavvanah,* mystical intention, is therefore a central component of worship. Looming before the religious individual at every moment is a crossroads that will determine his fate; not surprisingly, then, when sitting at the table, one has the potential for either holiness or impurity; it is an arena that is fraught with the potential for worship of the Divinity or of the demonic realm (*Zohar* 3:186b).[26] There are a variety of actions related to dining that observe and reinscribe the distinction between the holy and demonic sides. For example, in one teaching, the reason for the prohibition against eating the sciatic nerve is that it is the site of the evil inclination and comes from the *Sitra Aḥra;* it is, however, permitted to the non-Jewish nations.[27] (*Zohar* 1:170b) Elsewhere, it is suggested that the sciatic nerve corresponds to the point of vulnerability of the *membrum virile* of the Divinity.[28] Without harmonizing in an apologetic manner, it should be noted that these two reasons are analogous insofar as the point of vulnerability of the phallus is the point at which the *Sitra Aḥra* or the evil inclination can come to dominate; the latter is merely a broader note expressive of the same protective instinct.

A homily in *Zohar Ḥadash* states that Adam's sin consists of eating from all seven species of grains and fruits that scripture associates with the Land of Israel—wheat, barley, grapes, figs, pomegranates, olives, and date honey (Deuteronomy 8:8) (*Zohar Ḥadash Tikkunim* 107a).[29] Drawing on the aggadic tradition, in which the rabbis debate the identity of "the forbidden fruit," one teaching in the *Zohar* claims that there was no dispute; rather, Adam used all seven of the cited fruits in his transgression against the divine will.[30] These in turn correspond to the seven stations of the netherworld, as well as to the seven degrees of poverty.[31] This interpretation depends on the *Zohar*'s identification of *kavvanah* as the determinant of an action's righteous or demonic nature. Because these seven fruits are the seven that bear special status as "fruits of the Land of Israel," they are understood to originate from the side of the *Shekhinah* and, as such, can be apprehended as a unity. Adam's error lay in eating the seven fruits as separate entities. Separating the *Shekhinah* from the rest of the *sefirot* is the ultimate sin, the "cutting of the shoots."[32] Eating inevitably entails a fusion of the imaginative and the physical parts of the human person; one is obliged to adopt a particular theological assessment and summon the proper image in mystical contemplation in order to eat properly, because the understanding borne by the initiate while eating impacts directly the way in which the food is ingested and internalized. Adam, and therefore everyone, is obliged to recognize the indivisibility between the seven fruits of the land and the larger paradigm of God's fruitfulness, between sustenance and its source and, ultimately, between immanence and transcendence.

The recital of blessings is one of the primary tactics employed by the kabbalists to facilitate the appropriate yoking of understanding and vision. Initially, the rabbis of ancient Judaism multiplied the number of blessings to be recited before and after every kind of food or drink as a strategy to inject consciousness of God as the source of creation. The kabbalists exploit and amplify this ritual for their own ends. For them, the injunction to recite blessings plays a role in resolving several primary tensions in the kabbalistic mindset: first, blessings offer an opportunity to cultivate a kabbalistic consciousness that will lead one into the camp of the *Shekhinah*, avoiding the *Sitra Aḥra;* second, they help one to navigate between the antagonistic impulses of the soul and the body; third, and most generally, they stake out a position in the debate between ritualistic and spiritualistic emphases in Jewish worship.[33]

In the cosmic and immanent battle between the domains of the sacred and the demonic, eating supplies occasions to recite blessings that will tip the balance.[34] In the rabbinic ethos, food is an essential component of living that is subsequently framed by liturgical regulations; here it is the blessings that are primary, and one seeks opportunities to say blessings rather than seeking opportunities to eat. To regard food as an opportunity to make a blessing decidedly puts the cart before the horse, privileging liturgy over sustenance. The clearest statement of this approach is the *Zohar*'s assertion that God delights when people eat, because they utter a blessing before eating (*Zohar* 2:218a). A couple of examples will suffice to demonstrate how blessings are used to put the holy and demonic camps in stark relief. Both the *Shekhinah* and the *Sitra Aḥra* stand at the ready beside the table, anticipating a portion arising from the meal; if the grace after the meal is recited, the *Shekhinah* rests upon the person; if not, the *Sitra Aḥra* claims its share and takes over.[35] Another example comes from the history of halakhah. Among the medieval jurists, there was a dispute regarding the recital of blessings over nonpermitted food. Tosafot, Rabad, and Rosh all rule that one should recite a blessing over forbidden food, while Maimonides rules against it, assuming that sancta such as blessings can only be recited over foodstuffs that fall within the purview of the sacred diet.[36] The *Zohar* follows Maimonides, because his more rigorous approach readily lends itself to the dualistic myth making of the *Zohar:* blessings and the category of holiness can only apply to food from the same domain, permitted food; conversely, the category of impurity should not be given any portion from that side. Blessings also help to resolve the tension between the body and soul. Baḥya ben Asher stresses that one must have highly focused intention when reciting blessings over food, because one is naturally attracted to the matters of the body when sitting to dine.[37] In an example of micromanagement of the meal, he advocates that one contemplate God with every mouthful.[38] Once one has identified particular foods or meals with specific *sefirot,* further explication inevitably leads to this level of detail.[39]

In addition to blessings, there is another way in which food plays a role in the liturgical economy. Before the recital of the grace after the meal, there is a liturgical unit called *zimun* (invitation) that is recited if three people have eaten together. In the performance of the *zimun,* there is a series of statements said in call-and-response fashion, in preparation for the blessing—the *zimun*-invitation is a quasi-blessing before the actual blessing of the grace. The *yanuka,* the child kabbalist, asks why there is no unit of invitation in the case of other blessings, whereas there is such an "invitation" to the grace after the meal (*Zohar* 3:186b). To explain, he launches into a discourse about the regulations of eating fruit from a new tree. According to biblical legislation, fruit from a tree is not permitted to be eaten during its first three years, during which time it is called *orlah,* the same term used to designate the foreskin precircumcision (Leviticus 19:23–25). Medieval Jewish commentators explain the valences of this association. Rashi interprets the root *rl* as referring to a closedness that indicates the Jews should "close themselves off" from enjoying this class of fruits. Abraham ibn Ezra correlates this food restriction with the others, attesting that the fruit is unhealthy and can do physiological damage, just like fish without fins and scales, carnivorous birds, or impure animals. In addition to this medical assessment, he identifies this usage of the term with other uses: "uncircumcised lips" (Exodus 6:12), "uncircumcised ear" (Jeremiah 6:10), and "uncircumcised flesh" (penis). To this list Moses ben Nahman adds the "uncircumcised heart"[40] (Jeremiah 44:9; Hosea 13:8). Each of these specified organs is defective, and the young fruit, ibn Ezra maintains, should be regarded similarly.

The *yanuka* explains that after the third year the fruit is permitted to be eaten and "calls" for a blessing; before that, the fruit does not constitute an invitation. The fruit thus serves a liturgical function: it is the liturgical unit of *hazmanah* (invitation) that precedes eating;[41] further, the food itself is important structurally in the pattern of eating and blessing. In addition, he goes on, during the first three years the fruit remains within the possession of the *Sitra Aḥra,* only being released in the fourth year, relying on a characteristically schematic evaluative process that equates the permitted with the holy and the forbidden with the side of evil.[42] We can find a similar phenomenon in the talmudic commentary of Tosafot, in its explanation of the Saturday night ritual of *havdalah,* the rite that marks the distinction between the holiness of the Sabbath and the profaneness of the week. The Tosafist expresses surprise at the rule that when a festival begins on Saturday night, the ritual of transition from one sacred time to another does not include the spices, which function normally to give consolation to the soul in its distress about the Sabbath's end. The author suggests that the distress, in this instance, is allayed by the festival's meal and drink; here the food has served a different ritual purpose.[43]

On the whole, the zoharic passage with the child is a good indicator of how the *Zohar* regards the interaction of the commandments and how they are components of the material world that comprise them. Ontically, at the most supernal level, all that exists are the commandments, which are channels of the Divinity. Foods, fruits, or anything else required in the performance of a commandment participate in those channels when used appropriately. Food is ingested because it has to be; yet one pursues that activity for the sake of praising God and its concomitant spiritual or theurgical benefits.[44] At the same time, though, it appears that the *Zohar* treats food as a situation, a window in the day. Like a coffee break in which coffee is the occasion for rest rather than the point of the interval, here it is not the food so much as the liturgical function it serves that is relevant.[45]

GRACE AFTER THE MEAL

One ritual that receives a great deal of attention in the zoharic kabbalah is the grace after the meal.[46] One homily delves into great detail, explaining the procedure regarding the grace after the meal, how many and who may participate in it, and the various theurgic services that it performs.[47] In an ironic twist, the narrative frame sets the homily at an inn in which the visiting kabbalists set out to educate the innkeeper's seemingly ignorant son-in-law about the laws needed to live a simple, observant life. He had appeared two months earlier, was given the hand of the innkeeper's daughter, and certain elders imposed a two-month stretch of silence upon him in view of his meager educational background. Upon the arrival of the companions, however, his term of silence expires, and he begins to expound upon kabbalistic secrets, ending with the homily about the grace. The young man finally reveals that he is the son of the late Rav Safra, whom he had not known.[48] The perennial surprise for the kabbalists that Divinity and divine teaching are found in the most humble persons is manifest here as the son-in-law and daughter are symbolic of the *sefirot Tif'eret* and *Malkhut*.[49] What gives the narrative its appealing irony is the narrator's boldness in assuming that he and his companions would teach these figures esoteric knowledge. Moreover, notwithstanding the hierarchies based on erudition that are reinscribed by this episode, the element of surprise acts as a democratizing force, as anyone could emerge as a mysterious kabbalist. This narrative device has both theological and social import: theologically, it inclines toward a more pantheistic vision, in which reality is shot through with holiness and the esoteric; on the social level, even the lowliest person must be treated with utmost respect, because he might be the bearer of brilliant lore. Different classes eat together because the hide-and-seek game of concealing and revealing played by God is enacted on the human realm as well.

Paragraph by paragraph, the passage gives a full analysis of the whole procedure of preparing for and reciting the lengthy blessing.[50] Primarily, reciting this blessing is said to increase power in the supernal realm. The text rules that the benediction over the cup of blessing should only be recited when three have eaten together (*Zohar* 2:168b).[51] As we have seen earlier with regard to Boaz's satiation, engendering a greater ability to offer blessing, so too here the rabbinically enjoined practice of *zimun,* the invitation to participate in the grace after the meal, is cued by a physiological condition, that is, satiation. The social grouping of three that invokes the *zimun* constitutes an ontological basis from which this blessing emerges: "What is the reason [that you need three men to recite the blessing over the cup?] Because the cup of blessing only receives blessing with three or more than three but not with less than three."[52] The triad, with two opposing forces being mediated by a third, is a significant figure in the kabbalah. The most common triad is that of *Hesed, Gevurah,* and *Tif'eret,* in which *Hesed*/Grace is tempered and opposed by *Gevurah*/Judgment both of which, in turn, are mediated and harmonized by *Tif'eret*/Splendor. In this passage, three men have the power to symbolically assume the positions of this kabbalistic triad.[53] Not an egalitarian triad, the cup for the grace is held in the right hand to indicate that the grace after the meal does not issue from the left side, which is more strongly linked to the *Sitra Aḥra*. Holding it in the right hand asserts the dominant power of *Ḥesed* on the right and subjugates the power of *Gevurah* on the left; this action demonstrates the denial of any portion of the food of Israel to the *Sitra Aḥra*. Further, the grace after the meal is said to be characterized by the right side, and it is essential that the blessing for the Land of Israel, the second blessing of the grace, be connected to the right, because this then attaches the *sefirah* of *Malkhut*, as symbolized by the land, to *Ḥesed*, as symbolized by the right (*Zohar* 2:169a).[54]

Women have a lesser obligation with regard to reciting the grace because of the second blessing's references to Torah study and the covenant of circumcision, both of which are commandments that women are exempt from performing.[55] The obligation or exemption is determined by the person's capacity to study the Torah and the physical marking with God's name, the kabbalah's inveterate signs of male virility. Blessing is here marked as another sign of that virility. This message is reinforced by the narrative in which the son-in-law avoided fulfilling his conjugal obligations until he learned the grace after the meal. The knowledge of the blessing apparently confers upon him the right and duty of conjugal union. Once he can recite the grace and thus attain union with the *Shekhinah*, he is entitled to consummate his relationship with his wife. The grace, particularly the blessing that refers to commandments in which the male is obligated, validates his attachment to the covenant and thus frees him to have conjugal relations with his wife. Although already married, the marriage is not confirmed through consummation until he has demonstrated that the outward form of circumcision is confirmed by his rightful claim to that circumcision as evidenced by his knowledge of the blessing. He has established his virility in demonstrating his knowledge of kabbalistic lore. The ability to perform the grace grants him entry into the domain of those on the side of holiness and completes his construction as a male.

Giving to the Poor

In its characteristic blend of mysticism and homiletics, the *Zohar* intercedes in many places on behalf of the poor.[56] Much of the *Zohar*'s stress on charitable giving addresses its novel demand that one feed the indigent from one's table, leading me to contextualize charitable activity as part of the eating habits of the kabbalists.[57] According to one zoharic passage, giving to the poor is the primary criterion for evaluating a person's behavior after his death (*Zohar* 2:199b).[58] There is also a persistent critique of the wealthy for not giving to the poor (*Zohar* 3:8b). In one of its listings of the rules of etiquette required at a meal, the *Zohar* includes a requirement that one give food to the poor (*Zohar Ḥadash* 87b, *Midrash Ruth*). This commandment, normatively requiring the charitable giving of 10 percent of one's income, is here attached specifically to the setting of meals. The commandment is best fulfilled if one gives the indigent from the finest delicacies that he himself is eating, because, the author explains, God receives benefit from the very food that the kabbalist gives to the poor person: "It is a superlative performance of the commandment to give from the food that he himself is eating, from the very delicacies that he most enjoys, since the Holy One, blessed be He, [enjoys] that food that he gives [to the poor person]. This is because that food that he gives provides comfort to the poor person's soul and causes him to rejoice."[59]

Giving to the poor and Torah study are the two main criteria that determine if one's table will be received in the world-to-come (*Zohar* 2:154a). The table, representative of one's spiritual accomplishment, is thus constituted by the religious claim of Torah study and the ethical claim of supporting the poor. Indeed, Baḥya ben Asher reports that there were pious philanthropists in France who had the custom of being buried in their tables because of the righteousness that they had performed there.[60] As we shall see, however, giving to the poor is not exclusively, or even primarily, a humanistic concern for the *Zohar*, as its ethics are not self-grounded but, rather, rooted in the higher realms.

In a teaching that is likely borrowed from the *Sefer ha-Yashar*, attributed to Rabbenu Tam, the *Zohar* says that a poor person is a gift given by God (*Zohar* 2:198a).[61] Whatever the meaning may be in *Sefer ha-Yashar*, for the *Zohar* the reason such a person is a gift is that he provides an opportunity for the host to participate in the promotion of the flow of divine blessing. Several benefits accrue from this charitable giving: one is able to perpetuate the movement of food from the divine realm to the lowest strata in human society; through this sustenance of another human being, one prompts the further showering of blessing onto oneself. Like the food that is instrumental in inducing the recital of blessing, here, the indigent is instrumental as the prompt for the charitable act. This latter dynamic occurs in a manner analogous to the bread on the table: the ethico-spiritual output of giving serves as the magnet for the divine blessing. Moreover, God is the recipient of divine benefit as well, because once the needy person is nourished, he will bless God, which is of benefit to God:

How pleasant is the matter with regard to one who gives charity to the poor person, because he makes peace above and makes peace below. He makes peace and increases peace between the supernal realm and the lower realm. This is because when a poor person is distressed and anguished, he is resentful toward his Creator, engages in contention with Him, and judges Him. When a meritorious person comes and gives him charity and the poor person eats and drinks from the money that he is given, he repents and blesses God, may He be blessed, and he engages with God in a more peaceful manner, requesting forgiveness and atonement from Him. Then there is peace.[62]

There is an implicitly antiascetic trend in this passage—hunger detracts from one's ability to be joyous and to bless God.[63] This is similar to the phenomenon, discussed earlier, regarding one's ability to bless God with greater power when satiated. Unlike other passages that we have examined, however, where the blessing is the sole aim of the eating, here, the sense of physical ease that motivates the blessing is just as essential. The antiasceticism is certainly not thoroughgoing, as the *Zohar* advocates fasting, interrupting sleep, and general abstinence in a variety of scenarios.[64] The impulse toward the antiascetic here is genuinely motivated by a sincere concern for the poor.

The opening section of the *Zohar* enumerates a listing of commandments, and, significantly, the list maintains that feeding the poor is the ninth commandment. In this passage, the *Zohar*'s conception of gender creates the matrix for understanding the relationship between rich and poor:

The ninth commandment: to be generous to the poor and to give them food, as it is written, "Let us make man in our image after our likeness" (Genesis 1:26). "Let us make man"—from a combination of masculine and feminine. "In our image"—the rich; "after our likeness"—the poor. For the rich are from the masculine side and the poor are from the feminine side. As they are in one combination, and one is concerned about the other, and one gives to the other, and bestowing goodness one upon the other, this is the way that people should be below: The rich and the poor should be in one unity, giving one to the other and bestowing goodness one upon the other. "They shall rule the fish of the sea." We see this mystery in a book of King Solomon: Whoever concerns himself with the poor with the intention of his heart, his image never changes from the image of Adam. Once the image of Adam is inscribed upon him, he can rule over all creatures of the world with that image. This is as is written, "The fear and the dread of you shall be upon all the beasts of the earth" (Genesis 9:2). All tremble and fear before that image that is inscribed upon him, because that is a supernal commandment that elevates human beings with this image of Adam beyond all other commandments. From where do we learn this? From Nebuchadnezzar. Even though he dreamed that dream, as long as he was generous toward the poor his dream did not rule over him.[65] Once he looked askance at giving to the poor, what was written? "The words were still on the king's lips [when a voice fell from heaven, . . . You are being driven away from men, and your habitation is to be with the beasts of the field. You are to be fed grass like cattle]" (Daniel 4:28–29). Immediately, his appearance was altered and he was banished from other people. (*Zohar* 1:13b)

Although there is a continuation of the theurgic notion that feeding the poor will unite the masculine and feminine aspects of the Divinity, here we have different social groupings symbolizing those sefirotic potencies. The use of male-female gender imagery to render male-male relationships is a common way for the *Zohar* to explain the stratification of society, with the powerful, wealthy, or wise in the position of the masculine, and the weak, impoverished, or ignorant in the position of the feminine.[66] Giving food to the poor is homologous to the sexual but, as a result, helps color the meaning of the *Zohar*'s understanding of sexuality as well. It helps us to understand the *Zohar*'s ubiquitous use of the term "support" (*mefarnes*) in the context of the divine romance in a more literal way, thus nuancing the nature of the relationship and vitiating its erotic charge.[67]

The *Zohar*'s portrayals of relationships of dependence link active males and passive females, and even active males with passive males, in erotic, economic, and spiritual matters, homologizing the different kinds of interaction. Thus, semen passed from male to female is homologized with the Torah given from teacher to student and the food given from the host to his indigent guests. Unsurprisingly, supporting one's donkey does not have a sexual valence except in the case of Balaam, whom the author of the *Zohar* loves to vilify.[68]

One is not only sustaining the impoverished person and restoring him to good standing in his relationship with God but is deemed by God to have actually created such a person's soul (*Zohar* 2:198a). Like Noah's engendering the animals and like Abraham's creation of souls in Ḥaran, feeding the poor is the work of the righteous and, as such, is associated with the *sefirah Yesod,* the fount of creativity (*Zohar* 3:168a).[69] Souls come into the world from the *sefirah Yesod* and are the fruit of the conjugation of *Yesod* with the *Shekhinah* (*Zohar* 1:13a). Because the righteous man is occupied with conversion, he too is a creator of souls. As with so many of the other idealized functions that a person can perform that are conceived as expressions of the phallic *sefirah Yesod,* so too is the ability to give food in that it is a soul-creating act.[70] Related to this is the zoharic notion that the master of the household passing bread to the guests at the table stands in the position of *Yesod* disseminating "his fruit" to the feminized recipients.[71] All of the crumbs are like drops of the divine seed, which, if wasted, invoke impoverishment upon the doer.[72] The food is not represented as fully formed "fruit" but rather as "seed"; the seed takes root and comes to fruition within the belly of the recipient. This is yet another instance of the symbolic impregnation of those in the recipient position, taking in the blessing of life from "above," as it were.

The *Zohar* attributes great significance to caring for the poor at the time of the festivals. The *Zohar* says, "Come and see. In all other seasons and holidays, a person has to rejoice and to give joy to the poor. If he rejoices on his own and does not give to the poor, his punishment is great, because he rejoices alone and is not giving joy to another. About such a person it is written, 'I will strew dung upon your faces, the dung of your festal sacrifices'"[73] (Malachi 2:3) (*Zohar* 2:88b). Interestingly, the Sabbath meals are generally exempted from this ethical requirement.[74] The *Zohar* precludes the Sabbath meals through midrashic-style exegesis of a verse in Malachi, which refers to the "festal sacrifices," apparently excluding those of the Sabbath.[75]

Failing to give to the poor is a sin nearly unrivalled in terms of the severity of punishment that can be invoked. For example, the feast that Abraham sets on the occasion of the birth of Isaac is a prompt for the satanic prosecutor to observe if poor people are being attended to and are invited to sit at the table (*Zohar* 1:10b–11a). Dressed as an indigent, Satan discovers that the poor are being ignored, and he invokes God's justice. The decree for the sacrifice of Isaac is subsequently issued, Sarah's death as a result of distress is provoked, and all of the joy of the festive scene is annulled.[76] All of this is prompted not only by Abraham's stinginess and insensitivity but also because it appears precisely at the occasion of a festive meal. Abraham's own physical well-being has failed to elicit caring for others.

This combination of the theurgic, ethical, and experiential elements is also found in the *Zohar's* description of the *ushpizin* (guests) on the festival of Sukkot. According to the *Zohar* (3:103b–104a), seven mystical guests— Abraham, Isaac, Jacob, Moses, Aaron, Joseph, and David—visit the *sukkah* during the seven days of the festival. These seven correspond to the bottom seven *sefirot.* The food that is set for the *ushpizin* is, in actuality, the portion for the poor; thus, in feeding the poor, one is really feeding the Divinity.[77]

Moreover, if one does not set out food for the poor, the *ushpizin* leave the meal in disgust. The intent of the passage is that one loses one's own attainment of *devekut* with the *Shekhinah,* as symbolized by the *sukkah* dwelling, and with the other *sefirot* symbolized by the divine guests.[78] Giving to the poor thus acts as a compendium of some of the main theurgic strategies that have been examined up to this point: sustaining the divine flow, creating the opportunity and physical and spiritual energy to offer blessing, and promoting joy in the supernal and lower realms. In the kabbalistic treatment of charitable giving to the poor, food plays a central role in the commandment. Further, the commandment is perceived by the *Zohar* as an expression of the interconnectivity of one's physical environment, one's own body, the bodies of one's guests, and the body of the Divinity.

Conclusion

FROM THE WEALTH OF worldly interaction in the zoharic kabbalah, one might infer a mystical fraternity that is fully engaged in community and matters of daily sustenance. And yet the kabbalists' relationship to the senses remains rather austere—after all that we have examined, there is precious little about eating, at least as conventionally imagined. Eating for the *Zohar* is highly stylized, without explicit interest in food per se, but it is interested in how the activity is framed. The *Zohar*'s primary concerns are in the posturing before and after, how one looks at the food (rather than how it looks!), the vocalizing and intentions that accompany it, the liturgical bracketing, and the intellectual/mystical exchange accompanying the meal. There is nothing comparable to that which is found later in the Hasidic literature about the taste, enjoyment, and aroma of food, all of which serve as sensory stimulants to the divine communion. The zoharic world, in which everything material is a cipher for a divine correlate, sets the stage for the comprehensive bodily participation in which the Hasidic literature delights.

A notable lacuna in the *Zohar*'s treatment of eating topics is that of the rabbinic dictum, in the name of Rabbi Yehudah, that ignorant persons are not allowed to eat meat.[1] Although not adopted as normative practice, this teaching receives considerable attention in the kabbalistic literature contemporary with and following shortly after the *Zohar*. In the works of Joseph Gikatilla, Joseph of Hamadan, Baḥya ben Asher, Joseph ben Shalom Ashkenazi, and the *Sefer ha-Kanah,* the prohibition against improper slaughter stems from a doctrine of resurrection that includes the possibility of a person's being reincarnated in the body of an animal. Because each beast may bear the soul of a human being that has acquired a certain spiritual imperfection, causing its bestial peregrination, one must be exceedingly careful in slaughtering, ensuring that the act be done as mercifully and as painlessly as possible.[2] The *Tikkunei ha-Zohar* teaches that one who eats without having prayed for his food will die like a field animal, that is, slaughtered with a flawed knife. The unnatural death resulting from impious behavior is at best a vague hint of the concerns about the ignorant eating meat (*Tikkunei ha-Zohar* 21, 59a).

In a discussion of the ethics of constructions of the body, Michel Feher notes the need to examine "which regions of the body are mobilized and which types of discipline are imposed on it in order to produce the soul of a hero, a saint, or a perfect courtier. Conversely, one may wonder what particular lack of discipline in gestures or features not only signifies depravity or ignominy but actually creates it, so that a feeling such as racial hatred becomes more the result of a specific cultural construction than of a universal fear of the 'other.'" Speaking of love, Feher emphasizes "the singularity of the emotions immanent in the ceremonies that produce them. Not that the transports of love are artificial; but they do not exist outside a certain setting, that is, a stylization of movements and poses, each of which includes its own particular intensifications and deviations."[3] For our purposes, we have considered how the oral cavity and stomach are mobilized to produce the soul of the mystical saint in the *Zohar.*

Notwithstanding these various aspects of dining behavior that the *Zohar* does not treat, what emerges from this study is a sense of the intense involvement of the physical body interacting with the material world in order to effect the various transformations within the Divine and within the individual kabbalist. This is not a fanciful intellectual enterprise but rather a rich collection of descriptions of lives lived with deep spiritual and mystical experience diffused throughout their daily activities, even in such ostensibly mundane activities as dining. What is noteworthy about this stance is that unlike ascetics, for whom the body might be treated instrumentally, the individual has a "communicative" relationship with the body. As shown by the sociologist Arthur Frank, the communicative attitude arises in situations in which there is emphasis on association among individuals. Though the kabbalists do not wholly identify themselves with their bodies, neither are they alienated from them. The relational fluidity described in the zoharic kabbalah, in which individuals are ever gaining from and contributing toward both the Divine and each other, neatly fits this paradigm. The human body becomes an entity constantly in flux, consisting of movement of things into and out of the body, being alternately feminine and masculine, restoring and destroying the internal harmony of right and left.[4]

Though I have been talking about the various practices associated with eating techniques, there is neither the sense of predictability that one might find in a magical text nor the sense of humility about the body's contingency.[5] Rather, with a certain spiritual self-confidence, the kabbalists talk about experiences to be had and effects to be produced through these various practices, always with the underlying knowledge that these processes depend on one's being spiritually fit. These are not technologies to be manipulated but rather traditions one participates in through considerable self-exertion and discipline. At the same time, however, this is not the model of a body that is subjected to a test of truth in a Foucauldian manner in which the figures are examined for the value of their *kavvanah*.[6] There is a certain reliance upon the communal and dialogical nature of these experiences — that they do not operate mechanistically, like a switch turning things on and off. Consequently, spiritual accomplishment will be attained without the need for a studied examination of the quality of that moment.

In one teaching by Moses de Leon, we find that in the future, man will not separate from his body upon death, and de Leon laments that the separation now is comparable to the destruction of the Temple.[7] Although this might appear hyperbolic, in fact the description is apt, given de Leon's assumptions. The destruction of the Temple marks the loss of the Divine Presence residing in its fullest glory among the people. The present loss of that divine immanence residing within the material is directly analogous to the departure of the divine soul from within the human body.[8] The mutability of the body, its contingency, and its distance from the purely spiritual are ultimately overcome, and, as I believe has been demonstrated, it is this kind of embodied spirituality that the *Zohar* values most. According to a modern kabbalistic aphorism,[9] one who is a talmudist is like one who has a fever, whereas one who is a kabbalist is like one who has a stomachache. A fever can be measured, and one can ascertain if the person is indeed suffering from his claimed ailment. A stomachache, on the other hand, cannot be verified, and the verity of the claim remains unknown. Rabbi Shimon bar Yoḥai's tests of the kabbalists' moods notwithstanding, the abilities of the zoharic kabbalists to attain the experiences attested to in their books remain unascertainable. The only records are the texts that they have left us.[10]

Concern for the body, its limitations, and its remarkable capabilities persists in Western culture today, in both popular and academic realms. Dieting, bodybuilding, bodily implants, organ transplantation, radical makeovers, genetic engineering, and cloning have made the dreams and nightmares of medieval kabbalists realities in our day-to-day living and scientific practice. The imaginative world of the kabbalists that produced symbol systems creating very particular kinds of bodies is imaginatively matched and physiologically surpassed by today's headlines. Though the symbolic structures of contemporary culture may not be as rich as those of the kabbalists, the relationships between identity and body, and physiological experience and imaginative self-fashioning, continue as central motifs for human self-understanding. Today's stress on the physicality of life does mark a turn in the interaction between the physical and spiritual axes that we have been considering. Perhaps the words of Jean Starobinski explain the current fixation:

> What I devote to an awareness of the body, I subtract from my presence in the world, from my investment in the *other*. . . . There is nothing very bold in drawing the only superficially banal conclusion that the present infatuation with the different modes of body consciousness is a symptom of the considerable narcissistic component characteristic of contemporary Western culture. . . . Perhaps one could also enter a plea on behalf of Narcissus (or at least invoke extenuating circumstances in his favor. In a world in which technological mastery has made such rapid strides, can one not understand that the desire to feel—and to feel *oneself*—should arise as a compensation, necessary, even its excesses, to our psychic survival?[11]

And yet there are other voices, particularly feminist voices, that have been striving for a reassessment of the body in ways that touch upon the theological concerns of my study. In a recent, powerful feminist theology, Grace Jantzen writes, "To have the capacity for transcendence does not entail having the capacity, now or in the future, to become disembodied, but rather to be embodied in loving, thoughtful, and creative ways. Transcendence is not the opposite of immanence: indeed, immanence is a necessary condition of transcendence, since no one can achieve intelligence or creativity without the requisite physical complexity. Rather, immanence and transcendence are together opposed to reductionism."[12] Jantzen, a scholar of medieval Christian female mysticism, presents a program for modern theology that bears this similarity to the kabbalists: they too are seeking to embody qualities of the Divinity, to serve as human instantiations of the transcendent One.

NOTES

Introduction

1. Peter Farb, *Consuming Passions: The Anthropology of Eating* (Boston: Houghton Mifflin, 1980), 3.

2. Roland Barthes, "Reading Brillat-Savarin," in *The Rustle of Language*, ed. François Wahl and trans. Richard Howard (Berkeley: University of California Press, 1986), 251.

3. Jenna Weissman Joselit, *The Wonders of America: Reinventing Jewish Culture, 1880–1950* (New York: Hill and Wang, 1994), 182–83.

4. Increasingly, kabbalah scholarship has drawn a line from the experiences and practices described in the *Zohar* to the kabbalists who authored and edited its texts. Throughout this study I use the generic term "kabbalists," or the writers of "zoharic" or "classical kabbalah," to refer to the kabbalists of late-thirteenth-century Spain (Castile, specifically) as well as Ra'aya Mehema and kabbalists such as Isaac of Acre and Menahem Recanati, and the author of the *Tikkunei ha-Zohar*. For an introduction to the literature of the *Zohar*, its authorship, and the doctrine of the *sefirot* and practice in relationship to them, see Arthur Green, *A Guide to the Zohar* (Stanford, Calif.: Stanford University Press, 2004).

5. *b. Yoma* 75a–76a. Numbers 11:8 characterizes manna as tasting like "the cream of oil" (*le-SHaD ha-Shamen*). The letters *shd*, meaning "cream" in this context, can also refer to the words *breast* and *demon*, yielding the meanings in the preceding text.

6. I have used the feminine pronoun whenever I speak in a generic, modern context. Because of the overwhelmingly male-centered nature of kabbalistic study and practice, all other instances will use the masculine form.

7. See, e.g., Seth Lance Brody, "Human Hands Dwell in Heavenly Heights: Worship and Mystical Experience in Thirteenth Century Kabbalah" (Ph.D. diss., University of Pennsylvania, 1991).

8. See Maurice Merleau-Ponty, *Phenomenology of Perception*, trans. Colin Smith, International Library of Philosophy and Scientific Method (London: Routledge and Kegan Paul, 1962), part 1, chap. 3.

9. Elizabeth Grosz, "Inscriptions and Body-Maps: Representations and the Corporeal," in *Feminine, Masculine, and Representation*, ed. Terry Threadgold and Ann Cranny-Francis (Sydney: Allen and Unwin, 1990), 73–74.

10. See, e.g., *Zohar* 1:64a, 74a, 84b, 87b, 183a, 203a, 225a, 251b; 2:28b, 244b, 247b–248a, 276b; 3:269a, 291b, 296a; *Zohar Ḥadash* 14b–c, 44d, 53c, 73a, 74a, 81a; in Lurianic kabbalah, see, e.g., *Sefer Ta'amei ha-Mizvot* 253b. In this latter source, it is

explicitly the mother-child relationship that is being invoked. In the kabbalah of Rabbi Isaac the Blind, suckling (*yenikah*) refers to a noncognitive mode of contemplation. See his commentary on *Sefer Yezirah* 1:1. Scholem has a valuable discussion of this passage in Gershom Scholem, *Origins of the Kabbalah*, ed. R. J. Zwi Werblowski and trans. Allan Arkush (1962; reprint, Philadelphia: Jewish Publication Society, 1987), 279–80. All citations from the *Zohar, Zohar Hadash*, and *Tikkunei ha-Zohar* are from Reuven Margaliot, ed., *Sefer ha-Zohar* (Jerusalem: Mosad ha-Rav Kuk, 1970); Reuven Margaliot, ed., *Zohar Hadash* (Jerusalem: Mosad ha-Rav Kuk, 1994); Reuven Margaliot, ed., *Tikkunei ha-Zohar* (Jerusalem: Mosad ha-Rav Kuk, 1994).

11. Hayyim Vital, *Sha'ar ha-Mizvot* (Jerusalem: Yeshivat Kol Yehudah Press, 1988), 59. My thanks to David Seidenberg for bringing this source to my attention.

12. Eating and destruction are etymologically linked (see, e.g., Exodus 3:2; Isaiah 1:20), enabling the kabbalists to identify these two conceptually, and also with mystical union, as an event that implies destruction of the self. See *Zohar* 1:51a.

13. Balaam, no doubt, is a satiric stand-in for the Christian priests, whose communion and consumption of the wafer must certainly have appeared to the kabbalists as a demonic meal.

14. See Caroline Walker Bynum, *Holy Feast and Holy Fast: The Religious Significance of Food to Medieval Women* (Berkeley: University of California Press, 1987), 60–61. Bynum says that greater emphasis is given to food presentation in the texts of the Christian mystics, for whom food served as central metaphor and vehicle for mystical experience.

15. Countless evocative descriptions of the *Shekhinah*, decorated by the righteous in their performance of commandments and mystical study of the Torah, yield little detail about her physical appearance (the color of her hair, her complexion, her carriage, the size or delicacy of her limbs). The only time that the *Zohar* engages in a lengthy description of a woman's appearance is in that of Lilith, the queen of demons, as she embarks on her role as demonic seductress. See *Zohar* 1:148a–b (*Sitrei Torah*); see Isaiah Tishby, *The Wisdom of the Zohar*, trans. David Goldstein (Oxford: Oxford University Press, 1989), 538–39.

16. Even if one were to argue that this jump from text to history is untenable, the significance of food in preparing oneself for mystical experience holds for the literary characters of the *Zohar*.

17. Hans-Georg Gadamer, *Truth and Method*, trans. Garret Barden and John Cumming (New York: Seabury/Continuum, 1975), 116–17, 147–48.

18. This approach has been taken up by scholars of various forms of mysticism as well as those of the kabbalah. In the study of Christian mysticism, see Nelson Pike, *Mystic Union: An Essay in the Phenomenology of Mysticism* (Ithaca, N.Y.: Cornell University Press, 1992), 174. In the hermeneutics of al-Ghazali, see Gerald L. Bruns, *Hermeneutics Ancient and Modern* (New Haven, Conn.: Yale University Press, 1992), 133–34. Moshe Idel uses the term "spiritualistic exegesis" to refer to the personal investment of the mystic in the allegoresis employed by Abraham Abulafia; Moshe Idel, *Language, Torah, and Hermeneutics in Abraham Abulafia*, trans. Menahem Kallus (Albany: State University of New York Press, 1989), xvii. In kabbalah, see Moshe Idel, *Kabbalah: New Perspectives* (New Haven, Conn.: Yale University Press, 1988),

234–49; Elliot R. Wolfson, *Through a Speculum That Shines: Visionary Experience and Imagination in Medieval Jewish Mysticism* (Princeton, N.J.: Princeton University Press, 1994), 330–32. Cf. Yehuda Liebes's formulation that "mythopoesis is myth itself," meaning that the description of a particular scenario serves to connect that supernal scenario to the individuals involved in the ritualized description. Yehuda Liebes, "Zohar and Eros," *Alpayim — A Multidisciplinary Publication for Contemporary Thought and Literature* 9 (1994): 93.

19. See, e.g., Wolfson, *Through a Speculum That Shines*, 374 and notes 164–65; Yehuda Liebes, "How the *Zohar* Was Written," *Jerusalem Studies in Jewish Thought* 8 (1989): 5 n. 16, 7; Yehuda Liebes, "How Was the *Zohar* Written?" in *Studies in the Zohar*, trans. Stephanie Nakache (Albany: State University of New York Press, 1993), 196 n. 19, 89; Liebes, "*Zohar* and Eros." See also Idel's general remarks in Idel, *Kabbalah*, 27–29.

20. *b. Berakhot* 43a.

21. Solomon ibn Adret, *Hidushei ha-Rashba: Berakhot*, Hiddushei ha-Rashba (Jerusalem: Mosad ha-Rav Kuk, 1982–83), 42b; Yom Tov ben Abraham Ishvili, *Hidushei ha-Ritba: Berakhot*, Hidushei ha-Ritva (Jerusalem: Mosad ha-Rav Kuk, 1984), 286.

22. It is possible that the *Zohar* is using the term "*haseibah*" in a technical sense to denote the intention of the diners: that the meal is the purpose of their gathering. See the comments of *Tosafot Berakhot* 42a, s.v. *haseibu;* Yom Tov ben Avraham Ishvili, *Hiddushei ha-Ritva*, Mosad ha-Rav Kuk (Jerusalem: Mosad ha-Rav Kuk, 1984), 1:287.

23. See, e.g., *Bahir* 82, 172. In Abrams's edition, see nos. 55, 116.

24. See, e.g., Isaac the Blind, "Commentary on *Sefer Yezirah*," ed. Gershom Scholem, in *ha-Kabbalah be-Provence*, ed. Rivkah Schatz (Jerusalem: Hebrew University of Jerusalem, 1970), 3:4; Ezra of Gerona, "Commentary on the Song of Songs," in *Kitvei Ramban* II, ed. Charles Chavel (Jerusalem: Mosad ha-Rav Kuk, 1966), 528; Rabbi Azriel, *Commentary on the Aggadot*, ed. Isaiah Tishby (Jerusalem: Magnes, 1983), 5 ; *Zohar* 2:142a–b, 3:139b, 141b (*Idra Raba*); Moses ben Shem Tov de Leon, *Sefer ha-Rimmon*, ed. Elliot R. Wolfson (Atlanta: Scholars Press, 1988), 13, 221, 222, 254; Moses ben Shem Tov de Leon, *Shushan Edut*, ed. Gershom Scholem, *Qovez al Yad*, n.s., 8 (1975): 353–54; *Tikkunei ha-Zohar*, 2nd Preface, 17a–17b; Bahya ben Asher, *Commentary on the Torah*, ed. Charles Chavel (Jerusalem: Mosad ha-Rav Kuk, 1982), 46–47. For a general discussion of the anatomical form of the *sefirot*, see Tishby, *Wisdom of the Zohar*, 295–302.

25. See, e.g., de Leon, *Sefer ha-Rimmon*, 132, 220.

26. *Sefer ha-Nefesh ha-Hakhamah*, 1, sig. 3, fol. 2a, cited in Tishby, *Wisdom of the Zohar*, 681. Regarding the authorship of the *Zohar*, for many years the scholarly consensus followed Scholem, who had argued that the *Zohar* was the work of Moses de Leon. Gershom Scholem, *Major Trends in Jewish Mysticism* (New York: Schocken, 1946), 156–204. In the 1980s, Yehuda Liebes argued for a group composition of the zoharic anthology. Liebes, "How the *Zohar* Was Written" (Hebrew); Liebes, "How Was the *Zohar* Written?" Recently, Ronit Meroz has undertaken research to uncover the layers of the authorship of the *Zohar*, leading ultimately to a kind of documentary archeology of the *Zohar*. See Ronit Meroz, "Zoharic Narratives and Their

Adaptations," *Hispania Judaica Bulletin* 3 (2000): 3–63. Last, Daniel Abrams contends that it is impossible to identify a text called *Sefes ha-Zohar* until it is printed. Moreover, he argues that Zoharic material was reworked by textual committees over hundreds of years. See Daniel Abrams, "The *Zohar* as a Book: On the Assumptions and Expectations of the Kabbalists and Modern Scholarship," *Kabbalah: Journal for the Study of Jewish Mystical Texts* 12 (2004): 201–32.

27. Regarding the cultural constructedness of the body, see Caroline Walker Bynum, "Introduction: The Complexity of Symbols," in *Gender and Religion: On the Complexity of Symbols,* ed. Caroline Walker Bynum, Stevan Harrell, and Paula Richman (Boston: Beacon, 1986), 7; Bynum, *Holy Feast and Holy Fast;* Peter Brown, *The Body and Society: Men, Women, and Sexual Renunciation in Early Christianity,* Lectures on the History of Religions, vol. 13 (New York: Columbia University Press, 1988); Julia Epstein and Kristina Straub, "Introduction: The Guarded Body," in *Body Guards: The Cultural Politics of Gender Ambiguity,* ed. Julia Epstein and Kristina Straub (New York: Routledge, 1991); Michel de Certeau, *The Mystic Fable: The Sixteenth and Seventeenth Centuries,* trans. Michael B. Smith (1982, in French; reprint, Chicago: University of Chicago Press, 1992); Jacques Le Goff, *The Medieval Imagination,* trans. Arthur Goldhammer (Chicago: University of Chicago Press, 1988); Thomas Laqueur, *Making Sex: Body and Gender from the Greeks to Freud* (Cambridge, Mass.: Harvard University Press, 1990); see also the essays collected in the Zone volumes, *Fragments for a History of the Body,* ed. Michel Feher (New York, Zone, 1989), parts 1–3. A volume of essays studying the nature of constructed embodiment in Jewish cultures is Howard Eilberg-Schwartz, ed., *People of the Body: Jews and Judaism from an Embodied Perspective* (Albany: State University of New York Press, 1992).

28. J. Wood, "Physiology of the Enteric Nervous System," in *Physiology of the Gastrointestinal Tract,* ed. L. R. Johnson (New York: Raven, 1987), 1–39.

29. Mikhail Bakhtin, *Rabelais and His World* (Bloomington: Indiana University Press, 1984), 278–367.

30. Tishby, *Wisdom of the Zohar,* 764.

31. Ibid. 765. A menstruant or a woman's uncovered hair both signify instances in which the body inhabits a demonic space. See also ibid., 1358–59.

32. Ibid., 763.

33. Ibid., 766.

34. Ibid., 767.

35. For discussions of these two functions of symbolism in kabbalah scholarship, see Idel, *Kabbalah,* 200–234; Susan A. Handelman, *Fragments of Redemption: Jewish Thought and Literary Theory in Benjamin, Scholem, and Levinas* (Bloomington: Indiana University Press, 1991), 93–115; Wolfson, *Through a Speculum That Shines,* 52–73; Steven M. Wasserstrom, *Religion after Religion: Gershom Scholem, Mircea Eliade, and Henry Corbin at Eranos* (Princeton, N.J.: Princeton University Press, 1999), 91–95.

36. Joseph Gikatilla, *Sefer Sha'arei Orah* (New York: Moriah Offset, 1985), 2b.

37. At the other extreme is a figure such as Joseph of Hamadan, who exploits anthropomorphism to the extent of considering the nature of divine body hair and other such (discomfiting) detail.

38. See Wolfson, *Through a Speculum That Shines*, 52–58.

39. Ibid., 61 and n. 38.

40. Howard Eilberg-Schwartz, "Introduction," in *People of the Body: Jews and Judaism from an Embodied Perspective*, ed. Howard Eilberg-Schwartz (Albany: State University of New York Press, 1992), 1–13.

41. See Caroline Walker Bynum, "Why All the Fuss about the Body? A Medievalist's Perspective," *Critical Inquiry* 22 (autumn 1995): 1–33.

42. Moses Maimonides, *The Guide of the Perplexed*, trans. Shlomo Pines (Chicago: University of Chicago Press, 1963). For an insightful discussion of Maimonides' attitudes toward the body and aesthetics, see Kalman P. Bland, "Medieval Jewish Aesthetics: Maimonides, Body, and Scripture in Profiat Duran," *Journal of the History of Ideas* 54, no. 4 (1993): 537–46. For examples of the critiques of Maimonides' position, see Charles Chavel, ed., *Iggeret ha-Kodesh, Kitvei Ramban* II (Jerusalem: Mosad ha-Rav Kuk 1988), 323.

43. See Bezalel Safran, "Rabbi Azriel and Moses ben Nahman: Two Views of the Fall of Man," in *Rabbi Moses ben Nahman (Ramban): Explorations in His Religious and Literary Virtuosity*, ed. Isadore Twersky (Cambridge, Mass.: Harvard University Press, 1983), 75–82.

44. See *Kitvei Ramban* II, 303–7; Safran, "Rabbi Azriel," 82; Jonathan Feldman, "The Power of the Soul over the Body: Corporeal Transformation and Attitudes towards the Body in the Thought of Moses ben Nahman" (Ph.D. diss., New York University, 1999).

45. Safran, "Rabbi Azriel," 83, 93. This position can be found in the *Commentary on the Torah* of Abraham ibn Ezra, as well, in which Moses becomes angelicized and therefore is no longer in need of food or drink. See his *Commentary on the Torah* (Jerusalem: Mosad ha-Rav Kuk, 1976), e.g., Exodus 23:21, 33:21; Numbers 20:8.

46. Safran, "Rabbi Azriel," 83. In theosophic kabbalah, the *Shekhinah* (or *Malkhut*) is the feminine aspect of the Divine and the lowest of the *sefirot*. For the kabbalists, union with the *Shekhinah* is one of the primary mystical experiences that is desired. Diana Lobel has shown that Moses ben Nahman' commentary to Deuteronomy 11:22, "And to cling to Him," the locus classicus of *devekut* in Moses ben Nahman, is a direct quote from the ibn Tibbon translation of Yehudah Halevi's *ha-Kuzari*. The latter in turn draws on a rich Islamic context from a variety of sources. See Diana Lobel, "A Dwelling Place for the Shekhinah," *Jewish Quarterly Review* 90, nos. 1–2 (1999): 103–25.

47. As, e.g., in Tishby, *Wisdom of the Zohar*, 749–73. Scholastic discussions of the nature of the body and food far surpass those of the kabbalists in their sophisticated use of medical models. For a comprehensive discussion, see Philip Lyndon Reynolds, *Food and the Body: Some Peculiar Questions in High Medieval Theology* (Leiden, Neth.: Brill, 1999).

48. Michael Jackson, *Paths toward a Clearing: Radical Empiricism and Ethnographic Inquiry* (Bloomington: Indiana University Press, 1989), 123.

49. Ibid., 135–36.

50. The most significant, groundbreaking work in this direction has been undertaken by Elliot R. Wolfson in a number of his studies. See, e.g., Elliot R. Wolfson, "Circumcision, Vision of God, and Textual Interpretation: From Midrashic Trope

to Mystical Symbol," *History of Religions* 27 (1986–87): 189–215; Wolfson, *Through a Speculum That Shines*, 326–92.

51. Moses Cordovero, *Siddur Tefillah le-Moshe le-ha-Ramak* (Ashdod, Isr.: Torah Treasures Institute, 2004), 242a. Normally these terms refer to the "simple meaning" and the "esoteric meaning" of texts. In context here, however, the referent is not textual but ontological.

52. Jackson, *Paths toward a Clearing*, 142.

53. Marcel Mauss, "Body Techniques," in *Sociology and Psychology*, trans. Ben Brewster (French ed., 1935; reprint, London: Routledge and Kegan Paul, 1979). On the ethics of gesture, see Jean-Claude Schmitt, "The Ethics of Gesture," trans. Ian Patterson, in *Fragments for a History of the Human Body, Part Two* (New York: Zone, 1989), 128–47.

54. Mauss, "Body Techniques," 101.

55. Emphasis in the original.

56. Mauss, "Body Techniques," 102–3.

57. Ibid., 120.

58. Ibid., 104.

59. Ibid., 104–5. Emphasis in the original.

60. Roland Barthes has written similarly that food is "a system of communication, a body of images, a protocol of usages, situations, and behavior." See Barthes, "Toward a Psychosociology of Contemporary Food Consumption," trans. Elborg Forster, in *Food and Drink in History: Selections from the Annales, Economies, Societes, Civilisations Vol. 5*, ed. Robert Forster and Orest Ranum (1961; reprint, Baltimore: Johns Hopkins University Press, 1979). Mauss's approach is strongly in accord with that of Maurice Merleau-Ponty: "Consciousness is being-towards-the-thing through the intermediary of the body. A movement is learned when the body has understood it, that is, when it has incorporated it into its 'world,' and to move one's body is to aim at things through it; it is to allow oneself to respond to their call, which is made upon it independently of any representation." Merleau-Ponty, *Phenomenology of Perception*, 139.

61. See Daniel Boyarin, *Carnal Israel: Reading Sex in Talmudic Culture* (Berkeley: University of California Press, 1993), 5. Cf. Burton Visotzky and Gwynn Kessler, "Intersexuality and the Reading of Talmudic Culture," *Arachne* 1, no. 2 (1995): 238–52; Naomi Seidman, "Carnal Knowledge: Sex and the Body in Jewish Studies," *Jewish Social Studies: History, Culture, and Society* 1, no. 1 (1994): 129–34; Jay M. Harris, "The Circumcised Heart" (Review of Daniel Boyarin's *A Radical Jew: Paul and the Politics of Identity*), *Commentary* 99, no. 6 (1995): 57–60.

62. Jean Soler, "The Semiotics of Food in the Bible," trans. Elborg Forster, in *Food and Drink in History: Selections from the Annales, Economies, Societes, Civilisations*, ed. Robert Forster and Orest Ranum (1973; reprint, Baltimore: Johns Hopkins University Press, 1979), 126.

63. Miguel-Angel Motis Dolader, "Mediterranean Jewish Diet and Traditions in the Middle Ages," in *Food: A Culinary History from Antiquity to the Present*, ed. Jean Louis Flandrin, Massimo Montanari, and Albert Sonnenfeld (New York: Columbia University Press, 1999), 236. Dolader's subject is such a wide survey of geographical and temporal practice that it is hard to know if this does indeed apply to late-thirteenth-century Castile. See also Bynum, *Holy Feast and Holy Fast*, 191.

64. Hans Conrad Peyer, "The Origins of Public Hostelries in Europe," in *Food: A Culinary History from Antiquity to the Present*, ed. Jean Louis Flandrin, Massimo Montanari, and Albert Sonnenfeld (New York: Columbia University Press, 1999), 289–94.

65. One study has drawn attention to the increased role of female innkeepers during this period in Castile. Heath Dillard, *Daughters of the Reconquest: Women in Castilian Town Society, 1100–1300* (Cambridge: Cambridge University Press, 1984), 163.

66. David Kraemer, *The Gastronomic Jew* (forthcoming).

67. Antoni Riera-Melis, "Society, Food, and Feudalism," in *Food: A Culinary History from Antiquity to the Present*, ed. Jean Louis Flandrin, Massimo Montanari, and Albert Sonnenfeld (New York: Columbia University Press, 1999), 261.

68. Arthur Green, "Shekhinah, the Virgin Mary, and the Song of Songs," *AJS Review* 26, no. 1 (2002): 1–52; Peter Schäfer, *Mirror of His Beauty: Feminine Images of God from the Bible to the Early Kabbalah* (Princeton, N.J.: Princeton University Press, 2002); Yehuda Liebes, "Christian Influences in the Zohar," *Jerusalem Studies in Jewish Thought* 2, no. 1 (1982–83): 72; Yehuda Liebes, "Christian Influences on the Zohar," in *Studies in the Zohar*, trans. Stephanie Nakache (Albany: State University of New York Press, 1993), 159–61.

69. Cited in Louis J. Lekai, *The Cistercians: Ideals and Reality* (Kent, Ohio: Kent State University Press, 1977), 368.

70. Ibid.

71. Yom Tov Assis has gathered information largely from the responsa of Rabbi Solomon ibn Adret about the diet and some of the recipes of the Jews in Aragon. Assis, *The Golden Age of Aragonese Jewry: Community and Society in the Crown of Aragon, 1213–1327* (Oxford: Littman Library of Jewish Civilization, 1997), 282–83.

72. It is noteworthy that the Last Supper similarly focuses more on symbolic actions than actual food eaten. See, e.g., John 13:1–30.

73. Tishby, *Wisdom of the Zohar*, 3.

Chapter 1

1. Andrea Beth Lieber, "God Incorporated: Feasting on the Divine Presence in Ancient Judaism" (Ph.D. diss., New York: Columbia University, 1998), 60.

2. There is, in fact, a large quail migration across the Sinai Peninsula that can give a naturalistic account for this happening: "These migratory birds of the pheasant family, scientifically known as *Coturnix coturnix*, are to this day caught in large numbers in northern Sinai and Egypt. They migrate in vast flocks from Central Europe to Africa in the autumn and return in the spring. They are small in size and make the long and tiring journey in stages. Flying low and landing exhausted, they are easily captured with nets or by hand." Nahum M. Sarna, *Exodus = [Shemot]: The Traditional Hebrew Text with the New JPS Translation/Commentary by Nahum M. Sarna* (Philadelphia: Jewish Publication Society, 1991), 88.

3. Here, too, scholars have offered a natural explanation. Brevard Childs has written, "The manna has been identified with a natural substance formed in the wilderness of northern Arabia. There forms from the sap of the tamarisk tree [*Tamarix manifera*] a species of yellowish-white flake or ball, which results from the activity of a type of plant lice (*Trabutina mannipara* and *Najococcus serpentinus*). The insect punc-

tures the fruit of the tree and excretes a substance from this juice. During the warmth of the day, it [the substance] melts, but it congeals when cold. It has a sweet taste. These pellets or cakes are gathered by the natives in the early morning and, when cooked, provide a sort of bread. The food decays quickly and attracts ants. The annual crop in the Sinai Peninsula is exceedingly small and some years fails completely. If the identification is correct, its ephemeral nature and its undependableness—appearing irregularly and only for several hours each day—would have stamped it as supernatural, originating in heaven." Brevard S. Childs, *The Book of Exodus: A Critical, Theological Commentary* (Philadelphia: Westminster, 1976), 282, cited in Jacob Milgrom, *The JPS Torah Commentary: Numbers* (Philadelphia: Jewish Publication Society, 1990), 84. In scripture, of course, the event is wholly supernatural and miraculous, evoking wonder.

4. Milgrom, *JPS Torah Commentary: Numbers*, 84. Cf. *Sifra Num* 88; *Sifrei Zuta* 195.

5. Levine, *Numbers,* 322. The word *nefesh* has multiple meanings, including throat, neck, desire, life, and person, only rarely bearing the notion of soul. It must be conceded that while Levine's interpretation is in line with my overall thesis, "throat " would appear to be the most appropriate translation in this instance. For a full discussion of the term *nefesh,* see Hans Walter Wolff, *Anthropology of the Old Testament,* trans. Margaret Kohl (Philadelphia: Fortress, 1974), 10–25.

6. Ellen F. Davis, *Swallowing the Scroll: Textuality and the Dynamics of Discourse in Ezekiel's Prophecy* (Worcester, UK: Sheffield Academic, 1989), 53.

7. Ibid., 52–53.

8. See, e.g., Genesis 14:18–20; 26:26–31; 29:22, 27–28; 31:44–46, 51–54; Joshua 9:3–15; Judges 9:26–28; 2 Samuel 3:20; 9:7, 10–11; Proverbs 15:17; 17:1.

9. Roland de Vaux, *Ancient Israel: Its Life and Institutions* (Grand Rapids, Mich.: W. B. Eerdmans, 1997), iv.

10. Lieber, "God Incorporated," 77.

11. This banquet scene seems to draw on the mytho-poetical theme of similar banquet scenarios in the contemporary Ugaritic texts. See T. C. Vriezen, "The Exegesis of Exodus 24:9–11," in *The Witness of Tradition* (Leiden, Neth.: Brill, 1972), 100–133; J. B. Lloyd, "The Banquet Theme in Ugaritic Narrative," *Ugarit-Forschungen* 4 (1972): 187–88; Kathryn L. Roberts, "God, Prophet, and King: Eating and Drinking on the Mountain in First Kings 18:41," *Catholic Biblical Quarterly* 62, no. 4 (2000): 639–40. Even the number 70 in Exodus 24:9 corresponds to the number of deities that join Baal for his banquet. These similarities do not necessitate direct borrowing but rather familiarity and use of similar motifs. Moreover, Ernest Nicholson contends that the similarities to Ugaritic banquets with the deities are superficial. In the Ugaritic literary traditions, the "banquets" held by El and Baal are for other gods to honor one another or to celebrate the erection of a temple, central elements that are missing here. Ernest W. Nicholson, "The Origin of the Tradition in Exodus 24:9–11," *Vetus Testamentum* 26, no. 2 (1976): 158.

12. Roberts, "God, Prophet, and King."

13. Ibid., 641.

14. Exodus 24:1–11 text has been subject to considerable analysis, and scholarship has generally broken it down into its apparent component parts: verses 1–2 and

9–11 are deemed to be one pericope, and verses 3–8 another. This reading mitigates the covenantal quality of the episode by separating the theophany and "eating and drinking" from the sacrificial offerings. Building on this assumption, Nicholson claims that "there is evidence that the expression 'to eat and drink,' or 'to eat bread,' or simply 'to eat' is sometimes used in the Old Testament to connote 'to live a prosperous life,' 'to enjoy life' or, again simply, 'to live.' . . . [For example,] in the days of Solomon 'the people of Judah and Israel were countless as the sands of the sea; they ate and drank, and enjoyed life' (1 Kings 4:20). See also Jeremiah 22:15; Ecclesiastes 5:16: *kol yamav ba-hoshekh yokhel* meaning 'all his days he shall live or spend in darkness.'" Nicholson, "Origin of the Tradition," 149.

15. Isaiah 27:1; see also 2 Baruch 29:4; 4 Ezra 6:52. See Erwin R. Goodenough, *Jewish Symbols in the Greco-Roman Period* (New York: Pantheon Books, 1953–68), re: fish 5:35–41.

16. Milgrom, *JPS Torah Commentary: Numbers*, 92.

17. Cf. Psalms 8:4–5; 105:14; Jeremiah 8:14, 9:15, 23:15.

18. Leviticus 7:11–18.

19. Gary A. Anderson, "Sacrifice and Sacrificial Offerings," in *Anchor Bible Dictionary*, ed. David Noel Freedman (New York: Doubleday, 1992), 879.

20. See, e.g., Deuteronomy 27:7; Joshua 8:31; 22:23–24.

21. Gary A. Anderson, *A Time to Mourn, A Time to Dance: The Expression of Grief and Joy in Israelite Religion* (University Park: Pennsylvania State University Press, 1991), 20.

22. Sarna, *Exodus*, 163; Regarding Rashi's explanation, cf. *Bereshit Raba* 79:6; 91:5. Cf. also Baruch A. Levine, *The JPS Torah Commentary: Leviticus* (Philadelphia: Jewish Publication Society, 1989), 165.

23. Jacob Milgrom, *The Anchor Bible: Leviticus 23–27, A New Translation with Introduction and Commentary* (New York: Doubleday, 2001), 2091.

24. Levine, *JPS Torah Commentary: Leviticus*, 165.

25. It was an ancient practice to display bread before a deity. In Egypt, there were offerings on an outer altar, but fresh bread was brought into the sanctuary and placed on mats before the god's table, where they were burned and sprinkled with wine. In the Hittite religion, one gave a bread offering on the table before death. Milgrom, *Anchor Bible: Leviticus 23–27*, 2091.

26. Gary A. Anderson, *Sacrifices and Offerings in Ancient Israel: Studies in Their Social and Political Importance* (Atlanta: Scholars, 1987), 14–16.

27. Levine, *JPS Torah Commentary: Leviticus*, 243. Much of the following draws upon Levine's analysis.

28. Genesis 6:19–25 describes two of every kind of animal being brought in without distinctions of pure and impure.

29. Mary Douglas, *Purity and Danger: An Analysis of Concepts of Pollution and Taboo* (1969; reprint, London: Routledge and Kegan Paul, 1978).

30. Ibid., 55.

31. Cf. Jean Soler, "The Semiotics of Food in the Bible," trans. Elborg Forster, in *Food and Culture: A Reader* (New York: Routledge, 1997), 55–66.

32. Robert Alter, "A New Theory of *Kashrut*," *Commentary* 68 (August 1979): 51.

33. Milgrom, *JPS Torah Commentary: Numbers*, 740.

34. Jeffrey H. Tigay, *The JPS Torah Commentary: Deuteronomy* (Philadelphia: Jewish Publication Society, 1996), 137ff.

35. Ibid., 138.

36. For a full critique of Milgrom's position, see David P. Wright, "Observations on the Ethical Foundations of the Biblical Dietary Law: A Response to Jacob Milgrom," in *Religion and Law: Biblical-Judaic and Islamic Perspectives*, ed. E. R. Firmage et al. (Winona Lake, Ind.: Eisenbrauns, 1990), 193–98.

37. Ibid., 197.

38. Levine, *JPS Torah Commentary: Leviticus*, 244.

39. Only the pre-Islamic Arabs had a similar sanction. Milgrom, *JPS Torah Commentary: Numbers*, 704.

40. Ibid. See also Leviticus 3:17; 7:26–27; 19:26; Deuteronomy 12:15–16, 20–28; 15:19–23; 1 Samuel 14:32–35; Ezekiel 33:25.

41. Milgrom, *JPS Torah Commentary: Numbers*, 740.

42. For a full discussion of profane slaughter and the priestly code, see Baruch J. Schwartz, "'Profane' Slaughter and the Integrity of the Priestly Code," *Hebrew Union College Annual* 67 (1996): 15–42.

43. See Levine, *JPS Torah Commentary: Leviticus*, 112–13; and John E. Hartley, *Leviticus* (Dallas: Word Biblical Commentary, 1992), 269–71. In any event, most families could not afford to eat of their livestock beyond the occasions of festivals because of the cost. Thus the imagined hardship may be overstated. Schwartz, "'Profane' Slaughter," 41.

44. Schwartz, "'Profane' Slaughter," 19.

45. Ibid., 24.

46. Ibid., 25.

47. Ibid., 39–40.

48. Milgrom, *JPS Torah Commentary: Numbers*, 712.

49. Levine, *JPS Torah Commentary: Leviticus*, 115.

50. Baruch J. Schwartz, "The Prohibitions Concerning the 'Eating' of Blood in Leviticus 17," in *Priesthood and Cult in Ancient Israel*, ed. Gary A. Anderson and Saul M. Olyan (Sheffield, UK: JSOT, 1991), 49. See p. 49 n. 5, where Schwartz adduces a range of medieval and modern interpreters who do read the passage as providing a metaphysical truth.

51. Ibid., 61–62.

52. Ibid., 64–65.

53. These verses provide justification for meat and dairy dishes and for the three different kinds of prohibitions associated with the cooking of meat and milk together (*b. Hullin* 113a-116a); see 115b for the source of the three different laws derived (23).

54. Moses Maimonides, *The Guide of the Perplexed*, Part 3, trans. Shlomo Pines (Chicago: University of Chicago Press, 1963), chap. 48, 599.

55. Modern scholars have noted that there are animal mother-child nursing images in ancient Near Eastern iconography and that the mythic meaning of such an image — that slaying calf and mother on the same day would disrupt the harmony of the cosmos — might have been internalized by the Israelites. Because the iconography does not portray particular deities, it would not have been immediately dis-

turbing to the Israelite mindset and could therefore have drawn sympathetic viewing. Milgrom, *JPS Torah Commentary: Numbers*, 740. Milgrom asserts that this was a common cultic practice, and Tigay affirms this position. Milgrom, *JPS Torah Commentary: Numbers*, 737; Tigay, *JPS Torah Commentary: Deuteronomy*, 138. Some scholars had offered a reading of a Ugaritic tablet recounting the birth of Shahar and Shalim, the children of El, that has words that could refer to seething a kid in milk; furthermore, the erotic themes suggest a fertility cult. Read in light of the biblical injunction, it seemed that the smoking gun had been found, the pagan practice that elicited the biblical response. Subsequent scholarship has argued persuasively, however, that this reading is erroneous and that the link is unfounded. Menahem Haran, "Seething a Kid in Its Mother's Milk," *Journal of Jewish Studies* 30 (1979): 25.

56. Milgrom, *JPS Torah Commentary: Numbers*, 742.

57. Haran, "Seething a Kid," 31.

58. Ibid., 29.

59. Earlier interpreters who explained along the same lines the prohibition of seething the kid in its mother's milk include Philo (*De Virtutibus*, 143–44), Abraham ibn Ezra (eleventh-century philosopher, exegete, grammarian, and poet), and Rashbam (Rabbi Shmuel ben Meir, twelfth-century biblical exegete).

60. Tigay, *JPS Torah Commentary: Deuteronomy*, 140.

61. Haran, "Seething a Kid," 35.

62. Baruch Bokser, *The Origins of the Seder: The Passover Rite and Early Rabbinic Judaism* (Berkeley: University of California Press, 1984), 27.

63. See Joshua 5:10–11; 2 Kings 23:21–24; Ezekiel 45:21; Ezra 6:19–22; 2 Chronicles 30:1–27, 35:1–19.

64. See Menahem Haran, "The Passover Sacrifice," *Vetus Testamentum Supplements* 23 (1972): 87–88.

65. Joseph Tabory, "Towards a History of the Paschal Meal," in *Passover and Easter: Origin and History to Modern Times*, ed. Paul F. Bradshaw and Lawrence A. Hoffman (Notre Dame, Ind.: Notre Dame University Press, 1999), 62–80.

66. Similarly, Tobit declares that after deportation to Assyria, "everyone of my kindred and nation ate gentile food; but I myself scrupulously avoided doing so" (Tobit 1:10). Judith, too, assiduously avoids unfit food, professing, "I will not eat any of it in case I should be breaking our law" (Judith 12:2). Cf. Judith 10:5. Most dramatically, the second and fourth books of Maccabees have stories of fortitude under the pressure of torture, describing a mother and seven sons who all undergo ghastly torture rather than eat of "unlawful swine's flesh," as well as others who sought martyrdom to demonstrate fear of God rather than preserving their lives. See chapters 6–7. The fourth book of Maccabees, written in the first half of the first century CE, concentrates on the efforts of Antiochus Epiphanes IV to force Jews "to eat unclean meats and thus abjure the Jewish religion" (4 Maccabees 4:26). There are a full thirteen chapters devoted to gruesome descriptions of the torture of Eleazar and the mother and her seven sons. See chapters 5–18. Lastly, The praise of Eleazar uses dietary laws as representative of the entire law: "O priest, worthy of the priesthood, you neither defiled your sacred teeth nor profaned your stomach, which had room only for reverence and purity, by eating defiling foods. O man in harmony with the law and philosopher of divine life!" (4 Maccabees 7:6–7). Cf. 1 Maccabees 1:62–63; 2 Maccabees 5:27.

67. Morton Smith, "The Dead Sea Sect in Relation to Ancient Judaism," *New Testament Studies* 7 (July 1961): 352. That said, for the purposes of my study it is the representation of eating in the period's literary documents that will be most useful, rather than the limited historical information that might be reaped from other kinds of historical sources. What can be said of the sectarians is that their sectarian behaviors were "acts of *protest*, of *separation* from other Jews, whose inadequate observance of the commandments of the Torah made communal life impossible." Albert I. Baumgarten, "Finding Oneself in a Sectarian Context: A Sectarian's Food and Its Implications," in *Self, Soul and Body in Religious Experience*, ed. A. I. Baumgarten, J. Assmann, and G. G. Stroumsa (Leiden, Neth.: Brill, 1998), 130.

68. Dennis E. Smith, *From Symposium to Eucharist: The Banquet in the Early Christian World* (Minneapolis, Minn.: Fortress, 2003), 1–3.

69. Ibid., 6.

70. Ibid., 8–13. As noted at the outset to this chapter, I will be limiting my discussion to the textual streams that had an impact on the development of the kabbalistic worldview. Excluding Qumran and New Testament approaches to food practices, the presentation is both limited and de-contextualized.

71. Anthony J. Saldarini, *Pharisees, Scribes and Sadducees in Palestinian Society: A Sociological Approach* (Wilmington, Del.: M. Glazier, 1988), 215.

72. See Ibid., 217.

73. Cf. *t. Demai* 2:2–3:9.

74. Baumgarten, "Finding Oneself in a Sectarian Context," 135.

75. Jacob Neusner, *The Rabbinic Traditions about the Pharisees Before 70* (Leiden, Neth.: Brill, 1971), 3:304.

76. Jacob Neusner, *From Politics to Piety: The Emergence of Pharisaic Judaism* (New York: Ktav, 1979), 83.

77. Mark 7:4. See also Luke 11:38.

78. Baumgarten, "Finding Oneself in a Sectarian Context," 136.

79. E. P. Sanders, *Jewish Law from Jesus to the Mishnah: Five Studies* (Philadelphia: Trinity, 1990), 245–54.

80. Hannah K. Harrington, "Did the Pharisees Eat Ordinary Food in a State of Ritual Purity?" *Journal for the Study of Judaism in the Persian, Hellenistic and Roman Period* 26 (April 1995): 54; Gedalyahu Alon, *Jews, Judaism, and the Classical World: Studies in Jewish History in the Times of the Second Temple and Talmud*, trans. Israel Abrahams (Jerusalem: Magnes, 1977), 219.

81. The rabbis developed a storehouse of blessings, responses to everything from sighting a rainbow to emerging from a latrine. The most well known, perhaps, are those recited before and after eating, themselves a varied group. These blessings categorize various kinds of foods according to the way in which they grow (from the ground, on a tree), or if they are one of the "seven fruits of the Land of Israel," or if they are uttered over bread. Considerations of space have prevented me from delving into this area of rabbinic response to food.

82. These teachings can be found first in Pseudo-Philo, *Liber Antiquitatum Biblicarum*, ed. Johanan Levy, Publication in Medieval Studies (Notre Dame, Ind.: University of Notre Dame, 1949), 20:8, and in Josephus, Jewish Antiquities Books

1–4, trans. St. J. Thackeray, Loeb Classical Library (Cambridge, Mass.: Harvard University Press, 1991), 3, 26.

83. *Mekhilta* II Lauterbach, p. 128 on Exodus 16:35, cited in Geza Vermes, "'He Is the Bread': Targum Neofiti Exodus 16:15," in *Post-Biblical Jewish Studies* (Leiden, Neth.: Brill, 1975), 142. Cf. *t. Sotah* 11:10.

84. A comprehensive analysis of this trope can be found in Ira Chernus, "'Nourished by the Splendor of the *Shekhinah*': A Mystical Motif in Rabbinic Midrash," in *Mysticism in Rabbinic Judaism* (Berlin: Walter de Gruyter, 1982), 74–87, and much of the present section relies on Chernus's presentation.

85. Jacob Z. Lauterbach, trans., *Mekilta de-Rabbi Ishmael* (Philadelphia: Jewish Publication Society, 1949), 1: 171. See also Qumran CDC 6:4 "The well is the Law" as cited in Vermes, "He Is the Bread."

86. Harry Wolfson used this term to signify the Kalam understanding of the Koran as a direct manifestation of God and his will. Harry Wolfson, *Philosophy of the Kalam* (Cambridge, Mass.: Harvard University Press, 1976); 263–303.

87. Vermes, "He Is the Bread," 143; Gershom Scholem, *Major Trends in Jewish Mysticism* (New York: Schocken, 1946), 7–8. For examples of current trends of bringing rabbinic myth to the foreground, see Michael Fishbane, "'The Holy One Sits and Roars': Mythopoesis and Midrashic Imagination," in *The Exegetical Imagination: On Jewish Thought and Theology* (Cambridge, Mass.: Harvard University Press, 1998), 22–40; Yehuda Liebes, "*De Natura Dei:* On the Development of Jewish Myth (Hebrew)," in *Massu'ot: Studies in Kabbalistic Literature and Jewish Philosophy*, ed. Michal Oron and Amos Goldreich (Jerusalem: Bialik Institute, 1994), 243–97; Yehuda Liebes, "'*De Natura Dei*': On the Development of the Jewish Myth," in *Studies in Jewish Myth and Jewish Messianism*, trans. Batya Stein (Albany: State University of New York Press, 1993), 119–48.

88. *Bereshit Raba* 70:5. Translation based on H. Freedman, *Midrash Rabah: Genesis,* Midrash Rabah (London: Soncino, 1961). The sources in *Bereshit Raba* are Palestinian amoraim of the latter half of the fourth century CE, making it one of the earlier aggadic Midrashim. See also *Shemot Raba* 25:8. Cf. the midrashic teaching on 1 Chronicles 4:18 in *b. Megillah* 13a. It explains the biblical name Yered—*yrd* means "descend"—by identifying him as Moses, "because manna descended (*yrd*) in his days."

89. *Shemot Raba* 47:5. S. M. Lehrman, trans., *Midrash Rabah: Exodus,* Midrash Rabah (London: Soncino, 1939), 3: 540–41 (with some minor variations). *Shemot Rabah* is a relatively late midrash, drawing widely on the Babylonian Talmud. It is generally believed to be redacted no earlier than the eighth century CE.

90. *Shemot Rabah* 47:7. Translation from Lehrman, *Midrash Rabah: Exodus,* 47:7, 542–43.

91. Cf. *Vayikra Rabah* 30:1; *Bamidbar Rabah* 8:9; 13:15; *Kohelet Rabah* 7:16; 10:19; *Midrash Tanḥuma Aḥarei Mot* 10; *Midrash Mishle* 31; *Midrash Tehillim* 34; *Tanna de-vei Eliyahu Zuta* 13; *Pesikta de-Rav Kahana* 11:9, 27:1; *Sifre Ekev* 9.

92. *b. Berakhot* 17a.

93. For suggestions that this "eating" has a sexual valence, see Daniel Boyarin, *Carnal Israel: Reading Sex in Talmudic Culture* (Berkeley: University of California

Press, 1993), 70–75, 116–17, 123; Elliot R. Wolfson, *Through a Speculum That Shines: Visionary Experience and Imagination in Medieval Jewish Mysticism* (Princeton, N.J.: Princeton University Press, 1994), 42–43. Regarding the integrative role of eating in rabbinic literature, see, e.g., *b. Bava Batra* 12b, where it says that before eating, one has two hearts; after eating, a person has one heart.

94. Peter Schäfer, ed., *Synopse Zur Hekhalot-Literatur* (Tübingen, Ger.: J. C. B. Mohr, 1981), #160. On visionary mysticism in the *heikhalot* literature, see Rachel Elior, "The Concept of God in Hekhalot Mysticism," in *Binah: Studies in Jewish Thought,* ed. Joseph Dan and trans. Dena Ordan (New York: Praeger, 1989), 97–129; Wolfson, *Through a Speculum That Shines,* 74–124.

95. *Avot de-Rabbi Natan* version A, chap. 1, p. 3a.

96. *Bereshit Raba* 2.2, p. 15.

97. *Pesikta Rabati* 16.2, 80a; *Bemidbar Rabah* 21:16. Consider also the following text from *Pesikta Rabati:* "The angels do not eat or drink or taste death. Why? Because they look upon the image of My glory and they are nourished by the splendor of the *Shekhinah.* For even though I have said that they do not see My glory, as Rabbi Isaac said, they see as though through a veil. 'In the light of a king's face there is life.' 'You alone are God . . . and You sustain all of them'" (*Pesikta Rabati* 48.3, 194a).

98. Schäfer, *Synopse,* #335, 142–43. Chernus suggests Rav would have agreed with this last text in that the vision was only possible after death. Ira Chernus, *Mysticism in Rabbinic Judaism: Studies in the History of Midrash* (Berlin: Walter de Gruyter, 1982), 76. Chernus's own caution is belied, however, by Rav's own proof text, Exodus 24:11. That is, if Moses, Aaron, Nadav, Avihu, and the seventy elders all survived this fearsome event, so might other mortals. The historicity of the *heikhalot* material is virtually impossible to determine: the scholarship remains heavily divided over the dating and provenance of this material, with suggestions ranging as late as the twelfth century, in the hands of the German Pietists who redacted this material. See Peter Schäfer, "Tradition and Redaction in Hekhalot Literature," *Journal for the Study of Judaism in the Persian, Hellenistic and Roman Period* 14, no. 2 (1983): 172–81.

99. Vermes, "He Is the Bread," 143.

100. Chernus, "Nourished by the Splendor," 79 n. 34.

101. *Bemidbar Raba* 2.25; *Pesikta de-Rav Kahana* 26.9, p. 396; *Vayikra Raba* 20:10; *Midrash Tanḥuma Aharei* 6; *Midrash Tanḥuma (Buber) Aḥarei* 7.

102. Chernus, "Nourished by the Splendor," 84.

103. The primary sources for the discussion are as follows: *t. Berakhot,* 4:8–9; 5; *y. Berakhot* 10d; *b. Berakhot* 43a (top); paschal meal in *m. Pesaḥim* 10:1–9; *t. Pesaḥim* 10:1–14.

104. Joseph Tabory, "Towards a History of the Paschal Meal," in *Passover and Easter: Origin and History to Modern Times,* ed. Paul F. Bradshaw and Lawrence A. Hoffman (Notre Dame, Ind.: University of Notre Dame Press, 1999), 69.

105. Siegfried Stein was the first to write about this similarity. Siegfried Stein, "The Influence of Symposia Literature on the Literary Form of the Pesah Haggadah," *Journal of Jewish Studies* 8, nos. 1–2 (1957): 13–44; Gordon J. Bahr, "The Seder of Passover and the Eucharistic Words," in *Essays in Greco-Roman and Related Talmudic Literature,* ed. Henry A. Fischel (New York: KTAV, 1977), 473–94. Baruch Bokser

argues against viewing the seder as a cultural borrowing from Roman culture, claiming that the seder was developed primarily to compensate for the loss of the lamb. Bokser, *Origins of the Seder,* 52–53. Joseph Tabory, however, has conclusively demonstrated the derivation of seder components from symposia. Tabory, "Towards a History." Dennis Smith has demonstrated some of the ways in which the Gospel of Luke consciously draws upon symposium motifs in his literary style. Dennis E. Smith, "Table Fellowship as a Literary Motif in the Gospel of Luke," *Journal of Biblical Literature* 106 (December 1987): 613–38.

106. Walter Burkert, "Oriental Symposia: Contrasts and Parallels," in *Dining in a Classical Context,* ed. William J. Slater (Ann Arbor: University of Michigan Press, 1991), 7.

107. Blake Leyerle, "Meal Customs in the Greco-Roman World," in *Passover and Easter: Origin and History to Modern Times,* ed. Paul F. Bradshaw and Lawrence A. Hoffman (Notre Dame, Ind.: University of Notre Dame Press, 1999), 29–61.

108. Tabory, "Towards a History," 72–73.

109. Leyerle, "Meal Customs in the Greco-Roman World," 37.

110. Bahr, "Seder of Passover," 479.

111. Ibid., 481.

112. *y. Berakhot* 10d; *m. Berakhot* 6:6.

113. *t. Berakhot* 5:5, 12. Bahr, "Seder of Passover," 482. See also Luke 22:24–27, where Jesus rebukes his disciples for arguing over their placement at the table.

114. *m. Pesahim* 10:4–5.

115. Tabory, "Towards a History," 74.

116. Gillian Feeley-Harnik, *The Lord's Table: The Meaning of Food in Early Judaism and Christianity* (Washington, D.C.: Smithsonian Institute, 1981), 11.

117. Tabory, "Towards a History," 62. Much of the following presentation regarding the ancient Passover ceremony is derived from Tabory's various studies.

118. *m. Pesahim* 10:5. Baruch Bokser, "Was the Last Supper a Passover Seder?" *Bible Review* 3, no. 2 (1987): 30.

119. Baruch Bokser, "Ritualizing the Seder," *Journal of the American Academy of Religion* 56, no. 3 (1988): 447.

120. Ibid., 448.

121. Ibid.

122. Ibid.

123. A fine introduction to the details of the contemporary practice of kashrut is Binyamin Forst, *The Laws of Kashrus: A Comprehensive Exposition of Their Underlying Concepts and Applications* (New York: Mesorah, 1994).

124. *b. Hullin* 113a–116b.

125. *b. Hullin* 108a; *b. Pesahim* 44b. Although anomalous, the Jewish practice of separating meat and milk is not unique. See Louis Evan Grivetti, "Dietary Separation of Meat and Milk: A Cultural-Geographical Inquiry," *Ecology of Food and Nutrition* 9 (1980): 203–17. My thanks to David Kraemer, who brought this source to my attention.

126. *b. Shabbat* 40b. A prominent modern authority has ruled that 113 degrees Fahrenheit marks the dividing line. See Forst, *Laws of Kashrus,* 111 n. 14.

127. *b. Avodah Zarah* 67a.

128. *b. Gittin* 54b.

129. *b. Ḥullin* 98a.

130. "Soaking is like cooking." (*Khavush harei ke-mevushal*). *b. Ḥullin* 97b, 111b; *Pesaḥim* 76a.

131. *b. Ḥullin* 105a; translation from I Epstein, ed., *Tractate Ḥullin*, trans. Maurice Simon, *Hebrew-English Edition of the Babylonian Talmud* (London: Soncino, 1963), 582.

132. In northern Europe, a tradition evolved that one could wait after a meat meal as little as an hour, or three hours according to some, before sitting down to a dairy meal. In Spain, North Africa, and the Near East, the practice consolidated at six hours, following the influential opinion of Maimonides in the twelfth century. The dispute centers on the reason for waiting between the meals: Is it a formalistic concern that one cannot eat dairy and meat at the same meal, so that even a short period can mark the necessary distinction; or, as Maimonides says, is the central concern that bits of meat may remain in one's teeth, and one must wait a longer period until such remains are gone, a period Maimonides fixed at six hours?

133. In his forthcoming study on the history of kashrut, *The Gastronomic Jew,* David Kraemer argues that the designation of pots for one specific use (meat or dairy) is a late development, occurring in early-modern Eastern Europe. I am grateful to him for sharing portions of his unpublished manuscript with me.

134. *b. Avodah Zarah* 55bff.

135. *m. Avoah Zarah* 2:6.

136. *b. Avodah Zarah* 29b; *b. Ḥullin* 116b.

137. *m. Avodah Zarah* 2:3. In this situation, one may not derive benefit from such wine.

138. *m. Avodah Zarah* 2:6.

139. *b. Avodah Zarah* 38a.

140. *b. Avodah Zarah* 36b, 64b.

141. Moses Maimonides, *Mishnah Torah*, ed. and trans. Philip Birnbaum (New York: Hebrew Publishing, 1967); *Hilkhot De'ot* 3:2, 50, with minor modifications.

142. Maimonides, *Guide of the Perplexed*, 598–99.

143. This medical argumentation is anticipated by Abraham ibn Ezra in his Torah commentary on Leviticus 19:23. The sixteenth-century commentator Abravanel argues strenuously against this type of explanation, contending that Maimonides has turned the Torah into a medical text. *Vayikra* 11.

144. Moses Maimonides, *Hanhagat ha-Beri'ut* (Jerusalem: n.p., 1957): 84–85, both cited in Moses Maimonides, "Moses Maimonides' Two Treatises on the Regimen of Health," ed. A. Bar-Sela, H. E. Hoff, and E. Faris, in *Transactions of the American Philosophical Society*, n.s., 54 (1964): part 4, 31.

145. Moses Maimonides, *Pirke Moshe Bi-Refu'ah*, trans. Natan ha-Meati, ed. Zisman Montner (Jerusalem: Mosad ha-Rav Kuk, 1959), 230, treatise xx, paragraph 19; Fred Rosner and Suessman Munter, eds. and trans., *The Medical Aphorisms of Moses Maimonides* (New York: Yeshiva University Press, 1970–71), ii, treatise xx.

146. Jacob Levinger, "Maimonides' *Guide of the Perplexed* on Forbidden Food in the Light of His Own Medical Opinion," in *Perspectives on Maimonides: Philosophical and Historical Studies,* ed. Joel L. Kraemer (London: Littman Library of Jewish Civilization, 1996), 199–201.

147. Ibid., 206.

148. Ibid.

149. Israel M. Ta-Shma, *The Revealed in the Concealed: The Halakhic Residue in the Zohar* (Hebrew) (Israel: Hakibbutz Hameuchad, 2001).

Chapter 2

1. Gershom Scholem, *Major Trends in Jewish Mysticism* (New York: Schocken, 1946), 4.

2. For instances that extend the metaphor, see Dov Mandelbaum, ed., *Pesikta de-Rav Kahana, Aser te'aser,* (New York: Jewish Theological Seminary, 1961), I:167; *Midrash Tanḥuma* (Warsaw) *Re'eh* 17; *Midrash Tanḥuma* (Buber) *Re'eh* 12; Maimonides, *Guide of the Perplexed,* 1: 46. The twelfth-century Tosafists also adopted an interpretive approach that is more literally somatic: "Before a person prays that the Torah should enter his body, he should pray that delicacies do not enter his body." Tosafot, *b. Ketubot* 104a, s.v. *lo neheneiti.* Moreover, one statement in the Talmud treats the Torah residing in one's body as serving an apotropaic function. *b. Sanhedrin* 106b.

3. This term was aptly coined by Daniel C. Matt in "Introduction," in *Zohar: The Book of Enlightenment* (Ramsey, N.J.: Paulist, 1983), 30.

4. See, e.g., *Zohar* 1:88b (*Sitrei Torah*), which refers to the "delight of Torah in his inmost parts (*ḥamidu de'oraita be-mei'oi*)." In this passage describing the resurrection of the dead, the *Zohar* assures the reader that people will regain the Torah that they had in their original incarnation and that, once again, it will reside within their bodies.

5. Elliot R. Wolfson, "Forms of Visionary Ascent as Ecstatic Experience in the Zoharic Literature," in *Gershom Scholem's Major Trends in Jewish Mysticism: 50 Years Later,* ed. Joseph Dan and Peter Schaefer (Tübingen, Ger.: J. C. B. Mohr, 1993), 222–23.

6. Isaiah Tishby, *The Wisdom of the Zohar,* trans. David Goldstein (Oxford: Oxford University Press, 1989), 955.

7. The *ke-zayit,* an olive's volume, is a standard measure in the Talmud and often serves as the volume that a person must consume in order to fulfill halakhic obligations, such as the eating of unleavened bread or the amount of bread required to generate the requirement for grace after a meal.

8. The theme of psychosomatic unity is one that has been used both in the philosophical literature regarding the problems of mind/body and self/other as well as in recent scholarship treating the history of the body. See, e.g., Mark Johnson, *The Body in the Mind: The Bodily Basis of Meaning, Imagination, and Reason* (Chicago: University of Chicago Press, 1987); Caroline Walker Bynum, *The Resurrection of the Body in Western Christianity, 200–1336* (New York: Columbia University Press, 1995); Michel Feher, "Introduction," in *Fragments for a History of the Body,* ed. Michel Feher (New York: Zone, 1989), 14–15. Bynum writes that the medieval preachers assumed a person to be a psychosomatic unity and so understood unusual body events to be expressions of the soul and that the body was a means of access to the Divine. See Caroline Walker Bynum, "The Female Body and Religious Practice in the Later Middle Ages," in *Fragments for a History of the Human Body,* ed. Michel Feher (New York: Zone, 1989), 196.

9. Scholem refers to this verse as one that best typifies the synesthetic experience of the mystic. Scholem, *Major Trends in Jewish Mysticism*, 4. Scholem is not referring to the actual act of eating in this instance.

10. Caroline Walker Bynum, *Holy Feast and Holy Fast: The Religious Significance of Food to Medieval Women* (Berkeley: University of California Press, 1987), 6, 246–56. Bynum suggests similarly that, because the flesh was associated with the feminine, somatic expressions characterize women's spirituality. Bynum, "The Female Body and Religious Practice," 196. Although this may explain some of the body-soul phenomena in the *Zohar,* what I am calling "psychosomatic experiences" are often not explicitly addressing the body-soul polarity.

11. Moshe Cordovero suggests that "the blessing of the holy name" refers to the reciting of the blessing "Who extracts bread from the earth" and that this blessing had the effect of drawing the aroma of the Garden of Eden into the manna. Moses Cordovero, *Or Yakar* (Jerusalem: Achuzat Israel, 1976), 8: 77–78.

12. In the *Zohar,* the Garden is generally a cognomen for the *Shekhinah;* thus this passage indicates that the manna has come from this particular gradation within the Godhead.

13. *b. Yoma* 75a. Caroline Walker Bynum has noted that the medieval feast was more an aesthetic and social event than a gastronomic one, being visually astounding in terms of illusions devised. Ordinary food was often an illusion, so it was not surprising that bread, meaning the Eucharist, should adopt various tastes. See Bynum, *Holy Feast and Holy Fast,* 60. It could be argued that the *Zohar's* direct adoption of an existing rabbinic source does not reflect personal experience. However, the pneumatic engagement of the text by the mystical fraternity militates against such reserve. Could it be that the Jews had similar feasts with visual and sensual surprises that made the rabbinic statement about the multiflavored manna more readily acceptable? This possibility must remain in the realm of conjecture.

14. See *Tanhuma* (Warsaw) *Beshalah* 20.

15. Cf. *Zohar* 3:287b, in which the kabbalist raises his hands during prayer and thus receives illumination. In that instance, the kabbalist induces the descent of the divine efflux as preparation for the revelation of esoterica.

16. A similar phenomenon of embodied mysticism occurs in relation to circumcision in which the physical opening obtained through the excision of the foreskin marks an opening within the heart's ability to gain mystical vision. See Elliot R. Wolfson, "Circumcision, Vision of God, and Textual Interpretation: From Midrashic Trope to Mystical Symbol," *History of Religions* 27 (1986–87): 27, 189–215.

17. In the writings of Bahya ben Asher we find considerable attention given to the idea that food will prepare one for supernal wisdom. See also *Zohar* 3:296a: "Knowledge is established in one's inward parts"; cf. *Zohar* 1:13a, 185a.

18. One talmudic statement says that different people had to travel different distances to gather the manna, depending on their spiritual status. *b. Yoma* 75a.

19. Cf. Nehemiah 9:26.

20. *Sefer ha-Rimmon,* Ms. British Museum 107b–108a, from the text cited in Scholem, *Major Trends in Jewish Mysticism,* 397–98 n. 154.

21. See, e.g., *Zohar* 2:62b–63a. For the common formulation that the manna is ground for the righteous in the heaven called *Shehakim,* see *b. Hagigah* 12b; *Zohar*

3:26a and other zoharic sources in Margaliot, *Nizozei Zohar,* n. 2; Joseph Gikatilla, *Sha'arei Orah,* ed. Yosef Ben-Shlomo (Jerusalem: Bialik Institute, 1981), 1: 155–56; Joseph Gikatilla, *Sefer Sha'arei Zedek* (Brooklyn: Moriah Offset, 1985), 16b. Cf. Joseph of Hamadan, "Sefer Toledot ha-Adam," in *Sefer ha-Malkhut* (Casablanca: Imprimerie Razon, 1930), 72a, which indicates that manna is ground for the righteous in the heaven called *zevul.* For other sources regarding the grinding of manna for the righteous in the world-to-come, see *Zohar* 3:292b (*Idra Zuta*), 3:236a; Moses ben Shem Tov de Leon, *Sefer ha-Rimmon,* ed. Elliot R. Wolfson (Atlanta: Scholars Press, 1988), 190, 404; *Seder Gan Eden,* in *Beit ha-Midrash,* ed. Adolph Jellinek (Jerusalem: Bamberger and Wahrmann, 1938), 139; Moses ben Shem Tov de Leon, *Sod Eser Sefirot Belimah,* in *Qovez al Yad,* n.s., 8, ed. Gershom Scholem (1975), mss. a, 379–80.

22. See, e.g., *Zohar* 3:246a, *Ra'aya Mehemna.* In his *Commentary on the Chariot,* Moses de Leon indicates that the wheels of the vision have a certain appearance and action; their action is grinding the manna for the righteous in the world-to-come. Moses de Leon, *R. Moses de Leon's Commentary to Ezekiel's Chariot,* ed. Asi Farber-Ginat (Los Angeles: Cherub, 1998), 71.

23. See also *Tikkunei ha-Zohar* ed. Reuven Margaliot (Jerusalem: Mosad ha-Rav Kuk, 1994), 3, 140b.

24. Bahya ben Asher has repeated emphasis on this aspect of the curse and on the simplified economics of gathering manna. Bahya ben Asher, *"Shulhan shel Arba,"* in *Kitve Rabbenu Bahya,* ed. Charles Chavel (Jerusalem: Mosad ha-Rav Kuk, 1987), 457–59, 493. Cf. *Zohar Ra'aya Mehemna* 3:229b; *Tikkunei ha-Zohar* 21:44a. In the rabbinic tradition, one comment offers that even God struggles to provide food for humanity. *b. Pesahim* 118a.

25. The question of the correct hermeneutic as a point of distinction between the kabbalists and the nonkabbalists as presented in the *Zohar, Ra'aya Mehemna,* and *Tikkunei ha-Zohar* has been treated in a number of studies. See Gershom Scholem, "The Meaning of the Torah in Jewish Mysticism," in *On the Kabbalah and Its Symbolism,* trans. Ralph Manheim (1960; reprint, New York: Schocken, 1965), 68–70; Tishby, *Wisdom of the Zohar,* 1090–112; Pinchas Giller, *The Enlightened Will Shine: Symbolization and Theurgy in the Later Strata of the Zohar* (Albany: State University of New York Press, 1993); Elliot R. Wolfson, "Beautiful Maiden Without Eyes: *Peshat* and *Sod* in Zoharic Hermeneutics," in *The Midrashic Imagination: Jewish Exegesis, Thought, and History,* ed. Michael Fishbane (Albany: State University of New York Press, 1993), 155–203.

26. Joseph of Hamadan, *Sefer Toledot ha-Adam,* 72b.

27. Bahya ben Asher, *"Shulhan shel Arba,"* 469.

28. I have translated according to the interpretation of the *Tikkunei ha-Zohar.* The Jewish Publication Society translation reads "No longer will they *need to* teach one another."

29. Moses ben Nahman, *Commentary on the Torah,* ed. Charles Chavel (Jerusalem: Mosad ha-Rav Kuk, 1960), 88–91.

30. Cf. Exodus 16:5.

31. Isaac ben Samuel of Acre, *Sefer Me'irat Einayim: Critical Edition,* by Amos Goldreich (Jerusalem: Akademon, 1981), 97 Hebrew pagination.

32. *Tikkunei ha-Zohar* 19, 41a–b.

33. *b. Sanhedrin* 59b.

34. See chapter 4, notes 73–80, where Moses' talent as food purveyor is subject to gender analysis.

35. *Tikkunei ha-Zohar* 19, 41a–b.

36. Cf. *Zohar* 3:33b. See Wolfson, "Circumcision."

37. See *b. Berakhot* 20b; see also *b. Yoma* 79b. On the nature of mystical intention, see Gershom Scholem, "The Concept of *Kavvanah* in the Early Kabbalah," in *Studies in Jewish Thought: An Anthology of German Jewish Scholarship*, ed. Alfred Jospe and trans. Noah J. Jacobs (Detroit: Wayne State University Press, 1981). For Scholem, the term *kavvanah*, as used by the early kabbalists, refers to a voluntaristic, meditative contemplation that leads to the form of *unio mystica* that was available to the kabbalists, i.e., to *sefirot* below the *Ein Sof*. In the later kabbalists, *kavvanah* takes on a magical meaning as well in terms of eliciting benefit for personal needs. See also Moshe Idel's remarks in "Kabbalistic Prayer and Colors," in *Approaches to Judaism in Medieval Times*, ed. David R. Blumenthal (Atlanta: Scholars, 1988), 20.

38. *b. Berakhot* 21a.

39. See Steven T. Katz, "Language, Epistemology, and Mysticism," in *Mysticism and Philosophical Analysis*, ed. Steven T. Katz (New York: Oxford University Press, 1978), 30.

40. On the hermeneutical function of the terms *vadai* and *mamash*, see Daniel C. Matt, "'New-Ancient Words': The Aura of Secrecy in the *Zohar*," in *Gershom Scholem's Major Trends in Jewish Mysticism: 50 Years Later*, ed. Joseph Dan and Peter Schaefer (Tübingen, Ger.: J. C. B. Mohr, 1993), 203–4; Wolfson, "Beautiful Maiden Without Eyes," 175–76, 199 n. 140.

41. There is one explicit statement in the *Zohar* saying that the physical human body can be nourished with "spiritual food." "The portion of the body is fortunate because it can be nourished by the food of the soul." *Zohar* 2:61b–62a. See chapter 3, analysis at notes 36–41.

42. Cf. *m. Menahot* 11:4.

43. Joseph of Hamadan, "A Critical Edition of the *Sefer Ta'amey ha-Mizwoth* (Book of Reasons of the Commandments) Attributed to Isaac Ibn Farhi," ed. Menachem Meier (Ph.D. diss., Brandeis University, 1974), 114.

44. In a rabbinic prefiguring of this phenomenon, Rabbi Hanina is praised for sustaining himself week to week on a meager diet of carob, which in turn maintains the world. *b. Berakhot* 17b, *Ta'anit* 24b, *Hullin* 86a. Cf. *Zohar* 3:216b.

45. The term *be'ito* refers to the *Shekhinah*. See *Zohar* 3:58a.

46. Unlike other passages that indicate that food comes from *Tif'eret*, here food is said to be coming from the *sefirah* of *Keter*. See *Zohar* 2:62a; Tishby, *Wisdom of the Zohar*, 962.

47. J. F. Baer, "The Historical Background of the *Ra'aya Mehemna*," *Zion*, n.s., 5, no. 1 (1939); Tishby, *Wisdom of the Zohar*, 1438–42; Giller, *Enlightened Will Shine*, 29–32. Scholem points out that the *Zohar* uses the same term for the poor as it does for the mystics themselves, *bnei heikhla de-malka*. Scholem, *Major Trends in Jewish Mysticism*, 234. Cf. *The Hebrew Writings*, 17, however, where the indigent is associated with *Yesod*. Tishby draws a distinction between "holy poverty" and the "holy

poor," and only the latter of the two is lauded. He argues that the righteous are equated with the poor, suggesting that the author and his class of scholars were indeed not well patronized.

48. *Zohar* 1:168a. See also *The Hebrew Writings*, 17, 19.

49. Cf. *Zohar* 3:226a. The passage analyzed earlier, however, is another example of the *Zohar*'s multifarious method of solving problems: it both harmonizes and maintains the privileges that stem from economic hierarchies. There are, again, dual ideals with regard to satiety: one physical and one spiritual.

50. Regarding the construction of the body through the dialectic of polarities, see Feher, "Introduction," 13–14; Arthur W. Frank, "For a Sociology of the Body: An Analytical Review," in *The Body: Social Process and Cultural Theory*, ed. Mike Featherstone, Mike Hepworth, and Bryan S. Turner (London: Sage, 1991), 47.

51. The ascetic orientation arises at least partly from the Neoplatonic ground in which soul/body binaries often lead to negative representations of the body and to sharp curtailment of the enjoyment of physical activities.

52. See, e.g., *Zohar* 1:88b, *Sitrei Torah*.

53. On rabbinic fasting, see S. Lowy, "The Motivation of Fasting in Talmudic Literature," *Journal of Jewish Studies* 9, nos. 1–2 (1958): 19–38; and, most recently, Eliezer Diamond, *Holy Men and Hunger Artists: Fasting and Asceticism in Rabbinic Culture* (Oxford: Oxford University Press, 2004). I regret that I was not able to examine Diamond's book before completing this study.

54. *b. Sanhedrin* 65b.

55. See, e.g., *Heikhalot Rabati* 308f; *Heikhalot Zutarti* 424; *Merkavah Rabah* 278f. and 677f; *Ma'aseh Merkavah* 560, 565. Regarding these preparatory techniques, see Ithamar Gruenwald, *Apocalyptic and Merkavah Mysticism* (Leiden, Neth.: Brill, 1980), 99ff.

56. *b. Berakhot* 17a; Maimonides, *Hilkhot Teshuvah* 8:1.

57. Commentary on Exodus 24:11.

58. Gershom Scholem, *Origins of the Kabbalah*, ed. R. J. Zwi Werblowski and trans. Allan Arkush (1962; reprint, Philadelphia: Jewish Publication Society, 1987), 307. Cf. de Leon, *Sefer ha-Rimmon*, 249–50.

59. *Zohar* 1:4a.

60. The Jewish Publication Society translates the passage as "since he had spoken with Him," but I have translated the verse according to de Leon's understanding of it.

61. See Tishby, *Wisdom of the Zohar*, 288–89, 875, 991; Elliot R. Wolfson, *Through a Speculum That Shines: Visionary Experience and Imagination in Medieval Jewish Mysticism* (Princeton, N.J.: Princeton University Press, 1994), 388; Yehuda Liebes, "Myth vs. Symbol in the *Zohar* and in Lurianic Kabbalah," trans. Eli Lederhandler, in *Essential Papers on Kabbalah*, ed. Lawrence Fine (New York: New York University Press, 1995), 213–17.

62. Moses ben Shem Tov de Leon, "She'eilot u-Teshuvot be-Inyanei Kabbalah," ed. Isaiah Tishby, in *Studies in the Kabbalah and Its Branches* (Jerusalem: Magnes Press, 1982), 1:74. De Leon's notion of a unique being at the apex of the species is most likely informed by Maimonides' discussion of this notion. See Maimonides, *Guide of the Perplexed*, 380.

63. de Leon, "She'eilot u-Teshuvot," 1:72–73.

64. *b. Berakhot* 17a.

65. These correspond to *Ḥokhmah, Tif'eret,* and *Shekhinah.*

66. Cf. *Zohar Ḥadash* 79d–80a, (*Midrash Ruth*) and translation in Tishby, *Wisdom of the Zohar,* 1515–17. See also de Leon, *Sefer ha-Rimmon,* 127–28; Bahya ben Asher, *Kad ha-Kemaḥ,* in *Kitve Rabbenu Baḥya,* ed. Charles Chavel (Jerusalem: Mosad he-Rav Kuk, 1987), 443; *Sefer ha-Kanah* 67b. Ben Asher adds that the tears that one cries during fasting are like the libation poured upon the altar. In *Sefer ha-Rimmon,* de Leon says that in prayer one must dedicate oneself to God so that it is as if one was sacrificing one's liver and blood to him. See de Leon, *Sefer ha-Rimmon,* 79.

67. Every aspect of the body's experience of the fast is thus translated into dedication to the Divine. The discomfort caused by the fast corresponds to the altar's fire, causing the stomach to shrink and the fat and blood to ascend. The halitosis of the noneater is also correlated to the atoning altar. See *Zohar* 2:20b. Regarding the effects of Rabbi Eliezer ben Horkenos's fetid breath, caused by fasting or eating dirt, see *Bereshit Raba* 41:1, p. 398; *Pirke Rabbi Eliezer,* chap. 1.

68. *Zohar* 2:119b.

69. See Michael Fishbane, "The Imagination of Death in Jewish Spirituality," in *Death, Ecstasy, and Other Worldly Journeys,* ed. John J. Collins and Michael Fishbane (Albany: State University of New York Press, 1995), 183–208, for a discussion of other forms of imaginary death.

70. *Zohar* 3:232a, *Ra'aya Mehemna.*

71. This teaching draws on the explanation given by Moses ben Naḥman.

72. See *b. Berakhot* 8b.

73. In "Sod Eser Sefirot Belimah," de Leon compares the ninth and the tenth of Tishrei to the *sefirot Yesod* and *Shekhinah.* de Leon, *Sod Eser Sefirot Belimah,* 381.

74. See de Leon, *Sefer ha-Rimmon,* 167–68. See also 320–21, which affirms this but also refers to the weakening of the body. It is also possible that the two components being referred to in the zoharic passage are the soul and the body, as the homily continues: "[Scripture says] 'your souls' to comprise everything, the body and the soul." Bahya ben Asher contends that the affliction is imposed upon the animalistic soul and not on the body. See Bahya ben Asher, "Kad ha-Kemaḥ," 441–43; Cordovero, Or Yakar (1985) 13:55. The fact that the word *et,* usually used to refer to the *Shekhinah,* is employed in this instance of exegesis suggests that the body-soul reading may be correct, as the relationship of the *Shekhinah* to the rest of the *sefirot* is often that of body to soul. See also de Leon, *Sefer ha-Rimmon,* 164, where it appears that the reason that one feasts on the ninth of Tishrei is so that one will fatten oneself in a personal physical offering to God.

75. de Leon, *Sod Eser Sefirot Belimah,* 381.

76. It is not wholly assimilable to prayer, though. See, e.g., *Zohar* 2:15a. It is said of Rabbi Shimon that he did not have to fast in order to have his needs fulfilled, but rather he would offer his petitions and God would fulfill them. See *Zohar* 3:288b. In this instance there is a hierarchy in which fasting, perhaps because of its dependence on the body or on physical discomfort, is considered a form of petition that is not as elevated as prayer. In the rabbinic tradition, fasting is employed to annul the decrees whose portents are announced in dreams, and this use of fasting is also adopted by

the *Zohar*. The *Zohar*, however, places emphasis on the need for the fast to follow the dream immediately, because "there is no day below that is not ruled by another day above." See *Zohar* 3:92a. Thus any given dream is correlated to a particular *sefirah*, whose needs must be ameliorated. See also *Zohar* 1:224a; 3:105b; de Leon, *Sefer ha-Rimmon*, 125–27. The rabbinic source is *b. Ta'anit* 12b. For other examples of fasts having theurgic effects, see Zohar 3:202b–3a, 214b; *Zohar Ḥadash, Ki Teze* 59a.

77. Note, however, de Leon's comment that bad wine inhibits the ability to distinguish left from right, which is deemed a dangerous mark of confusion. Moses ben Shem Tov de Leon, *R. Moses de Leon's Sefer Shekel ha-Kodesh*, ed. Charles Mopsik (Los Angeles: Cherub, 1996), 36–37.

78. *Zohar* 2:207a–b. Further, according to rabbinic teaching, if one fasts on the Sabbath to prophylactically repair the damage a dream portends, one must fast another day because of having neglected the obligation to rejoice on the Sabbath. See *b. Ta'anit* 12b; Maimonides, *Hilkhot Ta'anit* 1:12.

79. Elsewhere fasting marks the increasing hiddenness of the light of the Torah. When Moses died, the light of Torah was hidden; the same thing happened with the death of King David. As the light of Torah continued to diminish each time someone died, a fast would be declared (*Zohar* 2:156b). Fasting here is hardly different from the rabbinic paradigm, where it is an expression of mourning. See *j. Mo'ed Katan* 17b.

80. *b. Berakhot* 31b; *Zohar* 2:165b, 3:89b. The rabbinic text concedes that the requirement for delight has been neglected, and so, to repair that lapse, one must fast again for having fasted at a less-than-ideal time. The zoharic text cited in this note adopts this solution but does not appear to give it the same status of reparation: the damage has been done. One passage, from a later stratum of the *Zohar*, reflects back on the *Zohar*'s own ambivalence, asking whether it is beneficial or detrimental to fast on the Sabbath (*Zohar* 3:105a–b); see also Joseph Gikatilla, *Sefer Sha'arei Zedek* (Brooklyn: Moriah Offset, 1985), 29a. Following some of the medieval commentators, the author of this section of the *Zohar* suggests that it is only if one is fasting to atone for a dream that one might be allowed to fast on the Sabbath. See *Tosafot Berakhot* 31b, s.v. *kol ha-yoshev;* Maimonides, *Hilkhot Ta'anit* 1:12. In contrast, Rashi says that one may fast on the Sabbath if one is suffering from a physical ailment that fasting will relieve. See *b. Ta'anit* 12b, s.v. *ve-afilu be-Shabbat*.

81. The text cites the scriptural verse with some minor deviation.

82. *b. Berakhot* 20b.

83. de Leon, *Sefer ha-Rimmon*, 104–5.

84. Regarding the body that is not a body, see Jean-Pierre Vernant, "Dim Body, Dazzling Body," in *Fragments for a History of the Human Body*, ed. Michel Feher (New York: Zone, 1989), 18–48.

85. Cf. de Leon, *Sefer ha-Rimmon*, 210, where there is a causal link of eating and the praise of God. The poor person responds automatically—giving praise is the natural response to eating.

86. See Ibid., note *ad loc.* See also *Zohar* 2:168b.

87. Cf. de Leon, "Sod Eser Sefirot Belimah," 381.

88. See *Sefer ha-Rimmon,* in which de Leon says that in the liturgical poem "Nishmat" the phrase "if our mouths" suggests that the praise of the body follows

that of the soul. de Leon, *Sefer ha-Rimmon*, 123. The Talmud commentaries of Rashi suggest similar notions of magical satiation and psychosomatic unity. In one passage (*b. Sanhedrin* 65b, s.v. *igla tilta*), two rabbis create a partially grown calf as a regular activity on Friday afternoons. Rashi says that they were sated by this calf, notwithstanding its small size. When an opinion in the Talmud suggests that one gains an extra soul on the Sabbath, Rashi says this means that "one's heart has greater capacity for rest and joy and is open to calmness. He will be able to eat and drink and his soul will be undisturbed" (*b. Beizah* 16a, s.v. *neshamah yeteirah*). In a parallel passage, he says, "his mind has greater capacity for eating and drinking" (*b. Ta'anit* 27b, s.v. *neshamah yeteirah*). Thus it appears that Rashi may have had conceptions of eating that are not entirely dissimilar from those of the *Zohar*. For another instance of preternatural satiation, see Rashi, *Commentary on the Torah*, Leviticus 26:6, s.v. *ve-akhaltem*. For another instance of a curse in the belly, see ibid., Leviticus 26:26, s.v. *ve-akhaltem*. The fullest treatment of Rashi's relationship to esoteric thought is in Ephraim Kanarfogel, *"Peering through the Lattices": Mystical, Magical, and Pietistic Dimensions in the Tosafist Period* (Detroit: Wayne State University Press, 2000), 144–53.

89. *b. Baba Bathra* 12b offers the following suggestive statement: "Before a person eats and drinks he has two hearts; after he eats and drinks he has only one heart." Though the rabbinic author may not be dealing with the strict dichotomy of body and soul assumed doctrinally by the kabbalists, the ability to appease the evil inclination and thus bring harmony between it and the good inclination suggests an understanding close to the psychosomatic unity that I suggest.

90. See *Midrash Ruth Rabah* 5:15.

91. See also *Zohar Hadash Ruth* 45c, 87c; *Zohar* 2:207b, 218a.

92. See *Midrash Ruth Rabah* 5:15.

93. The prominence of the word *tov* (good) in various forms in the fourth blessing of the grace after meals may also have led to this particular application.

94. *Zohar* 2:218a.

95. As we shall see in the following discussion of giving food to the poor, it appears that part of the reason for giving charity, especially food, is that it leads to the poor person's immediate response of praising God. See chapter 6 at notes 59 and 62, and, e.g., de Leon, *Sefer ha-Rimmon*, 210.

96. In a similar vein, Gerald Bruns has suggested that, in the Islamic tradition, grief is a hermeneutical emotion. See Gerald L. Bruns, *Hermeneutics Ancient and Modern* (New Haven, Conn.: Yale University Press, 1992), 129.

Chapter 3

1. Bahya ben Asher, *"Shulhan shel Arba,"* in *Kitve Rabbenu Bahya*, ed. Charles Chavel (Jerusalem: Mosad ha-Rav Kuk, 1987), 492. Cf. 501.

2. Bahya ben Asher, *Shulhan shel Arba*, 493.

3. Cf. Bahya ben Asher, *Commentary on the Torah*, ed. Charles Chavel (Jerusalem: Mosad ha-Rav Kuk, 1982); Exodus 25:3.

4. Bahya ben Asher, *Shulhan shel Arba*, 494.

5. *Zohar* 1:257b; 2:62a; 3:226a; *Tikkunei ha-Zohar* 10, 25b. These sources are

interpretations of the statement in *Mo'ed Katan* 28a that life, children, and food depend not on merit but on one's astrological chart. In different places in the *Zohar,* and in the writings of Moses de Leon and Joseph Gikatilla, *mazal* corresponds to different sefirotic values. Usually, however, *mazal* corresponds to *Keter.* Other instances of this usage include *Zohar* 1:24a (*Tikkunei ha-Zohar*), 47b, 115a, 181a, 156b, 159b, 160b, 181a, 207b; 2:6a, 252b, 257b; 3:25b; Joseph Gikatilla, *Sefer Sha'arei Zedek* (Brooklyn: Moriah Offset, 1985), 17a, 29b. As another example of food coming from *Keter,* the *Zohar* describes the most privileged kabbalist as "sucking from the honey of the supernal oil," which comes from the overflow of *Arikh Anpin* (*Zohar* 2:153a). Elsewhere the *Zohar* says that on the Sabbath, the souls of the righteous delight in the delicacies (*tafnukim*) of *Atika Kadisha* (*Zohar* 2:89a). In some instances, wine is said to come from *Atika Kadisha* (*Zohar* 3:189a).

6. *Zohar* 2:62b, 183a.

7. *Zohar* 2:6a, 97b, 252b; 3:79b (see notes in *Nizozei Zohar*); *Zohar Hadash* 87c–d, *Midrash Ruth;* Moses ben Shem Tov de Leon, *Sefer ha-Rimmon,* ed. Elliot R. Wolfson (Atlanta: Scholars Press, 1988), 198.

8. *Zohar* 1:88a, 239b; 3:4a (*Ra'aya Mehemna*), 33b (*Ra'aya Mehemna*), 40a, 40b, 127a.

9. *Zohar* 1:24a (*Tikkunei ha-Zohar*), 217a; 2:40a, 61b, 183a; 3:25b, 95b, 292b (*Idra Zuta*); de Leon, *Sefer ha-Rimmon,* 200; Yosef Gikatilla, *Sha'arei Orah* 2:83. The passage in *Zohar* 1:24a refers to *Tif'eret* as the Tree of Food (*ilana de-mezona*). See Isaiah Tishby, *The Wisdom of the Zohar,* trans. David Goldstein (Oxford: Oxford University Press, 1989), 1105; Daniel C. Matt, *Zohar: The Book of Enlightenment* (New York: Paulist, 1983), 113–16, 245–47.

10. Throughout the *Zohar* and the Hebrew writings of Moses de Leon, it is said that the prophets suckle from this pair of *sefirot.* See *Zohar* 3:58a; *Shekel ha-Kodesh,* p. 58; Moses ben Shem Tov de Leon, *Shushan Edut,* ed. Gershom Scholem, *Qovez al Yad,* n.s., 8 (1975): 335; Moses ben Shem Tov de Leon, *Sod Eser Sefirot Belimah,* in *Qovez al Yad,* n.s., 8, ed. Gershom Scholem (1975), 379 mss. b. See also Gikatilla, *Sha'arei Orah,* 1:158; Gikatilla, *Sefer Sha'arei Zedek,* 15b, 17a. In *Sha'arei Orah* 2:83, Gikatilla says that the prophets suckle from *Tif'eret* rather than from these two.

11. *Zohar* 1:60a, 208a; 3:236a, 261b (*Hashmatot*); de Leon, *Sefer ha-Rimmon,* 193–94. See also Gikatilla, *Sha'arei Orah,* 1:135–36.

12. *Zohar* 1:107a, 217a, 226b, 246a; 2:40a, 183a, 205a; 3:245a. Throughout kabbalistic literature we see nourishment ascribed to God in a more general sense as well; this, of course, goes back to biblical promises of sustenance. See, e.g., Gikatilla, *Sha'arei Orah,* 1:57.

13. See *Zohar* 3:217b, which has food for the righteous coming from *Arikh Anpin* (Large Countenance) and *Ze'ir Anpin* (Small Countenance), as well as from the "trees." The "trees" signify the individual *sefirot* within those configurations. A passage from the late-thirteenth-century kabbalist Isaac of Acre suggests the direction that these notions of eating can lead:

Proper *devekut* [is that in which] the soul is consumed upon consuming. That is to say, if it pursues and attains the intelligibles they will be enclosed and engraved within it. This is the mystery of eating. Concerning this eating and *devekut,* it is said: "Taste and see that the Lord is good." Let the soul adhere to the Divine Intellect and It [the Divine Intellect] will adhere to it [the soul], for "the cow desires to suckle even more than the calf wants to nurse." [Psalm 34:9] [*b. Pesaḥim* 112a] The soul and the intellect become one entity, just as all [of the water] becomes one when one pours a pitcher of water into a flowing stream.

See *Ozar ha-Hayyim*, p. 111a; cited in Seth Lance Brody, "Human Hands Dwell in Heavenly Heights: Worship and Mystical Experience in Thirteenth Century Kabbalah" (Ph.D. diss., University of Pennsylvania, 1991), 279 (with minor variations).

14. See also de Leon, *Sefer ha-Rimmon*, 375; *Zohar* 2:126a. The *Tikkunei ha-Zohar* indicates that, although food has its origins in the divine world on the Sabbath, during the week it proceeds from Metatron, the primary figure in the angelic world. *Tikkunei ha-Zohar* 54b.

15. The biblical text says, "I will rain down bread for you from the heavens" (Exodus 16:4). Because the term "heavens" (*shamayim*) is conceived as a cognomen for the *sefirah Tif'eret*, the manna is said to come directly from that source. See *Zohar* 1:157b, 246a; 2:40a, 61b–63a, 88a–b, 183a–b; 3:95b, 96a, 97b, 156a, 196a, 292b; Moses ben Naḥman, *Commentary on the Torah*, ed. Charles Chavel (Jerusalem: Mosad ha-Rav Kuk, 1960), Commentary on Exodus 16:4, 6; Matt, *Zohar*, 66. In some places, the manna is said to come from the place called *Sheḥakim;* in *b. Ḥagigah* 12b, this refers to one of the seven heavens; in the *Zohar*, however, it refers more frequently to the *sefirot* of *Nezaḥ* and *Hod*, places of grinding that prepare the flow of divine light for dissemination from *Yesod*. Further, in some passages, the manna is said to be ground from the dew that is emitted from the skull of *Atika Kadisha;* see *Zohar* 3:128b, 292b. See *Zohar* 3:292b n. 6. See also Joseph of Hamadan, "Joseph of Hamadan's *Sefer Tashak*: Critical Edition with Introduction," ed. Jeremy Zwelling (Ph.D. diss., Brandeis University, 1975), 308–9. Elsewhere Joseph says that holy manna comes from the nostrils. It derives from the sixth light that comes from the eye/*ḥokhmah* of the supernal body, the light that illuminates the divine nostrils. Joseph of Hamadan, *Sefer Toledot ha-Adam*, in *Sefer ha-Malkhut* (Casablanca: Imprimerie Razon, 1930), 57b.

16. For bread as Torah, see e.g., *Bereshit Raba* 43:6.

17. *Zohar* 3:236a; see *Bereshit Raba* 43:6.

18. See Elliot R. Wolfson, "Mystical Rationalization of the Commandments in *Sefer ha-Rimmon*," *Hebrew Union College Annual* 59 (1989): 241–44. The *Sitra Aḥra* is the demonic realm in the theosophic worldview. It is often represented as the demonic counterpart to the *sefirotic* structure. See Gershom Scholem, "*Sitra Aḥra*: Good and Evil in the Kabbalah," in *On the Mystical Shape of the Godhead*, ed. Jonathan Chipman, trans. Joachim Neugroschel (New York: Schocken, 1991).

19. See, e.g., *Tikkunei ha-Zohar* 21, 51a–b, in which God asks for good food, referring to the positive commandments and prayer. Cf. *Tikkunei ha-Zohar* 21, 55a–b. In one teaching from this period, the *Ein Sof* is food for the Godhead, reversing the direction of the flow and indicating a rough unity of all things spiritual. Joseph of Hamadan, *Sefer Tashak*, 104.

20. Joseph of Hamadan, *Sefer Toledot ha-Adam*, 62b.

21. See Ivan G. Marcus, *Rituals of Childhood: Jewish Acculturation in Medieval Europe* (New Haven, Conn.: Yale University Press, 1990).

22. Cf. Goldstein's translation in Tishby, *Wisdom of the Zohar,* 651. See also *Zohar* 3:155b.

23. On the concretization of the spiritual in Neoplatonic thought, see Tishby, *Wisdom of the Zohar,* 551–55; Dorit Cohen-Alloro, *The Secret of the Garment in the Zohar,* Research Projects of the Institute of Jewish Studies, Monograph Series 13 (Jerusalem: Hebrew University of Jerusalem, 1987), 43–44. See also *Zohar* 1:19b–20a; 2:61b; 3:292b.

24. Yehuda Liebes has written about the *Zohar*'s attitude to Christianity and its attempts to distance itself doctrinally from Christianity. See Yehuda Liebes, "Christian Influences in the Zohar," *Jerusalem Studies in Jewish Thought* 2, no. 1 (1982–83); an abbreviated, English version of the article appears in his collection, Liebes, "Christian Influences on the *Zohar.*"

25. Part of the reason for the emphasis on the degradation of the manna is the textual context, which is a longer homily about the fallen angels Uzza and Uzzael (see Tishby, *Wisdom of the Zohar,* 650–52.) The short homily on manna serves as a proof text for the Zohar's contention that descent into this world marks a degradation of the substance involved. See also *Zohar Ḥadash* 48c, *Midrash ha-Ne'elam,* where the upper manna is said to be uncolored and uncongealed, whereas the lower manna is colored, tasting like honey. This text thus indicates that the sense of taste too is of a lower ontological quality; higher entities are pristinely bland. While this caution may be seen as hesitancy in view of Christian conceptions of eating the Divinity, it is important to remember that each tradition develops its own manners of referring to mystical encounters. Thus it may be that the kabbalist does not eat God, not because he is polemically countering the Christian, but rather because one eats unleavened bread or the like and experiences God in the process. The fact that the manner in which God is engaged is through eating, in some instances, makes room for the anatomical siting of the experience. See Michael A. Sells, *Mystical Languages of Unsaying* (Chicago: University of Chicago Press, 1994), 11–12.

26. Regarding the ontology of the manna's descent and materialization, see Moses ben Shem Tov de Leon, *She'eilot u-Teshuvot be-Inyanei Kabbalah,* ed. Isaiah Tishby, in *Studies in the Kabbalah and Its Branches* (Jerusalem: Magnes Press, 1982), 63.

27. Joseph of Hamadan, *Sefer Tashak,* 309.

28. Of the literature that she has studied, Bynum says that references to myroblytes (sweet-smelling bodies) refer primarily to women in the medieval period, though she notes that this phenomenon is told of men in antiquity, as well. See Caroline Walker Bynum, *Holy Feast and Holy Fast: The Religious Significance of Food to Medieval Women* (Berkeley: University of California Press, 1987), 201. It is difficult to imagine that the zoharic kabbalists were food preparers, and so the association with food here means something other than it does in Bynum's material. In the *Zohar,* the idealized male body is a body of procreation, blessing, and production, albeit in a more figurative sense than in the material that Bynum analyzes.

29. Yehuda Liebes, "The Messiah of the *Zohar* (in Hebrew)," in *The Messianic Idea in Jewish Thought: A Study Conference in Honour of the Eightieth Birthday of*

Gershom Scholem, ed. Shemuel Rom (Jerusalem: Israel Academy of Sciences and Humanities, 1982), 141; Yehuda Liebes, "The Messiah of the *Zohar:* On R. Simeon Bar Yohai as a Messianic Figure (in English)," in *Studies in the Zohar,* trans. Arnold Schwartz and Devora Gamelieli (Albany: State University of New York Press, 1993), 28; Elliot R. Wolfson, *Through a Speculum That Shines: Visionary Experience and Imagination in Medieval Jewish Mysticism* (Princeton, N.J.: Princeton University Press, 1994), 371 n. 155.

30. See *b. Yoma* 75b.

31. Similarly, the judge who judges righteously is brought to the Garden of Eden and receives a taste from the Tree of Life; here too the tasting occurs after death (*Zohar* 2:117a). Significantly, in a number of instances, erotic union with the *Shekhinah* is said to occur after death. See Liebes, "The Messiah of the *Zohar* (in Hebrew)," 191–94; Liebes, "The Messiah of the *Zohar* (in English)," 63–65.

32. See Genesis 32:33.

33. de Leon, *Sefer ha-Rimmon,* 318. Apparently this particular passage was taken from Joseph of Hamadan, *Sefer Ta'amei ha-Mizvot.* Alexander Altmann, "Regarding the Question of the Authorship of *Sefer Ta'amei ha-Mitsvot* Attributed to Rabbi Yitshak Ibn Farkhi," *Kiryat Sefer* 40 (1965): 275. See also *Zohar* 2:41b; *Tikkunei ha-Zohar* 56, 91a.

34. According to rabbinic legend, one of the reasons that Nadav and Avihu met their fate was because they had consumed wine. See *Vayikra Rabah* 12:1; *Midrash Tanhuma Aharei Mot* 6.

35. I thank Joseph Davis for suggesting this latter point to me.

36. The *sefirah Malkhut.*

37. The *sefirah Tif'eret.*

38. Trans. from Tishby, *Wisdom of the Zohar,* 766, with some additions. Cf. Matt, *Zohar,* 113–16 and notes.

39. Tishby, *Wisdom of the Zohar,* 766.

40. Translated according to the midrashic understanding of the verse.

41. Judah Theodor and Chanoch Albeck, eds., *Bereshit Raba* (Jerusalem: Wahrmann, 1965), 48, pt. 2, 488. The notes contend that midrash indicates "support" for heart, not food.

42. Hayyim Vital underscores the problem, asking, "Why are they naturally weaker than the rest? It should be the reverse!" See *Derekh Emet* in Margaliot, *Zohar.*

43. On the dialectic of ideal body and real body, see chapter 2, note 50. In Moses Cordovero's version of the zoharic text, the food that the standard text refers to as "bread of angels" (*lehem avirim*) is called instead "miserable food" (*lehem kelokel*), using the epithet of complaint from Numbers 21:5. The meaning in the Ramaq's version is that, because the manna does not nourish the body, the masses do not appreciate it. Cordovero elucidates that the kabbalists appreciate the divine food and appreciate the resulting body; the ingratiate masses of Israel, weighted down by their bodies, find the ethereal food disgusting.

44. Derived from Ezekiel 44:7.

45. See Elliot R. Wolfson, "Forms of Visionary Ascent as Ecstatic Experience in the Zoharic Literature," in *Gershom Scholem's Major Trends in Jewish Mysticism: 50 Years Later,* ed. Joseph Dan and Peter Schaefer (Tübingen, Ger.: J. C. B. Mohr, 1993),

222–23. See also *Zohar* 1:136a (*Midrash ha-Ne'elam*), which, in a Maimonidean vein, portrays God using various lures to induce Israel to obey the commandments, satiety being the biggest lure of them all. Thus, in the manna narrative, God promises them food. Similarly, the rabbis promised Israel a great feast in the world-to-come to help them get through the exile, and the *Zohar* reveals that the food of that feast is the joy and laughter in God. Here, the food is explicitly and consciously spiritualized, following the approach of the more philosophically oriented *Midrash ha-Ne'elam*.

46. This is partly based on the rabbinic teaching that one should not eat until after the morning prayers. *b. Berakhot* 28b.

47. This is a homiletical development of Proverbs 13:25.

48. See also *Midrash ha-Ne'elam, Parashat Aharei, Ma'mar 2–3 Se'udot be-Shabbat*. It also indicates that there are two different kinds of gathering and two different grades of manna: the uncolored, uncongealed type and the colored type, tasting like honey, which is of a lower grade.

49. Leviticus 23:17.

50. Translation from Elliot R. Wolfson, "Light through Darkness: The Ideal of Human Perfection in the Zohar," *Harvard Theological Review* 81, no. 1 (1988): 92–93.

51. According to Joseph Gikatilla, in a passage from his "Commentary on the Haggadah," Israel is commanded to give an offering of leavened bread during the festival of Shavuot because one should always verbally confess one's sins with reference to the evil inclination, here symbolized by the leaven. Unlike in the *Zohar*, where evil is refined and assimilated to the holy realm, for Gikatilla, here, evil appears irredeemable. The best that can be done is to repent and move on, if not to effect full restitution. Joseph Gikatilla, "Commentary on the Haggadah," in *Haggadah Sheleimah*, ed. Menahem Mendel Kasher (New York: Sentry, 1967), 112–13. It should be noted that this is an unusual representation of evil on the part of Gikatilla. In his *Sod ha-Nahash u-Mishpato*, evil is, primordially, a benign force outside the domain of the sacred that, if left alone, would have harmoniously promoted "growth and procreation from the outside." See Gershom Scholem, "Good and Evil in the Kabbalah," in *On the Mystical Shape of the Godhead,* ed. Jonathan Chipman and trans. Joachim Neugroschel (New York: Schocken, 1991), 78–80. Similarly, in *Sha'arei Orah,* Gikatilla seems to believe that, at the redemption, the evil forces will be restored to their proper role in subservience to the realm of the sacred. See Yosef Ben-Shlomo, "General Introduction," in *Joseph Gikatilla: Sha'arei Orah,* ed. Yosef Ben-Shlomo (Jerusalem: Bialik Institute, 1981), 34–41. Generally, Gikatilla's representation of evil is more moderate than that of the *Zohar*. In his discussion of Gikatilla's writings, Ben-Shlomo does include the "Commentary on the Haggadah," so the contradiction needs to be addressed.

52. While this passage could be translated as "they may have leaven," it seems appropriate, given the *Zohar*'s predilection for visionary mysticism and the role of the visual, to translate it more literally.

53. A number of the kabbalistic commentaries on this passage are troubled by the *Zohar*'s assertion that the loaves are intended to be burnt when, in fact, according to scripture and accepted halakhic opinion, leaven offerings are not burnt but rather eaten by the priests. See Maimonides, *Hilkhot Ma'aseh ha-Korbanot* 12:3; *Nizozei*

Orot n. 1; *Nizozei Zohar* n. 1; *Hagahot Moreinu ha-Rav Hayyim Vital* n. 1. The *Zohar*'s misconstrual of the law could arise from ambiguity in the scriptural text (Leviticus 23:17,20), in Maimonides' explanation of the laws (*Hilkhot Temidin u-Musafin* 8:1) or, more likely, from the fact that leaven is, in fact, burnt on the eve of Passover and that burning would be the primary association that the author would have with leaven rather than with the priestly obligations.

54. Translation in Elliot R. Wolfson, "Left Contained in the Right: A Study in Zoharic Hermeneutics," *AJS Review* 11, no. 1 (1986): 50–51, where he discusses this passage. I have continued the translation where his ends.

55. In contrast, Gikatilla explains that, at Shavuot, one must articulate one's sin and that confessing it, before the sacrificial offering of leaven that represents the sin, elicits God's forgiveness. Gikatilla, "Commentary on the Haggadah," 112–13. It appears that the sin remains wholly spiritual and the bread symbolically expressive of one's contrition.

56. See also *Pesikta Rabati Piska* 3.2: "Another comment: As the roots of a tree spread in all directions, so words of Torah enter and spread through the whole body of a man." The midrashic interpretation indicates that "understanding is something more than a mental state." See Gerald L. Bruns, "Midrash and Allegory: The Beginnings of Scriptural Interpretation," in *The Literary Guide to the Bible*, ed. Robert Alter and Frank Kermode (Cambridge, Mass.: Harvard University Press, 1987), 633.

57. de Leon, *Sefer ha-Rimmon*, 172–73.

58. For a different approach to this problem, see Wolfson, "Left Contained in the Right," 51; Wolfson, "Light through Darkness," 92–93.

59. For more on this theme of the giving of the Torah causing the evil inclination to pass from Israel, see *b. Shabbat* 146a, *b. Yevamot* 103b, *b. Avodah Zarah* 22b. The rabbinic sources say that the filth that passes away was first deposited in Eve and then passed onto Israel. The *Zohar* makes ample use of this aggadic story; see *Zohar* 1:36b, 52b, 63b, 126b, 228a; 2:94a, 193b, 236b; 3:14b; *Zohar Hadash* 83a (*Midrash Ruth*). See also Brody, "Human Hands Dwell in Heavenly Heights," 349–51.

60. Joseph of Hamadan, *Sefer Ta'amey ha-Mizwoth*, 223.

61. *b. Shabbat* 146a.

62. de Leon, *Shushan Edut*, 362.

63. This homily is then borne out by a story about a man who bought an herb in the market that gave him a stomachache (literally: "an ache was born in his stomach"). Subsequently, he sired a son with the same illness. De Leon explains that this person was like Adam in the garden and that what Adam ate was far more significant, so it affected *all* his limbs. Consequently, Adam caused death to all of humanity. The naturalistic and scientific approach adopted by de Leon is noteworthy, because he brings empirical data to support his mystical homily. De Leon alludes to a great mystery about lowering supernal souls into human bodies to achieve great purpose in this regard. It would appear that there is a requirement to introduce new souls to restore the purity of the gene pool, so to speak. See also Gikatilla, *Sha'arei Orah*, 1:257 and n. 150.

64. This is a refutation of Maimonides' contention to that effect. Moses Maimonides, *The Guide of the Perplexed*, trans. Shlomo Pines (Chicago: University of Chicago Press, 1963) 1:23–26.

65. The ability of foods to have detrimental effects upon the soul is discussed by Moses ben Nahman, *Commentary on the Torah*, Exodus 22:30, Deuteronomy 14:3. Foods are deemed to have eugenic impact in Moses ben Nahman's commentary on Leviticus 11:13, and this theme receives considerable attention in *Iggeret ha-Kodesh*, in *Kitve Ramban*, ed. Charles Chavel (Jerusalem: Mosad ha-Rav Kuk, 1964), 329–30. The latter source also provides a taxonomy of the different effects of eating the various kinds of prohibited foods.

66. *Shushan Edut*, p. 306. See Deuteronomy 12:23.

67. Regarding the doctrine of the soul, see Gershom Scholem, *Major Trends in Jewish Mysticism* (New York: Schocken, 1946), 240–41; Tishby, *Wisdom of the Zohar*, 684–92; *Zohar* 1:109a–b (*Midrash ha-Ne'elam*); *Zohar Hadash* 6d, 9a, 14b (*Midrash ha-Ne'elam*); Moses ben Shem Tov de Leon, "*Sefer ha-Mishkal:* Text and Study," ed. Jochanan Wijnhoven (Ph.D. diss., Brandeis University, 1964), 38–47. See also de Leon, *Sefer ha-Rimmon*, 406, which refers to the five names of the soul, whose literary source is *Bereshit Raba* 14:9, p. 132. The middle element is *ruah* and the uppermost is *neshamah*.

68. Cf. Moses ben Nahman, *Commentary on the Torah*, 2:126. In his comments on Leviticus 19:26 ("You shall not eat anything with its blood"), Moses ben Nahman explains that violating the prohibition constitutes a sin against the name of God contained within the prohibition itself.

69. On the last blood spurting out of a vein, see *m. Keritut* 5:1. On blood that can be squeezed from an animal's flesh, see *t. Makhshirin* 3:13.

70. de Leon, *Sefer ha-Rimmon*, 407. There is a characteristic problem in zoharic kabbalah here. It is unclear why the *nefesh*, a spiritual entity, should feel drawn after the coarse, material body; superior entities usually enfold inferior ones within their sphere of influence. The *sefirotic* parallel would be that the *Shekhinah* is actually drawn after the *Sitra Ahra*, rather than that, in her vulnerability, she is dominated by the demonic realm. This is characteristic of the *Zohar*'s dilemma in resolving the tension between determinism and voluntarism of human beings and divine entities.

71. Gikatilla, *Sha'arei Orah*, 1:229; cf. *Zohar Hadash* Ruth 86c.

72. *b. Berakhot* 10b; de Leon, *Sefer ha-Rimmon*, 304.

73. See Conclusion, note 2. De Leon may also have conflated the restriction against eating with the interdiction against judges drinking wine before passing judgment. He may have been led to this association because of the common linking of meat and wine in the rabbinic imagination as sources of joy and foodstuffs that are restricted in certain contexts.

74. Gikatilla, *Sha'arei Orah*, 2:11–12. Yosef Ben-Shlomo notes that Gikatilla interprets the talmudic dictum according to its plain meaning, not the esoteric one entailing a human soul having undergone metempsychosis, being reincarnated in this animal (12 n. 12). Nonetheless, the conversion of one creature into another through eating is not the simple meaning of the restriction against the ignorant eating meat, either. The Talmud's concern, it would appear, is that the unlettered, wholly unfamiliar with the detailed laws regarding the slaughter of animals, will slaughter improperly and come to eat forbidden food. See Rabbeinu Nissim Gerondi, 16b (according to pagination of Alfasi). See Jonathan Brumberg-Kraus, "Meat-Eating and Jewish Identity: Ritualization of the Priestly 'Torah If Beast and Fowl' [Lev.

11:46] in Rabbinic Judaism and Medieval Kabbalah," *AJS Review* 24, no. 2 (1999): 227–62.

75. See Leon R. Kass, *The Hungry Soul: Eating and the Perfecting of Our Nature* (New York: Free Press, 1994), 54.

76. For a slightly different formulation of the same idea, see Baḥya ben Asher, "*Shulḥan shel Arba,*" 496.

77. Joseph of Hamadan, *Sefer Tashak*, 92.

78. Theodor and Albeck, *Bereshit Raba*, 65:1. The midrash compares Esau to the pig, with Esau as a symbolic stand-in for the Roman legion who had the wild boar emblazoned upon their shields. In the Middle Ages, Esau and the pig in this midrash, by extension, represented the church and all Christians. Condemnation of the pig here is also a religious and social polemic.

79. Joseph of Hamadan, *Sefer Tashak*, 334–35.

80. This is a common theme in Hasidic literature. See, e.g., Rivka Schatz Uffenheimer, ed., "Commentary of the Baal Shem Tov on Psalm 107" (Jerusalem: Magnes, 1988) 203.

81. de Leon, *Sefer ha-Rimmon*, 309. Cf. Uffenheimer, "Commentary of the Baal Shem Tov," 161, 166, and *Zohar* 1:59b.

82. If we reverse the metaphor and consider the conception and parenting of children, disturbing implications can be drawn, implications that would easily justify, for example, Abraham's binding of Isaac.

83. Grace M. Jantzen, *Becoming Divine: Towards a Feminist Philosophy of Religion* (Bloomington: Indiana University Press, 1999), 233.

84. William James, *The Varieties of Religious Experience: A Study in Human Nature* (1902; reprint, New York: Macmillan, 1961), 299–302; Wayne Proudfoot, *Religious Experience* (Berkeley: University of California Press, 1985), 136–37.

85. See *b. Yoma* 75a–b; Solomon Buber, ed., *Midrash Tanhuma* (Jerusalem: Eshkol, 1972); *be-Shalaḥ* 20–21; *Shemot Rabah Be-shalaḥ* 25:2–3, 7; *t. Sotah* 4:1; *Mekhilta be-shalaḥ* 2; Rashi on Exodus 16:7.

86. See Solomon Buber, ed., *Tanhuma* (Jerusalem: Eshkol, 1972), *be-Shalaḥ* 20.

87. See also Moses ben Nahman, *Commentary on the Torah*, Exodus 16:6, in which he offers a metaphysical-psychological explanation for the sustenance by the manna. Through the intellect's apprehension of the supernal light, the animal soul (*nefesh*) experiences the wonders of the manna. That wisdom can be held within the body is found in de Leon's descriptions of corpses, as well. Thus, for example, he says that there is a knowledge that is held by corpses that stays in the body until resurrection. Moses ben Shem Tov de Leon, *Sefer Shekel ha-Kodesh*, ed. Charles Mopsik (Los Angeles: Cherub, 1996), 35.

88. On manna and Torah, see Daniel Abrams, ed., *The Book Bahir: An Edition Based on the Earliest Manuscripts* (Los Angeles: Cherub, 1994), 127–28, pp. 209, 211. For references to the wine of Torah, usually referring to the *sefirah* of *Gevurah*, see *Zohar* 2:124b; 3:39a, 216b *Ra'aya Mehemna*; de Leon, *Sefer ha-Rimmon*, 319; Joseph of Hamadan, *Sefer Tashak*, 11, 20. For the rabbinic comparison of Torah to wine, see *b. Ta'anit* 7a. The *Zohar* (3:216b) follows the rabbinic comparison of *yayin* to *sod* because of their numerical equivalency (*b. Eruvin* 65a, *Sanhedrin* 38a). As is so often the case in zoharic kabbalah, wine too has a bivalent potential, meaning that it can be used for both holy and demonic wisdom: there is both good and bad wine. This

is largely due to wine's red color and consequent association with the *sefirah* of *Gevurah* and because of its ability to intoxicate. In one of his Hebrew works, Moses de Leon writes that bad wine intoxicates until one cannot distinguish right from left—the ultimate epistemological error. There is thus consumption of food with negative cognitive effects. Further, Adam, Noah, and Aaron's sons, Nadav and Avihu, all sinned with this wine. The distinction between the good and bad uses of wine is sharpened so that there is a difference between those who are intoxicated (*shetuyei yayin*) and those who are drunk; according to the halakhah, the former can still pray. Whereas Adam and Noah drank a lot because of their great desire for the wine, Nadav and Avihu drank in order *to see*. Drinking "good wine," in their moment of fervent spiritual desire, they also drank some of the "bad wine." Last, because of the association of wine with *Gevurah*, wine without water (*Hesed*) is deemed to be dangerous. De Leon, *Sefer Shekel ha-Kodesh*, 36–38. See also *Zohar* 1:238b; Joseph of Hamadan, *Sefer Tashak*, 100. Forbidden wine (*yayin nesekh*), that which has been handled by non-Jews, presumably for idolatrous purposes, is a deep mystery and is forbidden because of its unmediated relationship to Judgment. Further, wine causes God and men to rejoice, and so wine is only given to Israel and not to the nations. De Leon, *Sefer ha-Rimmon*, 319; *Zohar* 1:238b; 2:246b; 3:12b, 40a. One passage in the *Zohar* says that "holiness cannot exist without wine" (*Zohar* 3:95a). There was a tradition of wine parties among the courtly Andalusian Jews, as well as more general carousing. Is it possible that the wine drinking that is criticized, say of Nadav and Avihu, could reflect a social criticism of wine parties that contemporaries of the *Zohar* engaged in? Our lack of biographical knowledge about the figures of the zoharic mystical fraternity again confounds our ability to draw conclusions in this respect, but the *Zohar*'s critique of contemporary licentiousness with Muslim slave girls suggests that this too could be a social critique. Bahya ben Asher gives an interesting psychological twist to the polyvalent nature of wine, saying that, while wine certainly enhances joy, when one increases joy overmuch it leads to sadness. See *Kad ha-Kemah*, 82. Being drunk is a frequent metaphor, cross-culturally, for the experience of mystic union. See, e.g., Bernard of Clairvaux, "Treatise on Loving God," in *Bernard of Clairvaux: Selected Works*, trans. G. R. Evans, Introduction by Jean Leclercq, Preface by Ewert H. Cousins (New York: Paulist Press, 1987), #27, 195, where he says that the mind is so "drunk with divine love" that it becomes "one with [God] in spirit." Cited in Nelson Pike, *Mystic Union: An Essay in the Phenomenology of Mysticism* (Ithaca, N.Y.: Cornell University Press, 1992), 33. Regarding the prohibition against drinking the wine of non-Jews, see *Zohar* 1:238b; 2:246b; 3:12b, 40a; de Leon, *Sefer ha-Rimmon*, 319, and see note to line 10; the "Mystery of Wine Used for Prohibited Libations" by Gikatilla, cited in Altmann, "Regarding the Question of the Authorship," 270–71.

89. It is commonplace in rabbinic and kabbalistic literature to associate bread with wisdom or with Torah. See, e.g., *b. Shabbat* 120a; *Bereshit Raba* 43:5; *Zohar* 1:260a; 3:236a (*Ra'aya Mehemna*); *Zohar Hadash* 58d; *Tikkunei ha-Zohar* 1b.

90. Interestingly, in this passage, it is not theosophic knowledge that one gains but practical knowledge that enables the practitioner to walk in upright ways. This appears to refer to pietistic behavior rather than theurgy. See *Zohar* 2:183b; this is the end of the passage bearing the parable of the king's sick son.

91. *Zohar* 1:157a–b. See Tishby, *Wisdom of the Zohar*, 1242–43 and 1242 n. 279;

Zohar 2:40a–b, 183b; 3:97b, 274a. See also Baḥya ben Asher, *Commentary on Exodus,*
16:12.

92. Joseph of Hamadan, *Sefer Tashak,* 309.

93. See *b. Berakhot* 40a; b. *Sanhedrin* 70b. In discussing the identity of the Tree
of Knowledge of good and evil, Rabbi Yehudah says, "It was wheat, for a child does
not know how to call for its father and mother until it has tasted the taste of grains."
See also *Bereshit Raba* 15:7: "From what kind of tree did Adam and Eve eat? Rabbi
Meir said, 'It was wheat, for when a person is lacking knowledge, people say that
such a person has never eaten bread from wheat in his life.'" Clearly, there was a notion
that knowledge was physiologically related to nutrition. See also *Pesikta* 20. In
Braude's and Kapstein's edition, p. 333 n. 10, they note, "Wheat was the first cereal to
be domesticated. Hence it is considered both source and symbol of wisdom."
Significantly, in his *Sefer ha-Mishkal,* de Leon makes a link between the child eating
bread and gaining knowledge of evil:

> On this verse [1 Chronicles 4:22], [the rabbis,] may their memory be for a bless-
> ing, said, "An infant never recognizes anything in the world as caused by the
> drawing of the sin that is within him until he eats bread [for until he has eaten
> bread] the drawing of that principle of evil is not imprinted upon him. Thus
> it is in his material nature from the beginning. After he eats bread, the infant
> will recognize that which he had not recognized before, that imprinted within
> him is that filth. This is like a blind man groping in the dark. Indeed, one should
> know that all of these gradations are found within a man from the day of his
> birth until he eats bread and comes to recognize a bit of the world. This is the
> beginning of his cognitive ability. This is the lowest gradation of those differ-
> ent gradations. (p. 154)

It would appear that the knowledge that the child gains is that of the material
world and of the potential for latent evil therein. Consequently, eating more ethereal
foods would invoke a more elevated form of knowledge. See also Rashi, *b. Sanhedrin*
70b s.v. *she-ein ha-tinok.* Part of the motivation for assigning this exalted status to
wheat is that the *gematriyah* of wheat (*ḥittah*) is 22, corresponding to the number of
letters in the Hebrew alphabet. See *Zohar* 3:188a.

94. See the parallel passage in de Leon, *Sefer ha-Rimmon,* 132–33. In both of these
passages, the *mazah* and the manna are conflated into one wisdom-giving bread.
Their ontological status lies in their being foods with biblical sources, whether narrative or legal. The rabbinic sources for this notion are in *b. Berakhot* 40a and *b.
Sanhedrin* 70b.

95. Gikatilla, "Commentary on the Haggadah," 111–14.

96. This is not to say, of course, that eating one particular kind of food magi-
cally bestows knowledge upon the diner—that would be an overly literal reading of
the kabbalistic material. What can be said, however, is that it *is* through engagement
with the material world—in this instance, through eating—that the "sons of the
palace" come to know God.

97. See Dorit Cohen-Alloro, "From Supernal Wisdom to the Wisdom of the
Leaves of the Tree: The *Zohar's* View of Magic as a Consequence of the Original Sin,"
Daat 19 (summer 1987): 31–65.

98. In *Sefer Shekel ha-Kodesh,* de Leon portrays Moses as having "drunk" violence in the Koraḥ episode and having been sated with anger (51). The English Revised Version of the Bible has the translation that accords with Moshe de Leon's use of it. Moses' body, that is, the human body as imaginatively experienced by the mystic, imbibes a negative attribute.

99. Tishby, *Wisdom of the Zohar,* 1289.

100. On the Jewish mystical use of the nut metaphor, whose prevalent usage was in the thought of Hasidei Ashkenaz, see Alexander Altmann, "Eleazar of Worms' *Hokhmat ha-'Egoz,*" *Journal of Jewish Studies* 11 (1960); Joseph Dan, "*Hokhmath ha-'Egoz,* Its Origin and Development," *Journal of Jewish Studies* 17 (1966); Joseph Dan, *The Esoteric Theology of Ashkenazi Hasidism* (Jerusalem: Bialik Institute, 1968), 207–10; Joseph Dan, "History of the Text of *Hokhmat ha-'Egoz,*" *Alei Sefer* 5 (1978); Asi Farber-Ginat, "The Conception of the Chariot in the Esoteric Theology of the Thirteenth Century: The *Sod ha-'Egoz* and Its Development," 2 vols.(Ph.D. diss., Hebrew University of Jerusalem, 1986); Daniel Abrams, *Sexual Symbolism and Merkavah Speculation in Medieval Germany* (Tübingen, Ger.: Mohr Siebeck, 1997). Regarding the use of the nut in the *Zohar* to describe the Divine, see *Zohar* 1:19b–20a; 2:108b, 140b–141a; 3:227a–b; *Tikkunei ha-Zohar* 18, 36a; Tishby, *Wisdom of the Zohar,* 463–64.

101. Translation from Tishby, *Wisdom of the Zohar,* 1083.

102. *Zohar Ḥadash Tikkunim* 118b; *Tikkunei ha-Zohar,* Introduction 11b, 69 114a. In rabbinic literature, the Torah is frequently represented by bread. See L. Finkelstein, ed., *Siphre ad Deuteronomium* (New York: Jewish Theological Seminary 1969), teaching 45, p. 104; b. *Shabbat* 120a; b. *Ḥagigah* 14a; b. *Sanhedrin* 104b; *Numbers Rabah* 13:16. For later use of bread as Torah study, see Maimonides, *Hilkhot Yesode ha-Torah* 4:13; Maimonides, *Guide of the Perplexed,* 1:30; see also b. *Berakhot* 64a; b. *Baba Bathra* 145b for use of the formula "master of wheat" to denote someone who has mastered oral traditions; on bread as a symbol for the Oral Law, see *Zohar Ḥadash* 50b, *Zohar* 3:33b (*Pikkudin*); Wolfson, "Beautiful Maiden without Eyes," 197 n. 108; see also *Zohar* 3:188b (*Yanuka*), where wheat is identified as the *Shekhinah,* comprising the 22 letters in herself.

103. Exodus 15:23.

104. *Tikkunei ha-Zohar* 21, 44a. See also *Zohar* 1:27a (Tikkunei ha-Zaher); 3:124a–b *Ra'aya Mehemna,* 151a (*Ra'aya Mehemna*); *Zohar Ḥadash* 98b (*Tikkunim*).

105. *Zohar Ḥadash* (*Tikkunim*) 107a–b. Examples of water describing the divine realm are ubiquitous, as the *sefirot* of *Binah* and *Ḥesed,* in particular, are frequently described as being wells of water or as rivers of light. See, e.g., *Zohar* 1:60a, 135b.

106. *Zohar* 3:98a–b (*Ra'aya Mehemna*), 252b–253a (*Ra'aya Mehemna*).

107. The distance between signifier and referent with regard to the nut imagery takes on special significance when the nut refers to the sign of circumcision. While the divine sexual organ, so to speak, was not to be eaten, the fact that it is compared to the edible kernel from a stalk of wheat is certainly suggestive.

108. The *Zohar* conflates this story of Elisha (2 Kings 4:1–7) with that of the Shunamite (2 Kings 4:8–37), referring to this indigent woman as the Shunamite as well. This interaction between Elisha and the Shunamite is clearly marked with an erotic charge. He asks if she has a "suitable table," an allusion to the feminine *Shekhinah,* and she responds in the affirmative, claiming to have a small amount of oil. Food becomes a prerequisite for the union with the Divine and for the subse-

quent flow of divine energy. In theosophic terms, there is an arousal from below in the form of the food, preparing for the arousal from above, the arrival of Elisha, who will bring divine favor into the Shunamite woman's home.

109. There is another way of reading this: it could be that being wise means merely performing the pietistic act of obedience in placing bread upon the table as was done by the high priest, but I believe that my reading reveals a deeper structure. This phenomenon of attaining wisdom through eating certain kinds of bread occurs with the manna, as well. See *Zohar* 2:183a–b: "It is with this bread that Israel was made wise with the supernal wisdom of the Torah and they followed in its ways. . . . The *mazah* is a remedy that enables one to ascend and to know the mystery of faith." Not only does the manna impart a certain kind of wisdom, but the ways in which it guides the Israelites suggest the experience that comes with the mystical performance of the commandments.

110. Matt, *Zohar,* 38–39. For discussion of this passage, see Daniel C. Matt, "'New-Ancient Words': The Aura of Secrecy in the *Zohar,*" 205–6; Wolfson, "Beautiful Maiden without Eyes," 171 and notes there; Yehuda Liebes, "How the *Zohar* Was Written," *Jerusalem Studies in Jewish Thought* 8 (1989): 17–18; Liebes, "How Was the *Zohar* Written?" 97. Liebes says that the *Zohar* is not talking about natural food at all, presumably because it refers to eating the raw kernel; in support of this position it can be argued that this is a rare passage that opens up the possibility of an actual kabbalistic gastronomy. Its rarity, in fact, suggests the absence of such a gastronomy. Nonetheless, as I have argued, I would suggest that the metaphor arises from the kabbalists' embodied experience of consumption.

111. I am indebted to Joseph Davis for this reading.

112. Gershom Scholem, "The Meaning of the Torah in Jewish Mysticism," in *On the Kabbalah and Its Symbolism,* trans. Ralph Manheim (1960; reprint, New York: Schocken, 1965) 32–86; Moshe Idel, "The Concept of the Torah in Heikhalot Literature and Its Metamorphoses in Kabbalah," *Jerusalem Studies in Jewish Thought* 1 (1981): 23–84; Moshe Idel, "Infinities of Torah in Kabbalah," in *Midrash and Literature,* ed. Geoffrey H. Hartman and Sanford Budick (New Haven, Conn.: Yale University Press, 1986) 141–57.

113. Moses de Leon writes that, for one who has understanding (*sekhel*) and knowledge (*mada*), unleavened bread will give knowledge of his creator. De Leon, *Sefer ha-Rimmon,* 135.

114. Regarding the use of food metaphors in the medieval Christian tradition to describe mystical union, see Bynum, *Holy Feast and Holy Fast,* 150–86. See also remarks by Efraim Gottlieb regarding eating and consuming as metaphors for *devekut.* See *Studies in the Kabbala Literature,* ed. Joseph R. Hacker (Jerusalem: Daf-Chen, 1976), 237; Idel has also traced the use of swallowing as a metaphor for *devekut.* See Moshe Idel, *Kabbalah: New Perspectives* (New Haven, Conn.: Yale University Press, 1988), 70–73.

115. Cf. Piero Camporesi, "The Consecrated Host: A Wondrous Excess," in *Fragments for a History of the Human Body,* ed. Michel Feher (New York: Zone, 1989) 221–37.

116. Here the contradictions of the "in/out" schema become most pronounced. As one ingests the food, one moves into another realm. This can be partially explained

by saying that it is a commonplace in the *Zohar* to describe a holy act by saying that one has moved into the holy domain, and vice versa. The problem arises, however, because there are references to the act of ingestion as such.

117. The *Sitra Aḥra*.

118. The *Shekhinah*.

119. See also *Zohar* 1:33a; *b. Pesaḥim* 115b–116a.

120. When the letter *vav*, which represents the *sefirah Tif'eret*, is added to a word that is understood to be a cognomen for the feminine *Shekhinah*, the author of the *Zohar* frequently understands it to be a unification of masculine and feminine potencies within the Divine. This is especially the case with the relationship of the words *mazah* and *mizvah*. See *Zohar* 2:235b; 3:251b (*Ra'aya Mehemna*); *Tikkunei ha-Zohar* 13, 30b; 51, 56a. Regarding the letter *vav* as masculine, and the significance of gender with regard to letters, see Elliot R. Wolfson, "Letter Symbolism and Merkavah Imagery in the *Zohar*," in *Alei Shefer: Studies in the Literature of Jewish Thought Presented to Rabbi Dr. Alexandre Safran*, ed. Moshe Halamish (Ramat-Gan, Isr.: Bar-Ilan University Press, 1990), 195–236.

121. This verse suggests a union of the two because the article *this* (*zot*) used in relation to the word *mizvah* is usually understood to refer to the feminine *Shekhinah*. See also *Zohar* 1:226b; de Leon, *Sefer ha-Rimmon*, 133.

122. *Zohar* 2:183a.

123. *Zohar* 2:182a.

124. The manna is connected to the masculine *Tif'eret*.

125. See *b. Pesaḥim* 118a, which juxtaposes these two verses but draws a different conclusion.

126. See *b. Berakhot* 17a; cf. Rashi s.v. *se'or she-be'isa*.

127. It is common in both rabbinic and zoharic literature for the kidneys and the gut to be represented as a source of both good and evil counsel. See, e.g., *b. Berakhot* 61a; *Shabbat* 33b; *Rosh ha-Shanah* 26a; *Ḥullin* 11a; *Avot de-Rabbi Nathan* 16; *Pesikta de-Rav Kahana Aser Te'aser* 6; *Tosafot Ketubot* 104a s.v. *lo ne'heneiti*; *Zohar* 1:52a; 3:296a. At the time of resurrection, the Torah that one has learned is restored to one's gut, where it sings praises. See *Zohar* 1:185a. For the gut as a reference to the female womb, see *Zohar* 1:13a.

128. Translation from Tishby, *Wisdom of the Zohar*, 1344, with some modifications. See also *Zohar* 1:226b; 2:40b (*Pikkudin*); 41a; 183a. For an alternative explanation of the leaven and unleavened bread in the writings of Moses de Leon and other kabbalists, see Tishby, *Wisdom of the Zohar*, 1278 n. 406. For eating as a contributor to the evil inclination in general, see *Zohar* 2:154b.

129. Hamadan is drawing on halakhic principles in which kosher food can nullify a small proportion of nonkosher food, even when the latter is a different kind of food than the former. In his example, it is the force of the camp of Michael, rather than a certain quantity, that enables the one to overpower the other.

130. Joseph of Hamadan, *Sefer Ta'amey ha-Mizwoth*, 221–23. See also *Zohar* 2:182a.

131. Cf. *Tikkunei ha-Zohar*, 70 130b.

132. Bahya ben Asher, "*Shulḥan shel Arba*," 505.

133. Ibid., 506.

134. De Leon, *Sefer ha-Rimmon*, 135. See also *Zohar* 1:226b; 3:95b.

135. *m. Avot* 3:3.

136. See also *Zohar* 2:213b, 253a.

137. Cordovero explains that without words of Torah the table and meal remain connected to the spiritual world and, while the body may be strengthened, nothing strengthens the soul. It is the words of Torah that strengthen the soul, and in that way the table is purified. *Or Yakar,* 10:26.

138. For rabbinic sources regarding eating alone with the king, see *b. Sukkah* 55b; Buber, *Midrash Tanhuma, Pinhas* 78b; *Pesikta de-Rav Kahana,* ed. Dov Mandelbaum (New York: Jewish Theological Seminary, 1962), 193b; Tishby, *Wisdom of the Zohar,* 1253 notes 394–95. Elsewhere it is used as a mark of the special intimacy enjoyed by those favored by the king; thus, in *Sifre* Numbers 119, those who are invited to eat at the king's table are clearly privileged over those who receive presents from the king. See the slightly different formulation of the trope in Revelation 3:20. The biblical source for the trope is 1 Kings 2:7.

139. On all of Israel fulfilling the will of God, see, e.g., *Zohar* 2:152b. On the idealized, preexilic Israel, see *Zohar* 1:84b; 3:209b. In a more materialist vein, the *Zohar* complains that the feast previously reserved for Israel is now given to the other nations. Presumably, in this instance, the feast refers metaphorically to the physical power and wealth held by the surrounding culture. This materialist and populist attitude comfortably stands next to more esoteric passages concerned with the superior hermeneutical abilities of the kabbalists.

140. See *Zohar* 3:197a.

141. See *b. Ta'anit* 10a; *Zohar* 1:84b; 3:209b.

142. See also *Zohar* 3:107b, 195b; *Zohar Hadash Ruth* 86a–c.

143. See Ezekiel 44:3; Rashi, *Commentary on Ezekiel.* Toward the end of the homily, the *Zohar* even raises the question of whether the intimacy of eating with the king at his table is indeed possible: "If you say that others eat at the king's table other than he [the beloved], this is not the case. Rather, the king eats first and then all of the nation. Those that eat with the king when he eats are those that are dear to him above all, and they are appointed to the king's table" (*Zohar* 2:153a). Elsewhere, the distinction regarding appropriate guests is made between Israel and the nations. See *Zohar* 3:256b (*Ra'aya Mehemna*). The parable of the king's table is a common rabbinic trope. See *Bereshit Raba* 56:8; *Vayikra Rabah* 22:8; *Bamidbar Rabah* 4:8, 15:82, 3:13; *Esther Rabah* 2:6; *Midrash Tanhuma* (Warsaw) *Beha'alotekha* 6; Buber, *Midrash Tanhuma, Beha'alotekha* 9; *Mas'ei* 9; *Midrash Tehillim* 4:8.

144. *Zohar* 3:104b.

145. See Daniel 1:8. See also *Zohar* 1:191a; Louis Ginzberg, *Legends of the Jews* (Philadelphia: Jewish Publication Society, 1968), 5:119–20.

146. *Nizozei Orot* n. 1.

147. In *Shushan Edut,* Moses de Leon claims that the sinner loses "his image." Moses ben Shem Tov de Leon, *Shushan Edut,* ed. Gershom Scholem, *Qovez al Yad,* n.s., 8 (1975): 354. See also *The Hebrew Writings,* 94. The term "image," referring to the image of God, is commonly used in the *Zohar;* usually it is used to refer to man as a mystical microcosm of the paradigmatic divine anthropos. In some instances, as in the previous passage, this characteristic has magical attributes. See Tishby, *Wisdom of the Zohar,* 770–73. In *Sefer ha-Mishkal,* de Leon offers a different explanation of the

reason for maintaining separation between these two foodstuffs. In an apparently anticarnivorous impulse, he says that meat is associated with the demonic realm, and milk with the holy realm, and this distinction of the holy and demonic must be sustained (146–47). The *Tikkunei ha-Zohar* posits that the prohibition against mixing meat and milk constitutes a mixing of species, which corresponds to the yoking together of ox and donkey. *Tikkunei ha-Zohar* 14, 30a; cf. *Zohar* 2:125a.

148. Moses de Leon, *Sefer ha-Mishkal*, 59.

149. Physiognomy and metoposcopy became important practices for the kabbalists of Safed. See Lawrence Fine, *Physician of the Soul, Healer of the Cosmos: Isaac Luria and His Kabbalistic Fellowship* (Stanford, Calif.: Stanford University Press, 2003), 153–63.

150. Maimonides, *Guide of the Perplexed*, 3:48, 598–600; Jacob ben Sheshet writes that eating prohibited foods would harm the body of one who was returning from communion with the divine. See ben Sheshet, *Sefer Meshiv Devarim Nekhohim*, ed. Georges Vajda (Jerusalem: Israel Academy of Sciences and Humanities, 1968), 82–83; Gikatilla, "Commentary on the Haggadah," 115.

151. There are other instances in which Moses de Leon advances a universalizing interpretation of the commandments. In his *Sefer Shekel ha-Kodesh*, in the course of his condemning those who have sexual relations with their Moslem maidservants, de Leon says that one aspect of the sin is that the Moslem women have a status of *nidah*, a category that only properly applies to Jewish women. De Leon, *Sefer Shekel ha-Kodesh*, 52–53. In contrast, see Joseph of Hamadan, *Sefer Ta'amei ha-Mizvot*, Negative Commandments mss. Paris 817, folio 150b (cited in Elliot R. Wolfson, "Mystical Rationalization of the Commandments in *Sefer ha-Rimmon*," *Hebrew Union College Annual* 59 (1989): 309 n. 1), who says that the non-Jews are not detrimentally affected by their consumption of impure foods because "like is drawn to like," and as they are impure, so is their food impure. For a similar position, see de Leon, *Sefer ha-Rimmon*, 308–9. In one place, de Leon writes that the meat of animals that are prohibited as *treifot* (animals that are on the verge of death) can be given to dogs as food because dogs have strong souls, presumably in opposition to those of Israel (313).

152. See *b. Pesahim* 56a, which recounts that Hizkiyah buried a book of medication, which, Rashi explains, allowed sick people to be healed immediately without appropriate contrition. See *b. Berakhot* 10b; Maimonides, *Commentary on the Mishnah*, ed. and trans. Yosef Kafih (Jerusalem: Mosad ha-Rav Kuk, 1987), *Pesahim* 4:10.

153. The *Zohar* has a decidedly ambivalent attitude toward magic. While a figure like Balaam is soundly condemned as a master sorcerer, there is a rabbinic tradition that describes King Solomon as a master of forbidden works, without attaching any negative judgment to that pursuit; this tradition is subsequently adopted in the kabbalah. See Moses ben Nahman, "Introduction" to his *Commentary on the Torah*, 6; *Zohar* 2:128a; 3:19a, 77a, 194b. On magic in the *Zohar*, see Wolfson, "Left Contained in the Right," 27–37; Cohen-Alloro, "From Supernal Wisdom."

154. Daniel Boyarin talks about the relationship of the two in rabbinic literature, arguing that they were treated similarly by the rabbis: each was viewed as being primarily an agent of the continuity of vitality and of life, with ancillary benefits, such

as pleasure and social intimacy. See Daniel Boyarin, *Carnal Israel: Reading Sex in Talmudic Culture* (Berkeley: University of California Press, 1993), 72–73, 109–19.

155. *Zohar* 1:240a. See *Shushan Edut*, 339; *Sod Eser Sefirot Belimah*, 381. See *Sefer ha-Rimmon*, 228–29, where it says that the *sefirah Yesod* quenches the Garden (*Malkhut*) with dew, an image of erotic nourishment.

156. Daniel C. Matt, *The Zohar: Pritzker Edition* (Stanford, Calif.: Stanford University Press, 2004), 177.

157. As cited in ibid., 177 n. 564.

158. *Zohar* 2:88a–b. In the Sabbath hymns of Rabbi Isaac Luria, the Sabbath delicacies serve as ornaments for the *Shekhinah* in preparation for her nuptials. See Yehuda Liebes, "Hymns for the Sabbath Meals of the Ari," *Molad*, n.s., 23 (February 1972): 544.

159. Roland Barthes, "Reading Brillat-Savarin," in *The Rustle of Language*, ed. François Wahl and trans. Richard Howard (Berkeley: University of California Press, 1986), 267.

160. *Ketubot* 62b; see *Zohar* 1:14a–b, 49b, 50a, 112a (*Midrash ha-Ne'elam*), 257a (*Hashmatot*); 2:63b, 136a, 204b; 3:78a, 143a (*Idra Raba*); *Tikkunei ha-Zohar* 21a, 38b, 57a, 61a, 78a, 90a. According to *Zohar* 2:89a, the fertility of the kabbalists is enhanced.

161. See also *Zohar* 1:246a; *Bereshit Raba* 86:6; *Shemot Rabah* 1:32; *Tanhuma* Exodus 11; Rashi on Genesis 39:6, Exodus 2:20; *Tosafot Menahot* 94a s.v. *shetei ha-lehem*.

162. Wolfson has written extensively on the containment of the feminine in the masculine in Jewish mysticism. As one example, see Elliot R. Wolfson, "Woman— the Feminine as Other in Theosophic Kabbalah: Some Philosophical Observations on the Divine Androgyne," in *The Other in Jewish Thought and History*, ed. L. Silberstein and R. Cohn (New York: New York University Press, 1994), 166–204.

163. Bernard McGinn has commented: "Much of the power of Western mysticism may come from its deliberate eroticizing of the relation between the human virgin and the Divine 'Better Bridegroom,' as if the absorption of the erotic element into the internal arena becomes more forceful and more total the more it negates all deliberate external expression." McGinn, *The Foundations of Mysticism* (New York: Crossroad, 1994), 214.

164. De Leon, *Sefer ha-Rimmon*, 314–15. See, however, de Leon, *Sefer ha-Mishkal*, 147, which offers another interpretation of the prohibition of meat and milk, saying that milk is related to the *sefirah* of *Hesed*, and meat to the demonic entity *Kez Kol Basar* ("End of all Flesh" from Genesis 5:13) and that these should never be mixed together. Another interpretation for the prohibition against mixing meat and milk is offered at *Zohar* 2:125a: "It is written, 'The choice first fruits of your soil [you shall bring to the house of the Lord your God.] You shall not boil a kid in its mother's milk' (Exodus 23:19), so that That Side will not suckle from the milk of its mother, holiness will not be rendered impure and judgments will not be aroused. . . . Whoever unites this food [meat and milk] as one, or in one hour or in one meal, causes a kid to be roasted in its skin before those above and support for impurity approaches it, causes judgements to be aroused in the world." This is an ideal example of the kabbalistic method of developing explanations of the commandments. A prohibition can be interpreted along any of the conventional lines that signify the arousal of evil in the world, whether through inducing judgments in the world or in eliciting other

illicit behaviors. In the last example, the reference to not eating meat and milk together in one hour is a sign of the Jewish Germanic influence upon the *Zohar*'s understanding of practice. The practice of Sephardim developing at the time was to wait six hours between meat and milk, whereas in Ashkenaz, one hour sufficed. Ta-Shma, *The Revealed in the Concealed*, 32.

165. In this instance "another land" is not a term for the demonic. See however, *Zohar* 1:244b and *Nizozei Zohar* n. 3, where Gad's adoption of land beyond the Jordan River for habitation is considered a spiritual flaw.

166. The main text of the *Zohar* has "flowing along in the body," and another alternate version has "it was swallowed in the body." I have chosen the first alternative version that Margaliot includes to highlight my point.

167. See *Zohar* 3:272a, which says that the bread distributed at the meal constitutes the points of the holy name and is called "the crumbs of the olive-sized portion"; these crumbs are said to receive drops of seed. Here too bread is homologized to divine seminal fluid. The *Zohar* says that it is for this reason that one who drops a piece of bread is condemned to poverty. See b. *Hullin 105b*.

168. See *Tikkunei ha-Zohar* 15, 30b, where bread serves as a symbol for the divine semen.

169. See also *Zohar* 2:62b.

170. See Elliot R. Wolfson, "Crossing Gender Boundaries in Kabbalistic Ritual and Myth," in *Circle in the Square: Studies in the Use of Gender in Kabbalistic Symbolism* (Albany: State University of New York Press, 1995), 110–21.

171. Ibid., 98–110.

172. *Zohar* 1:15a.

173. *Tikkunei ha-Zohar* 16, 41a–b; 21, 52b.

Chapter 4

1. Isaiah Tishby, *The Wisdom of the Zohar*, trans. David Goldstein (Oxford: Oxford University Press, 1989), 9–12.

2. Michel Jeanneret, *A Feast of Words: Banquets and Table Talk in the Renaissance*, trans. Jeremy Whiteley and Emma Hughes (1987; reprint, Chicago: University of Chicago Press, 1991), 260.

3. Tishby, *Wisdom of the Zohar*, 1236. Though the *Zohar* usually refers to the *sefirot* with the nomenclature of the ten *sefirot*, *Keter* through *Shekhinah/Malkhut*, some passages refer to three configurations of the *sefirot*, *Atika Kadisha* (the Holy Ancient One), *Ze'ir Anpin* (the Impatient One), and *Hakal Tapuhin Kadishin* (the Field of Holy Apples). According to this configuration, *Atika Kadisha* corresponds to the most recondite area of the Godhead, including *Ein Sof* and the *sefirah Keter*; *Ze'ir Anpin* corresponds to the next eight *sefirot*, *Hokhmah* through *Yesod* with *Tif'eret* as the primary focus; and, *Hakal Tapuhin Kadishin* corresponds to *Shekhinah*.

4. See, e.g., *Zohar* 2:88a-88b; *Tikkunei ha-Zohar* 24, 69b–70a; 47, 84a; Tishby, *Wisdom of the Zohar*, 874, 1233, 1235; Elliot K. Ginsburg, *The Sabbath in the Classical Kabbalah* (Albany: State University of New York Press, 1989), 83, 117. Cf., however, Joseph of Hamadan, "A Critical Edition of the *Sefer Ta'amey ha-Mizwoth* (Book of Reasons of the Commandments) Attributed to Isaac Ibn Farhi," ed. Menachem Meier (Ph.D. diss., Brandeis University, 1974), 114–16, where the table refers to the

sefirah Tif'eret. In *The Hebrew Writings*, 48, the table represents Metatron and the table legs represent Michael, Gabriel, Raphael, and Nuriel. For a discussion of unifications at the Sabbath table in the literature of *Ra'aya Mehemna* and *Tikkunei ha-Zohar*, see Pinchas Giller, *The Enlightened Will Shine: Symbolization and Theurgy in the Later Strata of the Zohar* (Albany: State University of New York Press, 1993), 111–14. See Exodus 26:35; *b. Yoma* 51b; *b. Menahot* 86b; *Zohar* 3:272b (*Ra'aya Mehemna*); *Tikkunei ha-Zohar* Introduction 13b, 14b; 47, 84a. In zoharic symbolism, north is the direction of the *sefirah* of *Gevurah*, and the table is illuminated by the candelabrum, which is in the south, thus symbolizing the flow of divine light from the *sefirah* of *Hesed* to the *sefirah* of *Gevurah*. See Moses ben Nahman, *Commentary on the Torah*, ed. Charles Chavel (Jerusalem: Mosad ha-Rav Kuk, 1960), Commentary on Exodus 25:30. Part of the reason for the interchangeable nature of the table and the altar is that the exchange can be found in scripture. See, e.g., Ezekiel 44:16.

5. The Jewish Publication Society translates this as, "Yea, all tables are covered with vomit and filth, so that no place (*maqom*) is left." For the biblical source of "sacrifices of the dead," see Psalm 106:28.

6. *The Mishnah*, trans. Herbert Danby (New York: Oxford University Press, 1985), 450; I have substituted "Torah" where Danby has "Law." See also *b. Megillah* 12b.

7. *b. Berakhot* 55a. See *Zohar* 2:168b.

8. See, e.g., *Zohar* 2:153a, 157a, 169a; 3:21b, 60b, 62a–b, 186a, 189b, 201b. For the normative prescription of reciting mystical sermons at the table, see *Zohar* 2:153b, 168b; 3:245b; *Zohar Hadash Ruth* 47a.

9. Usually the world-to-come is a cognomen for the sefirah *Binah*. See, e.g., *Zohar* 1:31a, 34a, 141b, 210a; 2:31b, 36b, 98a, 132a; 3:26a, 40a, 41a, 290b.

10. Ronald L. Grimes, *Beginnings in Ritual Studies* (reprint; 1985, Columbia: University of South Carolina Press, 1995), 28–29.

11. One section of the *Zohar* lists ten rituals of the Sabbath meals and suggests that these ten correspond to the *sefirot*. *Zohar* 3:271b–272b; *Zohar Hadash Ruth* 46a–b. This is an example of the theurgic anagogy of the *Zohar:* the lower world is modeled after the upper world as a means to energize the upper and to draw it down into the lower. In this passage, it is the performative value of the meal that is significant for the *Zohar*'s goals rather than the appearance or taste of the food, because only one of the ten acts is directly related to the physical act of eating; such diverse rituals as inviting poor people to the table, reciting the grace after meals, and the exchange of words of Torah are all included in the list, suggesting that it is the ritualization of the meal, rather than the eating itself, with which the *Zohar* is concerned.

12. See Caroline Walker Bynum, *Holy Feast and Holy Fast: The Religious Significance of Food to Medieval Women* (Berkeley: University of California Press, 1987), 60–61; Jeanneret, *Feast of Words*, 55. Bynum concludes that it is the lability of the presentation of the food that further enables the Christian figures she studies to have transformative experiences in the context of dining. The texts that we are considering bear the same lability in terms of the food's signification and the experience that it engenders, but without the variety and emphasis on visual prompts to which Bynum points.

13. Cf. *b. Pesaḥim* 105a. This talmudic passage represents rabbis sitting down for a meal and the meal prompting a halakhic discussion about the meal itself. Moreover, Rav Hemnuna Saba is one of the primary figures in this drama and is a central figure in the zoharic narratives, as well. In *b. Pesaḥim* 103b and *Ḥullin* 86b, Rav Yeiva Saba, another one of the main actors in the zoharic drama, is represented as a waiter at meals, chastising the other rabbis for improper practice.

14. The *yanuka* is referring to Numbers 15:19 and Genesis 40:10, the two verses that he has just expounded upon.

15. See also *Zohar* 3:60b, 62a–b.

16. One teaching in the *Tikkunei ha-Zohar* explains the original sin with regard to the commandment to separate a portion of bread (*ḥallah*) for the priests. Wheat was the fruit of the Tree of Life, and improper use of it led to the fall. The scope of the sin is magnified because the bread is deemed to comprise all seven species of the Land of Israel, foods that enjoy special scriptural and rabbinic status. *Tikkunei ha-Zohar* 16, 31a. Tying one more scriptural/rabbinic datum to the symbol of bread intensifies the latter's power as a symbol and emphasizes the totalizing nature of Adam and Eve's sin.

17. See also *Zohar* 1:238b–239b, 240a. For an observation of a similar cycle of contemplative ascent and blessing, see Seth Lance Brody, "Human Hands Dwell in Heavenly Heights: Worship and Mystical Experience in Thirteenth Century Kabbalah" (Ph.D. diss., University of Pennsylvania, 1991), 459.

18. See also, e.g., *Zohar* 1:238b–240b. This is the anthropological side of the coin, whose flip side is the spiritual ecosystem in which food turns into homilies, which in turn serves as food.

19. Or "about this meal."

20. The following homily (*Zohar* 2:153a–b) indicates that satiety is a technical term and that the grace after meals can be recited, according to the normative halakhah, even if only an olive's-worth (*ke-zayit*) has been eaten. There is a continuing tension between a pleasure-affirming embodied experience that leads to communion with the Divine and a more modest physical experience that must be accompanied by certain mystical intentions to attain that same degree of experience.

21. A similar result occurs when the kabbalists are joined together in love. The simple meaning of their joining is that they will sit together; but the term *yithaber* is never innocent of polysemic valence, and, as is stated explicitly in the mysterious riddling of the Old Man of *Mishpatim,* the physical union of the kabbalists entails a mystical union of one with the other as well. Furthermore, each of the kisses that the kabbalists bestow upon each other following the delivery of mystical homilies, as at the beginning of the previously cited passage, while continuing a behavior that was current among the rabbis of the Talmud, entails a union as well. In rabbinic literature, see *j. Ḥagigah* 2:1, 77a; *t. Ḥagigah* 2:1; in zoharic literature, see e.g. *Zohar* 1:6a, 12a, 51a, 61a, 64b, 70a, 72a, 89b, 92b, 148b, 239b; 2:12a, 169a, 170a, 190a, 199b, 203a, 209a; 3:187b, 189b, 191b, 196b, 261a, 303a. For the kiss as a metaphor for the union of different entities in zoharic literature, see, e.g., *Zohar* 1:137a, 168a; 2:38a, 97a, 124b, 146a–b, 254a; 3:59b, 130b, 201b; *Zohar Ḥadash* 60c, 63d-64b; see also *Sefer Yezirah* 6:4. Regarding the meaning of kissing in the *Zohar,* see Yehuda Liebes, "*Zohar* and Eros," *Alpayim—A Multidisciplinary Publication for Contemporary Thought and*

Literature 9 (1994): 105–8. See also *b. Berakhot* 64a, which says that participating in a meal with a sage is like benefiting from the *Shekhinah.*

22. The liturgical declaration of God's unity. The ritual entails the recitation of Deuteronomy 6:4–9, Deuteronomy 11:13–21, and Numbers 15:37–41 as part of the morning and evening rites.

23. *Zohar* 3:186a. The ability of the *yanuka* to apprehend a quality of the soul through the olfactory sense is an echo of the biblical story of Isaac smelling Jacob's clothing. According to Rashi's commentary, Isaac smelled the fragrant aroma of the Garden of Eden rather than the smell of the hunt or of sheep. See Rashi, Commentary on Genesis 27:27. See *Bereshit Raba* 65:22; *b. Ta'anit* 29b. A passage in *Zohar* 3:233b compares the first five words of the *Shema* (Deuteronomy 6:4) to the leaves of the lily, with its beautiful fragrance. See the comments of Azulai, *Nizozei Orot* in *Zohar* 3:186a n. 3. Caroline Bynum refers to the myroblites, the women with sweet-smelling bodies, as one of the ways in which there was somatic expression of personal sanctity. Whereas in the medieval period this phenomenon was noted with regard to women only, in antiquity it was reported of men as well. See Bynum, *Holy Feast and Holy Fast,* 201. For instances of scent as a marker of the divine presence, see *Zohar* 3:67a, 98b; Joseph of Hamadan, "Joseph of Hamadan's *Sefer Tashak*: Critical Edition with Introduction," ed. Jeremy Zwelling (Ph.D. diss., Brandeis University, 1975), 14–16, 26. When righteous souls ascend heavenward, the archangel Michael sacrifices them on the supernal altar. The fragrance they exude gives comfort to God. Charles Mopsik, *Les Grands Textes de la Cabale: Les Rites Qui Font Dieu* (Paris: Verdier, 1993), 198–99.

24. *Zohar* 3:186a.

25. *Zohar* 3:272b (*Ra'aya Mehemna*).

26. In fact, it seems that the second source, from the *Ra'aya Mehemna,* is a homiletic reinterpretation of the original zoharic text.

27. Jeanneret, *Feast of Words,* 35.

28. On Mauss's *techniques du corp,* see chapter 1, notes 53–59.

29. For a short survey of the meditative use of sitting in the history of kabbalistic literature, see Mark Verman, *The History and Varieties of Jewish Meditation* (Northvale, N.J.: Jason Aronson, 1996), 72–77.

30. Elliot R. Wolfson, "*Yeridah la-Merkavah:* Typology of Ecstasy and Enthronement in Ancient Jewish Mysticism," in *Mystics of the Book: Themes, Topics, and Typologies,* ed. R. A. Herrera (New York: Peter Lang, 1993), 21–22.

31. See, e.g., *Zohar* 1:64b, 84a; 2:38b; 3:53b, 266b, 304a (*Tosafot*).

32. See, e.g., *Zohar* 3:161b.

33. See, e.g., *Zohar* 2:36b; 3:201b, 161b, 221b, 266b.

34. See *Zohar* 1:87a.

35. See, e.g., *Zohar* 1:289a; 3:20b, 21a, 268b. The images of sitting under a rock or sitting in a cave evoke the representation of Moses attaining a vision of God while in the cleft of the rock. See Exodus 33:22.

36. See, e.g., *Zohar* 2:15a, 16b; *Zohar Hadash* 8a (*Midrash ha-Ne'elam*), 10a–b *Midrash ha-Ne'elam,* Va-yeshev 29a, 29b (*Sitrei Torah*) 50c–d. See Liebes's analyses regarding the significance of place and being established in a particular place. *Sections of the Zohar Lexicon* (Ph.D. diss., Hebrew University of Jerusalem, 1976), 362–66.

37. *Zohar* 3:71a.

38. See, e.g., *Zohar* 1:233a; 2:10b; 3:53b, 64a. One consideration that requires further study with regard to the significance attached to sitting in the zoharic literature is the relationship of sitting to standing. In normative Jewish practice, the seminal part of the worship service, performed three times a day, is the *amidah*, the silent prayer, performed while standing. How a shift of valence from the normative stance to that of sitting occurs invokes the questions of the relationship of nonnormative practice to normative, mystical to nonmystical, and the interaction of mystical praxis with ordinary life. For a full survey of physical gestures performed during the daily prayers, see Eric Zimmer, "Poses and Postures during Prayer," *Sidra* 5 (1989): 89–130. As to the privileging of standing over sitting for prayer, see, e.g., *b. Berakhot* 30a; Uri Ehrlich, *The Non-Verbal Language of Jewish Prayer* (Jerusalem: Magnes, 1999), 17–18.

39. See *Zohar* 1:223a. The *Zohar* is interpreting Moses' comment "I remained on the mountain" (Deuteronomy 9:9).

40. See Margaliot, *Nizozei Zohar* 86b n. 9.

41. Hayyim Yosef David Azulai, *Nizozei Orot* to *Zohar* 1:72a, notes 2–3. He glosses a comment in the *Zohar* that says, "Words of Torah require preparation (*tikuna*) of the body and preparation (*tikuna*) of the heart." For Azulai, the body's preparation is a garment, and this is paralleled by the *kavvanah* that serves as a garment for the heart.

42. Many more examples can be adduced. See, e.g., *Zohar* 1:92b–93a, 94a–b, 155b, 200a, 241b; 2:20a, 36b, 37a, 38b; 3:7a, 64a, 84b, 157b, 193a, 233a, 268a. Note *Zohar Hadash Va-yeze* 28b (*Midrash ha-Ne'elam*): "Rabbi Yose was sitting and engaged with the Torah. Rabbi Abba approached him. Rabbi Yose said, 'You are a master of teaching.' He came before him. They sat and engaged themselves with the Torah. Before they sat down, night fell. They sat and engaged [in Torah study] until the middle of the night." In some of these passages, it is apparent that even if the term "they sat" (*yatvu*) refers primarily to "remaining," it bears the additional meaning of sitting. Other examples of sitting include sitting and crying, sitting while waiting for someone, sitting and having visions, and sitting and uniting as a group.

43. See also *Zohar* 2:166a.

44. *b. Berakhot* 46b.

45. This was the practice of Roman feasts; chairs were used only for ordinary meals. Paul Veyne, "The Roman Empire," in *A History of Private Life: From Pagan Rome to Byzantium*, ed. Paul Veyne and trans. Arthur Goldhammer (Cambridge, Mass.: Belknap, 1987), 187–88.

46. It is a euphemistic usage in rabbinic literature to refer to females as "beds" and one that is frequently carried over into the kabbalistic literature. See *b. Pesahim* 112a–b; *b. Megillah* 13a; *b. Ketubot* 62b; *b. Gittin* 70a; *b. Bava Kama* 82a; *b. Nidah* 17a, 31a, 43a; *j. Pesahim* 28a; *Bereshit Raba* 64:5; *Vayikra Rabah* 21:8; *Midrash Tehillim* 73:4. The phrase *shimesh mitato*, which means literally "to serve one's bed," is an idiom meaning to perform one's conjugal obligations, thus blurring the line between bed and wife. See Eliezer ben Yehuda, *A Complete Dictionary of Ancient and Modern Hebrew* (Jerusalem and Tel Aviv: La'am Publishing, 1925), 6:2945. There is some ambiguous usage of the term *mishkav* in rabbinic literature, referring to both "bed" and "wife." See *Midrash Tannaim*, ed. David Zvi Hoffman (Israel: Books Export Enterprises,

1980), commenting on Deuteronomy 23:22, page 152; *b. Rosh ha-Shanah* 6a; *b. Sanhedrin* 22a. My thanks to Herb Basser and Admiel Kosman for their help with this material. In the *Zohar*, see, e.g., 1:37a, 225b, 226b, 248b, 250b; 2:5a, 48b; 3:60a, 210b; *Zohar Ḥadash* 25c. Gikatilla refers to each of the body's limbs as a "throne " for the corresponding *sefirah*. Gikatilla, *Sha'arei Orah*, 1:49–50.

47. Joseph of Hamadan, *Sefer Tashak*, 244, 332. Richard Sennett has written about sitting as subservience in classical antiquity: "To sit was also to submit, as when a young girl came to the house of her new husband and signified her submission to his rule in a ritual which made her sit for the first time by this hearth. Vase paintings depict urban slaves, also, performing their tasks either sitting down or crouching down. The theatre put this aspect of sitting to use in tragedy: the seated audience was literally in a position to empathize with a vulnerable protagonist, for both the spectators' and actors' bodies were placed in a humble, submissive position to a higher law." See Richard Sennett, *Flesh and Stone: The Body and the City in Western Civilization* (New York: Norton, 1994), 60. As we have seen, the zoharic kabbalists are no strangers to hierarchies, either in the divine, human, or divine-human domains. Nonetheless, the value that is assigned to the subjectivity of the individual kabbalists in their desire to attain union—by assuming a supine position—with God, as well as with the *Shekhinah*, who adopts the submissive role in relationship to the blessed Holy One, resists an overly neat equation between the classical seating and that of the kabbalists.

48. The *Idra Raba* is located in *Zohar* 3:127b–145a. Regarding the theosophic significance of the seating arrangement at the Idra Raba, see Liebes, "The Messiah of the *Zohar* (in Hebrew)," 130–32; Yehuda Liebes, "The Messiah of the *Zohar* (in Hebrew)," in *The Messianic Idea in Jewish Thought: A Study Conference in Honour of the Eightieth Birthday of Gershom Scholem*, ed. Shemuel Rom (Jerusalem: Israel Academy of Sciences and Humanities, 1982), 20–21.

49. See *Zohar* 2:14b; 3:60a, 180a, 203a; Liebes, "Messiah of the Zohar," 129 n. 179, and *Sections of the Zohar Lexicon*, 359 n. 48 and 362–66.

50. See Ezekiel 1:7; *b. Berakhot* 10b. The role of the seating plans can be seen further in *Zohar* 3:272a, where the guest leads the introductory *zimmun* to the grace after the meal so that he can bless "the master of the house." The double meaning of "master of the house" includes both his human host and the divine master. My interest here is the human dynamic of the relationship between guest and host, where the arrangement of persons at the table reflects the dynamics of the supernal paradigm above.

51. See also *Zohar* 2:88b, where Rabbi Shimon would announce the designation of each of the Sabbath meals and then "sit and rejoice."

52. See Arthur W. Frank, "For a Sociology of the Body: An Analytical Review," in *The Body: Social Process and Cultural Theory*, ed. Mike Featherstone, Mike Hepworth, and Bryan S. Turner (London: Sage, 1991), 53, 79–89.

53. See Melila Hellner-Eshed, "'A River Goes out from Eden': The Language of Mystical Invocation in the *Zohar*," *Kabbalah: Journal for the Study of Jewish Mystical Texts* 2 (1997): 287–310, who suggests that one of the ways in which the *Zohar* functions as a literary text is in the performative modality, trying to elicit mystical praxis from, and evoke mystical experience in, the reader of the text.

54. Catherine Bell, *Ritual Theory, Ritual Practice* (New York: Oxford University Press, 1992), 70.

55. Ibid., 94–117.

56. See Margaret Visser, *The Rituals of Dinner: The Origins, Evolution, Eccentricities, and Meaning of Table Manners* (New York: Grove Weidenfeld, 1991).

57. The minor tractates *Derekh Erez* and *Derekh Erez Zuta* do contain several statements regarding one's conduct during eating that cover the issue of manners, i.e., prescriptions against belching, licking one's fingers, eating while standing, etc. See chapters 5–6. Interestingly, the *Zohar* does not appear to be drawing upon these works at all. Bahya ben Asher, however, makes full use of these texts in his treatise on dining. See Bahya ben Asher, "*Shulḥan shel Arba,*" in *Kitve Rabbenu Bahya*, ed. Charles Chavel (Jerusalem: Mosad ha-Rav Kuk, 1987), 497–501.

58. Although most of the prescribed activities originate in normative rabbinic behavior, in context their meaning may shift. See *b. Berakhot* 46a–47a.

59. See Moses ben Shem Tov de Leon, *Sefer ha-Rimmon*, ed. Elliot R. Wolfson (Atlanta: Scholars Press, 1988), 104. Cf. *b. Berakhot* 55a; *Ḥagigah* 27a; *Menaḥot* 97a.

60. See *Bereshit Raba* 43:6; *Midrash Mishlei* 31:4; *Midrash Tehillim* 41:7; *Seder Eliyahu Rabah* 25:5; *Seder Eliyahu Zuta* 14:3. There are also ten matters related to the cup of blessing, deriving from *b. Berakhot* 51a, similarly associated with the ten *sefirot*. See *Zohar* 3:273b.

61. The zoharic text as cited in Menaḥem Recanati's *Commentary on the Torah* phrases this in the positive. Recanati, *Commentary on the Torah* (Jerusalem: Mordekhai Attia, 1961), 84c. See also *Zohar* 1:138b, 2:168b, 3:198b, 236a (*Ra'aya Mehemna*); *Tikkunei ha-Zohar* 140b. See *Zohar* 3:246a, which adds that, as one should not swallow one's food but rather chew carefully, one should utter words of Torah or prayer with the same deliberation. This connection between eating and praying or studying as activities of the oral cavity is, however, only allusive rather than suggesting an ontological link or phenomenological link. On this point, see *Zohar* 3:236a (*Ra'aya Mehemna*). Regarding the avoidance of gluttony, see *Ozar Midrashim* 27:38. See *Zohar* 3:272a, which, in its list of eating norms, prescribes that one should give out large pieces of bread at his table so that he should not appear to be a glutton. Regarding the importance of eating slowly, see *b. Shabbat* 76a. Regarding chewing in the rabbinic tradition, see *b. Sanhedrin* 103b; Tosafot, *Ḥagigah* 27a s.v. *shulḥano shel adam mekhaper alav*. These sources could be referring merely to the requirement to give food to the needy, but the locution regarding chewing is provocative in that it offers a rare comment on the physical act of eating and digesting. For the alternate interpretation, see Rashi, *Sanhedrin* 103b, s.v. *shulḥano shel adam mekhaper alav*.

62. See *Zohar* 2:168b; *b. Yoma* 39a; *Bereshit Raba* 45:5; *Devarim Rabah* 6:11; *Kohelet Rabah* 2:23. In the *Ra'aya Mehemna* version of these rules, the text reads, "One should not be ravenous and gluttonous, at the table of the king," whereas the *Zohar Ḥadash* version says, "One should not be ravenous and gluttonous but rather *like* one who is eating before the king." In this example, the mythical dimension is more pronounced in the *Ra'aya Mehemna*, as one does sit at the table of the king rather than just adopt appropriate behavior for such a situation. The literal formulation used in the *Zohar* is that "one should not be a swallower (*bela'an*) and a glutton (*gargaran*)." In rabbinic materials, this latter term is also used to refer to someone with an uncon-

trollable sexual appetite. See *m. Niddah* 10:8. See also *b. Ḥagigah* 14b, which suggests that Ben Zoma appears to have fallen prey to this temptation, as he is described as one who ate more than his fill of honey.

63. In a different portrayal of gluttony, Joseph of Hamadan interprets Pharaoh's second dream from Genesis 41. He suggests that the "thin and scorched ears [of grain]" are from Lilith, a concubine who receives sustenance through proscribed seminal emissions. They take in the overflow through swallowing, as indicated in the biblical text (v. 7). Joseph of Hamadan, *Sefer Toledot ha-Adam*, in *Sefer ha-Malkhut* (Casablanca: Imprimerie Razon, 1930), 98a. Lack of restraint in the sexual arena is inexorably followed by gluttony of a different sort.

64. See also *Zohar* 3:41a–b.

65. An alternative medical model is offered, saying that swallowing one's food causes one to choke. See *b. Ta'anit* 5b. Interestingly, this rabbinic source advocates that one avoid discussion during one's meal because this will lead to choking. The *Zohar*, which so strongly affirms the importance of exchanging words of Torah at one's meal, selectively excludes this part of the explanation.

66. See, e.g., Elliot R. Wolfson, *Through a Speculum That Shines: Visionary Experience and Imagination in Medieval Jewish Mysticism* (Princeton, N.J.: Princeton University Press, 1994), 336–45, 357–68.

67. See also *Zohar* 2:183a–b. In this latter source, the distinction is drawn between the *mazah* and the manna as two different breads that the Israelites ate, thus suggesting a different bodily ability to consume different kinds of comestibles contingent upon their spiritual attainment. There is a midrashic tradition that establishes circumcision as the prerequisite for eating the manna; see *Shemot Rabah* 19:6; Elliot R. Wolfson, "Left Contained in the Right: A Study in Zoharic Hermeneutics," *AJS Review* 11, no. 1 (1986): 51 and n.107.

68. The term "bread of angels" (*leḥem avirim*) originates in the Standard Revised Version of Psalm 78:25. The Jewish Publication Society translation has "a hero's meal." See also *Zohar* 2:40a.

69. The halakhah distinguishes between two stages in the ritual of circumcision, *milah* and *peri'ah*. The first is the cutting of the foreskin, and the second entails pulling down the membrane to reveal the corona. The kabbalists considered these two stages to correspond to the masculine and feminine aspects of the Divine, the *sefirot Yesod* and *Shekhinah*. See *Zohar* 1:13a, 32a–b, 47b, 69a, 71b, 72b, 117a; 2:40a, 60b, 125b; 3:14a, 91b, 115b, 163a.

70. Note that there is a strong connection between the biblical restriction against non-Jews eating the Passover offering and the rabbinic prohibition against teaching Torah to non-Jews. See Exodus 12:48; *b. Ḥagigah* 13a. In both instances, the presence of the foreskin is the impediment.

71. The Jewish body is thus similarly superior to the body of a Moslem for, according to the *Zohar*, Islamic law requires only the cutting away of the foreskin, whereas Jewish law also prescribes the peeling away of the remaining flesh to reveal the corona of the boy's penis. This secondary action results in the union with the male aspect of the Divine, whereas the former only allows for union with the *Shekhinah*. See *Zohar* 2:32a, 86a, 87a; Moses de Leon, *Sefer Shekel ha-Kodesh*, 67; Ronald C. Kiener, "The Image of Islam in the *Zohar*," *Jerusalem Studies in Jewish Thought* 8 (1989): 55–59.

72. Women are apparently excluded from the eating of the *maẓah* and the manna, whereas in the desert, according to the biblical account, one presumes women's participation. The *Zohar* is a strongly androcentric and idealizing text, imagining the ideal community as one of kabbalistic scholars engaged in material and spiritual communion. At the same time, it should be noted that, unlike rabbinic culture, which has been characterized by Boyarin as "androcentric, not gynephobic," the kabbalah on the whole has a much more troubled relationship with females and the feminine than do the rabbis in their androcentric milieu. Daniel Boyarin, *Carnal Israel: Reading Sex in Talmudic Culture* (Berkeley: University of California Press, 1993), 94.

73. In a Persian kabbalistic song written to honor Rabbi Shimon bar Yoḥai, we find the lyric, "Happy is the man who merited to see you and happy are those who eat your bread. . . . Bar Yoḥai, the one who birthed you shall rejoice, your father and mother will be happy," *Hillula Raba* (Baghdad: n.p. 1908), 61b, cited in Moshe Hallamish, "Problems in the Research of the Influence of Kabbalah on Prayer," in *Kabbalah: In Liturgy, Law, and Custom* (Ramat-Gan, Isr.: Bar Ilan University Press, 2000), 24 n. 16.

74. The Jewish Publication Society translation of the Hebrew Bible has "We have come to loathe." I have translated the term *nafsheinu* as "our souls" because of the kabbalah's proclivity for essentializing.

75. The term used for flaw, *pagim*, is the same term used to denote the mark of the covenant on the improperly used male sexual organ. See *Zohar* 1:50a, 200b, 201a, 240b; 2:108b, 214b; 3:5b, 34a, 44b, 77a, 78a, 90a.

76. See *b. Ta'anit* 9a; *Zohar* 2:190b; 3:102b. Note that Aaron is considered to be on the right, Naḥshon ben Aminadav on the left. While Aaron is normally placed on the left in relation to Moses, he is placed on the right here because Moses is aligned with the paradigmatic masculine potency, Tif'eret.

77. An aggadic teaching recounts that Moses warns God to forgive Israel after the episode with the calf or else people of the world will say that his power has faded like a woman's. b. *Berakhot* 32a.

78. See Gershom Scholem, "Shekhinah: The Feminine Element in Divinity," in *On the Mystical Shape of the Godhead*, ed. Joachim Neugroschel (New York: Schocken, 1991), 189–90.

79. See Thomas Laqueur, *Making Sex: Body and Gender from the Greeks to Freud* (Cambridge, Mass.: Harvard University Press, 1990), 35–36, 41–43, 14–106. This should be seen in contrast to the lactation imagery attributed to Jesus and other male figures studied by Caroline Walker Bynum. See Caroline Walker Bynum, "Jesus as Mother and Abbot as Mother: Some Themes in Twelfth-Century Cistercian Writing," in *Jesus as Mother: Studies in the Spirituality of the High Middle Ages* (Berkeley: University of California Press, 1982) 110–69. Further, in the medieval pietistic and mystical literature of the figures she has studied, producing, preparing, and serving food are paradigmatic functions of womanhood. See Bynum, *Holy Feast and Holy Fast*, 190–93, 220–22, 233–34.

80. Rabbi Naḥman of Braẓlav spells out the possibility of one man receiving "semen" from another in the following remarkable passage: "And why is advice referred to as an aspect of marriage? Because (*b. Berakhot* 61a) the organs excrete, and the organs are the organs of engenderment, the organs of semen. Thus, when you

receive advice from a man, it is as if you receive semen from him." *Likkutei Moharan* 7:3; cited in Nathaniel Deutsch, "Rabbi Nahman of Bratslav: The Zaddik as Androgyne," in *God's Voice from the Void,* ed. Shaul Magid (Albany: State University of New York Press, 2000), 200.

81. On the role of humor in the *Zohar,* see Liebes, "*Zohar* and Eros," 80–85. Although I believe that Liebes has looked at an important component of the literary charm of the *Zohar,* his assumption that even the *Zohar's* treatment of evil should be understood ironically seems overstated. On irony in the *Zohar,* see Mikhal Oron, "'Place Me as a Seal upon Your Heart': Studies in the Poetics of the Author of the *Zohar* in the Saba of Mishpatim Section," in *Massu'ot: Studies in Kabbalistic Literature and Jewish Philosophy,* ed. Mikhal Oron and Amos Goldreich (Jerusalem: Bialik Institute, 1994) 1–24.

82. Regarding the literary use of weapons in the *Zohar,* see Liebes, "Messiah of the *Zohar* (in Hebrew)," 132–33; Liebes, " Messiah of the *Zohar* (in English)," 21–22. There is a venerable tradition of competitive and even violent imagery representing the sages and their interactions. Most explicitly, *b. Sanhedrin* 24a refers to the sages of Babylon as assaulting each other (*mehavlim zeh ba-zeh be-halakhah*), in contrast to the sages of Palestine, who behave pleasantly with each other. This critique of the competitive nature of Babylonian discourse falls by the wayside among the tide of competitive interactions within the talmudic corpus. In the same tractate, we read that the "war of Torah" is waged by those who bear "bundles of *mishnayot*" (*b. Sanhedrin* 42a). See also *b. Berakhot* 27b; *b. Kiddushin* 30a–b.

83. *b. Nidah* 43a. For a remarkable instance of the homoerotic link of weapons and male interaction, see Ḥayyim Vital, "Inyan Shaul Ve-Yehonatan Ve-David," in *Likkutei Torah,* ed. Yehudah Ashlag (Jerusalem: Yeshivat Kol Yehudah Press, 1988), 294–95. My appreciation to Rabbi J. H. Worch for bringing this source to my attention. Regarding the link between the delivery of homilies or writing to male potency, see Moshe Idel, *The Mystical Experience in Abraham Abulafia,* ed. Jonathan Chipman (Albany: State University of New York Press, 1988), 190–95. Competition at feasts is rooted in the Islamic-Spanish-Jewish culture preceding that of the kabbalists. Consider, for example, the following citation from the thirteenth-century poet and translator Judah al-Ḥarizi: "In the days of my youth, I was in a gathering of scholars, men so clever as to shame the sages and to silence wits. As we were discussing rhetorical speeches and clever figures, weaving poems into robes of honor with golden studs of beauty." The figure proceeds to boast about his poetic abilities sounding like the playful competitiveness of the members of the zoharic fraternity. Cited in Raymond P. Scheindlin, *Wine, Women, and Death: Medieval Hebrew Poems on the Good Life* (Philadelphia: Jewish Publication Society, 1986), 22. For the use of metaphors of combat in intellectual engagement in Roman culture, see Maud W. Gleason, *Making Men: Sophists and Self-Presentation in Ancient Rome* (Princeton, N.J.: Princeton University Press, 1995), 123. See Boyarin's comments on rabbinic weaponry—Torah study—in Daniel Boyarin, *Unheroic Conduct: The Rise of Heterosexuality and the Invention of the Jewish Man* (Berkeley: University of California Press, 1997), 127–50. Unlike Boyarin's analysis of rabbinic narratives, in which the ironic transvaluation of masculinity takes place through the substitution of the scholar model for the Roman gladiator model, in the *Zohar* this irony does not exist, as the only model of masculinity is that of the

kabbalistic adept. No non-Jews brandishing real weapons appear to suggest that the kabbalistic version of masculinity is anything but ideal.

84. *Kirta* appears to be one of the *Zohar*'s invented words. It is used in similar contexts to refer to a sling. As to the association of the child and King David, the text links the *kirta* to the five stones that David picked up to kill Goliath, stones that united as one (1 Samuel 17:40). The *Tikkunei ha-Zohar* 21, 11a, says that these five correspond to the first five words of the *Shema* prayer, the sixth word being "one," signifying the unity of the five words, five stones, and, of course, Divinity. There are several logical grounds for associating the *yanuka* with David: first, because of their shared youthfulness; second, David declares that it is the word of God that would defeat the giant (1 Samuel 17:45), and it is words of God that serve as the primary weapons of the child kabbalist too. See also *Tikkunei ha-Zohar* 21, 43b; *The Hebrew Writings*, 140, 141.

85. The tone of that passage, when read in the light of passages such as this one or others that portray the competitiveness of the kabbalists, also has a competitive resonance.

86. In a different narrative involving the *yanuka*, the child is told to cook his meal ("*tevashel bishulakh*"), the intent being that he should deliver a homily. He replies that he has not "cooked it" yet; that is, he has no innovative teachings of his own but can deliver a teaching that he had heard from his father. *Zohar* 2:29a. The child's boastfulness is muted, but he can still supply the necessary rations.

87. The playfulness here can be contrasted with the no-holds-barred style of the rabbis in the Babylonian Talmud and the midrash. Aryeh Cohen has shared an unpublished paper in which he makes a case for the trope of Torah study as a discourse of violence. See *b. Hagigah* 14a; *b. Kiddushin* 30a; *j. Ta'anit* 69b (4:7); *b. Sanhedrin* 24a, 42a; *Eikhah Rabah* 2:4; *Bamidbar Rabah* 11:3. Cohen quotes approvingly Richard Kalmin's observation regarding the famous denouement of the Reish Lakish-R. Yohanan partnership: "The passion which makes one a great brigand, the story teaches, also makes one a great Torah scholar. The study house and the battlefield are similar arenas. Debates in the study house are a matter of life and death, every bit as dangerous as a fight to the death between brigands." Richard Kalmin, *The Sage in Jewish Society of Late Antiquity* (London: Routledge, 1999), 4. My thanks to Aryeh for his generosity.

88. In his sociology of "interactionism," Erving Goffman writes about the dramaturgical performance in which one is inevitably involved in interaction in community. Goffman, *The Presentation of Self in Everyday Life* (New York: Anchor, 1959), 1–16.

89. There are other instances in zoharic literature in which one is enjoined to adopt a certain mood or action, but it is not explicitly directed toward an observer's watching of that action. For example, "one should clean one's home for Shabbat beyond what one normally does during the week. Another change in one's [normal] activity: If one is sad during the week, he should be joyful on the Sabbath. If he had an argument during the week with someone or with his wife, he should be at peace with her on Shabbat." *Tikkunei ha-Zohar* 21, 57a.

90. These terms, "members of the faith" (*benei mehemnuta*), "scions of the king" (*benei malka*), and "members of the palace" (*benei heikhalei*) are ubiquitous in the

Zohar and refer alternatively to the kabbalists or to Israel as a whole. *b. Shabbat* 67a; cf. *Zohar* 2:26b, top; Cf. Reuven Margaliot, ed., *Sefer ha-Bahir* (Jerusalem: Mosad ha-Rav Kuk, 1994) 113, 129; Daniel Abrams, ed., *The Book Bahir: An Edition Based on the Earliest Manuscripts* (Los Angeles: Cherub, 1994), 82, 89. See also *Zohar Ḥadesh* 106d–107a (Tikkunim); *The Hebrew Writings of the Author of Tiqqunei Zohar and Ra'aya Mehemna*, ed. Efraim Gottlieb (Jersusalem: Israel Academy of Sciences and Humanities, 2003) 6–7, 13, 129.

91. Cordovero writes that the meals testify that Israel inherits from three levels. See Moses Cordovero, *Or Yakar* (Jerusalem: Achuzat Israel, 1976), 8:223.

92. Elsewhere one shows oneself to be from the side of impurity (or purity) and being known to be from that side. See *Zohar* 3:73a. Other benefits accrue to those who are "sons of faith." See *Zohar* 2:62b.

93. Goffman has been critiqued for this understanding of human interaction because of its atomized view of people and for creating a model in which people bear no cultural history but are subject, rather, to the buffeting of external social perceptions. See, e.g., Alasdair MacIntyre, *After Virtue: A Study in Moral Theory* (Notre Dame, Ind.: University of Notre Dame Press, 1981), 115–17. The aptness of Goffman's analysis as applied to the kabbalists effectively undermines this critique.

94. There is a rabbinic motif that the *Shekhinah* only rests upon one who is joyous. See *j. Sukkah* 5:1; *b. Shabbat* 30b; Solomon Buber, ed., *Midrash Tehillim* (Jerusalem: Ḥ. Wagshal, 1977), 24:3, 204. In a discussion of theurgic weeping, Idel suggests that Vital's emphasis on weeping, even for the nonsaintly, indicates a shift from theurgy based on theosophic knowledge to a sympathetic theurgy, easing the popularization of the practice. See Moshe Idel, *Kabbalah: New Perspectives* (New Haven, Conn.: Yale University Press, 1988), 198–99. The *Zohar* also recognizes the problem of prescribing a heteronymous emotional norm. See *Zohar* 2:165a.

95. Moshe Hallamish has studied the way in which the requirement for love among the kabbalistic fraternities was generated into a normative kabbalistic practice. See Hallamish, "The Evolution of a Kabbalistic Custom: 'I Accept upon Myself the Obligation to Fulfill the Positive Commandment of "You Shall Love Your Fellow as Yourself,"'" *Kabbalah: In Liturgy, Halakhah, and Custom* (Ramat-Gan, Isr.: Bar-Ilan University, 2000), 356–82.

96. Trans. in Liebes, "Messiah of the *Zohar* (in English)," 37–38. See also 3:59b, 62b, 128a (*Idra Raba*); *Sefer ha-Rimmon*, 118. In other passages, the individual is instructed to show joy and delight in worship, e.g., *Zohar* 1:229b, 248a; 2:165b. In these examples, the display of joy has a theurgic effect. See also, e.g., *Zohar* 1:180b; 3:89b. In general, one's actions must be overtly demonstrative of the world above. See, e.g., *Zohar* 3:86b.

To date, the phenomenon of love among the kabbalists of the zoharic narrative has been studied primarily by Yehudah Liebes and Elliot Wolfson. Liebes has emphasized the notion that the fraternal love among the companions issues license to Rabbi Shimon to disclose secrets of the highest order, effects the *tikkunim* of union above, and enables union between Rabbi Shimon and the *Shekhinah*. Both he and Wolfson have drawn attention to the homoerotic component that is sublimated in their exchange of mystical homilies in the context of a loving conventicle. Liebes, "Messiah of the *Zohar* (in Hebrew)," 157–65; Liebes, "Messiah of the *Zohar* (in English)," 37–43;

Liebes, "*Zohar* and Eros," 107–10; Wolfson, *Through a Speculum That Shines*, 368–77; Wolfson, "Crossing Gender Boundaries in Kabbalistic Ritual and Myth," 107–10.

97. Regarding the role of physiognomy in the *Zohar*, see *Zohar* 2:70b–78a (parallel version in *Raza de Razin*), 272b–276a; *Zohar Hadash* 35b–37c; *Tikkunei ha-Zohar* 70, 121a–135b. For a different interpretation of this passage, see Bahya ben Asher, *Commentary on the Torah*, Exodus 18:21. For studies of the history of chiromancy, physiognomy, and metoposcopy in the Jewish esoteric traditions, see Gershom Scholem, "Chiromancy in the *Zohar*," *The Quest* 17 (1926): 255–56; Gershom Scholem, "Physiognomy and Chiromancy," in *Sefer Asaf*, ed. M. D. Casuto, J. Klausner, and J. Gutman (Jerusalem: Mosad ha-Rav Kuk, 1953); Ithamar Gruenwald, "Further Jewish Physiognomic and Chiromantic Fragments," *Tarbiz* 40 (1971): 305; Ithamar Gruenwald, *Apocalyptic and Merkavah Mysticism* (Leiden, Neth.: Brill, 1980); Lawrence Fine, "The Art of Metoposcopy: A Study in Isaac Luria's Charismatic Knowledge (Reprinted in *Essential Papers on Kabbalah*, 1995)," *AJS Review* 11, no. 1 (1986): esp. 334 n. 12.

98. Clifford Geertz, "Religion as a Cultural System," in *The Interpretation of Cultures: Selected Essays* (New York: Basic, 1973), 90, 95.

99. Gary A. Anderson, *A Time to Mourn, A Time to Dance: The Expression of Grief and Joy in Israelite Religion* (University Park: Pennsylvania State University Press, 1991), 2.

100. Ibid., 4–5.

101. For examples of biblical texts that command one to "rejoice before the Lord," see Leviticus 23:40; Numbers 10:10; Deuteronomy 12:7, 12, 18; 14:26; 16:11, 14, 15; 26:11; 27:7. There are many injunctions to be joyful before God in connection with feasting, sacrifices, and the pilgrimage festivals. See Deuteronomy 12:2. "The minimal legal requirement to rejoice entails talking one's sacred animal to the Temple, having it slaughtered, and consuming it amid the gathered family." Anderson, *Time to Mourn*, 20. See also Nehemiah 8:12, 17; Ezra 6:22; 2 Chronicles 30:21, 23, 25; Esther 8:15–17; 9:17–19,22. For rabbinic texts that associate joy with the cultic sacrifices, see *b. Shabbat* 148b; *b. Pesahim* 60a–61a, 109a; *b. Megillah* 5a, 16b; *Hagigah* 2b–3a, 6b, 7b, 8a; *b. Zevahim* 99b; *b. Beizah* 19b; *Mekhilta de R. Ishmael, be-Shalah* 3:1; *Sifre* 53, 64, 69, 107, 135, 138, 193, 303; *Sifra* 13:6, 102:4.

102. George A. Lindbeck, *The Nature of Doctrine: Religion and Theology in a Post-Liberal Age* (Philadelphia: Westminster, 1984), 33–34.

103. See chapter 2, text near notes 37–44.

104. De Leon, *Sefer ha-Rimmon*, 104–5. Cf. *Zohar* 1:207b.

105. See *b. Berakhot* 45a; Maimonides, *Hilkhot Berakhot* 3:12; *Shulhan Arukh Orah Hayyim* 210.

106. Another passage juxtaposes the verses "Out of the eater (*okhel*) came something to eat" (Judges 14:14) and "The righteous man eats fully sating his soul (*zaddiq okhel le-sova nafsho*)" (Proverbs 13:25). The author explains that the "eater" eats fully, corresponding to the fullness of the *Zaddiq/Yesod*, who then gives to his soul/*Shekhinah*. *Zohar* 1:240a. Here we see the linkage of sexuality and eating within the divine realm alone, with the masculine *sefirah Yesod* "eating" his fill and then bestowing that fullness upon the feminine *Shekhinah*. Cf. also *Tikkunei ha-Zohar* 16, 31a.

107. Cf. *Zohar* 3:38b.

108. I have translated literally in accord with the *Zohar*'s interpretation of the verse. The Jewish Publication Society has "The righteous man eats to his heart's content."

109. De Leon, *Sefer ha-Rimmon*, 58–59.

110. See note 107.

111. Mopsik insightfully describes the body's role in replicating the Divine through the wearing of phylacteries and ritual fringes as per the *Zohar*: "Le fait de revêtir ces parures rituelles remodèle le corps physique en rectifiant sa forme de telle façon qu'elle rappelle la structure du monde divin. Ces parures sont des sortes d'idéogrammes, signes d'écriture en même temps que dessins. Célébrant et ranimant l'union nuptiale des pôles masculin et féminin du plérome, le corps du fidèle est le support vivant des hiéroglyphes de laine et de cuir qu'il porte comme une toile un tableau." Mopsik, *Les Grands Textes de la Cabale*, 210.

112. See *Zohar* 1:208a, where one is required to adopt a stance of either satiety or hunger, depending on whether it is the Lord or the *Sitra Aḥra* that is dominant at the time. Elsewhere, the *Zohar* says that giving the appearance of satiety at a time of famine suggests or causes a weakness in the supernal realm and is thus forbidden (two homilies offer the two different approaches, one cognitive, the other theurgic: *Zohar* 3:92b). It is not the satisfying eating that is condemned, but merely the outward display of that contentment; here, the *Zohar* makes explicit that it is the performative dimension that is being fashioned. Elsewhere, the *Zohar* cautions against walking around the marketplace during a famine. Moses Cordovero explains the limitation, saying that the demon Hunger (*Kafna*) wanders around during a famine, harming even those who are well fed. See *Zohar* 1:204b; 2:253b; Cordovero, *Or Yakar*, 6:141. This is part of a more general warning in rabbinic literature that warns against roaming. See *b. Bava Kama* 60b; *Zohar* 1:63a, and Margaliot's n. 1 there. One is also enjoined not to display joy when Israel is in exile, which would mark a disparity between one's outward comportment, the historical situation, and its corresponding sefirotic fissure. See *Zohar* 3:118a.

113. On this combined display of satiety and joy, see de Leon, *Sefer ha-Rimmon*, 118, 120–21. In this latter source, the increased joy from satiety expresses itself in the sexual act as well. In contrast, the lack of joy or sadness is referred to, in the *Zohar*, as a lack and flaw. *Zohar* 1:216b.

114. This is the *Zohar*'s explanation of the halakhic distinction between the grace after the meal and prayer. One may recite the blessing for the food when one is drunk, but one is not permitted to pray when inebriated. *b. Berakhot* 31a and Tosafot. s.v. *mi-kan*. The *Zohar* explains that this is because prayer goes to a higher place. See *Zohar* 2:116a; de Leon, *Sefer ha-Rimmon*, 375. The latter text explains that scripture indicates an alignment of the words "and you shall eat" with eating, "and be satiated" with drinking, "and bless the Lord your God" (*u-verakhta et adonai elohekha*) with the particle *et* referring to the *Shekhinah*, the beneficiary of the blessing. Therefore one can be drunk and still recite the blessing. In fact, de Leon says, it is the drinking that brings on the joy required for the blessing. The *Zohar* maintains a distinction between eating and drinking as different levels within the Godhead, a common cross-cultural distinction. In the *Zohar*, see, e.g., 1:87a. For an anthropological discussion of this distinction, see Raymond Firth, *Symbols: Public and Private* (Ithaca, N.Y.: Cornell University Press, 1973), 247–48. As food might

be thought of as more material than drink, the *Zohar* places the former on a higher level because of its greater role in sustenance. The tension among the dualistic impulse, degrading the material, and the more abstract symbolic impulse—valuing the life-sustaining abilities of food—is here resolved in favor of the former.

115. Cf. Rashi *b. Berakhot* 31a s.v. *be-khol ezev yihiyeh motar.* In the context of a discussion of the preparation before prayer, he comments, "When a person shows himself to be sad he will receive reward."

116. This is to be contrasted with the ataraxy that is an integral part of the preparation for mystical experience as often described in the Jewish mystical and pietistic tradition. See Isaac of Isaac ben Samuel of Acre, *Sefer Me'irat Einayim: Critical Edition,* by Amos Goldreich (Jerusalem: Akademon, 1981), 2:218; Ḥayyim Vital, *Sha'ar ha-Mizvot* (Jerusalem: Yeshivat Kol Yehudah Press, 1988), 3:4. For discussions of ataraxy in the scholarly literature, see Gershom Scholem, *Major Trends in Jewish Mysticism* (New York: Schocken, 1946), 96–97, 372 n. 59; R. J. Zwi Werblowsky, *Joseph Karo: Lawyer and Mystic* (Philadelphia: Jewish Publication Society of America, 1977), 161–62; Moshe Idel, *Studies in Ecstatic Kabbalah* (Albany: State University of New York Press, 1988), 107–64. In the modern context, for a presentation of a remarkable example of manipulation of emotions as a mystical ideal, see Nehemia Polen, *The Holy Fire: The Teachings of Rabbi Kalonymus Kalman Shapira, the Rebbe of the Warsaw Ghetto* (Northvale, N.J.: Jason Aronson, 1994).

117. The passage continues, contrasting this prescribed practice with that of those who serve Saturn. They fast, showing sadness and anxiety, wearing black clothes, and avoiding all forms of sensual pleasure and social contact. This apparently anti-Gentile, antiascetic polemic stands in contrast to the *Zohar*'s own advocacy of fasting and ascetic practices at certain times. Margaliot has identified both of these passages as being from the *Sitrei Torah* section of the *Zohar.* See the intratextual note on *Zohar Ḥadash,* 35b. See parallel on 2:275a; see also *Zohar* 2:252b; *The Hebrew Writings,* 87.

118. Cf. Maimonides' version of *m. Pesaḥim* 10:5. Maimonides, *Commentary on the Mishnah,* ed. and trans. Yosef Kafih (Jerusalem: Mosad ha-Rav Kuk, 1987).

119. See Idel, *Kabbalah,* 198–99. Idel talks about the movement from the emphasis on the anthropomorphic structure and theosophy of medieval kabbalah toward the anthropopathic focus in Hasidism, citing passages from Yaakov Zemah's *Zohar ha-Rakia* as a significant turning point. My argument demonstrates that the roots of the emotional focus in Hasidism can be traced back yet further.

120. The record of the kabbalists' death is at *Zohar* 2:142b. For a discussion of the differences between the *Idra de-vei Mashkena* and the *Idra Raba,* see Liebes, "Messiah of the *Zohar* (in Hebrew)," 157–65; Liebes, "Messiah of the *Zohar* (in English)," 37–43.

121. Literally, "stands upon him."

122. Elliot Ginsburg notes the role of coronation images on Friday night specifically with regard to the *kiddush* and prayers. Ginsburg, *Sabbath in the Classical Kabbalah,* 201.

123. See also de Leon, *Sefer ha-Rimmon,* 104.

124. Elliot R. Wolfson, "Weeping, Death, and Spiritual Ascent in Sixteenth-Century Jewish Mysticism," in *Death, Ecstasy, and Other Worldly Journeys,* ed. John J. Collins and Michael Fishbane (Albany: State University of New York Press, 1995), 220–28. See *Zohar* 2:157b, which charges that the cup of blessing, associated with the

Shekhinah, is to be given from between the right and the left hands, symbolizing *Ḥesed* and *Gevurah.* It thus effects the downward movement of the divine blessing from between the two poles of Grace and Judgment. The mandate to look at the cup of wine derives from *b. Berakhot* 51a.

125. Cf. Genesis 33:10. See *j. Eruvin* 5:1, 22b: "Whoever receives the face of his teacher, it is as if he has received the face of the *Shekhinah.* . . . One who receives the face of his friend, it is as if he has received the face of the *Shekhinah.*"

126. Translation from Daniel C. Matt, ed. and trans., *The Essential Kabbalah: The Heart of Jewish Mysticism* (New York: HarperSan Francisco, 1994), 210.

127. *Talmud Yerushalmi, Tractate Sanhedrin* 58a. See Joseph of Hamadan's use of this text in Joseph of Hamadan, *Fragment d'un Commentaire sur la Genese,* ed. and trans. Charles Mopsik, Les Dix Paroles (Paris: Editions Verdier, 1998), 7.

128. See Oron, "Place Me as a Seal upon Your Heart," 3 n. 9.

129. Wolfson, *Through a Speculum That Shines,* 357–68, 396–97. Regarding the crown as a symbol for mystical union, see Elliot R. Wolfson, "Mystical Rationalization of the Commandments in *Sefer ha-Rimmon,*" *Hebrew Union College Annual* 59 (1989): 52–55.

130. In this instance, the adept's emotional mood serves as the crown for his guest. Whereas in other situations the recipient, such as an indigent, receives his good materially, here the guest is enfolded in the divine economy simply by receiving the mood of his host. I use the term "homosocial dynamic" to refer to the patterns of what would be called "male-bonding" in our culture that are framed by heterosexual rhetoric as a way of masking the homoerotic dynamic beneath. For a man to be crowning another means to be completing the other as a man by restoring the feminine to him. For a helpful discussion of the phrase "male homosocial desire," see Eve Kosofsky Sedgwick, *Between Men: English Literature and Male Homosocial Desire* (New York: Columbia University Press, 1985), 1–5.

131. The previously cited passages regarding the female innkeeper and the narrative frame of the *yanuka,* whose mother hovers in the background, are also suggestive of interactions with female figures around kabbalistic topics. Consider also the following: "A woman must light the Sabbath candles with joy in her heart and with longing, for it is a great honor to her" (*Zohar* 1:48b). Moreover, in the seventeenth-century prayer book of Isaiah Horowitz, *Siddur Sha'ar ha-Shamayim,* the author refers to this passage's prescriptions for the Friday night scene and says that the angels must see the rejoicing of the husband and his wife. Lawrence Fine raises the question of the intentionality of kabbalists' wives. See Lawrence Fine, *Physician of the Soul, Healer of the Cosmos: Isaac Luria and His Kabbalistic Fellowship* (Stanford, Calif.: Stanford University Press, 2003), 201–5.

132. See Goffman, op. cit., 17, 72–76. It is unclear how much effort is being expended in gaining the desired affect. See Goffman, *Presentation of Self in Everyday Life,* 33. Regarding the flowering of concern for gesture and the appropriate expression of mood in the twelfth and thirteenth centuries, see Jean-Claude Schmitt, "The Ethics of Gesture," trans. Ian Patterson, in *Fragments for a History of the Human Body, Part Two* (New York: Zone, 1989), 136–43.

133. Regarding pneumatic hermeneutics in mystical texts, see Gerald L. Bruns, *Hermeneutics Ancient and Modern* (New Haven, Conn.: Yale University Press, 1992),

133–34; Wolfson, *Through a Speculum That Shines,* 330. See also Scholem in *Major Trends in Jewish Mysticism,* 205.

134. Stanley Tambiah, *Culture, Thought and Social Action* (Cambridge, Mass.: Harvard University Press, 1985), 132.

135. Ronald L. Grimes, "Defining Nascent Ritual," in *Beginnings in Ritual Studies* (Columbia: University of South Carolina, 1995), 64.

136. See *Zohar* 2:34a, where the text explains Job's cyclical fortunes, saying that God has to show (*ahazei* — the same term used for the demonstrative performances of the kabbalists) that a good-bad cycle will always entail a return to the good. God, like the kabbalists, is in the teaching profession.

Chapter 5

1. Moshe Idel, *Kabbalah: New Perspectives* (New Haven, Conn.: Yale University Press, 1988), 157, and see further, 157–70.

2. For a study of the use of language for talismanic power, see Moshe Idel, "On Talismatic Language in Jewish Mysticism," *Diogenes* 43/2, no. 170 (1995): 23–41.

3. Catherine Bell strives to efface this dichotomy. Bell, *Ritual Theory, Ritual Practice* (New York: Oxford University Press, 1992).

4. Melkhizedeq "brought out the bread and wine (*hozi lehem ve-yayin*)" (Genesis 14:18), and in the creation story "the earth brought forth vegetation" (*va-tozei ha-arez deshe eisev*). Genesis 1:12.

5. I am not suggesting that a single author wrote both homilies and that the second represents a reaction to the first. We do not yet know enough about the redaction of the *Zohar* to make that argument here.

6. *b. Berakhot* 4b. One recital precedes the morning statutory prayer, the second is near its conclusion in a section called *Kedushah de-Sidra,* and the third precedes the afternoon prayer.

7. The other theurgic dynamic connected to this verse is that of centering *Malkhut* between the respective flows of *Hesed* and *Gevurah* so that she can receive from them and transmit food to the lower realms. See *Zohar* 3:119b–120a; Moses ben Shem Tov de Leon, *Sefer ha-Rimmon,* ed. Elliot R. Wolfson (Atlanta: Scholars Press, 1988), 65.

8. *Tikkunei ha-Zohar,* 51b, 55a, 55b; *The Hebrew Writings,* 41, 178.

9. *Zohar* 1:199b. Isaac of Acre, a kabbalist who lived at the same time as the kabbalists of the zoharic circle, elucidates the story of Abraham offering a meal to the angels. He explains that Abraham did not actually intend to feed the angels; rather, his intention was to induce blessing from God so that an extra dollop of the holy spirit would be drawn down onto him. When he brought the food before the angels, it was consumed as if it were on an altar, implying that it was a sacrificial offering, and yet the magical intent of this food suggests something closer to the notion of talismanic theurgy than either magic or traditional understandings of sacrificial offerings, albeit with an extra component of exchange. Isaac ben Samuel of Acre, *Sefer Me'irat Einayim: Critical Edition,* by Amos Goldreich (Jerusalem: Akademon, 1981), 49.

10. See previous note.

11. *b. Berakhot* 10b.

12. It should be noted that in the first textual instance of the story, the homily continues, delivered by another mysterious figure, offering an injunction that it is a fit time to study Torah. The seam between narrative and homily, creating a merger between food and Torah, underscores the experience of Torah being assimilated into one's body through study.

13. The lines preceding the homily that I have cited indicate that the supernal food becomes manifest in the material food below. See Ḥayyim Yosef David Azulai, *Niẓoẓei Orot* on *Zohar,* ed. Margaliot, 2:62b n. 1.

14. A parallel passage charges the reader that he should follow the example of Rabbi Yeisa, one who fears the Lord, taking time after this petition to prepare his meal. *Zohar* 2:62b. It would appear that some time was required to allow for God's blessing to ensue. Cordovero explains that it is at the hour at which prayer is allowed that the flow from *Ḥesed* is initiated, generating the transmission of food. See Moses Cordovero, *Or Yakar* (Jerusalem: Achuzat Israel, 1976), 8:78.

15. See *Zohar* 1:88b, 155b.

16. See *m. Menaḥot* 11:7. Notably, the *Zohar* refrains from referring to the qualifying statement by Rabbi Yose in the Babylonian Talmud, in which he explains that it was only at night that the rack had to be full—during the daytime, the bread's absence was acceptable. *b. Menaḥot* 99b.

17. *b. Berakhot* 40a; *Sukkah* 46a–b.

18. See *b. Sanhedrin* 92a; Rashi s.v. *ve-ha.*'

19. Charles Mopsik emphasizes that in the *Zohar,* on the contrary, the stress is on the ability to effect illumination above rather than to draw it down, that is, in his words, establishment-theurgy rather than attraction-theurgy. Mopsik, *Les Grands Textes de la Cabale: Les Rites Qui Font Dieu* (Paris: Editions Verdier, 1993), 202.

20. This practice derives from medieval German halakhic practice. See Israel M. Ta-Shma, *Minhag Ashkenaz ha-Kadmon: Ḥeker Ve-Iyyun* (Jerusalem: Magnes Press, 1992), 269–70; Ta-Shma, *The Revealed in the Concealed: The Halakhic Residue in the Zohar* (Israel: Hakibbutz Hameuchad, 2001), 28. (Hebrew)

21. See also *Zohar* 1:88b, 240a; 2:63b, 87b–88a, 154b–155a, 157b; 3:34a; Joseph of Hamadan, "A Critical Edition of the *Sefer Ta'amey ha-Miẓwoth* (Book of Reasons of the Commandments) Attributed to Isaac Ibn Farhi," ed. Menachem Meier (Ph.D. diss., Brandeis University, 1974), 114–16. A passage from de Leon's *Sefer ha-Rimmon* articulates the Neoplatonic heritage of this principle: "Know that the sages of old, knowers of wisdom who understand science have made us aware, and it is a tradition that we possess from the rabbis, may their memory serve as a blessing, that a supernal entity can only have an influence on something that is prepared to receive. Something from above will not rest upon something empty, as they have said, 'One should not recite the grace over an empty table.'" See de Leon, *Sefer ha-Rimmon,* 270. There is an interesting complement to this motif in an alternate text in *Zohar* 2:67a, which says that "it is the habit [of impurity] to rest upon an empty place." Further, one can infer an ethical corollary that one cannot learn without appropriate humility, a factor that becomes central in the kabbalistic-ethical literature of the sixteenth century.

22. See also *Zohar* 1:88b.

23. See also *Zohar* 2:157b.

24. See *b. Berakhot* 55a: "When the temple was standing the altar atoned for all of Israel; now a person's table atones for him." Cf. *b. Ḥagigah* 27a.

25. A similar motif can be found in the writings of Isaac of Acre who tells "the story of a particular pious man who gave all he had in his hand to the alms collector save for one *zuz*. With that one *zuz* he bought wheat and put it in storage. His wife came and asked him, 'Where is the money that you had?' He answered her, 'I bought wheat with it and, look, it is in the storage room.' She went and found the entire storeroom filled with wheat." *Me'irat Einayim*, 124. There are, of course, ancient parallels to the phenomenon of producing bounty from scarce resources. As one of the most obvious examples, consider the story of Jesus' multiplication of loaves and fish. See John 6:1–14.

26. See Moses ben Naḥman, *Commentary on the Torah*, ed. Charles Chavel (Jerusalem: Mosad ha-Rav Kuk, 1960), Commentary on Exodus 25:24, 461. See also *Zohar* 2:168b, where the blessing on the land is said to draw blessing down to the land from which all food comes. The land from which all food comes is the *sefirah* of *Malkhut*, but it is that *sefirotic* potency as symbolically represented by the Land of Israel. Similarly, Joseph of Hamadan writes, "The Holy One, blessed be He, said, 'Bring before me the first fruits that are brought at Shavuot so that future fruit will be blessed.' The same is true with regard to the water libation at Sukkot invoking blessing on the water." See Joseph of Hamadan, "Joseph of Hamadan's *Sefer Tashak*: Critical Edition with Introduction," ed. Jeremy Zwelling (Ph.D. diss., Brandeis University, 1975), 188.

27. Bahya ben Asher, "*Shulḥan shel Arba*," in *Kitve Rabbenu Bahya*, ed. Charles Chavel (Jerusalem: Mosad ha-Rav Kuk, 1987), 477.

28. Ibid.

29. Moses ben Shem Tov de Leon, "*Sefer ha-Mishkal*: Text and Study," ed. Jochanan Wijnhoven (Ph.D. diss., Brandeis University, 1964), 87–88. On the matter of resurrection from a small bone, see Menaḥem Recanati, *Commentary on the Torah* (Jerusalem: Mordekhai Attia, 1961), 25:30. See also *Zohar* 2:151b regarding kosher slaughter (*sheḥitah*), in which it says that if one does not perform *sheḥitah* properly the *Sitra Aḥra* comes to rest upon the meat. This is similar, the *Zohar* says, to bodies that are buried outside of the Land of Israel. Thus there is a divine blessing that is preserved within the animal when slaughtered properly as there is within the human corpse when buried properly.

30. I have translated according to Bahya ben Asher's understanding of the verse here. The Jewish Publication Society translation offers the following: "With no survivor to enjoy it, His fortune will not prosper." The Revised Standard Version, from which I partially borrowed, has "There was nothing left after he had eaten, / therefore his prosperity will not endure."

31. Bahya ben Asher, "*Shulḥan shel Arba*," 477. In his commentary on Exodus 25:23, he states that the talismanic theurgy is the simple, that is, nonkabbalistic, meaning: "According to the simple meaning (*al derekh ha-peshat*) the table that is in the house of the Lord requires the bread that is upon it to serve as a root in which the blessing will rest." Bahya ben Asher, *Commentary on the Torah*, ed. Charles Chavel (Jerusalem: Mosad ha-Rav Kuk, 1982), Commentary on Exodus 25:23, 279. His explanation here is largely an expansion upon that of Moses ben Nahman, cited in note 26. See also Recanati, *Commentary on the Torah*, 49b.

32. *Zohar* 2:155a.

33. The *Zohar* is punning on the normal vocalization of the word "*pnym*" as well.

See *m. Menaḥot* 11:4 in which Ben Zoma emphasizes that the bread should have "faces."

34. The upper countenances are *Tif'eret* and *Yesod*. See Tishby, op. cit., 916 n. 50. Translation on p. 916.

35. Affinities between *sefirot* that are alike are quite common, thus explaining the relationship between the righteous Isaac associated with Judgment and his close relationship to his demonic son Esau. See, e.g., de Leon, *Sefer ha-Rimmon*, 144, and the *Zohar* citations adduced in the notes. This formula of "like with like" is used explicitly in this work by de Leon (244). It is also characteristic of the inclination in zoharic kabbalah to place everything in its appropriate slot. See *Zohar* 1:20b; 3:263b (*Ra'aya Mehemna*); cf. *b. Bava Kama* 92b; Daniel C. Matt, "*Matnita Dilan:* A Technique of Innovation in the *Zohar*," *Jerusalem Studies in Jewish Thought* 8 (1989): 135; Dorit Cohen-Alloro, "From Supernal Wisdom to the Wisdom of the Leaves of the Tree: The *Zohar*'s View of Magic as a Consequence of the Original Sin," *Daat* 19 (summer 1987): 32 n. 5.

36. See, e.g., *Zohar* 1:35a, 77b, 86b, 88a, 210b, 235a; 2:30a, 31b, 232b; 3:36b, 45a–b, 92a–b, 105a, 112b, 118a. Given the hierarchical direction of the flow of divine blessing, the arousal from below could only arise as a result of the previous influence of the supernal gradations. In some of the previously cited passages, the *Zohar* confronts this problem implicitly. See *Zohar* 1:77b, 88a.

37. Joseph of Hamadan, *Sefer Toledot ha-Adam*, in *Sefer ha-Malkhut* (Casablanca: Imprimerie Razon, 1930), 97b.

38. See Charles Mopsik, "The Body of Engenderment in the Hebrew Bible, the Rabbinic Tradition, and the Kabbalah," in *Fragments for a History of the Human Body Part I*, ed. Ramona Naddaff and Nadia Tazi Michael Feher (New York: Zone, 1989), 48–73.

39. *b. Berakhot* 23a. See de Leon, *Sefer ha-Rimmon*, 56, 80, where he refers to the need to vacate waste from one's body and to wear clean clothing before prayer. These two requirements—for clean clothing and a clean body—received considerable attention in the writings of the German pietists. See *Sefer Hasidim* (Parma) #1612–1613; *Sefer Hasidim* (Bologna) #18, 371, 522, 824, 827; Eleazar of Worms, *Sefer ha-Roke'ah, Hilkhot Ḥasidut Shoresh Taharah Perishut u'Zehirut*, (Jerusalem: Oẓar ha-Poskim, 1967), 14.

40. See *b. Berakhot* 53b.

41. See also *Zohar Ḥadash* 87a, (*Midrash Ruth*). Compare to Baḥya ben Asher, who stresses the number ten in the hand washing. See Baḥya ben Asher, "*Shulḥan shel Arba*," 464.

42. See also *Zohar* 1:10b; 3:186a.

43. See *Zohar* 1:20b. *Sefer Yeẓirah* is the first text to refer to the sanctity of the fingers and their relationship to the divine. See *Sefer Yeẓirah* 1:3.

44. To prove that the left is contained in the right, the *Zohar* says, "The sign of this (*simanakh*) is that one who washes his hands has the vessel in his right hand first in order to give it to the left and not from the left to the right" (*Zohar* 2:154b). Because this is the praxis of the knowing adept, the observer understands the ontological reality. See also *Zohar* 2:167a. For a discussion of the motif of the left hand contained within the right, see Elliot R. Wolfson, "Left Contained in the Right: A Study in Zoharic Hermeneutics," *AJS Review* 11, no. 1 (1986): 42–46.

45. *b. Sotah* 4b.

46. Regarding the raising of the hands during prayer, See Daniel Abrams, ed., *The Book Bahir: An Edition Based on the Earliest Manuscripts* (Los Angeles: Cherub, 1994), 177.

47. The *Zohar* here takes a stand on an unresolved issue in the halakhah of its time. For a brief discussion, see *Tur Orah Hayyim* 181. Cf., however, Bahya ben Asher, "*Shulhan shel Arba,*" 463, where the washing after the meal serves the same holy purpose as the washing before the meal, and p. 476, where he says that a blessing is recited before this washing.

48. Later in the same passage the text states that individuals should unite with the angels in order to derive the same nourishment as them. See *Zohar Hadash* 87b, (*Midrash Ruth*). Note de Leon, *Sefer ha-Rimmon,* 104, where it says that a person draws his food down by virtue of his attributes (*al pi midotav*). Assuming that these are the human attributes that are being referred to, we see how one's entire being, both physical and spiritual, is mobilized to draw food down from the supernal realms.

49. See also *Zohar* 1:250a.

50. See also *Zohar* 2:88b, where failing to celebrate the three Sabbath meals with the proper ceremony will demonstrate and effect a flaw in the *sefirot* and serve as evidence that the practitioner is in fact not one of the members of faith. With regard to the layout of the furniture, it is reckoned essential that the table upon which one eats have four legs, thus replicating the table in the Temple. See *Zohar* 3:245a; *Tikkunei ha-Zohar* 84a. This became the regular practice of Isaac Luria as noted in *Peri Ez Hayyim Sha'ar ha-Shabbat* 17. Cited in Margaliot, ed., *Tikkunei ha-Zohar* (Jerusalem: Mosad ha-Rav Kuk, 1994), 84a n. 22.

51. See also *Tikkunei ha-Zohar* 24, 70a. This latter statement in the *Tikkunei ha-Zohar* presents the obligation as incumbent upon all of Israel, thus attempting to popularize the presumably esoteric practice.

52. Although I would not argue for historical continuity, the role of the visual as demonstrated thus far has strong similarities to the way in which the Hasidim observe their rebbe eat. He too assumes a role, displaying the proper mode of cutting, observing, chewing, and swallowing one's food.

53. Here the setting of the table promotes supernal joy, a theurgic effect in the divine realm resulting from the same act.

54. See also *Zohar Hadash* 3:48c–d, in which the elevation of the table is referred to more explicitly as an offering. Tishby has noted that this latter source, attributed to *Sitrei Torah,* is probably a later addition. See Tishby, *Wisdom of the Zohar,* 126 n.223. The rabbinic source for the notion of the two angels accompanying a person home is *b. Shabbat* 119b. According to the zoharic text, along with this blessing comes the benefit of the extra soul. See *b. Beizah* 16a. Another version of the homily has the angel Suria elevating an image of the table, as formed by the words of Torah recited over it, before God, rather than the table itself (*Zohar* 2:154a). This homily directly precedes the one about the two angels cited earlier and suggests a spiritual version of the latter. The "great angel Suria" is elsewhere depicted as receiving souls on their ascent after death and smelling their fragrance to determine their standing (*Zohar* 2:213b). See also *Zohar* 2:253a and *Nizozei Zohar* n. 2. The name of the angel Suria may be derived from the name given to the Prince of the Presence Suri'el, referred to in *b. Berakhot* 51a. See also *Zohar* 2:252b, which describes that

when all of the tables are set on Friday night, myriads of angels observe and answer "amen" to the blessing.

55. See, e.g., *Zohar* 2:98b–99a; 3:152a; Elliot R. Wolfson, "Occultation of the Feminine and the Body of Secrecy in Medieval Kabbalah," in *Rending the Veil: Concealment and Secrecy in the History of Religions,* ed. Elliot R. Wolfson (New York: Seven Bridges, 1999), 113–54.

56. See Mopsik, "Body of Engenderment," 57–68.

57. *b. Berakhot* 55b.

58. The upper *sefirot* are *Keter, Hokhmah,* and *Binah,* and the latter seven refer to the *sefirot Hesed* through *Malkhut.*

59. See *b. Yoma* 53b.

60. See *b. Bava Kama* 60b.

61. The degree of faith here is not a body of theological knowledge attained by the kabbalist but rather a measure of spiritual success that can be measured in terms of experiential categories such as mystical union, theurgy, illumination, and visionary experience. Cf. Tishby, *Wisdom of the Zohar,* 1289 n. 83. There is no explicit indication that the kabbalists were involved in the actual cooking but, given that the Talmud tells of amoraim — postmishnaic rabbis of the Talmud — cooking some of the food for the Sabbath themselves, it certainly seems plausible that the kabbalists were as well. On the other hand, the representation of these rabbinic kabbalists keeps them far from mundane activities, unlike their talmudic models. See *b. Kiddushin* 41a; and see Introduction, text near notes 19–22.

62. See also *Zohar* 2:63b, where preparation is the key to receiving divine blessing. The common statement that blessing does not rest in an empty place refers here not to bread that is left over but rather to the preparation of the table on the eve of the Sabbath.

63. Tishby says that all of Israel is on this level because their souls come from the *sefirot.* See Tishby, *Wisdom of the Zohar,* 1287 n. 57. This would seem not to be correct, as the context is already dealing within the framework of those of Israel that have the obligation; from amongst that group, there is a subgroup who prepares the table in the desirable manner. Similarly, consider the formulation in *Zohar* 2:89a about the kabbalists knowing the mystery about when to have sex on Friday nights; *kavanah* is referred to explicitly.

64. This statement was adopted by Luria as part of the introduction to each of his three Sabbath hymns. See *Peri Ez Hayyim Sha'ar ha-Shabbat* 17. For a study of these hymns, see Yehuda Liebes, "Hymns for the Sabbath Meals of the Ari," *Molad,* n.s., 23 (February 1972): 540–55.

65. Tishby, *Wisdom of the Zohar,* 1288.

66. In the biblical story, Pharaoh sends for his magicians in the competition with Moses and Aaron, and in the *Zohar,* too, he has magicians in tow, but he is the master of impurity, rather than actually being a magician himself. On Balaam as magician, see *Targum Pseudo-Jonathan* Numbers 24.3, 31.8; *Tanhuma* Balak 4–5; *b. Sanhedrin* 105a; Solomon Buber, ed., *Midrash Tanhuma* (Jerusalem: Eshkol, 1972), 4, 134–35; *Bemidbar Rabah* 20.18. On Balaam as the master of impurity, see Moses ben Shem Tov de Leon, *R. Moses de Leon's Sefer Shekel ha-Kodesh,* ed. Charles Mopsik (Los Angeles: Cherub, 1996), 14–15, and *She'eilot u-Teshuvot be-Inyanei Kabbalah,* ed.

Isaiah Tishby, in *Studies in the Kabbalah and Its Branches* (Jerusalem: Magnes Press, 1982), 74–75. One of the ways in which Balaam is most strongly condemned is for having intercourse with his donkey as a means of gaining the demonic overflow that he required for his version of prophecy and magic. See, e.g., *Zohar* 1:125b; de Leon, *Sefer Shekel ha-Kodesh*, 14–15, and "She'eilot u-Teshuvot be-'Inyanei Kabbalah," 75. This motif is originally found in rabbinic sources. See, e.g., *b. Avodah Zarah* 4b; *Sanhedrin* 105a–b; *Targum Pseudo-Jonathan* Numbers 22:30. On Balaam's practice of drawing prophecy from the demonic realm, see Cohen-Alloro, *The Secret of the Garment in the Zohar*, 75–81; Roland Goetschel, "The Conception of Prophecy in the Works of R. Moses de Leon and R. Yosef Gikatilla," *Jerusalem Studies in Jewish Thought* 8 (1989): 235–36. It certainly seems plausible that the portrait of Balaam has a polemical edge, targeting the ritual of communion, with Balaam's demonic altar symbolizing the Christian one.

67. See Numbers 22:5; Deuteronomy 23:5. The lexicon *Arukh ha-Shalem* suggests that "Pator" is related to the term *patar*, meaning "to interpret dreams." See Natan ben Yehiel of Rome, *Arukh ha-Shalem*, ed. Hanokh Y. Kohut (Vienna: Menorah, 1926), 467–468. See also *Tanhuma* Balak 4, where he is referred to as a money changer, apparently because of the similarity of the term money changer (*shulhani*) to the Hebrew word for table (*shulhan*). See also Solomon Buber, ed., *Midrash Tanhuma* (Jerusalem: Eshkol, 1982), 4:141, where there is a contrast drawn between Israel's Passover meal and Balaam's offerings at his altar.

68. Cf. *The Hebrew Writings*, 135–36. Even Balaam's blessings do not function as blessings but necessarily align themselves with the Other Side.

69. See *Bamidbar Rabah* 14:19 in which a parable compares Balaam to a chef who knows what the king is about to eat; so too does Balaam know in advance what will be "on God's plate." This midrash is later cited by Moses ben Nahman in his commentary on Numbers 23:23.

70. A teaching in the sixteenth-century compendium of three major *Zohar* commentaries, the *Or ha-Hamah*, comments here about the relationship of holiness (*kedushah*) and profanity (*kelipah*) to material things, explaining that all material entities have two causes: one from the holy realm, connecting them to the upper elements, and one from the *kelipah*, which causes decay in this world. *Or ha-Hamah* 3:52b. Cohen-Alloro argues that the sole distinction between positive magic and negative magic is the nature of the intention underlying it. See Cohen-Alloro, "From Supernal Wisdom," 34.

71. *Zohar* 3:193a.

72. The verse is more correctly translated as "A good name is better than fragrant oil," but I have translated according to the *Zohar*'s use of the verse.

73. Cf. *Tanhuma* (ed. Buber) *Va'era*, 236.

74. Cf. *Bereshit Raba* 13:3. The divine name can only be uttered and revelation can only occur if it is revealed in concealment, in connection with the world.

75. See also *Zohar* 2:88a.

76. See Elliot R. Wolfson, "Woman—the Feminine as Other in Theosophic Kabbalah: Some Philosophical Observations on the Divine Androgyne," in *The Other in Jewish Thought and History*, ed. L. Silberstein and R. Cohn (New York: New York University Press, 1994), 166–204.

77. Michel de Certeau, *The Mystic Fable: The Sixteenth and Seventeenth Centuries,* trans. Michael B. Smith (1982, in French; reprint, Chicago: University of Chicago Press, 1992), 80–81.

78. Ibid., 14. Consider also the following comment of Marcel Mauss: "We are faced everywhere with physio-psycho-sociological assemblages of actions. . . . I believe precisely that at the bottom of all our mystical states there are body techniques which we have not studied, but which were studied fully in China and India even in very remote periods." Marcel Mauss, "Body Techniques," in *Sociology and Psychology,* trans. Ben Brewster (French ed., 1935; reprint, London: Routledge and Kegan Paul, 1979), 120–22. Mauss's remarks suggest the "naturalness" of the experience of eating, exchanging words of Torah, and offering blessings.

79. See also *Zohar* 2:183a–b.

80. In an attempt to vitiate the miraculous nature of the claim that the kabbalists were consuming manna, the *Zohar* settles for a quantitative solution, apparently suggesting that these scholars get half-rations, reverting to the realm of economics.

81. See *m. Avot* 3:3. An alternate version of the text explicates the requirement of "words of Torah," saying that reciting the grace after the meal fulfills one's obligation, as it contains words of Torah within it. This is a leniency introduced in the halakhah to accommodate the unlettered or as a more charitable rendition of the law.

82. See also *Zohar* 2:168b, where words of Torah "strengthen one's Master." There is an interesting midrash that, relying on a juxtaposition of two different uses of the term "remember," says that as the Sabbath table should be appropriately adorned to ensure its proper observance, the table should be laid bare to observe the obligation to eradicate the memory of Amalek (*Midrash Tanhuma* Warsaw *Ki Tezei* 7:7 s.v. *zakhor et*).

83. Interestingly, if a person eats alone, his blessings are sufficient to requite the demand for words of Torah at the table, *Zohar Hadash* 86d. (*Midrash Ruth*). The requirement for mystical homilies has been omitted. It would appear that words unheard are not valued. Although there are models in rabbinic Judaism for reciting words of Torah solo, for the *Zohar,* words, as efficacious as they may be, require a human listener serving as recipient in order to be fully valued. Thus, at a typical meal, there are two recipients of the mystical homilies, the table and the audience. Each in its own way completes the theurgical circuit. The acceptability of words of Torah uttered unaccompanied can be seen quite clearly with regard to the injunction to ask questions regarding the Passover exodus at the festival meal. See *b. Pesahim* 116a; Maimonides, *Hilkhot Hamez u-Mazah* 7:3.

84. The aggadic teaching about God's difficulty in procuring food for people is originally found at *b. Pesahim* 118a.

Chapter 6

1. See, e.g., *Zohar* 2:218a. For a full discussion of sefirotic correspondences of the various components of the Sabbath meal, see Isaiah Tishby, *The Wisdom of the Zohar,* trans. David Goldstein (Oxford: Oxford University Press, 1989), 1234–36.

2. There are other symbolic correspondences between the various meals and the *sefirot.* See, e.g., *Zohar* 2:88a–b; 3:288b (*Idra Zuta*). See also the discussion in

Tishby, *Wisdom of the Zohar,* 1235–36, 1269 n.209; Joseph Gikatilla, *Sha'arei Orah,* ed. Yosef Ben-Shlomo (Jerusalem: Bialik Institute, 1981), 1:113. According to one rabbinic tradition, observing the three meals saves one from three kinds of torment. See *b. Sabbath* 117b.

3. This is only one of the sets of correspondences proposed by the *Zohar* and is the one that was adopted by Luria. See also Hayyim Vital, *Shaar Ma'amerei Rashbi,* ed. Yehudah Ashlag (Jerusalem: Yeshivat Kol Yehudah Press, 1988), 19b, which comments on this zoharic passage. Regarding the importance attached by the rabbis to the three meals on the Sabbath, see *b. Shabbat* 118b.

4. *Zohar* 1:246a; 3:272b–273a (*Ra'aya Mehemna*); Joseph of Hamadan, "A Critical Edition of the *Sefer Ta'amey ha-Mizwoth* (Book of Reasons of the Commandments) Attributed to Isaac Ibn Farhi," ed. Menachem Meier (Ph.D. diss., Brandeis University, 1974), 189.

5. *Zohar* 1:246a; 3:98a (*Ra'aya Mehemna*). See also *Zohar Hadash* 86a (*Midrash Ruth*) regarding the six grains that Boaz gives to Ruth. These six grains symbolize the six *sefirot* that connect *Binah* to the *Shekhinah* and thus give Ruth soteriological benefit as well as providing the necessary theurgic unification. While this section of the *Zohar* tends to be strongly allegorical, it does not seem to lose its concrete meaning in this case.

6. *Zohar* 3:244b (*Ra'aya Mehemna*).

7. *Zohar* 3:245a (*Ra'aya Mehemna*); see also *Zohar Hadash* 48c–d, which recommends twelve loaves. The rabbinic prescription was for two loaves at each meal, upon which the *Ra'aya Mehemna* embroiders this new ritual. See *b. Berakhot* 39b; *Shabbat* 117b.

8. *Tikkunei ha-Zohar* 47, 84a–b.

9. *b. Sanhedrin* 102b; see also *Derekh Erez Zuta* 6:3. This requirement is also mentioned in the work of Abraham of Narbonne, *Sefer ha-Eshkol, Hilkhot Netilat Yadayim ve-'Inyanei ha-Se'udah* 1. See also *Zohar* 2:121a (*Ra'aya Mehemna*).

10. The feminine does contribute to that final state, as it is the oven in which that finalization occurs. See *Zohar* 3:252b (*Ra'aya Mehemna*). See also *Zohar* 3:272a in the midst of the same discussion, where bread is identified with the letter *heh;* see also 2:120b. The exegetical opportunity created by the "marked" part of the bread does not disturb the *Zohar*'s more regular association of bread with the *Shekhinah.* One rabbinic teaching considers eating an uncooked part of the bread to cause the forgetting of Torah and eating the best-cooked part of the bread to restore the loss. See *b. Horayot* 13b.

11. See *b. Shabbat* 119b; *b. Ketubot* 103a; *b. Nedarim* 41a; *b. Menahot* 86b; *Tikkunei ha-Zohar* 47, 84a.

12. See also *Zohar* 3:272a–b; *Zohar Hadash* 87b (*Ra'aya Mehemna*); and *t. Berakhot* 38b s.v. "*Ve-hilkhata ha-mozi.*" Cf. *Tikkunei ha-Zohar* 17, 31a.

13. For the association of the Tree of Knowledge with wheat, see *b. Berakhot* 40a; *Bereshit Raba* 15:7; *Zohar* 3:188b, 189a; 3:275a; *Zohar Hadash* (*Tikkunim*) 100c, 107a, *Tikkunei ha-Zohar* 16, 31a; 24, 69a.

14. See *Zohar* 1:2a; 2:168a–b, 231b; 3:98a (*Ra'aya Mehemna*); *Tikkunei ha-Zohar* 22, 68a.

15. The source for the relatively unusual formulation of "*ha-mozi*" rather than

"*mozi*" arises from the desire to avoid the repetition of the consonantal sound "m" at the end of the word "*olam*" that precedes it. See *j. Berakhot* 6:1. This is another example of the *Zohar*'s use of a minor detail from halakhah as the jumping-off point for theurgical praxes.

16. The most recent treatment of the dating of *Sefer Yezirah* is in Steven M. Wasserstrom, "Further Thoughts on the Origins of 'Sefer Yesirah,'" *Aleph* 2 (2002): 201–21.

17. Ithamar Gruenwald, "A Preliminary Critical Edition of *Sefer Yezirah*," *Israel Oriental Studies* 1, no. 3 (1971): 141; in the traditional text the citation is 1:3.

18. On kabbalistic orthography, see Elliot R. Wolfson, "The Anthropomorphic and Symbolic Image of the Letters in the *Zohar*," *Jerusalem Studies in Jewish Thought* 8 (1989): 147–81.

19. A midrashic tradition compares the numerical value of wine to the seventy faces of the Torah. See *Bamidbar Rabah* 13:15. In general, the failure to maintain the divine name results in not receiving the divine food. See, e.g., *Zohar* 3:7a–b.

20. See Ḥavivah Pedayah, "Flaw and Rectification of the Divine in the Kabbalah of Rabbi Isaac the Blind (in Hebrew)," *Jerusalem Studies in Jewish Thought* 6 (1987): 157–285. In general, blessings are effective theurgically, creating harmony above. See, e.g., Moses ben Shem Tov de Leon, *Sefer ha-Rimmon*, 105–6.

21. Menaḥem Recanati cites the talmudic passage from *b. Sotah* 4b, "Whoever eats [bread] without washing his hands, it is as if he has had sexual relations with a harlot, as it is said, 'The last loaf of bread will go for a harlot'" (Proverbs 6:26). He then adds the following approbation: "Understand this statement well because it is wondrous." Recanati, *Commentary on the Torah* (Jerusalem: Mordekhai Attia, 1961), 84a. In his commentary to the passage, Mordekhai Jaffe explains it in terms of the next passage that refers to the submission of the Levite washing the hands of the Kohen, that is, that the lower entity must strive to reach for the higher and demonstrate his subservience. Similarly, the individual Jew must not submit to the desire for bread, homologized to the lust for promiscuous coupling with an unworthy woman; rather, he must demonstrate his rejection/subjection of that inferior entity by striving for the higher ideal, in this instance through delaying his eating. This apt interpretation considers both eating and sexuality to be actions of conquering and consumption: as sexuality must be properly bounded, so must food be properly eaten and digested.

22. The reason given for not mixing meat and milk is that the former refers to the *Shekhinah*, the latter to the *Sitra Aḥra*, and so it is essential that these categories not be mixed. For the rabbinic warnings against this practice, see *b. Sotah* 4b.

23. The rabbinic source for hand washing is *b. Ḥullin* 105a; see also *b. Sotah* 4b. There is similar reasoning for the waters used after the meal to wash off whatever filth might have stuck to one's fingers. See *Zohar* 3:273b. See also Moshe Idel, "Some Remarks on Ritual and Mysticism in Geronese Kabbalah," *Journal of Jewish Thought and Philosophy* 3, no. 1 (1993): 113.

24. *Zohar* 2:208a.

25. Rachel Elior, "The Concept of God in Hekhalot Mysticism," *Jerusalem Studies in Jewish Thought*, no. 6:1–2 (1987): 13–58 (in Hebrew).

26. In the enumeration of the commandments in *Sefer ha-Rimmon*, the recita-

tion of the grace after the meal holds the seventh position immediately following the knowledge of God and immediately preceding the study of Torah and observance of the Sabbath. In some of the medieval orderings of the commandments, the rationale of classification often becomes less apparent after the first few commandments. It might be suggested in this instance, however, that de Leon is following the liturgical order of the day, in which the meal and its ritual appurtenances immediately follow the morning prayers, which would be accounted for by the first six commandments that deal with fearing and loving God, unifying his name, etc. De Leon, *Sefer ha-Rimmon*, 15.

27. Alexander Altmann demonstrated that this passage is taken from *Sefer Taʾamei ha-Mizvot* of Rabbi Joseph of Hamadan. Alexander Altmann, "Regarding the Question of the Authorship of *Sefer Taamei ha-Mitsvot* Attributed to Rabbi Yitshak Ibn Farkhi," *Kiryat Sefer* 40 (1965): 275.

28. De Leon, *Sefer ha-Rimmon*, 318. See also *Zohar* 2:41b.

29. The scriptural source is Deuteronomy 8:8. See also *Tikkunei ha-Zohar* 24, 69a.

30. The rabbinic sources for the debate are *b. Berakhot* 40a, and *b. Sanhedrin* 70a–b. Most frequently, the *Zohar* considers the fateful fruit to have been either wheat or grapes. Part of the significance of wheat is that the *gematriyah* of *ḥitah* equals twenty-two, the number of letters in the Hebrew alphabet. See *Zohar* 3:188b, 272a (*Raʾaya Mehemna*); *Tikkunei ha-Zohar* 16, 31a. Because the letters of the alphabet constitute the very stuff from which the divine body was formed, they are considered to be of the Divine itself. Regarding grapes as the problematic fruit, see *Zohar* 1:36a, 192a; 2:144a, 267b; 3:127a, 158b; *Tikkunei ha-Zohar* 24, 69a; *Bereshit Raba* 19:5.

31. See *Midrash Tanhuma* (Vilna) *Be-har* 3.

32. See *Zohar* 1:12a–b, 35b–36a, 52a–b, 75a–b, 83a, 221a–b, 262a; 2:191a, 237a; 3:42a.

33. Isaiah Tishby uses this dichotomy to trace the different impulses of those who have written about devotion to God in the history of Jewish spirituality. Tishby, *Wisdom of the Zohar*, 941–55.

34. Regarding the theurgic value of reciting blessings, see *Zohar* 3:271a (*Pikkudin*), *Zohar Ḥadash*, 86c–d (*Midrash Ruth*); *Sefer ha-Rimmon*, 362. Cf. Recanati, Recanati, *Commentary on the Torah* (Jerusalem: Mordekhai Attia, 1961), 82a–b, which has a slightly different version of the passage from Ruth *Zohar Ḥadash*, (*Midrash Ruth*) 86c–d. On Recanati's exposure to and uses of the *Zohar*, see Moshe Idel, *R. Menahem Recanati the Kabbalist* (Jerusalem: Schocken, 1998), 101–10.

35. In a parallel passage of zoharic material cited by Menahem Recanati, the requirement for *kavvanah*, mentioned twice in our version of *Zohar Ḥadash*, *Midrash Ruth*, is not mentioned. Menahen, Recanati, *Commentary on the Torah* (Jerusalem: Mordekhai Attia, 1961), 84b. It seems to me that there are several possible interpretations for this variance between the current printed version and that found in Recanati. First, there were many versions of *Midrash ha-Neʾelam* on Ruth in Italy in the fourteenth century, and Recanati's version simply lacked the requirement for *kavvanah*. Second, *kavvanah* was a later addition to the zoharic text. Last, the two versions may be adopting different halakhic stances with regard to the requirement for *kavvanah* in the performance of commandments. This question was very much

a live issue for the halakhic authorities of the High Middle Ages, and the *Zohar*'s stance is more pietistic. On this issue, see Moshe Hallamish, "The Confrontation with the Duty of *Kavvanah*," in *Kabbalah: In Liturgy, Halakhah, and Custom* (Reprint; 1996, Ramat-Gan, Isr.: Bar-Ilan University, 2000), 71–105.

36. Maimonides, *Hilkhot Berakhot* 1:19 and surrounding commentaries.

37. See Baḥya ben Asher, "*Kad ha-Kemaḥ*," in *Kitve Rabbenu Baḥya*, ed. Charles Chavel (Jerusalem: Mosad he-Rav Kuk, 1987), 80, 187. Building on Moses ben Naḥman' teaching about *devekut* in his commentary on the theophanic feast of the elders at Mount Sinai, he says that one can have visions of God even while eating.

38. Baḥya ben Asher, *Shulḥan shel Arba*, in *Kitve Rabbenu Baḥya*, ed. Charles Chavel (Jerusalem: Mosad ha-Rav Kuk, 1987), 494.

39. This phenomenon becomes most pronounced among Hasidim who differentiate the grades of holiness pertaining to different species of fish and different kinds of *kugel*, a traditional pudding eaten on the Sabbath, customarily made of noodles or potatoes. See Alan Nadler, "Holy Kugel! The Sanctification of East European Jewish Ethnic Foods at the Hasidic Tish," in *15th Annual Klutznick-Harris Symposium: Food and Judaism*, ed. Leonard Greenspoon (Omaha, Neb.: Creighton University Press, 2005).

40. Abraham ibn Ezra, *Commentary on the Torah*, Leviticus 19:23; Moses ben Naḥman, *Commentary on the Torah*, ed. Charles Chavel (Jerusalem: Mosad ha-Rav Kuk, 1960), Commentary on Leviticus 19:23.

41. This is not dissimilar to the bottle in *Alice's Adventures in Wonderland*, inscribed with the plea "Drink Me!"

42. In the *Tikkunei ha-Zohar*, the four years are compared to the talmudic story of the four who entered the Pardes with only one of the four, Rabbi Akiva, emerging whole, corresponding to the permitted status of the fruit of the fourth year. *Tikkunei ha-Zohar* 55, 88b.

43. Tosafot *Pesaḥim* 102b s.v. *rav amar yqnh*. R. Asher ben Yeḥiel (Rosh) fourteenth-century Talmud commentator, says that covering the table with a cloth and reciting the sanctification of the Sabbath (*kiddush*) and a new blessing over bread suffices to indicate that one has finished the old meal and that the previous meal can be concluded with grace. These activities substitute for the *zimmun*, whereas in the *Zohar* the fruit constitutes the *zimmun* by providing the opportunity for the grace after the meal. Asher ben Yeḥiel, *Commentary on Arvei Pesaḥim*, no. 7.

44. According to Baḥya ben Asher, blessings recited over food serve primarily to increase the divine overflow of food back into the world. Blessings thus maintain a circular theurgical dynamic of the consumption of food, blessings, and theurgic overflow of more food. See ben Asher, "*Kad ha-Kemaḥ*," 78.

45. See Roland Barthes, "Toward a Psychosociology of Contemporary Food Consumption," trans. Elborg Forster, in *Food and Drink in History: Selections from the Annales, Economies, Societes, Civilisations Vol. 5*, ed. Robert Forster and Orest Ranum (1961; reprint, Baltimore: Johns Hopkins University Press, 1979), 172. Baḥya ben Asher suggests that the oral cavity was created primarily for the purpose of praising God and only secondarily for eating. See Baḥya ben Asher, *Shulḥan shel Arba*, 475.

46. Menaḥem Recanati wrote a short treatise on the grace after the meal, but at

the time of this writing I have been unable to examine it. It is found appended to manuscript copies of his *Sefer Ta'amei ha-Mizvot*, specifically mss. Munich 103, 171a and Vatican 209, 41a, as cited in Moshe Idel, *R. Menahem Recanati the Kabbalist* (Jerusalem: Schocken, 1998), 101.

47. *Zohar* 2:165b–169a. See the parallel version in *Zohar Hadash* 86c–87d (*Midrash ha-Ne'elam*) and a similar narrative in *Zohar* 3:272a (*Ra'aya Mehemna*). The latter version appears to be the early version. Both narrative frames refer to the young man's lack of knowledge of even the grace after the meal, a rudimentary bit of religious knowledge. In the *Midrash ha-Ne'elam* version, the boy launches immediately into a discussion of issues related to eating and grace; in the version from the *Ra'aya Mehemna*, however, a series of homilies treating other topics intervene before the discussion of dining ensues. Menahem Kasher notes that part of Bahya ben Asher's *Shulhan shel Arba* was inserted in the *Ra'aya Mehemna* treatment. Menahem Kasher, *Sinai*, Jubilee Volume 1958, cited in Gershom Scholem, *Gershom Scholem's Annotated Zohar* (Jerusalem: Magnes, 1992), note to 3:274a.

48. Scenarios with orphaned child geniuses occur sporadically in the *Zohar*. It seems quite plausible that the detail about the son not knowing the father is inserted to indicate that the child is, in fact, the reincarnation of the father's soul, one of the *Zohar*'s deepest secrets. There is only one passage in the *Zohar* that discusses this theme at length, and it is characterized as among the most esoteric of doctrines. See *Zohar* 2:94b–114a. Regarding reincarnation, see Gershom Scholem, "*Gilgul*: The Transmigration of Souls," in *On the Mystical Shape of the Godhead*, ed. Jonathan Chipman and trans. Joachim Neugroschel (Reprint; 1962, New York: Schocken, 1991) 179–250; Ronit Meroz, "Selections from Ephraim Penzieri: Luria's Sermon in Jerusalem and the *Kavvanah* in Taking Food," *Jerusalem Studies in Jewish Thought* 10 (1992): 211–57.

49. The wisdom that is found in the mouths of innocents in the zoharic literature, however, is not like that of the romanticized innocents trumpeted in Buberian characterizations of Hasidism. It is not pithy statements that these zoharic youths enunciate, but the same kind of recondite, articulate, and lengthy homilies modeled by the kabbalistic masters. The ethical teaching that emerges then is not so much that one should greet innocents with humility, for they may be wise indeed, but rather that one should comport oneself modestly.

50. See de Leon, *Sefer ha-Rimmon*, 104; Joseph of Hamadan, *Sefer Ta'amey ha-Mizwoth*, 84–87.

51. See also *Zohar Hadash* 87c (*Midrash Ruth*); *Zohar* 3:274a *Ra'aya Mehemna; b. Pesahim* 105b, 117b, where the requirement that the grace after the meal be recited over a cup of wine appears to apply not only to a group of three but even to an individual. See *Tosafot* s.v. "*shema minah berakhah*"; *Tur Orah Hayyim* no. 182 on requiring a blessing over a cup with one individual. Luria's practice was to require three. See Hayyim Vital, *Ta'amei ha-Mizvot*, ed. Yehudah Ashlag (Jerusalem: Yeshivat Kol Yehudah Press, 1988), *Ekev*, 258.

52. I have quoted from the parallel text in *Midrash ha-Ne'elam* 87c.

53. While the male triad suggests a mystical erotic relationship with the *Shekhinah*, women and children have a relationship with the cup of blessing too, as they are obli-

gated in its observance to hear the *zimmun* and grace recited over the cup. *Zohar* 2:190a; see Margaliot's n. 2 there.

54. See *b. Berakhot* 51a.

55. See *b. Berakhot* 20b; *Tosafot* s.v. "*nashim.*"

56. See, e.g., *Zohar* 1:3a; 2:88b, 168b; *Zohar Ḥadash* 86d (*Midrash Ruth*).

57. On the question of the *Zohar*'s attitude toward charity and the poor, see J. F. Baer, "The Historical Background of the *Ra'aya Mehemna*," *Zion*, n.s., 5, no. 1 (1939)1–44; Scholem, *Major Trends in Jewish Mysticism*, 234–35; Tishby, *Wisdom of the Zohar*, 1438–47.

58. See also de Leon, *Sefer ha-Rimmon*, 140. One possible explanation is that one's table atones when one gives to the poor. See Rabbenu Ḥananel, *Commentaries of Rabbenu Ḥananel*, ed. David Metzger (Jerusalem: Lev Sameah Foundation, 1990), 127; Rashi, *Ḥagigah* 27a s.v. *shulḥano mekhaper alav*, and *Sanhedrin* 103b, s.v. *legimah*.

59. Cf. *Zohar* 1:10b.

60. Baḥya ben Asher, "*Shulḥan shel Arba*," 474.

61. See also *Zohar* 1:104a, 208a.

62. Moses ben Shem Tov de Leon, *Shushan Edut*, ed. Gershom Scholem, *Qovez al Yad*, n.s., 8 (1975): 356–57. See parallel in *Zohar Ḥadash* 75c–d (*Midrash ha-Ne'elam*), and also *Zohar Ḥadash* 49a (*Sitrei Torah*), and de Leon, *Sefer ha-Rimmon*, 210. This latter source goes so far as to say that a person who sins before God when he is poor is held by God to be innocent of the iniquity, because a poor person "is not in his right mind." This accusation that is laid by the indigent and then resolved is reminiscent of the accusation that is laid by the *Sitra Aḥra*, when it does not get the nourishment that it calls for. Every place on the ontological map must have its needs met with the proper apportioning in every direction. At an earlier point in *Sefer ha-Rimmon*, de Leon says that giving to the indigent prevents him from stealing, committing murder, and other crimes. De Leon, *Sefer ha-Rimmon*, 117. The ethical situation below is clearly an anagogical model of what transpires above: if one perpetuates the divine flow, one prevents evil from occurring at the lower reaches. Sometimes that refers to the *Shekhinah*, sometimes to the poor person, though, ultimately, the one implies the other. See also de Leon, *Sefer ha-Rimmon*, 302; Azriel of Gerona, *Commentary on Talmudic Aggadoth*, ed. Isaiah Tishby (Jerusalem: Magnes, 1982), 38–39.

63. For another example of concern for the indigent and the welfare and interplay of bodies and souls, see de Leon, *Sefer ha-Rimmon*, 304. To be sure, there are passages that credit the poor with a special ability to gain God's ear and benefit from his closeness. See, e.g., *Zohar* 1:168b; 2:61a, 86b; 3:9a, 108b, 195a–b; *Zohar Ḥadash* 77c (*Midrash Ruth*), 82a. King David is able to transform himself contemplatively so that he should be treated by God like a poor person. See *Zohar* 3:223a (*Ra'aya Mehemna*). Similarly, Jacob advises his sons to travel in Egypt in the garb of the needy so that they should receive divine protection. See *Zohar Ḥadash* 67a (*Shir ha-Shirim*). In both of these instances, we observe the *Zohar*'s proclivity for prescribing modes of performance, including appearance, and not simply behaviors or intentions.

64. Regarding asceticism in the *Zohar*, see, e.g., *Zohar* 1:180b; 2:183b–184a, 187a–b; 3:90b; *Zohar Ḥadash* 8d (*Midrash ha-Ne'elam*), 22c (*Midrash ha-Ne'elam*), 97a

(*Midrash ha-Ne'elam*); Tishby, *Wisdom of the Zohar,* 764–65, 1331–32. See also *Zohar* 2:154b, which says, explicating the verse "Lest, being sated, I renounce, [saying, 'Who is the Lord?']" (Proverbs 30:9), that "it is from food and drink that the evil inclination is increased in a person's belly." See *Avot de-Rabbi Nathan* 16, which locates the evil inclination in the belly.

65. The reference is to the dream in which Nebuchadnezzar is transformed into a beast. See Daniel 4:7–14.

66. See also *Zohar* 1:208a; 3:153b. Tishby suggests that because the *Zohar* attributes these symbolic significations to the religious actions of giving charity, it is primarily this mystical meaning that lends religious significance to these acts. See Tishby, *Wisdom of the Zohar,* 1166–67. While this is undoubtedly true, I would suggest that the "place" in which these actions occur are more this-worldly than Tishby's comments allow. In other words, it may not be a supernal realm ontologically removed from our daily existence with which the *Zohar* is concerned here; the union of the masculine and feminine potencies among the *sefirot* is an action that occurs in this world.

67. One narrative describes two donkey drivers, the *Zohar's* idiosyncratic hierophants, who feed their donkeys before eating themselves (*Zohar* 3:21a). See Genesis 43:24 and Proverbs 12:10 as possible scriptural roots for this idea, and *b. Berakhot* 40a, which creates the norm. Note also the irony at the beginning of the Saba of Mishpatim section in which the donkey-feeding Saba is excluded from the rabbis' meal even though he is fulfilling the superior duty.

68. See *Zohar* 1:125b; 2:264a; *Zohar Ḥadash* 47c (*Midrash ha-Ne'elam*), 47c; the rabbinic sources for this are *b. Sanhedrin* 105b, and *b. Avodah Zarah* 4a–b. There are a wide variety of sources using the term feeding (*zan*) to refer to the sexual relationship between *Tif'eret* and *Malkhut*. See, e.g., Moses ben Shem Tov de Leon, *Sod Eser Sefirot Belimah,* in *Qovez al Yad,* n.s., 8, ed. Gershom Scholem (1975), 381; *Zohar* 1:208b, 240a; 2:170a, 206a.

69. See also *Zohar* 1:79a, 130a *Midrash ha-Ne'elam;* 2:147b.

70. There is a link between Torah study and giving to the poor (see *Zohar* 1:87b–88a; 3:9a) and a link between unifying the divine name and giving charity (see *Zohar* 3:113b).

71. *Zohar* 3:272a, *Ra'aya Mehemna.*

72. See *Zohar* 3:244a; *Tikkunei ha-Zohar* 15, 30b; *b. Berakhot* 52b, *Tosafot.* s.v. *peirurin de-leit behu ke-zayit.*

73. See de Leon, *Sefer ha-Rimmon,* 16, 140. On p. 16, the obligation to give joy to the poor utilizes the proof text from Genesis 47:22, emphasizing eating. Eating is thus perceived as the primary experience of abundance.

74. In the long discussion of the etiquette for meals, dealing primarily with the meals on the Sabbath, the *Ra'aya Mehemna* refers to the need to have extra food at one's table so that the indigent can come. See *Zohar* 3:271b–274a (*Ra'aya Mehemna*).

75. See also Deuteronomy 16:11 and Rashi's comment there. The verse specifies the need to take care of the needy in the context of the festivals. This requirement finds its way into normative Jewish law in Maimonides' code, *Hilkhot Yom Tov* 6:18. There does not seem to be an earlier rabbinic source for it, and the *Zohar's* deliberations appear to arise from the fact that the law specifies this charitable giving, in both

its scriptural and legal contexts, in relation to the festivals. Predictably, the laws regarding charity do not make such distinctions.

76. Interestingly, though it is ostensibly Abraham's tight-fisted, elitist behavior and his consorting exclusively with the aristocrats of his community that invite punishment, it is only when Sarah skeptically laughs at her good fortune that justice is meted out. This reflects the *Zohar*'s general proclivity to attribute sin to women; God's anger at Sarah for doubting his abilities serves as an exegetical hook—becoming the last straw—for God's growing rage. Ironically, Sarah is portrayed as nursing all of the children brought to her, demonstrating a generosity that Abraham lacks. In typical fashion, the *Zohar* blunts its posturing with conflicting impulses, showing that, in this instance, it is ultimately not an ethical matter that invokes the array of punishments.

77. *Zohar* 3:104a.

78. There are also other more typically ethical injunctions that the *Zohar* enjoins with regard to feeding the poor. One should give a sufficient quantity of food so that they will not be embarrassed (*Zohar* 2:198a); one should first give to the poor and then eat oneself (*Zohar* 3:104a).

Conclusion

1. *b. Pesahim* 49b.

2. See, e.g., Joseph Gikatilla, *Sefer Sha'arei Orah* (New York: Moriah Offset, 1985), 2, 11–12; Joseph of Hamadan, "Joseph of Hamadan's *Sefer Tashak*: Critical Edition with Introduction," ed. Jeremy Zwelling (Ph.D. diss., Brandeis University, 1975), 92; Joseph of Hamadan, "A Critical Edition of the *Sefer Ta'amey ha-Mizwoth* (Book of Reasons of the Commandments) Attributed to Isaac Ibn Farhi," ed. Menachem Meier (Ph.D. diss., Brandeis University, 1974), 309–10; *Sefer ha-Kanah*, 66a, 119b, 129a, 131a, 132a. The concern about the worthiness and intention of the person performing ritual slaughter receives considerable attention in *Sefer ha-Kanah*. Part of the concern for these works' emphasis on the spiritual fitness of the carnivore is that he is not only a meat eater, but, it would appear, is engaging in homophagy— he is a soul eater. In the *Zohar*, slaughter is invariably a cruel act, hence the unusual assertion that the priests in the Temple did not perform the ritual slaughter there. *Zohar* 3:124a, 180b. See Margaliot *Nizozzei Zohar*, n. 6. When there is reference to ritual slaughter of human beings, it is always in the more figurative sense, performed by the *Sitra Ahra*. See, e.g., *Zohar* 3:33a (*Ra'aya Mehemna*). In one brief homily that is similar to some of the concerns of the *Sefer ha-Kanah*, the *Zohar* says that the reincarnated souls masters of the academy do not require slaughter but only gathering, as is the case with fish. See *Zohar* 3:42a. As punishment for minor faults, the righteous find their new embodiment in fish, which are not subjected to the agony of slaughter. In the *Zohar*, the meaning is homiletical: when the scholars are taken out of their sea, the sea of Torah, they die immediately and do not require slaughter. For a different explanation for the prohibition against an ignoramus eating meat, see Bahya ben Asher, "*Shulhan shel Arba*," in *Kitve Rabbenu Bahya*, ed. Charles Chavel (Jerusalem: Mosad ha-Rav Kuk, 1987), 496. See also *Zohar Hadash* 11d (*Midrash ha-Ne'elam*), which notes that one does not require any special intentions to perform

slaughtering, running counter to the doctrines seen earlier. On reincarnation into liv-
ing beings, see Ronit Meroz, "Selections from Ephraim Penzieri: Luria's Sermon in
Jerusalem and the *Kavvanah* in Taking Food," *Jerusalem Studies in Jewish Thought* 10
(1992): 211–57; Moshe Hallamish, "The Kabbalistic Meaning of Eating Fish on
Shabbat," in *Alei Shefer: Studies in the Literature of Jewish Thought Presented to Rabbi
Dr. Alexandre Safran,* ed. Moshe Hallamish (Ramat-Gan, Isr.: Bar-Ilan University
Press, 1990), 67–87 (Hebrew section).

3. Michel Feher, "Introduction," in *Fragments for a History of the Body,* ed. Michel
Feher (New York: Zone, 1989), 14.

4. The kabbalistic notion of the body's penetrability coheres with one rendition
of a halakhic understanding of the body. Moses ben Nahman writes in his commentary on the tractate *Berakhot* that "[the rabbis] did not sanction blessings recited for
pleasures that do not enter into the body, such as washing with cold or hot water or
like the pleasure gained from a breeze. This is true all the more for light that does not
touch the body at all. They [only required that blessings be recited for pleasurable
items] if they enter the body and the body derives pleasure from them, such as eating
and drinking. Fragrances also enter the body and give nourishment and are thus similar to eating and drinking." Moses ben Naḥman, *Ḥiddushei ha-Ramban: Berakhot,* ed.
Moshe David Weinberger (Jerusalem: Foundation for the Complete Israeli Talmud,
1986), 42. It must be noted that Moses ben Nahman was an important kabbalist and,
while there are only two explicit references to kabbalistic matters in his halakhic writings, it is certainly plausible that the kabbalistic style of thinking affected his jurispru-
dence as well. Another way in which the body's borders are overcome in halakhic
literature can be seen in the context of the laws regarding carrying objects on the
Sabbath. Consider the way in which a walking stick is considered part of the body.
Shulḥan Arukh Oraḥ Ḥayyim 301:17. Merleau-Ponty writes that the blind man's stick
is "no longer an object perceived by the blind man, but an instrument *with* which he
perceives." Maurice Merleau-Ponty, *Phenomenology of Perception,* trans. Colin Smith,
International Library of Philosophy and Scientific Method (London: Routledge and
Kegan Paul, 1962), 152.

5. See Jean-Pierre Vernant, "Dim Body, Dazzling Body," in *Fragments for a
History of the Human Body,* ed. Michel Feher (New York: Zone, 1989), 32; Arthur W.
Frank, "For a Sociology of the Body: An Analytical Review," in *The Body: Social Process
and Cultural Theory,* ed. Mike Featherstone, Mike Hepworth, and Bryan S. Turner
(London: Sage, 1991), 51.

6. This is, of course, notwithstanding my comments in chapter 4 about performative affect.

7. Moses ben Shem Tov de Leon, *R. Moses de Leon's Sefer Shekel ha-Kodesh,* ed.
Charles Mopsik (Los Angeles: Cherub, 1996), 34.

8. In an adjacent passage, de Leon contends that even after death, there is a
kind of knowledge that is maintained residing within the corpse. Ibid., 35.

9. Source unknown.

10. Nelson Pike draws attention to the problem of developing a phenomenol-
ogy based only on historical documents and calls the analysis phenomenography.
Nelson Pike, *Mystic Union: An Essay in the Phenomenology of Mysticism* (Ithaca, N.Y.:
Cornell University Press, 1992), 166–75.

11. Jean Starobinski, "The Natural and Literary History of Bodily Sensation," in *Fragments for a History of the Human Body,* ed. Michel Feher, Ramona Naddaff, and Nadia Tazi (New York: Zone, 1989), 369–70.

12. Grace M. Jantzen, *Becoming Divine: Towards a Feminist Philosophy of Religion* (Bloomington: Indiana University Press, 1999), 271.

BIBLIOGRAPHY

Primary Sources

Abraham of Narbonne. *Sefer ha-Eshkol.*

Asher ben Yeḥiel. *Commentary on Arvei Pesaḥim.*

Azriel of Gerona. *Commentary on Talmudic Aggadoth.* Ed. Isaiah Tishby. Jerusalem: Magnes, 1982.

Baḥya ben Asher. *Commentary on the Torah.* Ed. Charles Chavel. Jerusalem: Mossad ha-Rav Kook, 1982.

———. *"Kad ha-Kemaḥ."* In *Kitve Rabbenu Baḥya,* ed. Charles Chavel, 17–451. Jerusalem: Mossad ha-Rav Kook, 1987.

———. *"Shulḥan Shel Arba."* In *Kitve Rabbenu Baḥya,* ed. Charles Chavel, 453–514. Jerusalem: Mossad ha-Rav Kook, 1987.

Bereshit Raba. Ed. Judah Theodor and Chanoch Albeck. Jerusalem: Wahrmann, 1965.

The Book Bahir: An Edition Based on the Earliest Manuscripts. Ed. Daniel Abrams. Los Angeles: Cherub, 1994.

Buber, Solomon, ed. *Midrash Tanhuma.* Jerusalem: Eshkol, 1972.

———, ed. *Midrash Tehillim.* Jerusalem: H. Wagshal, 1977.

Cordovero, Moses. *Or Yakar.* Jerusalem: H. Wagshal, 1962–89.

———. *Siddur Tefillah le-Moshe le-ha-Ramak.* Ashdod, Isr.: Torah Treasures Institute, 2004.

Epstein, I, ed. *Tractate Ḥullin.* Hebrew-English Edition of the Babylonian Talmud. Trans. Maurice Simon. London: Soncino, 1963.

Gikatilla, Joseph. "Commentary on the Haggadah." In *Haggadah Sheleimah,* ed. Menahem Mendel Kasher, 111–120. New York: Sentry, 1967.

———. *Sefer Sha'arei Orah.* Brooklyn: Moriah, 1985.

———. *Sefer Sha'arei Zedek.* Brooklyn: Moriah, 1985.

———. *Sha'arei Orah,* ed. Yosef Ben-Shlomo. Jerusalem: Bialik Institute, 1981.

ibn Adret, Solomon. *Ḥiddushei ha-Rashba: Berakhot. Ḥiddushei ha-Rashba.* Jerusalem: Mossad ha-Rav Kook, 1982–83.

Isaac of Acre. *"Sefer Me'irat Einayim* by R. Isaac of Acre: A Critical Edition." Ed. Amos Goldreich. Ph.D. diss., Hebrew University of Jerusalem, 1981.

Ishvili, Yom Tov ben Abraham. *Hiddushei ha-Ritva: Berakhot. Hiddushei ha-Ritva.* Jerusalem: Mossad ha-Rav Kook, 1984.

Jacob ben Sheshet. *Sefer Meshiv Devarim Nekhoḥim.* Ed. Georges Vajda. Jerusalem: Israel Academy of Sciences and Humanities, 1968.

Joseph of Hamadan. "A Critical Edition of the *Sefer Ta'amey ha-Miẓwoth* ('Book of

Reasons of the Commandments') Attributed to Isaac Ibn Farhi." Ed. Menachem
    Meier. Ph.D. diss., Brandeis University, 1974.
——. *Fragment d'un Commentaire sur la Genese.* Ed. and trans. Charles Mopsik. *Les
    Dix Paroles.* Paris: Editions Verdier, 1998.
——. "Joseph of Hamadan's *Sefer Tashak*: Critical Edition with Introduction." Ed.
    Jeremy Zwelling. Ph.D. diss., Brandeis University, 1975.
——. *Sefer Toledot ha-Adam.* In *Sefer ha-Malkhut,* 53a–104b. Casablanca: Imprimerie
    Razon, 1930.
Maimonides, Moses. *The Guide of the Perplexed.* Trans. Shlomo Pines. Chicago:
    University of Chicago Press, 1963.
——. *Mishneh Torah.* Ed. and trans. Philip Birnbaum. New York: Hebrew, 1967.
——. "Moses Maimonides' Two Treatises on the Regimen of Health." Ed. A. Bar-
    Sela, H. E. Hoff, and E. Faris. *Transactions of the American Philosophical Society,*
    n.s., 54 (1964).
——. *Pirke Moshe bi-Refu'ah.* Jerusalem: Yeshivat Kol Yehudah Press, 1959.
Margaliot, Reuven, ed. *Sefer ha-Bahir.* Jerusalem: Mossad ha-Rav Kook, 1994.
——, ed. *Sefer ha-Zohar.* Jerusalem: Mossad ha-Rav Kook. 1970.
——, ed. *Tikkunei ha-Zohar.* Jerusalem: Mossad ha-Rav Kook, 1994.
Matt, Daniel, ed. and trans. *The Zohar: Pritzker Edition.* Stanford, Calif.: Stanford
    University Press, 2004.
——, ed. and trans. *Zohar: The Book of Enlightenment.* New York: Paulist, 1983.
Moses ben Naḥman. *Commentary on the Torah.* Ed. Charles Chavel. Jerusalem:
    Mossad ha-Rav Kook, 1960.
——. *Ḥiddushei ha-Ramban: Berakhot.* Ed. Moshe David Weinberger. Jerusalem:
    Foundation for the Complete Israeli Talmud, 1986.
Moses ben Shem Tov de Leon. ——. *R. Moses de Leon's Commentary to Ezekiel's
    Chariot.* Ed. Asi Farber-Ginat. Los Angeles: Cherub, 1998.
——.*R. Moses de Leon's Sefer Shekel ha-Kodesh.* Ed. Charles Mopsik. Los Angeles:
    Cherub, 1996.
——. "*Sefer ha-Mishkal*: Text and Study; Edited by Jochanan Wijnhoven." Ph.D.
    diss., Brandeis University, 1964.
——. *Sefer ha-Rimmon.* Ed. Elliot R. Wolfson. Atlanta: Scholars, 1988.
——. "*She'eilot u-Teshuvot be-'Inyanei Kabbalah.*" Ed. Isaiah Tishby. In *Studies in the
    Kabbalah and Its Branches,* vol. 1, 36–75. Jerusalem: Magnes Press, 1982.
——. *Shushan Edut.* Ed. Gershom Scholem. *Kovez al Yad,* n.s., 8 (1975): 325–70.
——. *Sod Eser Sefirot Belimah.* Ed. Gershom Scholem. *Kovez al Yad,* n.s., 8
    (1975):371–84.
Rabbenu Hananel. *Commentaries of Rabbenu Ḥananel.* Ed. David Metzger.
    Jerusalem: Lev Sameah Foundation, 1990.
Recanati, Menaḥem. *Commentary on the Torah.* Jerusalem: Mordekhai Attia, 1961.
Schäfer, Peter, ed. *Synopse Zur Hekhalot-Literatur.* Tübingen, Ger.: J. C. B. Mohr, 1981.
The Hebrew Writings of the Author of Tiqquni Zohar and Ra'aya Mehemna. Ed. Efraim
    Gottlieb. Jerusalem: Israel Academy of Sciences and Humanities, 2003.
Vital, Ḥayyim. "Inyan Shaul Ve-Yehonatan Ve-David." In *Likkutei Torah,* ed. Yehudah
    Ashlag, 294–95. Jerusalem: Yeshivat Kol Yehudah Press, 1988.
——. *Sha'ar ha-Mizvot.* Jerusalem: Yeshivat Kol Yehuda Press, 1988.

——. *Sha'ar Ma'amerei Rashbi*. Ed. Yehudah Ashlag. Jerusalem: Yeshivat Kol Yehudah Press, 1988.

——. *Ta'amei ha-Mizvot*. Ed. Yehudah Ashlag. Jerusalem: Yeshivat Kol Yehudah Press, 1988.

Secondary Sources

Abrams, Daniel. *Sexual Symbolism and Merkavah Speculation in Medieval Germany.* Tübingen, Ger.: Mohr Siebeck, 1997.

Alon, Gedalyahu. *Jews, Judaism, and the Classical World: Studies in Jewish History in the Times of the Second Temple and Talmud.* Trans. Israel Abrahams. Jerusalem: Magnes, 1977.

Alter, Robert. "A New Theory of *Kashrut.*" *Commentary* 68 (August 1979): 46–52.

Altmann, Alexander. "Eleazar of Worms' *Hokhmat ha-'Egoz.*" *Journal of Jewish Studies* 11 (1960): 101–13.

——. "Regarding the Question of the Authorship of *Sefer Taamei ha-Mitsvot* Attributed to Rabbi Yitshak Ibn Farkhi." *Qiryat Sefer* 40 (1965): 256–76, 405–12.

Anderson, Gary A. "Sacrifice and Sacrificial Offerings." In *Anchor Bible Dictionary,* vol. 5, ed. David Noel Freedman, 870–86. New York: Doubleday, 1992.

——. *Sacrifices and Offerings in Ancient Israel: Studies in Their Social and Political Importance.* Atlanta: Scholars, 1987.

——. *A Time to Mourn, a Time to Dance: The Expression of Grief and Joy in Israelite Religion.* University Park: Pennsylvania State University Press, 1991.

Assis, Yom Tov. *The Golden Age of Aragonese Jewry: Community and Society in the Crown of Aragon, 1213–1327.* Oxford: Littman Library of Jewish Civilization, 1997.

Baer, J. F. "The Historical Background of the *Ra'aya Mehemna.*" *Zion,* n.s., 5, no. 1 (1939): 1–44.

Bahr, Gordon J. "The Seder of Passover and the Eucharistic Words." In *Essays in Greco-Roman and Related Talmudic Literature,* ed. Henry A. Fischel, 473–94. New York: KTAV, 1977.

Bakhtin, Mikhail. *Rabelais and His World.* Bloomington: Indiana University Press, 1984.

Barthes, Roland. "Reading Brillat-Savarin." In *The Rustle of Language,* ed. François Wahl and trans. Richard Howard, 250–70. Berkeley: University of California Press, 1986.

——. "Toward a Psychosociology of Contemporary Food Consumption." Trans. Elborg Forster. In *Food and Culture: A Reader,* ed. Carole Couniham and Peggy Van Eserik, 20–27. New York: Routledge, 1997.

Baumgarten, Albert I. "Finding Oneself in a Sectarian Context: A Sectarian's Food and Its Implications." In *Self, Soul and Body in Religious Experience,* ed. A. I. Baumgarten, J. Assmann, and G. G. Stroumsa, 125–47. Leiden: E. J. Brill, 1998.

Bell, Catherine. *Ritual Theory, Ritual Practice.* New York: Oxford University Press, 1992.

Ben-Shlomo, Yosef. "General Introduction." In *Joseph Gikatilla: Sha'arei Orah,* ed. Yosef Ben-Shlomo, 7–41. Jerusalem: Bialik Institute, 1981.

Bland, Kalman P. "Medieval Jewish Aesthetics: Maimonides, Body, and Scripture in Profiat Duran." *Journal of the History of Ideas* 54, no. 4 (1993): 533–59.

Bokser, Baruch. *The Origins of the Seder: The Passover Rite and Early Rabbinic Judaism.* Berkeley: University of California Press, 1984.

——. "Ritualizing the Seder." *Journal of the American Academy of Religion* 56, no. 3 (1988): 443–71.

——. "Was the Last Supper a Passover Seder?" *Bible Review* 3, no. 2 (1987): 24–33.

Boyarin, Daniel. *Carnal Israel: Reading Sex in Talmudic Culture.* Berkeley: University of California Press, 1993.

——. *Unheroic Conduct: The Rise of Heterosexuality and the Invention of the Jewish Man.* Berkeley: University of California Press, 1997.

Brody, Seth Lance. "Human Hands Dwell in Heavenly Heights: Worship and Mystical Experience in Thirteenth Century Kabbalah." Ph.D. dissertation. University of Pennsylvania, 1991.

Brown, Peter. *The Body and Society: Men, Women, and Sexual Renunciation in Early Christianity.* Lectures on the History of Religions, vol. 13. New York: Columbia University Press, 1988.

Brumberg-Kraus, Jonathan. "Meat-Eating and Jewish Identity: Ritualization of the Priestly 'Torah If Beast and Fowl' [Lev. 11:46] in Rabbinic Judaism and Medieval Kabbalah." *AJS Review* 24, no. 2 (1999): 227–62.

Bruns, Gerald L. *Hermeneutics Ancient and Modern.* New Haven, Conn.: Yale University Press, 1992.

——. "Midrash and Allegory: The Beginnings of Scriptural Interpretation." In *The Literary Guide to the Bible.* Cambridge, Mass.: Harvard University Press, 1987.

Burkert, Walter. "Oriental Symposia: Contrasts and Parallels." In *Dining in a Classical Context,* ed. William J. Slater, 7–24. Ann Arbor: University of Michigan Press, 1991.

Bynum, Caroline Walker. "The Female Body and Religious Practice in the Later Middle Ages." In *Fragments for a History of the Human Body,* ed. Michel Feher. New York: Zone, 1989.

——. *Holy Feast and Holy Fast: The Religious Significance of Food to Medieval Women.* Berkeley: University of California Press, 1987.

——. "Introduction: The Complexity of Symbols." In *Gender and Religion: On the Complexity of Symbols,* ed. Caroline Walker Bynum, Stevan Harrell, and Paula Richman, 1–20. Boston: Beacon, 1986.

——. "Jesus as Mother and Abbot as Mother: Some Themes in Twelfth-Century Cistercian Writing." In *Jesus as Mother: Studies in the Spirituality of the High Middle Ages.* 110–69. Berkeley: University of California Press, 1982.

——. *The Resurrection of the Body in Western Christianity, 200–1336.* New York: Columbia University Press, 1995.

——. "Why All the Fuss about the Body? A Medievalist's Perspective." *Critical Inquiry* 22 (autumn 1995): 1–33.

Camporesi, Piero. "The Consecrated Host: A Wondrous Excess." In *Fragments for a History of the Human Body,* ed. Michel Feher, 220–37. New York: Zone, 1989.

Chernus, Ira. *Mysticism in Rabbinic Judaism: Studies in the History of Midrash.* Berlin: Walter de Gruyter, 1982.

——. "'Nourished by the Splendor of the *Shekhinah*:' A Mystical Motif in Rabbinic

Midrash." In *Mysticism in Rabbinic Judaism: Studies in the History of Midrash,* 74–87. Berlin: Walter de Gruyter, 1982.

Childs, Brevard S. *The Book of Exodus,: A Critical, Theological Commentary.* Philadelphia: Westminster, 1976.

Cohen-Alloro, Dorit. "From Supernal Wisdom to the Wisdom of the Leaves of the Tree: The *Zohar*'s View of Magic as a Consequence of the Original Sin." *Daat* 19 (summer 1987): 31–65.

———. *The Secret of the Garment in the Zohar.* Research Projects of the Institute of Jewish Studies, Monograph Series 13. Jerusalem: Hebrew University of Jerusalem, 1987.

Dan, Joseph. *The Esoteric Theology of Ashkenazi Hasidism.* Jerusalem: Bialik Institute, 1968.

———. "Toward a History of the Text of Hokhmat ha-Egoz." *Alei Sefer* 5 (1978): 49–52.

———. "*Hokhmath ha-'Egoz,* Its Origin and Development." *Journal of Jewish Studies* 17 (1966): 73–82.

Davis, Ellen F. *Swallowing the Scroll: Textuality and the Dynamics of Discourse in Ezekiel's Prophecy.* Worcester, UK: Sheffield, 1989.

de Certeau, Michel. *The Mystic Fable: The Sixteenth and Seventeenth Centuries.* Trans. Michael B. Smith. [1982, in French]. Chicago: University of Chicago Press, 1992.

Deutsch, Nathaniel. "Rabbi Nahman of Bratslav: The Zaddik as Androgyne." In *God's Voice from the Void,* ed. Shaul Magid, 193–215. Albany: State University of New York Press, 2000.

de Vaux, Roland. *Ancient Israel: Its Life and Institutions.* Grand Rapids, Mich.: W. B. Eerdmans, 1997.

Diamond, Eliezer. *Holy Men and Hunger Artists: Fasting and Asceticism in Rabbinic Culture.* Oxford: Oxford University Press, 2004.

Dillard, Heath. *Daughters of the Reconquest: Women in Castilian Town Society, 1100–1300.* Cambridge: Cambridge University Press, 1984.

Ehrlich, Uri. *The Non-Verbal Language of Jewish Prayer.* Jerusalem: Hebrew University Magnes Press, 1999.

Eilberg-Schwartz, Howard, ed. *People of the Body: Jews and Judaism from an Embodied Perspective.* Albany: State University of New York Press, 1992.

———. "Introduction." In *People of the Body: Jews and Judaism from an Embodied Perspective,* ed. Howard Eilberg-Schwartz, 1–13. Albany: State University of New York Press, 1992.

Elior, Rachel. "The Concept of God in Hekhalot Mysticism." *Jerusalem Studies in Jewish Thought,* no. 6:1–2 (1987): 13–58 (in Hebrew).

———. *The Concept of God in Hekhalot Mysticism.* In *Binah: Studies in Jewish Thought,* ed. Joseph Dan and trans. Dena Ordan, 97–129. New York: Praeger, 1989.

Epstein, Julia, and Kristina Straub. "Introduction: The Guarded Body." In *Body Guards: The Cultural Politics of Gender Ambiguity,* ed. Julia Epstein and Kristina Straub, 1–28. New York: Routledge, 1991.

Farb, Peter. *Consuming Passions: The Anthropology of Eating.* Boston: Houghton Mifflin, 1980.

Farber, Asi. *The Conception of the Chariot in the Esoteric Theology of the Thirteenth Century: The Sod ha-'Egoz and Its Development.* Ph.D. diss., Hebrew University of Jerusalem, 1986.

Feeley-Harnik, Gillian. *The Lord's Table: The Meaning of Food in Early Judaism and Christianity.* Washington, D.C.: Smithsonian Institute, 1981.

Feher, Michel. "Introduction." In *Fragments for a History of the Body,* ed. Michel Feher. New York: Zone, 1989.

Feldman, Jonathan. "The Power of the Soul over the Body: Corporeal Transformation and Attitudes towards the Body in the Thought of Naḥmanides." Ph.D. dissertation. New York University, 1999.

Fine, Lawrence. "The Art of Metoposcopy: A Study in Isaac Luria's Charismatic Knowledge (Reprinted in *Essential Papers on Kabbalah,* 1995)." *AJS Review* 11, no. 1 (1986): 79–101.

——. *Physician of the Soul, Healer of the Cosmos: Isaac Luria and His Kabbalistic Fellowship.* Stanford, Calif.: Stanford University Press, 2003.

Firth, Raymond. *Symbols: Public and Private.* Ithaca, N.Y.: Cornell University Press, 1973.

Fishbane, Michael. "'The Holy One Sits and Roars': Mythopoesis and Midrashic Imagination." In *The Exegetical Imagination: On Jewish Thought and Theology,* 22–40. Cambridge, Mass.: Harvard University Press, 1998.

——. "The Imagination of Death in Jewish Spirituality." In *Death, Ecstasy, and Other Worldly Journeys,* ed. John J. Collins and Michael Fishbane, 183–208. Albany: State University of New York Press, 1995.

Forst, Binyamin. *The Laws of Kashrus: A Comprehensive Exposition of Their Underlying Concepts and Applications.* New York: Mesorah, 1994.

Frank, Arthur W. "For a Sociology of the Body: An Analytical Review." In *The Body: Social Process and Cultural Theory,* ed. Mike Featherstone, Mike Hepworth, and Bryan S. Turner. London: Sage, 1991.

Freedman, H. *Midrash Rabah: Genesis.* Midrash Rabah. London: Soncino, 1961.

Gadamer, Hans-Georg. *Truth and Method,* trans. Garret Barden and John Cumming. New York: Seabury, Continuum, 1975.

Geertz, Clifford. "Religion as a Cultural System." In *The Interpretation of Cultures,* 87–125. New York: Basic, 1973.

Giller, Pinchas. *The Enlightened Will Shine: Symbolization and Theurgy in the Later Strata of the* Zohar. Albany: State University of New York Press, 1993.

Ginsburg, Elliot K. *The Sabbath in the Classical Kabbalah.* Albany: State University of New York Press, 1989.

Gleason, Maud W. *Making Men: Sophists and Self-Presentation in Ancient Rome.* Princeton, N.J.: Princeton University Press, 1995.

Goetschel, Roland. "The Conception of Prophecy in the Works of R. Moses de Leon and R. Yosef Gikatilla." *Jerusalem Studies in Jewish Thought* 8 (1989): 217–37.

Goffman, Erving. *The Presentation of Self in Everyday Life.* New York: Anchor, 1959.

Green, Arthur. *A Guide to the Zohar.* Stanford, Calif.: Stanford University Press, 2004.

——. "Shekhinah, the Virgin Mary, and the Song of Songs." *AJS Review* 26, no. 1 (2002): 1–52.

Grimes, Ronald L. *Beginnings in Ritual Studies.* 1985. Reprint, Columbia: University of South Carolina Press, 1995.

——. "Defining Nascent Ritual." In *Beginnings in Ritual Studies,* 58–74. Columbia: University of South Carolina, 1995.

Grivetti, Louis Evan. "Dietary Separation of Meat and Milk: A Cultural-Geographical Inquiry." *Ecology of Food and Nutrition* 9 (1980): 203–17.

Grosz, Elizabeth. "Inscriptions and Body-Maps: Representations and the Corporeal." In *Feminine, Masculine, and Representation,* ed. Terry Threadgold and Ann Cranny-Francis, 62–74. Sydney: Allen and Unwin, 1990.

Gruenwald, Ithamar. *Apocalyptic and Merkavah Mysticism.* Leiden, Neth.: E. J. Brill, 1980.

———. "Further Jewish Physiognomic and Chiromantic Fragments." *Tarbiz* 40 (1971): 301–19.

———. "A Preliminary Critical Edition of *Sefer Yezirah.*" *Israel Oriental Studies* 1 (1971): 132–77.

Hallamish, Moshe. "The Confrontation with the Duty of *Kavvanah.*" In *Kabbalah: In Liturgy, Halakhah, and Custom,* 71–105. 1996. Reprint, Ramat-Gan, Isr.: Bar-Ilan University, 2000.

———. "The Evolution of a Kabbalistic Custom: 'I Accept upon Myself the Obligation to Fulfill the Positive Commandment of 'You Shall Love Your Fellow as Yourself.'"' *Qiryat Sefer* 53 (July 1978): 534–56.

———. *Kabbalah: In Liturgy, Halakhah, and Custom.* Ramat-Gan, Isr.: Bar-Ilan University, 2000.

———. "The Kabbalistic Meaning of Eating Fish on Shabbat." In *'Alei Shefer: Studies in the Literature of Jewish Thought Presented to Rabbi Dr. Alexandre Safran,* ed. Moshe Hallamish, 67–87 (Hebrew section). Ramat-Gan, Isr.: Bar-Ilan University Press, 1990.

———. "Problems in the Research of the Influence of Kabbalah on Prayer." In *Kabbalah: In Liturgy, Law, and Custom,* 21–44. Ramat-Gan, Isr.: Bar Ilan University Press, 2000.

Handelman, Susan A. *Fragments of Redemption: Jewish Thought and Literary Theory in Benjamin, Scholem, and Levinas.* Bloomington: Indiana University Press, 1991.

Haran, Menahem. "The Passover Sacrifice." In *Studies in the Religion of Ancient Israel,* 86–116. Leiden, Neth.: E. J. Brill, 1972.

———. "Seething a Kid in Its Mother's Milk." *Journal of Jewish Studies* 30 (1979): 23–39.

Harrington, Hannah K. "Did the Pharisees Eat Ordinary Food in a State of Ritual Purity?" *Journal for the Study of Judaism in the Persian, Hellenistic and Roman Period* 26 (April 1995): 42–54.

Harris, Jay M. "The Circumcised Heart." Review of *A Radical Jew: Paul and the Politics of Identity,* by Daniel Boyarin. *Commentary* 99, no. 6 (1995): 57–60.

Hartley, John E. *Leviticus.* Dallas: Word Biblical Commentary, 1992.

Hellner-Eshed, Melilah. "'A River Goes out from Eden': The Language of Mystical Invocation in the *Zohar.*" *Kabbalah: Journal for the Study of Jewish Mystical Texts* 2 (1997): 287–310.

Idel, Moshe. "The Concept of the Torah in Heikhalot Literature and Its Metamorphoses in Kabbalah." *Jerusalem Studies in Jewish Thought* 1 (1981): 23–84.

———. "Infinities of Torah in Kabbalah." In *Midrash and Literature,* ed. Geoffrey H. Hartman and Sanford Budick, 141–57. New Haven, Conn.: Yale University Press, 1986.

———. *Kabbalah: New Perspectives.* New Haven, Conn.: Yale University Press, 1988.

———. "Kabbalistic Prayer and Colors." In *Approaches to Judaism in Medieval Times,* ed. David R. Blumenthal, 17–27. Atlanta: Scholars, 1988.

———. *Language, Torah, and Hermeneutics in Abraham Abulafia.* Trans. Menahem Kallus. Albany: State University of New York Press, 1989.

———. *The Mystical Experience in Abraham Abulafia.* Ed. Jonathan Chipman. Albany: State University of New York Press, 1988.

———. "On Talismatic Language in Jewish Mysticism." *Diogenes* 43/2, no. 170 (1995): 23–41.

———. *R. Menaḥem Recanati the Kabbalist.* Jerusalem: Schocken, 1998.

———. "Some Remarks on Ritual and Mysticism in Geronese Kabbalah." *Journal of Jewish Thought and Philosophy* 3, no. 1 (1993): 111–30.

———. *Studies in Ecstatic Kabbalah.* Albany: State University of New York Press, 1988.

Jackson, Michael. *Paths toward a Clearing: Radical Empiricism and Ethnographic Inquiry.* Bloomington: Indiana University Press, 1989.

James, William. *The Varieties of Religious Experience: A Study in Human Nature.* 1902. Reprint, New York: Macmillan, 1961.

Jantzen, Grace M. *Becoming Divine: Towards a Feminist Philosophy of Religion.* Bloomington: Indiana University Press, 1999.

Jeanneret, Michel. *A Feast of Words: Banquets and Table Talk in the Renaissance.* Trans. Jeremy Whiteley and Emma Hughes. 1987. Reprint, Chicago: University of Chicago Press, 1991.

Johnson, Mark. *The Body in the Mind: The Bodily Basis of Meaning, Imagination, and Reason.* Chicago: University of Chicago Press, 1987.

Joselit, Jenna Weissman. *The Wonders of America: Reinventing Jewish Culture, 1880–1950.* New York: Hill and Wang, 1994.

Kanarfogel, Ephraim. *"Peering Through the Lattices": Mystical, Magical, and Pietistic Dimensions in the Tosafist Period.* Detroit: Wayne State University Press, 2000.

Kass, Leon R. *The Hungry Soul: Eating and the Perfecting of Our Nature.* New York: Free Press, 1994.

Katz, Steven T. "Language, Epistemology, and Mysticism." In *Mysticism and Philosophical Analysis,* ed. Steven T. Katz, 22–74. New York: Oxford University Press, 1978.

Kiener, Ronald C. "The Image of Islam in the *Zohar.*" *Jerusalem Studies in Jewish Thought* 8 (1989): 43–65.

Klawans, Jonathan. *Impurity and Sin in Ancient Judaism.* New York: Oxford University Press, 2000.

Laqueur, Thomas. *Making Sex: Body and Gender from the Greeks to Freud.* Cambridge, Mass.: Harvard University Press, 1990.

Lauterbach, Jacob Z., trans. *Mekilta de-Rabbi Ishmael.* Philadelphia: Jewish Publication Society, 1949.

Le Goff, Jacques. *The Medieval Imagination.* Trans. Arthur Goldhammer. [1985 in French.] Chicago: University of Chicago Press, 1988.

Lehrman, S. M., trans. *Midrash Rabah: Exodus.* London: Soncino, 1939.

Lekai, Louis J. *The Cistercians: Ideals and Reality.* Kent, Ohio: Kent State University Press, 1977.

Levine, Baruch A. *The JPS Torah Commentary: Leviticus.* Philadelphia: Jewish Publication Society, 1989.

——. *Numbers 1–20 : A New Translation with Introduction and Commentary.* New York: Anchor Bible/Doubleday, 1993.

Levinger, Jacob. "Maimonides' *Guide of the Perplexed* on Forbidden Food in the Light of His Own Medical Opinion." In *Perspectives on Maimonides: Philosophical and Historical Studies,* ed. Joel L. Kraemer, 195–208. London: Littman Library of Jewish Civilization, 1996.

Leyerle, Blake. "Meal Customs in the Greco-Roman World." In *Passover and Easter: Origin and History to Modern Times,* ed. Paul F. Bradshaw and Lawrence A. Hoffman, 29–61. South Bend, Ind.: University of Notre Dame Press, 1999.

Lieber, Andrea Beth. "God Incorporated: Feasting on the Divine Presence in Ancient Judaism." Ph.D. diss., Columbia University, 1998.

Liebes, Yehuda. "Christian Influences in the Zohar." *Jerusalem Studies in Jewish Thought* 2, no. 1 (1982–83): 43–74.

——. "Christian Influences on the *Zohar*." In *Studies in the Zohar,* 139–61. Albany: State University of New York Press, 1993.

——. "*De Natura Dei:* On the Development of Jewish Myth (Hebrew)." In *Massu'ot: Studies in Kabbalistic Literature and Jewish Philosophy,* ed. Michal Oron and Amos Goldreich, 243–97. Jerusalem: Bialik Institute, 1994.

——. "'*De Natura Dei*': On the Development of the Jewish Myth." In *Studies in Jewish Myth and Jewish Messianism,* trans. Batya Stein, 119–48. Albany: State University of New York Press, 1993.

——. "How the *Zohar* Was Written." *Jerusalem Studies in Jewish Thought* 8 (1989): 1–71 (in Hebrew).

——. "How Was the *Zohar* Written?" In *Studies in the Zohar,* trans. Stephanie Nakache, 85–138, 194–227 [in English]. Albany: State University of New York Press, 1993.

——. "Hymns for the Sabbath Meals of the Ari." *Molad,* n.s., 23 (February 1972): 540–55.

——. "The Messiah of the *Zohar* (in Hebrew)." In *The Messianic Idea in Jewish Thought: A Study Conference in Honour of the Eightieth Birthday of Gershom Scholem.* 236–87. Jerusalem: Israel Academy of Sciences and Humanities, 1982.

——. "The Messiah of the *Zohar:* On R. Simeon Bar Yohai as a Messianic Figure [in English]." In *Studies in the Zohar,* trans. Arnold Schwartz, Stephanie Nakache, and Penina Peli, 1–84, 163–94. Albany: State University of New York Press, 1993.

——. "Myth vs. Symbol in the *Zohar* and in Lurianic Kabbalah." Trans. Eli Lederhandler. In *Essential Papers on Kabbalah,* ed. Lawrence Fine, 212–42. New York: New York University Press, 1995.

——. "*Zohar* and Eros." *Alpayim—A Multidisciplinary Publication for Contemporary Thought and Literature* 9 (1994): 67–119.

Lindbeck, George A. *The Nature of Doctrine: Religion and Theology in a Post-Liberal Age.* Philadelphia: Westminster, 1984.

Lloyd, J. B. "The Banquet Theme in Ugaritic Narrative." *Ugarit-Forschungen* 4 (1972): 169–93.

Lobel, Diana. "A Dwelling Place for the Shekhinah." *Jewish Quarterly Review* 90, nos. 1–2 (1999): 103–25.

Lowy, S. "The Motivation of Fasting in Talmudic Literature." *Journal of Jewish Studies* 9, nos. 1–2 (1958): 19–38.

MacIntyre, Alasdair. *After Virtue: A Study in Moral Theory.* South Bend, Ind.: University of Notre Dame Press, 1981.

Marcus, Ivan G. *Rituals of Childhood: Jewish Acculturation in Medieval Europe.* New Haven, Conn.: Yale University Press, 1990.

Matt, Daniel C., ed. and trans. *The Essential Kabbalah: The Heart of Jewish Mysticism.* New York: Harper San Francisco, 1994.

——. "Introduction." In *Zohar: The Book of Enlightenment.* Ramsey, N.J.: Paulist, 1983.

——. "*Matnita Dilan:* A Technique of Innovation in the *Zohar.*" *Jerusalem Studies in Jewish Thought* 8 (1989): 123–45.

——. "'New-Ancient Words': The Aura of Secrecy in the *Zohar.*" In *Gershom Scholem's Major Trends in Jewish Mysticism: 50 Years Later,* ed. Joseph Dan and Peter Schaefer, 181–207. Tübingen, Ger.: J. C. B. Mohr, 1993.

Mauss, Marcel. "Body Techniques." In *Sociology and Psychology,* trans. Ben Brewster [1935 in French], 97–123. London: Routledge and Kegan Paul, 1979.

McGinn, Bernard. *The Foundations of Mysticism.* New York: Crossroad, 1994.

Merleau-Ponty, Maurice. *Phenomenology of Perception.* Trans. Colin Smith. International Library of Philosophy and Scientific Method. London: Routledge and Kegan Paul, 1962.

Meroz, Ronit. "Selections from Ephraim Penzieri: Luria's Sermon in Jerusalem and the *Kavvanah* in Taking Food." *Jerusalem Studies in Jewish Thought* 10 (1992): 211–57.

——. "Zoharic Narratives and Their Adaptations." *Hispania Judaica Bulletin* 3 (2000): 3–63.

Milgrom, Jacob. *The Anchor Bible: Leviticus 23–27, a New Translation with Introduction and Commentary.* New York: Doubleday, 2001.

——. *The JPS Torah Commentary: Numbers.* Philadelphia: Jewish Publication Society, 1990.

Mopsik, Charles. "The Body of Engenderment in the Hebrew Bible, the Rabbinic Tradition, and the Kabbalah." In *Fragments for a History of the Human Body Part I,* ed. Ramona Naddaff and Nadia Tazi Michael Feher, 48–73. New York: Zone, 1989.

——. *Les Grands Textes de la Cabale: Les Rites Qui Font Dieu.* Paris: Verdier, 1993.

Motis Dolader, Miguel-Angel. "Mediterranean Jewish Diet and Traditions in the Middle Ages." In *Food: A Culinary History from Antiquity to the Present,* ed. Jean-Louis Flandrin, Massimo Montanari, and Albert Sonnenfeld, 225–44. New York: Columbia University Press, 1999.

Nadler, Alan. "Holy Kugel! The Sanctification of East European Jewish Ethnic Foods at the Hasidic Tish." In *15th Annual Klutznick-Harris Symposium: Food and Judaism,* ed. Leonard Greenspoon. Omaha, Neb.: Creighton University Press, 2005.

Neusner, Jacob. *From Politics to Piety: The Emergence of Pharisaic Judaism.* New York: Ktav, 1979.

——. *The Rabbinic Traditions about the Pharisees Before 70.* Leiden, Neth.: E. J. Brill, 1971.

Nicholson, Ernest W. "The Origin of the Tradition in Exodus 24:9–11." *Vetus Testamentum* 26 (April 1976): 148–60.

Oron, Mikhal. "'Place Me as a Seal upon Your Heart': Studies in the Poetics of the Author of the *Zohar* in the Saba of Mishpatim Section." In *Massu'ot: Studies in Kabbalistic Literature and Jewish Philosophy,* ed. Mikhal Oron and Amos Goldreich, 1–24. Jerusalem: Bialik Institute, 1994.

Pedaya, Havivah. "Flaw and Rectification of the Divine in the Kabbalah of Rabbi Isaac the Blind [in Hebrew]." *Jerusalem Studies in Jewish Thought* 6 (1987): 157–285.

Peyer, Hans Conrad. "The Origins of Public Hostelries in Europe." In *Food: A Culinary History from Antiquity to the Present,* ed. Jean-Louis Flandrin, Massimo Montanari, and Albert Sonnenfeld, 287–94. New York: Columbia University Press, 1999.

Pike, Nelson. *Mystic Union: An Essay in the Phenomenology of Mysticism.* Ithaca, N.Y.: Cornell University Press, 1992.

Polen, Nehemia. *The Holy Fire: The Teachings of Rabbi Kalonymus Kalman Shapira, the Rebbe of the Warsaw Ghetto.* Northvale, N.J.: Jason Aronson, 1994.

Proudfoot, Wayne. *Religious Experience.* Berkeley: University of California Press, 1985.

Reynolds, Philip Lyndon. *Food and the Body: Some Peculiar Questions in High Medieval Theology.* Leiden, Neth.: E. J. Brill, 1999.

Riera-Melis, Antoni. "Society, Food, and Feudalism." In *Food: A Culinary History from Antiquity to the Present,* ed. Jean-Louis Flandrin, Massimo Montanari, and Albert Sonnenfeld, 251–67. New York: Columbia University Press, 1999.

Roberts, Kathryn L. "God, Prophet, and King: Eating and Drinking on the Mountain in First Kings 18:41." *Catholic Biblical Quarterly* 62, no. 4 (2000): 632–44.

Rosner, Fred, and Suessman Munter, eds. and trans. *The Medical Aphorisms of Moses Maimonides.* New York: Yeshiva University Press, 1970–71.

Safran, Bezalel. "Rabbi Azriel and Naḥmanides: Two Views of the Fall of Man." In *Rabbi Moses Naḥmanides (Ramban): Explorations in His Religious and Literary Virtuosity,* ed. Isadore Twersky, 75–106. Cambridge, Mass.: Harvard University Press, 1983.

Saldarini, Anthony J. *Pharisees, Scribes and Sadducees in Palestinian Society : A Sociological Approach.* Wilmington, Del.: M. Glazier, 1988.

Sanders, E. P. *Jewish Law from Jesus to the Mishnah: Five Studies.* Philadelphia: Trinity, 1990.

Sarna, Nahum M. *Exodus = [Shemot]: The Traditional Hebrew Text with the New JPS Translation/Commentary by Nahum M. Sarna.* Philadelphia: Jewish Publication Society, 1991.

Schäfer, Peter. *Mirror of His Beauty: Feminine Images of God from the Bible to the Early Kabbalah.* Princeton, N.J.: Princeton University Press, 2002.

———. "Tradition and Redaction in Hekhalot Literature." *Journal for the Study of Judaism in the Persian, Hellenistic and Roman Period* 14, no. 2 (1983): 172–81.

Scheindlin, Raymond P. *Wine, Women, and Death: Medieval Hebrew Poems on the Good Life.* Philadelphia: Jewish Publication Society, 1986.

Schmitt, Jean-Claude. "The Ethics of Gesture." Trans. Ian Patterson. In *Fragments for a History of the Human Body, Part Two,* ed. Michel Feher and Ramona Naddaf, 128–47. New York: Zone, 1989.

Scholem, Gershom. "Chiromancy in the *Zohar*." *The Quest* 17 (1926): 255–56.
———. "The Concept of *Kavvanah* in the Early Kabbalah." In *Studies in Jewish Thought: An Anthology of German Jewish Scholarship,* ed. Alfred Jospe and trans. Noah J. Jacobs. Detroit: Wayne State University Press, 1981.
———. *Gershom Scholem's Annotated Zohar.* Jerusalem: Magnes, 1992.
———. "*Gilgul:* The Transmigration of Souls." In *On the Mystical Shape of the Godhead,* ed. Jonathan Chipman and trans. Joachim Neugroschel, 197–250, 300–312. 1962. Reprint, New York: Schocken, 1991.
———. *Major Trends in Jewish Mysticism.* New York: Schocken, 1946.
———. "The Meaning of the Torah in Jewish Mysticism." In *On the Kabbalah and Its Symbolism,* trans. Ralph Manheim. 1960. Reprint, New York: Schocken, 1965.
———. *Origins of the Kabbalah.* Ed. R. J. Zwi Werblowski and trans. Allan Arkush. 1962. Reprint, Philadelphia: Jewish Publication Society, 1987.
———. "Physiognomy and Chiromancy." In *Sefer Asaf,* ed. M.D. Casuto, J. Klausner, and J. Gutman. Jerusalem: Mossad ha-Rav Kook, 1953.
———. "Shekhinah: The Feminine Element in Divinity." In *On the Mystical Shape of the Godhead,* trans. Joachim Neugroschel, 140–96, 293–300. New York: Schocken, 1991.
———. "*Sitra Aḥra:* Good and Evil in the Kabbalah." In *On the Mystical Shape of the Godhead,* ed. Jonathan Chipman and trans. Joachim Neugroschel, 56–87, 281–83. New York: Schocken, 1991.
Schwartz, Baruch J. "'Profane' Slaughter and the Integrity of the Priestly Code." *Hebrew Union College Annual* 67 (1996): 15–42.
———. "The Prohibitions Concerning the 'Eating' of Blood in Leviticus 17." In *Priesthood and Cult in Ancient Israel,* ed. Gary A. Anderson and Saul M. Olyan, 34–66. Sheffield, UK: JSOT, 1991.
Sedgwick, Eve Kosofsky. *Between Men: English Literature and Male Homosocial Desire.* New York: Columbia University Press, 1985.
Seidman, Naomi. "Carnal Knowledge: Sex and the Body in Jewish Studies." *Jewish Social Studies: History, Culture and Society* 1, no. 1 (1994): 1–21.
Sells, Michael A. *Mystical Languages of Unsaying.* Chicago: University of Chicago Press, 1994.
Smith, Dennis E. *From Symposium to Eucharist: The Banquet in the Early Christian World.* Minneapolis: Fortress, 2003.
———. "Table Fellowship as a Literary Motif in the Gospel of Luke." *Journal of Biblical Literature* 106 (December 1987): 613–38.
Smith, Morton. "The Dead Sea Sect in Relation to Ancient Judaism." *New Testament Studies* 7 (July 1961): 347–61.
Soler, Jean. "The Semiotics of Food in the Bible." Trans. Elborg Forster. In *Food and Culture: A Reader,* 55–66. New York: Routledge, 1997.
Starobinski, Jean. "The Natural and Literary History of Bodily Sensation." In *Fragments for a History of the Human Body, Part 2,* ed. Michel Feher, Ramona Naddaff, and Nadia Tazi, and trans. Lydia Davis, 350–93. New York: Zone, 1989.
Stein, Siegfried. "The Influence of Symposia Literature on the Literary Form of the Pesah Haggadah." *Journal of Jewish Studies* 8, nos. 1–2 (1957): 13–44.
Studies in Jewish Mysticism, Philosophy, and Ethical Literature: Presented to Isaiah Tishby

on His Seventy-Fifth Birthday. Ed. J. Dan and J. Hacker. Jerusalem: Magnes Press, 1986.

Tabory, Joseph. "Towards a History of the Paschal Meal." In *Passover and Easter: Origin and History to Modern Times,* ed. Paul F. Bradshaw and Lawrence A. Hoffman, 62–80. South Bend, Ind.: University of Notre Dame Press, 1999.

Tambiah, Stanley. *Culture, Thought and Social Action.* Cambridge, Mass.: Harvard University Press, 1985.

Ta-Shma, Israel M. *Minhag Ashkenaz ha-Kadmon: Ḥeker Ve-Iyyun.* Jerusalem: Magnes, 1992.

———. *The Revealed in the Concealed: The Halakhic Residue in the Zohar (Hebrew).* Israel: Hakibbutz Hameuchad, 2001.

Theodor, Judah, and Chanoch Albeck, eds. *Bereshit Raba.* Jerusalem: Wahrmann, 1965.

Tigay, Jeffrey H. *The JPS Torah Commentary: Deuteronomy.* Philadelphia: Jewish Publication Society, 1996.

Tishby, Isaiah. *The Wisdom of the Zohar.* Trans. David Goldstein. The Littman Library of Jewish Civilization. Oxford: Oxford University Press, 1989.

Verman, Mark. *The History and Varieties of Jewish Meditation.* Northvale, N.J.: Jason Aronson, 1996.

Vermes, Geza. "'He Is the Bread': Targum Neofiti Exodus 16:15." In *Post-Biblical Jewish Studies,* 139–46. Leiden, Neth.: E. J. Brill, 1975.

Vernant, Jean-Pierre. "Dim Body, Dazzling Body." In *Fragments for a History of the Human Body,* ed. Michel Feher, 18–48. New York: Zone, 1989.

Veyne, Paul. "The Roman Empire." In *A History of Private Life: From Pagan Rome to Byzantium,* ed. Paul Veyne and trans. Arthur Goldhammer, 5–233. Cambridge, Mass.: Belknap, 1987.

Visotzky, Burton, and Gwynn Kessler. "Intersexuality and the Reading of Talmudic Culture." *Arachne* 1, no. 2 (1995): 238–52.

Visser, Margaret. *The Rituals of Dinner: The Origins, Evolution, Eccentricities, and Meaning of Table Manners.* New York: Grove Weidenfeld, 1991.

Vriezen, T. C. "The Exegesis of Exodus 24:9–11." In *The Witness of Tradition,* 100–133. Leiden, Neth.: E. J. Brill, 1972.

Wasserstrom, Steven M. "Further Thoughts on the Origins of 'Sefer Yesirah.'" *Aleph* 2 (2002): 201–2.

———. "Religion after Religion." In *Religion after Religion: Gershom Scholem, Mircea Eliade, and Henry Corbin at Eranos.* Princeton, N.J.: Princeton University Press, 1999.

Werblowsky, R. J. Zwi. *Joseph Karo: Lawyer and Mystic.* Philadelphia: Jewish Publication Society of America, 1977.

Wolff, Hans Walter. *Anthropology of the Old Testament.* Trans. Margaret Kohl. Philadelphia: Fortress, 1974.

Wolfson, Elliot R. "The Anthropomorphic and Symbolic Image of the Letters in the Zohar." *Jerusalem Studies in Jewish Thought* 8 (1989): 147–81.

———. "Beautiful Maiden without Eyes: *Peshat* and *Sod* in Zoharic Hermeneutics." In *The Midrashic Imagination: Jewish Exegesis, Thought, and History,* ed. Michael Fishbane, 155–203. Albany: State University of New York Press, 1993.

——. "Circumcision, Vision of God, and Textual Interpretation: From Midrashic Trope to Mystical Symbol." *History of Religions* 27 (1986–87): 189–215.

——. "Crossing Gender Boundaries in Kabbalistic Ritual and Myth." In *Circle in the Square: Studies in the Use of Gender in Kabbalistic Symbolism.* 79–121. Albany: State University of New York Press, 1995.

——. "Forms of Visionary Ascent as Ecstatic Experience in the Zoharic Literature." In *Gershom Scholem's Major Trends in Jewish Mysticism: 50 Years Later,* ed. Joseph Dan and Peter Schaefer, 209–35. Tübingen, Ger.: J. C. B. Mohr, 1993.

——. "Left Contained in the Right: A Study in Zoharic Hermeneutics." *AJS Review* 11, no. 1 (1986): 27–52.

——. "Letter Symbolism and Merkavah Imagery in the *Zohar.*" In *Alei Shefer: Studies in the Literature of Jewish Thought Presented to Rabbi Dr. Alexandre Safran,* ed. Moshe Halamish, 195–236. Ramat Gan, Isr.: Bar-Ilan University Press, 1990.

——. "Light through Darkness: The Ideal of Human Perfection in the Zohar." *Harvard Theological Review* 81, no. 1 (1988): 73–95.

——. "Mystical Rationalization of the Commandments in *Sefer ha-Rimmon.*" *Hebrew Union College Annual* 59 (1989): 217–51.

——. "Occultation of the Feminine and the Body of Secrecy in Medieval Kabbalah." In *Rending the Veil: Concealment and Secrecy in the History of Religions,* ed. Elliot R. Wolfson, 113–54. New York: Seven Bridges, 1999.

——. *Through a Speculum That Shines: Visionary Experience and Imagination in Medieval Jewish Mysticism.* Princeton, N.J.: Princeton University Press, 1994.

——. "Weeping, Death, and Spiritual Ascent in Sixteenth-Century Jewish Mysticism." In *Death, Ecstasy, and Other Worldly Journeys,* ed. John J. Collins and Michael Fishbane, 209–47. Albany: State University of New York Press, 1995.

——. "Woman—the Feminine as Other in Theosophic Kabbalah: Some Philosophical Observations on the Divine Androgyne." In *The Other in Jewish Thought and History,* ed. L. Silberstein and R. Cohn, 166–204. New York: New York University Press, 1994.

——. "*Yeridah la-Merkavah:* Typology of Ecstasy and Enthronement in Ancient Jewish Mysticism." In *Mystics of the Book: Themes, Topics, and Typologies.* 13–44. New York: Peter Lang, 1993.

Wolfson, Harry. *Philosophy of the Kalam.* Cambridge, Mass.: Harvard University Press, 1976.

Wright, David P. "Observations on the Ethical Foundations of the Biblical Dietary Law: A Response to Jacob Milgrom." In *Religion and Law: Biblical-Judaic and Islamic Perspectives,* ed. E. R. Firmage, Bernard G. Weiss, and John W. Welch, 193–98. Winona Lake, Ind.: Eisenbrauns, 1990.

Zimmer, Eric. "Poses and Postures during Prayer." *Sidra* 5 (1989): 89–130.